LIBRARY OF ART

PUBLISHER - DIRECTOR: GEORGE RAYAS

GREEK POPULAR
MUSICAL INSTRUMENTS

Pandhoúra or trichordhon. A four century B. C. relief from Mantineia. National Archaeological Museum, Athens.

FIVOS ANOYANAKIS

GREEK POPULAR
MUSICAL INSTRUMENTS

2nd EDITION

"MELISSA" PUBLISHING HOUSE

Collaborator: FIVI CARAMEROU
Translation from the Greek: CHRISTOPHER N.W. KLINT
Design and lay-out: TAKIS KATSOULIDIS, artist-engraver
Proof-reading and make up of the letterpress supervised by MARIA A. GAVRILIS
Printing: A. PETROULAKIS A.B.E.E.

Pages: 416. Dimensions of volume: 30×25 cm.
Color reproductions: 169. Black and white illustrations: 58. Drawings: 178

ISBN: 960-204-004-1

*To all Greek popular musicians
and popular musical instrument - makers*

CONTENTS

FOREWORD

The re-publication of this work marks forty years since the beginning of the research which led to its compilation, twenty since it was designed and fifteen since the first publication (1st Greek ed., 1976, 1st English ed., 1979). Its warm reception at the time by both the Greek and the international erudite and cultivated public, which led to its being rapidly sold out and to an increasing demand for its re-issue, prove its importance. Research in ethnomusicology has advanced very little from 1976 to the present: the creation of a university chair in Crete, the founding of the "Museum of Greek Popular Musical Instruments" and the publication of a limited number of specialized studies and records is of course important, but not sufficient for the study of an area of particular national and cultural significance. The need for effective agents and generous donors is strongly in evidence here: valuable work has created the conditions for its completion and true appreciation.

The re-publication of my work gives me the opportunity to once more thank all those who helped me then in its production and particularly the National Bank of Greece which published the first edition and gave permission for the second edition, Stelios Papadopoulos who guided its creation from its inception to the final stage and Fivi Caramerou for her ardent and valuable assistance. Finally, I would like to thank Y. Rayas, the director of "MELISSA" Publications, who has undertaken the re-publication and distribution of the book.

F. ANOYANAKIS

INTRODUCTION

INTRODUCTION

Greece is a crossroads between East and West. Situated in the middle of two cultural currents of such great difference, Greece was subjected to and assimilated creatively diverse influences. The fall of Constantinople in 1453 completed the collapse of the Byzantine Empire. The four hundred years of slavery which followed, lasting until the 1821 War of Independence and the subsequent creation of a sovereign Greek state, hampered the natural development of Hellenism and restricted its spiritual evolution.[1]

Those years had an especially inhibitive influence on music. From the twelfth or thirteenth century onwards, while the West was enjoying a continual social and intellectual progress, an economically exhausted Byzantium, weary of long years of strife —of factional rebellions, religious disputes, crusades and invasions— was spiralling downwards towards its fated end. While the new technique of polyphony was developing in the West, the Orthodox Eastern Church in Byzantium —initially for reasons of dogma, and later out of opposition to the Church of Rome— fanatically resisted any kind of change. Thus Byzantine music remained monophonic, and without any form of instrumental accompaniment. In other words, it was deprived of polyphony and instrumental accompaniment, those elements which, in the West, contributed to an unimpeded development of art, and which gave promise of the superb musical structure of the centuries to come — the music of Bach, Mozart, and Beethoven.

However, the isolation of Byzantium which kept music away from polyphony, together with the passage of so many centuries of continuous culture, enabled monophonic music to develop so as to reach the greatest heights of perfection. If Byzantium failed to bequeath us polyphonic music equivalent to that produced by the West, it nevertheless presented us with a melodic treasure of inestimable value for its rhythmical variety and expressive power, the monophonic *Byzantine chant*.

Along with the Byzantine chant —which constituted a form of 'art' musical creation— from the late Byzantine years until the present day the Greek people also cultivated the *folk song*.

The origins of Greek folk song

The origins of Greek folk song *(dhimotikó traghoúdhi)* can be traced back to the first centuries of Christianity; more precisely to the orchestic and pantomimic performances as these were formed under the new social and intellectual conditions that prevailed after the third century A.D.

As early as the first century A.D., ancient Greek tragedy —at its peak an harmonious unity incorporating poetry, music and dance— had disintegrated into its component elements. Actor-tragedians continued to perform only certain parts of dialogue from the tragedies, while others endowed with good voices, sang the vocal parts of the tragedy. During this same period, there also arose a *gesticulator* whose role was to illustrate with pantomimic gestures whatever the actor-tragedian was singing. The result was the gradual transformation of the old Attic tragedy and comedy into the 'tragic pantomime' of the imperial years, a spectacle-cum-concert including dance, mime, recitation and song. The extent to which these tragedian-singers travelled throughout the vast territories of the Roman Empire has been recorded by many writers, among them Plutarch, Philostratus et alii. Furthermore, the reactions of the Church Fathers and the continuous stream of condemnatory decisions and excommunications issued by the ecumenical synods indicate the popularity of these spectacle-concerts in multi-ethnic Byzantium, and the influence of the mime performances on the austere moral code of the Christians for many centuries to come.

What is of principal interest here is that the tragic pantomime, however much a product of disturbed times and adapted to what the ill-educated masses wanted to see, preserved many elements of ancient Greek poetry, elements which have been recognised by philological researchers in modern Greek folk poetry. The word *paraloghí* (narrative song or 'ballad') probably stems from the ancient Greek *parakataloghí*, a form of musical recitation somewhere between recitation and ode (pure melody), which was also used in tragedies.[2] In the *paraloghés*, or at least in their nucleus, philological research has revealed ancient myths that were once "popular with the theatre". In the theme of the song *The Exile's Return,* Nicolaos Politis has distinguished the incident of Penelope's recognition of Ulysses. In a Pontic *paraloghí* in which a wife consents to sacrifice half the years of her life so that her husband might be saved, we encounter the myth of Alcestes, who agreed to die in place of her husband. Further evidence of the relationship between folk song and ancient Greek poetry and music is the derivation of the words *traghoúdhi* (song) and *traghoudhó* (to sing) from *traghodhía* (tragedy) and *traghodhó* (to act).[3]

Musicological research has also proved rewarding in the domain of the Greek folk song. It has unearthed valuable evidence linking the modern Greek folk song to ancient Greek music. It would not, of course, be feasible to seek this relationship in any similarities of modern Greek folk melodies with those few melodies bequeathed to us by Greek antiquity. The passage of so many centuries, and the profound changes in the style of music caused by Christianity obviously preclude any such attempt. Nor should we forget the substantial difference between the ancient and the modern Greek language. The prosody of the ancient Greek language was *quantitative,* a recitation which clearly marked the difference between long and short syllables. That is, thanks to its vowels each word had an elementary rhythmical form as well as a rough melodic line. In contrast, the modern Greek language is based on the so-called *tonic* prosody (strong accentuation): its words simply have accentuated or non-accentuated syllables.

This change however, which took its final form in the early years of Christianity, combined with other factors, influenced in a decisive manner the formation of a new melodic concept, radically different from that of the classical era. It is true that today no similarity between modern Greek folk melodies and the melodies of Greek antiquity is recognised, but musicological research has revealed something of far greater significance. Despite the change from *quantitative* to *tonic* prosody and the passage of so many centuries, the ancient Greek rhythmical formations live on in the modern Greek folk melody. The researches of Professors Thrasyvoulos Georgiadis and Samuel Baud-Bóvy demonstrate that 7/8 time, found throughout Greece, is

1.　　*Triangular psaltery (kanonáki). Miniature, 12th cent., Codex 911, f. 2v. Stavronikita Monastery, Mount Athos.*

3.	*Bagpipe, flute (?). Icon: Nativity (detail), 17th-18th cent. Church of Bethlehem, Jerusalem.*

→

2.	*Bowed stringed-instrument, lute, trumpet, lute, psaltery (kanonáki). Wall-painting: Praise ye the Lord (detail), 16th cent. Philanthropinon Monastery, Ioannina (Island).*

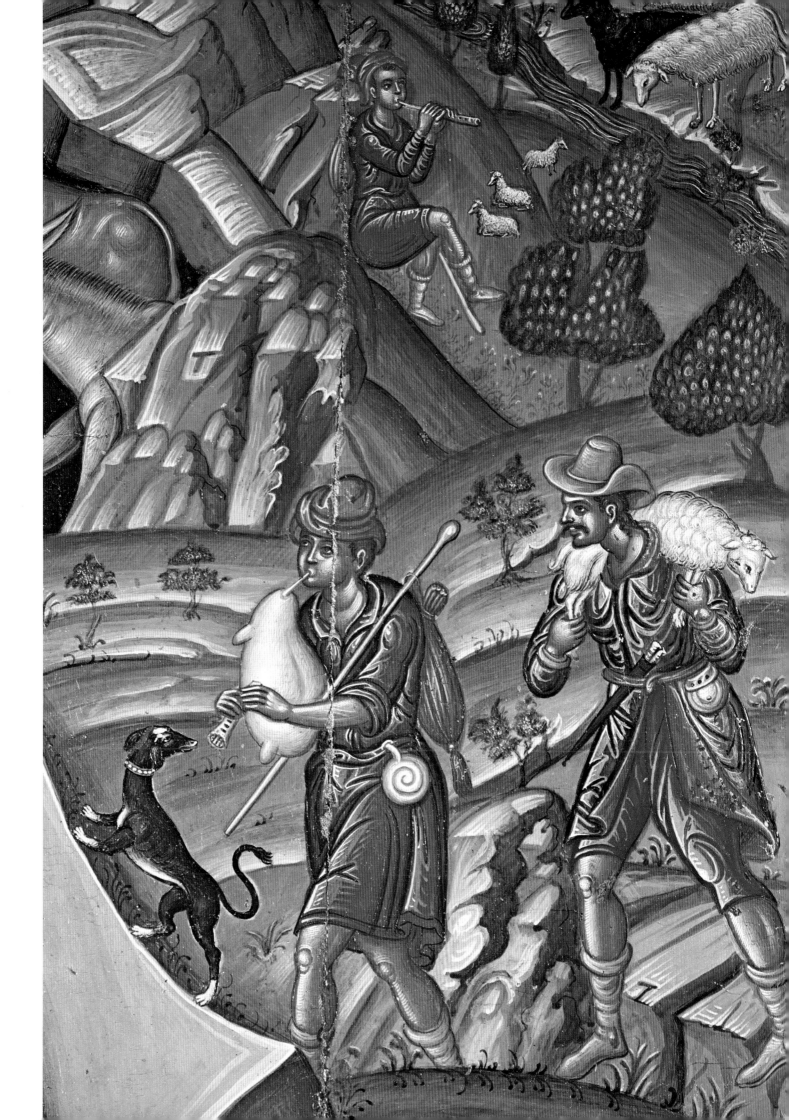

5. *Pellet-bells on silver gold-plated censer (1622). Great Lavra Monastery, Mount Athos.*

4. *Pellet-bells on silver incense-boat (c. 1800). Great Lavra Monastery, Mount Athos.*

6.   *Miniatures of the Romance of Alexander the Great, 14th cent., Ms. of the Greek Institute in Venice : 1. Flute, trumpet, tambourás, f. 49 v.*

2. *Flute, tambourás, f. 75 r.*

3. *Tambourás, flute, clappers, harp, f. 91 r.*

7. *Shawm. Wall-painting: Parable of Dives and Lazarus (detail), 16th-17th cent. Loukous Monastery, Astros, Kynouria.*

none other than the heroic hexameter in which the Homeric epics were recited.[4] Their work has also pointed out the relationship between the tuning of the ancient Greek lyre and modern Greek folk music,[5] and that the two basic ancient Greek rhythmical genera — the *dhiplásion* (double, 1:2) and the *hemiolic* (1:1 1/2), survive with their ancient characteristics fully preserved, especially in the *syrtós* dances in 2/4 and 7/8 (or 7/16) time.[6] What is more, the word *syrtós*, which is applied to the most common form of circular dance in today's Greece, is known to have existed as early as the first century A.D., from an ancient Greek inscription.[7] In addition, this dance formation can be recognised in archaeological finds (representations on vases, statuettes, and terracottas). All of these represent the dancers linked either hand-on-shoulder or hand-in-hand, and with the instrumentalist in the centre — a picture to be seen today in every Greeek village and at every Greek fair. Finally, we should note the relationship between modern Greek folk melody and Byzantine music, illustrated, among others, in Samuel Baud-Bovy's recent work *Folk Songs of Western Crete*.[8]

Greek folk song

Greek folk song may be divided into two principal cycles. The first of these is the *akritic cycle*, created between the ninth and the eleventh century, and expressing the life and struggles of the *akrites* (frontier guards) of the Byzantine Empire. The second or *klephtic cycle* came into being between the late Byzantine period and 1821. The *klephtic cycle*, together with other songs of the same period —historical songs, *paraloghés*, love-songs, wedding-songs, songs of exile, dirges, etc.— express the life of Greeks of more recent centuries. Given the epic spirit of the *akritic* songs, the proud tone of the *klephtic* songs, and the sheer lyricism of the island melodies, these two song-cycles reflect —in an indivisible unity of words, music and dance— the Greek people's struggles for freedom, their joys and sorrows, their attitudes towards love and death. (*Klephtis*, or thief, in time came to mean the combatant for liberty).[9]

Apart from the term *dhimotikó traghoúdhi* (English, folk song; French, chanson folklorique; German, Volkslied), the term *laïkó traghoúdhi* (English, popular song; French, chanson populaire; German, volkstümliches Lied) is also employed interchangeably, even by specialists in the field of folk music. As far as musicology is concerned, however, these two terms are not always considered to mean the same thing. 'Folk song' by definition, refers to the old songs of a given people, whereas 'popular song' refers to more recent musical creations. The specific chronological dividing line between these two categories depends in each case upon the historical and social conditions prevailing in the particular country in question.

In Greece, the category of 'folk song' includes all those songs created before the 1821 War of Independence — those songs belonging to the *akritic* and *klephtic* cycles. That of 'popular song' extends to cover all the more recent songs, such as "Uncle-Yianni with the jugs", the *Athenian cantádha*, modern *rebétika* songs, etc.

The same two terms also apply to Greek musical instruments. The *líra, laghoúto* (lute), *tambourás, gáida* (bagpipe), *zournás* (shawm), *daoúli* (drum) and other instruments belong to the category of *folk* musical instruments. By contrast, instruments such as the violin *(violí)*, clarinet *(klaríno)* and the guitar *(kithára)*, which have all come into general use in more recent times, belong to the *popular* category. Despite this distinction, the term *popular musical instruments* has acquired a certain predominance in usage, regardless of the age of the instruments in any given instance.

The establishment of the year 1821 as a measure to divide 'folk' from 'popular' songs, is obviously no more than an arbitrary methodological delineation, which simply helps classification and study in the field. Representing as it does the end of one epoch and the beginning of another in Greek history, nevertheless many features of the pre-independence period survive into the subsequent age, and many of the roots of the life-style of the sovereign state can be traced back to the years before 1821. This observation holds true for the songs of the Greek people as well; the ultimate criteria for assigning individual songs to one or the other category are entirely literary and musical.

Nowadays, given their increased knowledge and new research methods, many ethnomusicologists reject this division of the songs of a nation into old and new with the corresponding designations folk song and popular song. They consider popular creativity an uniform phenomenon, as a continuous stream of invention, and so use a single term: *laïkó traghoúdhi* (popular song, chanson populaire, Volkslied). The position of ethnomusicology regarding popular musical instruments is similar. The alternative term proposed, however, *ethnic musical instruments* (instruments de musique ethnique)[10] is not easily incorporated into the Greek language, as it tends to create confusion. The Greek adjective *ethnikos* in current usage most closely corresponds to the English and French 'national' and only minimally or not at all to what is implied by the term 'ethnic'.

Greek folk song —diatonic or chromatic, in syllabic or melismatic style— like Byzantine music is monophonic and modal in structure. In other words, without any harmonic accompaniment its melodies are based on a different sequence of intervals than that of the major and minor modes of the West. The primitive 'harmonic' accompaniment —intervals of fourths, fifths, and occasional periodic, momentary dissonances— which we encounter in the playing of certain popular instruments—such as the *líra, kementzés, tsaboúna* (island bagpipe), and *gáida* (mainland bagpipe), etc.,— in no way detract from its monophonic character. To some extent, it owes its peculiar colour to its monophonic character. As is true of any monophonic music, the Greek folk song is performed on the *natural* rather than on the Western *tempered scale*.[11]

Natural Scale

	C	D	E	F	G	A	B	C
Length of strings	1	8/9	4/5	3/4	2/3	16/27	8/15	1/2
Number of vibrations	1	9/8	5/4	4/3	3/2	27/16	15/8	2
Intervals		9/8	10/9	16/15	9/8	9/8	10/9	16/15

Tempered Scale

	C	D	E	F	G	A	B	C
Length of strings	1	8/9	64/81	3/4	2/3	16/27	128/243	1/2
Number of vibrations	1	9/8	81/64	4/3	3/2	27/16	243/128	2
Intervals		9/8	9/8	256/243	9/8	9/8	9/8	256/243

Certain songs of northern Epirus, sung in polyphony without any instrumental accompaniment, constitute an exception to the bulk of Greek monophonic and modal folk songs. The robust character of this popular polyphony in three or four voices, based chiefly on the fourth and fifth intervals and aided by a drone in the lowest voice, recalls the earliest medieval attempts at polyphony.[12] A form of "primitive two-voice singing" is also encountered in certain songs from Karpathos. "These songs for two voices are sung by two women —almost always elderly, as the younger women have given up singing them— who sit arm-in-arm, or rather each with her arm around the other's neck. One of them begins. The other, her partner, takes up the vocal drone, which consists of only two notes, the subtonic and the tonic of the melody... These strange songs must certainly have come from an imitation of the playing of the *tsaboúna* (island bagpipe)... This is not difficult to explain; women, not in a position to pay for instruments whenever they wanted to dance among themselves, imitated the playing of the *tsaboúna*".[13]

From the point of view of rhythm, the Greek folk song is divisible into two broad categories: melodies of *periodical rhythmical type,* and those of *free rhythmical type.* The former are characterised by the periodic repetition of a given rhythmical formula, as in all dance tunes, while the latter are characterised by a free (non-periodical) flow of various rhythmical patterns, as in the songs of the *távla* (table-songs) and others.

Popular instruments — Ziyiá — Companía

Along with singing and clapping, the Greek people have since early times used every available combination of instruments to provide the musical accompaniment for their singing and dancing. Apart from any chance combinations which were usually dictated by the mood of the revellers and the instruments at hand, however, certain instrumental combinations came in time to acquire a definite status as instrumental groups typical of the music of particular regions. Examples of this are the combination of the pear-shaped *líra* with the large *dacharés* (tambourine) in Macedonia, and more recently, the marriage of the pear-shaped *líra* with the *laghoúto* (lute) in Crete. Of these popular groups, the best known throughout Greece are the island *ziyiá* of violin and lute *(violí* and *laghoúto)*, the *ziyiá* of a shawm and drum *(zournás* and *daoúli)* in mainland Greece,[14] and the *companía* consisting of a clarinet, violin, lute and dulcimer *(klaríno, violí, laghoúto* and *sandoúri)*.[15]

The *ziyiá* of shawm and drum, with its loud piercing sound, was, and continues to be wherever it is still to be found, the perfect instrumental group for open spaces, for the fair or feast-day celebrated in the village square. The *companía,* on the other hand, with the clarinet its principal melodic instrument, is today the instrumental combination of mainland Greece *par excellence,* especially adapted to closed spaces because of the soft and flexible nuances of sound its instruments can create. The *companía* is often, though not invariably, joined by a singer, and the number of instruments may vary. None of these variations, however, affect its classical synthesis of clarinet, violin, lute and dulcimer. It is gradually taking the place of the *ziyiá* of shawm and drum, just as the violin is slowly but surely replacing the pear-shaped *líra* throughout the country.

Popular players — Instrument-makers

When monophonic folk song is sung by vocalists who still follow tradition, or performed by players who have not been affected by the catastrophic influence of Western music with its tempered scales and polyphonic technique, then one can enjoy the difference between the major, minor and minim-minor tones of the *natural scale,* and the attractive power of certain principal notes over the secondary; the smaller than semitone intervals; the slight differences, the omission or addition of a few notes by one of the two or more instruments playing in unison the same melody (the ancient Greek *heterophony*). In other words, all these features, in conjunction with the characteristic modes (scales) and rhythmic formations, connect folk song with Byzantine music, and even further back, with ancient Greek music.

The different ways in which popular performers manage to play the *natural scale* intervals and the above-mentioned micro-intervals are quite characteristic. This applies not only to popular instruments —which are made by the players themselves or by popular craftsmen in workshops— but also to such instruments as the clarinet, designed for example, to produce the intervals of the tempered scale. On unfretted chordophones —such as the pear-shaped *líra,* the bottle-shaped *líra (kementzés),* the violin and others— the popular musician who still follows tradition can produce the intervals at will by slightly opening or closing the fingers of his left hand, and especially by sliding the fingers in rapid and expressive glissandi, thus playing the smaller than semitone intervals. "He doesn't stop the strings; he licks the notes" is said of a good violinist, while the *líra*-player is said to "resurrect people's hearts with his fingers". Similar effects can be achieved with aerophones —pipes, bagpipes, shawms, clarinets, etc.— by the complete or partial closing of the fingerholes and through the use of appropriate blowing techniques.

It is to such popular musicians, and above all to those who play instruments suitable for open-air village fair, the shawm and drum *(zournás* and *daoúli)* for instance, that the Greek of the countryside owes his sense of traditional music. Those self-taught players bore upon their shoulders the entire weight of Greek musical tradition, as the dwindling number of their successors continue to do today. This is the tradition not only of the performer, but of the maker of the popular instruments of Greece, for more often than not, the players would perform on instruments of their own manufacture. Thus, in a single person would be united the experience of the musical performer and that of the instrument-maker, each of these two types of experience complementing the other.

A good player's instrument remains, one might say, under continuous manufacture. The island *líra*-player or the drummer of Roumeli (the mainland) will perform at a village fair or wedding, and at the same time will constantly work on his *líra* or *daoúli*. He adds, removes, or alters a spare part, not so much because it has been damaged by long hours of playing, nor yet because it happened to break in mid-performance, but because the player is himself 'obsessed' ('eaten', as the popular Greek expression has it) by his instrument. He is constantly endeavouring to improve its sound, to make it less difficult to play, to increase its resonance so that it can be heard at greater distances, to insure that the notes all sound at the correct intervals, and so on. It is to this constant care and attention that we may attribute the perfection of those instruments made by the player/craftsman of old.

The great differences to be found in the dimensions, the decorations and even the wide variety of shapes of the many different instruments, are all due to the same reason. Each instrument, however faithful the maker's adherance to tradition, bears the personal stamp of its player/manufacturer owner. Island *líras*, for example, differ so much from each other that it would be no exaggeration were one to say no two of them are alike in height, breadth, depth, the lenght of the strings which vibrate when bowed, the head dimensions, the positioning of the pegs, etc. Although they all retain the same pear-shaped outline, some are long and narrow, and may be of greater or lesser depth; others are short and wide-based; some have thin necks, while others have wide ones, and so on.

Popular instruments' workshops

Together with today's players/manufacturers,[16] there also exist several workshops where popular musical instruments are made. These began to appear in the second half of the nineteenth century, first in Athens, and later in Piraeus, Thessaloniki and elsewhere (especially after 1922, which saw the influx of musicians and instrument-makers from Asia Minor and Constantinople).[17] They owed their existence to an ever-increasing demand for instruments of the lute family (*oúti*, *laghoúto*, *tambourás*, etc.). They reached their zenith in the four decades extending from the end of the nineteenth century up to the beginning of the Second World War, a period which coincided with the development of the instrumental combinations, the island *ziyiá* and the *companía*.

The craftsmen in these workshops supplied the popular players with magnificent instruments. These players, travelling from village to village and from region to region with their groups *(ziyiés* and *companíes)*, kept the folk melodies alive. In addition to popular instruments, the same craftsmen also made instruments for 'art music', such as the mandolin, the guitar, the *mandóla* and the *mandolocéllo*, which were widely played up to the Second World War in the instrumental combination called the *mandolináta*. A few of these 'art' instruments have also been used in the performance of folk music.

Listed below are the most important of the craftsmen whose names are linked with the manufacture of instruments of folk and 'art music' in Greece:

In Athens: Emmanuel Z. Veloudios (1810-1875), from Aivali (Asia Minor), the earliest known lute-maker;[18] Dimitrios Mourtzinos (1857-1931), from Aegina; Emmanuel N. Kopeliadis (1852-1934), from Hydra; Nikolaos E. Kopeliadis (1905-1957); Fotis Avyeris (1888-1963), from Terovo (Epirus); Ioannis G. Gombakis, Ioannis G. Stathopoulos, George and Vassilios Panayis, Yiannis Paleologos, Kostas Angelidis, and others. In Piraeus: Michael Skenderidis (1893-1966), from Caesarea in Asia Minor; Yiannis Mouratidis, Stavros Dipapidis, and others.

cantádha, which became especially popular in Athens following the union of the Ionian islands with Greece in 1863.

The folk-like or Italianate melodies, which are sung either by a single voice accompanied by a guitar, piano, or other instruments, or by two voices in a *primo-secondo* arrangement accompanied by the same instruments, likewise belong to the major and minor modes of the music of the West. Of these folk-like melodies, still sung by the Greek people as though they were true folk songs, examples are "To Erinaki" (Little Irene), "To Melachrino" (The Dark-skinned One), "I Smirnia" (The Woman from Smyrna), etc.[25] These songs are accompanied by popular instruments, either the island *ziyiá* (violin and lute), or by the *companía* (violin, clarinet, dulcimer and lute).

The rebétiko song

The *rebétiko* song[26] which emerged in urban centres throughout Greece, especially those with large harbours, constitute the most recent kind of popular urban song. It originally sprang from and appealed to a restricted audience of convicts, dock workers, those who had refuge in hashish and other narcotics; in other words, to the 'down and out' segment of society. The *rebétiko* song is gloomy and fatalistic in content, and was always sung by a single voice.[27] In time its popularity increased until it came to be embraced by a great majority of the working class, reaching its classical period between the years 1940-1950. At that time the principal instruments of the *rebétiko* song, the *bouzoúki, baghlamás,* and guitar, became the established musical accompaniment.

It was then that the "songs became wide, with words that touched on the times and stirred up people's longings on two primal, genuinely modern Greek subjects, *escape* and *love,* a love which has been unsatisfied for three thousand years".[28] In the classic songs of the *rebétiko* tradition, distinguished for their sincerity of passion and power of expression, one can discern the contributions made by elements of folk song, Byzantine chant, and the popular music of the East. After this period, with few exceptions the *rebétiko* cames to be marked by the commercialised over-production of stereotyped, popular-like music and lyrics with mellifluous *primo-secondo* melodies, and by the deafening electronic over-amplification of performances. The ever-increasing number of instruments in the orchestra,[29] together with the transformation of the principal plucked instruments *(bouzoúki, baghlamás,* and guitar) into electronic sound machines, have destroyed whatever else was once peculiar to the *rebétiko* performance. The subtle, silvery sound natural to the *bouzoúki* has become an impersonal blaring devoid of any expression. In this new guise the *rebétiko* has conquered not only the urban centres of Greece, but also the Greek countryside. Gramophone recordings and the radio have carried it to the most remote villages in the country, gradually displacing the traditional folk song in the process.

These two song-cycles, the Heptanesian and Athenian *cantádhes,* as well as the *rebétiko,* nevertheless belong in essence to the realm of 'art' musical composition. Their melodies, many of them the creations of well known composers, were published in the same way as the works of composers of 'art music', and were performed on instruments also belonging to 'art music' (guitar, mandolin, piano, etc.), or on instruments belonging to both 'art' and popular music. These types of song are mentioned here because, loved and sung by the Greek people for many years, they have themselves become popular songs.

The modern term 'popular composer' has come into use along with the term 'popular music'. A 'popular composer' may be a person with a musical education —as is often the case with composers of Heptanesian and Athenian *cantádhes*— or quite the opposite, a self-taught musician. Most of the *rebétiko* composers never studied music; whatever rudimentary musical knowledge they possess is the result of the considerable experience they have acquired professionally, especially in the last few years, through collaboration with musicians of the so-called 'light music' genre. Naturally gifted musically, they 'compose' their melodies by playing them on their respective musical instruments. When their songs are published, the musical notation is undertaken on their behalf by some other musically educated person from their professional milieu. These popular songs show certain fundamental differences regarding the procedure by which they are brought into being and their popular reception in comparison to true folk songs.

Folk melody was transmitted orally from one generation to the other, during which transmission from mouth to mouth it was constantly reworked. It owes its perfection of form to the long centuries of cultivation and processing. By contrast, the modern popular song *(cantádha* and *rebétiko)* is never subjected to this kind of processing. The product of a single man's creative inspiration, it adheres to the laws governing artistic composition in establishing and transmitting itself. The form accorded it by its original creator is imposed on all and sundry through musical notation and via modern mass communication media (gramophone recordings, radio, and television). In this manner, whatever weaknesses it may possess are perpetuated along with its more positive attributes.

Folk song today

The Second World War, the German occupation of the country, and the upheavals of the years immediately following, all decisively influenced the course taken by the folk song in Greece. After the war, the invasion of every house in every village throughout the country by 'light music', dealt a crushing *coup de grâce* to traditional folk melody. It may be said of the latter that at this point the folk song passed into the final stage of its development.

Since the end of the First World War, particulary following the Asia Minor debacle of 1922, the trend towards urban living focused on the Greek capital, and gradually drove the popular musicians from all parts of Greece to Athens. There, in 1928, they founded their professional society, the "Athens and Piraeus Musicians' Society: Mutual Aid" (See note 17). However, their isolation from their home villages and their severance from the countryside, where folk song is preserved and renewed in spirit and in practice, has decisively influenced both its bearers, the popular musicians and singers, and its audience. This audience, composed of city dwellers, was in time transformed into a more passive receptor, incapable of making any contribution to the renewal and creation of folk melody.

Until the early years of this century, musical tradition was preserved in the villages of Greece, tight communities having little contact with the outside world. This was the milieu in which the last great popular musicians lived and performed their music, far removed from the influence of the music of the West. It was a relatively peaceful life for such musicians and those who lived around them. The events and social changes that came with the twentieth century, however, directly affected the course of folk music. The results were first realised in the urban centres, such as Athens, Piraeus, Thessaloniki and Patras, where, as has been mentioned, many popular musicians had gathered; the effects were felt in the villages immediately afterwards. The Balkan wars and the Asia Minor debacle, the invasion of Western music via the gramophone, the radio, and more recently television, did not merely influence the folk song in Greece; they decided its very fate.

It is possible to maintain that free intercourse with northern Greece and the islands following the wars of 1912-1913 had the effect of 'enriching' the repertoire of musicians from 'old Greece' with dances and songs from Epirus, Macedonia and Thrace.[30] The opposite holds true as well, for northern Greek musicians were 'enriched' by the songs and dances of 'old Greece'. On closer examination, however, one can see that this dissemination of music was not a natural process in either direction. By 'natural process' is meant that which is imposed by time in some remote village or village region, as the seasons slowly pass from fair to fair and from wedding to wedding. There, a musician only fulfills the needs and demands of his native region. The movement towards the satisfaction of the demands of a more panhellenic 'clientèle' of a Macedonian in 'old Greece' or a Peloponnesian in Macedonia was dictated by commercial motives. Ultimately, that 'enrichment' was clearly at the expense of quality, at the expense of traditional style and traditional technique. Much the same process, albeit at a stepped-up pace, took place among the Greeks who migrated from Asia Minor. Thousands of them brought their

8.   *Small bell. Wall-painting: St. George, 14th cent. Church of St. John Chrysostom, Yeraki, Laconia.*

←

9.   *Hand-semanterion. Wall-painting: The death of Ephraim the Syrian (detail), 16th cent. Anapafsas Monastery, Meteora.*

10. *Cymbals, horn. Wall-painting: Jesus is mocked (detail), 16th cent. Great Lavra Monastery, Mount Athos.*

11. *Hand-semanterion. Great Lavra Monastery, Mount Athos.*

←

12. *Tambourás. Wall-painting: Parable of the Prodigal Son, 19th cent. Great Lavra Monastery, Mount Athos.*

13.   *Liras and drum (daoúli). Anastenaria, Aghia Eleni, Serres (1970).*

14. *Liras and drum (daoúli) under the icons, in the "konaki", the private sanctuary of the chief Anastenaris. Anastenaria, Aghia Eleni, Serres (1970).*

15. *Hand-cymbals, bowed stringed-instrument, drum, flute and hand-clapping (?). Miniature, 11th cent., Codex Taphou 14, f. 310 v. Patriarchal Library of Jerusalem (see note 147).*

own songs and dances to the Greek mainland and to the islands, while at the same time they acquired those of their adopted homes. This was an 'obligatory' violent exchange — no less violent indeed, than their forced uprooting from the land of their fathers.

During those years, after 1922, the 'light music' of the West began to infiltrate even more deeply into the lower social strata, thanks to the gramophone and later the radio. This process of infiltration began in the large towns, subsequently spreading to the outlying villages. Today, the popular players and singers still go to perform at fairs and weddings. Now, however, night and day they are exposed to the influence of 'light music' in the towns they live in, with the result that their traditional sensitivity of ear has been blunted, with serious consequences. They have begun to lose their feeling for the modal structure of folk melody and for the *natural scale,* so that the *tempered scale* of the West creeps into their playing and singing, and western harmonisation has begun to appear in their songs and instrumental accompaniments. Aside from all these changes, these same players and singers have begun to learn and adapt the 'techniques' and 'aesthetics' of the gramophone and radio studios. This 'adaptation' creates severe enough problems for performers of 'art music'; for the folk musician it has proved destructive.

A folk musician can only 'function' properly in his natural environment (village fair, wedding, feast), and this invariably entails a close rapport with the singers and dancers. Moreover, the duration of any such wedding-feast or other festivity is never decided in advance; it always depends on the mood and expertise of the dancers, singers and musicians, who constitute a unified and indivisible whole. This many-sided 'dialogue', typical of any authentic traditional performance of folk music, has disintegrated before the onslaught of radio and gramophone studios; the musicians are now isolated in the closed space of a single room, and perform at a specified hour and for a specified length of time. The result is a dead, stylised rendering of folk melody — a living organism whose nature is very sensitive and utterly opposed to any predetermined framework of expression.

The gramophone and radio —and more recently, television— have finally succeeded in 'monopolising' folk music. Once, the seat of folk song was the village, whence its dissemination to the towns; nowadays, the reverse applies. The centre of folk music is now the large town, and particularly the city of Athens. From Athens the commercialised folk song, via gramophone, recordings and radio broadcasts, spreads in all directions, reaching even the most remote Greek villages. The authentic songs and dances which the villager has enjoyed since childhood together with his fellow countrymen are no longer a model or a measure of judgement; it has been replaced by the stylised performances of the gramophone recording and the radio, and by those modern 'folk songs' written by popular musicians. The latter, once they have made recordings of all the old, genuine melodies they can remember, begin to produce 'folk songs' of their own composition. They begin by writing new lyrics to authentic folk tunes, changing the latter just enough to ensure copyright protection for themselves. In time, however, they begin to write new music as well, either by combining motifs from various folk songs, or by composing 'folksy' melodies which they pass off as authentic folk music. Again, their purpose is to ensure themselves the copyrights, and the handsome profits that accompany them.

Despite all these developments, a few popular singers and performers are still to be found in remote villages, keeping tradition alive and themselves unspoiled by the 'civilisation' of technocratic age. Strangely enough, some of these can be found in Athens itself. Such musicians lead humble lives, but they are full of wisdom, and in the very questions they ask one may find instruction. These players —now a *lira*-player from Karpathos, now a bagpiper from Thrace— represent all that has survived today of the true Greek folk song, the accumulated spiritual capital of centuries of tradition.

The study of Greek folk song

The study of Greek folk song is a relatively recent development. Following the liberation of Greece from the Turkish yoke and the creation of the modern Greek state, Greek intellectuals turned their attention almost exclusively to ancient Greece and to the study of ancient Greek civilisation. This trend was reinforced by the Western European travellers who began visiting Greece as early as the Middle Ages, by successive excavations leading to the discovery of the monuments of ancient Greece, and by students of ancient Greek culture —especially literary scholars— and the atmosphere of antiquarianism their many-faceted researches brought to life.

A signal role was played by the musical 'upbringing' of the young nation, first at the hands of musical bands (philharmonics) —especially the Bavarian military band which accompanied King Otto to Greece in 1834— and then, most notably, through the Italian melodrama groups, who literally invaded Athens in successive waves from 1840 to the end of the nineteenth century. Together they provided the sole musical entertainment and education of the Greeks. One can easily imagine the impression those German marches and Italian arias, the harmonised melody, the resounding band, and the theatrical orchestra, made on their Greek audience, then so innocent of any kind of European musical education. Greek urban listeners began to think their monophonic folk music, so closely connected with the tortured years of slavery (1453-1821), somewhat 'poor' in comparison with the polyphonic music of Western Europe; this feeling gradually drew them away from their musical tradition. Withdrawal quickly became indifference, and, not uncommonly, contempt, especially in the upper social strata and among the majority of Greek intellectuals. The latter turned almost exclusively to the music of the Europe of Bach and Beethoven. It should also be pointed out that, to this very day Greek folk song has never been included systematically in school curricula, and is not taught in Greek conservatories. Moreover, there is no chair in musicology in any of the Greek universities.

The earliest impetus towards research and the collecting and publication of Greek folk songs was provided by foreign scholars. Their interest in the spiritual manifestations of the common people dates from the early nineteenth century, and stemmed from the Romantic movement of that time. The two volumes of the first[31] such collection, that of the Frenchman Claude Fauriel, were published in 1824-1825.[32] From then on, the collection and publication of folk songs was undertaken by Greek and foreign literary scholars alike. These collections, however, were only concerned with the verse texts of the songs. An inventory of folk melodies was undertaken at a much later date. With the exception of a few isolated publications in periodicals of the preceding century, the first comprehensive musical collection as such —that of L.A. Bourgault-Ducoudray— was published in Paris in 1876.[33]

This collection, however, as well as many of those that followed, although they will always be of some value in themselves are of little use to the modern student of the music of folk song.[34] Recording in European notation —although some collections were also made in Byzantine notation— was used to designate only the principal notes of each melody. A host of other details were left out, details which are distinctive features of Greek folk song. These include grace notes, gruppetti and trills which embellish every melodic note, the glissandi, the peculiar breathings or pauses, and others. The fact that the cylinder gramophone of the period was not used was responsible for the use of intervals of the tempered scale for the transcription of these melodies in European notation, even though monophonic folk song is sung in the *natural scale* and, what is more, employs intervals smaller than a semitone.

One should not forget that what is known today as 'Greek folk song' constitutes an indivisible unity of lyrics, music and dance. Even if the various scholars divided up this unity for the purpose of study —so that philologists studied the poetry, musicologists the music, and ethnologists and choreographers the dances, each branch treated separately— such a division is quite meaningless for those simple people for whom tradition is still a part of their lives. If one were to ask a rural countryman to recite the words of a song, he would do so to the appropriate tune. This same song (lyrics and music) would be fully realised were he to dance to it at the same time — assuming that it is in fact a dancing song. On the other hand, were one to insiste upon his reciting the lyrics alone, one would soon see that he could not manage to do so; if he tried, he would make mistakes, forgetting words and phrases and eventually coming to a halt. The same would happen were he asked to sing a tune softly, without its lyrics, or again, were he asked to demonstrate the steps of a dance without its music.

This union of words, music and dance is encountered in other manifestations of daily life. For example, a mother will sing melodies of simple words and sequences of intervals —the so-called *tachtarísmata*— to her small child, at the same time dandling the latter on her knees to the rhythm of the song. The same holds true of the lullabies or *nanourísmata*, where the song itself, the gentle rocking of the child in the mother's arms or in its cradle, and the mother's footsteps —themselves a kind of gentle dance-step— all combine rhythmically with the melody sung by the mother until her child falls asleep. Again, in the performance of dirges, or *miroló-yia,* the women gathered to keen over the corpse perform certain movements, always in time with the rhythm of the dirge tune; they rock their bodies to and fro from the waist up, beat their breasts with their hands, shake their heads back and forth of from side to side while grasping their head-kerchiefs at the edges, tear their hair, and so forth. All of this begins quietly enough in a ritualistic manner, but grows in intensity and grief as the hours pass, while the song itself reaches the level of screaming.

In more recent times, between the years 1930-1940, and particularly following the Second World War, collections of folk songs have begun to measure up to the standards of modern musicology. The gramophone and tape-recorder have been pressed into service, and, more importantly, research has been conducted by scholars with adequate philological and musical training. In Greece, the founder of rigorous ethnomusicological scholarship and research into folk song was the neo-Hellenist scholar, musicologist, and conductor, Professor Samuel Baud-Bovy. Thanks to his work, which includes all the most significant studies, transcriptions and publications of Greek folk song, Greece today occupies a position among the family of nations in this branch of study.

The study of popular instruments

Since the appearance of the first collections, those of L.A. Bourgault-Ducoudray (1876), Epaminondas Stamatiadis (1880), and Hubert Pernot (1903), the gathering and study of folk songs has undoubtedly made considerable progress, although there remains the lack of a corpus of all the songs (lyrics and music) of the Greek people. Although positive albeit few steps have been taken in this area of study, the popular instruments of Greece, the very bearers of folk song, remain the *terra incognita* of Greek ethnomusicology. In all of the already published collections a simple listing of the instruments together with a few comments exhausts the subject, which has today become a special branch of research and study in itself. Two studies by Despina Mazaraki on the popular clarinet *(klaríno)* and the shepherd's flute *(floyéra)* respectively,[35] as well as a handful of studies all written within the last few decades, constitute the entire specialised literature on the members of the modern Greek popular *instrumentarium*.[36]

The study of musical instruments sheds light not only on the history of music, as one might suppose, but also on other problems related to acoustics, technology, and decoration, as well as on certain aspects of sociology, religion, economy, and —at a broader level— of history in general. The discovery of a certain musical instrument some place far from its home has frequently helped establish the existence of links and mutual influences between cultures. Moreover, it is generally agreed that a musical instrument has always been one of the "most widely circulating of objects",[37] and that it has always been accorded special significance regardless of the cultural level of the land it belongs to.

Many theories have been proposed concerning the origins of musical instruments. Nowadays, the most widely accepted theory seeks these origins in the early forms of magico-religious dance. Dance and the musical instrument are closely bound up with each other in derivation.[38] Hand-clapping, foot-stamping, and the beating of breast and thighs with the hands; the sound made by a variety of objects, small stones, bones, teeth and others, and later by small bells suspended from ankles, wrists and waists; various cries, usually in a voice disguised by either dancers's masks —which act as a kind of soundbox— or changed on purpose, nasal, throaty, or ventriloquous, during the dance —all of these comprised the first sound-producers used to 'accompany' dancing, magical rituals, work, and other activities.[39] The first 'musical instrument' was man's own body, which, either alone or with the aid of certain objects, can create the two basic components of music: rhythm and sound/noise, as well as yet another musical component, one of particular importance to the study of that distant epoch of the non-European peoples today: that of timbre — a musical element discovered only in recent years by the music of the West.

Ethnomusicology

The study of popular musical instruments is the concern of organology, a branch of ethnomusicology at present most highly developed. Its scope includes not only those instruments still extant (whether or not they are still used), but also those whose former existence is known from literary evidence or from certain representations of them that have been preserved. The development of ethnomusicology over the last fifty years, aided by the gramophone in the early stages and then by the tape-recorder, has not merely widened the horizons of our musical knowledge, but has helped us to understand European music itself much better. Thus, hitherto unsuspected links and exchanges of influence have been identified, and we have come to realise that the debt of Western Europeans is owed not only to ancient Greece, but extends much further, all the way to the Far East. The study of non-European music, and traditional music in general, has had a decisive influence on many of our ideas concerning the Renaissance and the significance of the ancient Hellenic-Roman culture; as a result, we have had to re-examine many issues and to revise ideas that once had been taken for granted.

Until very recently, the appreciation of any non-European culture always took place according to the standards of European humanism. The guideline was always the music of Europe as it developed from the Middle Ages to the turn of the century. Only in recent years have various non-European musical cultures been examined, not from the technique and aesthetic standards of the music of the West, but as self-contained cultures of a certain period, and according to the laws and standards imposed by those very same cultures. Today, the approach of the researcher regarding the musical culture of Cambodia or Bali, for example, is entirely different from what it once was. He is no longer the European who at each step compares and measures and categorises with the yardstick of Western classical music. Instead, he is the researcher who knows very well that before him he has yet another kind of musical culture, having its own laws, its own 'ethos' and its own sence of aesthetics.

The term *ethnomusicology* was coined fairly recently, and has come into use internationally only within the last few decades. Previously, the descriptive terms *comparative musicology, musical ethnology* were used in its stead for the same subject, as well as phrases like *non-European music, musical geography, musical folklore, primitive music,* etc. Whatever the acceptance of the term ethnomusicology in international bibliography, and however much it is taught in the universities as a branch of classical musicology, many facets of this new field are still debated and today it has no generally recognised history.

In contrast to classical musicology, which is primarily the study of all written music, ethnomusicology researches and studies traditional music and traditional musical instruments. In other words, it deals primarily with unwritten music handed down from father to son, from generation to generation. And since 'written' music is, by virtue of a strict system of notation, the 'art music' of the West only,[40] all other non-European music belongs to the realm of ethnomusicology. For this reason one of the definitions of ethnomusicology is "the science and the study of world music with the exception of artistic Western music". Today, the most prevalent definition of ethnomusicology is "the science that studies the musical cultures of the so-called 'primitive' societies, the traditional music[41] of non-European cultures (e.g. China, Japan, India, Arabia, etc.), and in general, folk music".[42]

44

Hence the musical phenomena studied by an ethnomusicologist more often than not belong to a cultural cycle foreign to him. The laws and attributes of the musical world under study (rhythm, scales, forms, structures, musical instruments, execution, etc.) differ radically from his own familiar Western musical system. Quite often he is ignorant of the language of the people or race whose music he studies, and often has to work with material gathered not by specialised researchers, but by travellers, missionaries, ethnologists, and others. Moreover, his ignorance of the environment in which the music under study developed compels him to discover for himself the social conditions both past and present, the relation of music to witchcraft, to religion, and to authority (as, for example, is found in various tribes of Africa and Australia), the language of the people (phonological laws, pronunciation, and accentuation) — all of which are elements bearing upon the music itself. Among the first noteworthy studies of exceptional musical interest are those of Père Amiot on the music of China (1779)[43] and Villoteau's early nineteenth century study of the music of Egypt.[44] The father of ethnomusicology, however, is considered to be the English physicist-mathematician and philologist Alexander John Ellis. His work *On the Musical Scales of Various Nations* (1885) laid the foundation of ethnomusicology as a self-contained science.[45] In his work, Ellis sets forth the conclusions of his observations of many non-European musical instruments, as well as a system by which one can accurately record the acoustical qualities of a musical interval in mathematical relationships. The conclusion of Alexander John Ellis' basic ethnomusicological work is that there exist not only the well-known scales of the West, but also several others based on different, but equally natural and logical principles. His system for the measurement of musical intervals is generally accepted today, and is considered to be most satisfactory in its clarity and exactness.

"Ethnomusicology could never have developed as an independent science if the gramophone had not been invented", maintains one of the discipline's most important representatives, the Dutch ethnomusicologist Jaap Kunst.[46] Indeed, the use of the gramophone, and consequently the tape-recorder, has proved invaluable.

Thanks to these devices, the very style of music can be preserved in addition to the intervals and the rhythm. Thus the nasal quality of the singing of an Indonesian woman or the high head voices of the Pygmies —elements as vital to the study of these musical cultures as tonality, scales and rhythm— can be preserved and studied. The gramophone was first used towards this end in America, in 1889, by W. Fewkes, who recorded melodies of the Zuni Indians. Five years later it was used in Europe by the Hungarian B. Vikas to record Hungarian folk music. Since then, thanks to the gramophone and tape-recorder, the scientific collection, study, classification and publication of ethnomusicological material has been the task of the different phonographic archives established throughout the world; first in America,[47] and later in Vienna circa 1900 by E. Exner; in Berlin in 1902 by S. Stumpf, et alii.

In Greece, the first to use the cylinder-phonograph to record folk songs was Hubert Pernot, in 1898-1899.[48] Almost ten years later, the Athens Conservatory entrusted Constantine Psachos, professor of Byzantine music, with the recording of folk songs in the village of Mourla (Aegion) in 1910, and in Lakki (Crete) in 1911; a phonograph was used both times.[49] Thenceforth, the recording of folk songs with the aid of the phonograph and subsequently with the use of tape-recorders has been undertaken by three institutions: the "Musical Folklore Archives" (1930), founded and directed by Melpo Merlier; the "Society for the Dissemination of National Music" (1929), founded and directed by Simon Karas; and above all, the "Greek Folklore Research Centre" of the Academy of Athens. The latter's musical archives today contain 21.000 recording of Greek folk songs and dances on tape.[50]

The present edition

The need for a work on modern Greek popular instruments has been strongly felt for many years now. It is a difficult undertaking, because, as is well-known, there is a lack of specialised monographs on specific topics — a necessary prerequisite for even a general study of the subject. The present publication is intended as a contribution to the study of the popular instruments of Greece; each of these instruments, however, still requires a special study, with musical examples and suitable illustrations (photographs and drawings), of the kind already undertaken by Despina Mazaraki on the popular clarinet,[51] Spyros Peristeris on the island bagpipe,[52] and, most recently, by Fivos Anoyanakis on the lute.[53]

The present study includes those popular instruments which today provide accompaniment for the songs and dances of the Greek people. The names by which they are introduced here in no way exhaust the variety of popular nomenclature and terminology given to any one instrument and its parts — a variety which distinguishes region from region, and sometimes even village from village. As a rule, we have retained the most widely applied name for each instrument.[54] This edition also examines certain sound-producing devices —such as the *símandro* (semanterion), the bell, the whistle, etc.— which are used in a multitude of ways towards as many ends: as apotropaic instruments, signalling devices, children's playthings, etc., from magic and religious rituals to daily labour and entertainment. Certain of these devices are occasionally used as musical instruments. The sound-producers, today as much the focus of ethnomusicological interest as true musical instruments, often led us to the very roots of 'art music', and revealed to us their close connection with magic — that human belief that sound can chase away evil spirits, break a magical spell, cure diseases, and much else besides.

Sound-producers have been widely used in Greece since early times. In church, for example, there were the semanterion and small silver bells of the senior priest's cope; in many traditional rituals *(dhrómena)*, bells were used at the carnival celebrations of Skyros, Sokhos, Nikissiani, and coins jangled on the chests of the *Boúles* (kilted men) in Naoussa; at work, the conch was sounded by sailors to announce the arrival or departure of a caique. Other sound-producers, such as the ratchet *(rokána)* played by adults and children alike at Carnival-time, are used in merry-making. Many children's toys are also sound-producers, as, for example, the different whistles made from tree-twigs of fruit-stones; these are also included in the present volume. After woman, the child is considered one of the most conservative bearer of traditional life-styles. Ethnomusicologists have discovered in many a child's plaything clear traces or even concrete manifestations of adult practices of an earlier epoch. "Children's games mainly consist of the imitation of the lives and pastimes of adults, a living picture of their deeds."[55]

Some toys evidence their original magical function very clearly, as is the case with the bullroarer *(voúga)*, still to be found in many countries under different names, either as sound-producers or as playthings. Originally a sound-producer in the hands of the magicians of socalled 'primitive' societies, in time the bull-roarer was restricted in use to a noisy device for scaring animals away from land under cultivation; in more recent times this usage was abandoned, and it became nothing more than a toy for small children (see *voúga*).

The 'musical instruments' made by the children themselves also belong to the category of sound-producers. Their attempts, first to 'fashion' and then to 'learn to play' a *tambourás* or a *líra*, give them the opportunity to come into contact with traditional musical instruments in the course of their play. Thus, they are able to develop a native talent for imitation, which plays so important a part in their psychological and, more generally, their intellectual development.

Towards the identification and classification of sound-producers and musical instruments, and their allotment to different categories on the basis of common characteristics, we have followed the system of E. von Hornbostel and C. Sachs.[56] This system, accepted nowadays by the majority of ethnomusicologists, divides musical instruments into four principle groups; *idiophones* (instruments whose materials are also the source of sound), *membranophones* (instruments using a membrane), *aerophones* (wind instruments), and *chordophones* (stringed instruments).

For each instrument —according to its nature, its place in the modern Greek instrumentarium, and all available information to date— we provide: the name or names of the instrument; names of its component parts; the construction of the instrument; shapes, dimensions, materials used and methods of construction; principles of construction; the techniques used in its playing;

its musical possibilities (posture of performer, way of holding the instrument, manner of producing sound, melodic and harmonic potential, timbre, dynamics, manner of tuning); when and where it is played, whether or not it is connected with particular rituals, and if so, which rituals; its presence in Greece (its origins, geographical propagation, documentation).[57] In this edition, apart from photographs (coloured and black-and-white) we have also made use of line-drawings, which are especially necessary to depict certain instruments and sound-producers whose construction and function cannot be clearly understood through the use of photographs alone.

In this book we do not deal with the following:

a) Certain instruments, known from church wall-paintings or literary references, which are no longer in use in Greece; for example, the straight and S-shaped trumpets, horns *(kérata)*, clappers *(krótala)*, and the spike bowl fiddle *(kemantzá)*, (fig. 179 in note 58).

b) Those instruments known to us only by name from literary sources, without any other descriptive information, and which are likewise unknown in Greece today; such are the *fengía, tzoukána, tavlabássia*,[58] and others.

c) The trumpet, cornet and trombone, still to be found accompanying dancing and singing in a few small towns in northern Greece; remnants of former philharmonic bands, whose incursion into the sphere of folk music has had no further effects on the latter.

d) The church bell *(kambána)*.[59]

e) The accordion, electric guitar, jazz (percussion) and electric organ — all instruments of 'art music' which have of late begun to infiltrate the territory of folk music, and, since the nation-wide adoption of the microphone and loudspeakers, to appear alongside the traditional popular instruments at fairs and popular festivities.

Collections of Greek musical instruments

Of the existing collections of Greek musical instruments, most important are those of the "Greek Folklore Research Centre" (Academy of Athens) (64 instruments), the "Musical Folklore Archives" of Melpo Merlier (45 instruments), Simon Karas' "Society for the Dissemination of National Music" (80 instruments), the private collection of Fivos Anoyanakis (300 instruments), and the collections of pipes *(floyéres, sourávlia* and *madoúres)* of Despina Mazaraki (150 instruments) and Maria Kinigou-Flamboura (84 instruments).

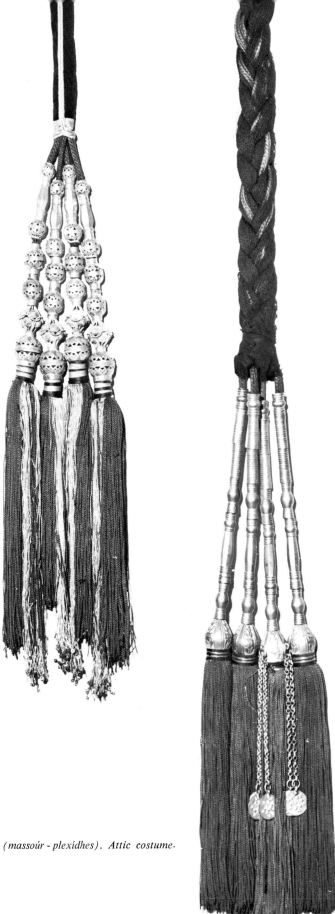

16. Ornament of hair - braids (massoúr - plexídhes). Attic costume. Benaki Museum, Athens.

IDIOPHONES

ZILIA (Cymbals)

Terminology

Zília, also called *tsíngles* (onomatopoeic?), *sachánia, sachanákia* (small frying pans), are small metal cymbals,[60] consisting of two slightly hollowed circular discs, usually of iron or bronze. Each cymbal has a small hole in the centre through which a string (cord, leather thong, etc.) is passed, and knotted on the inside of the disc. When played, the *zília* are held, one in each hand, by these strings; quite often a single string unites both discs. The sound produced is of indeterminate pitch.

Construction

The dimensions of the *zília* vary. Some players —at Megara[61] for instance— prefer large and correspondingly thick, deeply hollowed cymbals, whereas others prefer them small, thin, and only slightly concave. The former produce a deep, 'thick' sound; the latter a thin brilliant sound. Consequently, cymbals of various sizes are encountered, some with diameters ranging from six to eight centimetres, and others, though more rarely, to as much as twelve or even fourteen centimetres.

   For the skilled player, however, the important factor is not the size of the cymbals but the quality of their construction. A pair of cymbals is considered satisfactory when the sound produced by the discs is clear, strong, and homogeneous. The men who make the *zília* —the blacksmiths and bronze-workers— flatten the periphery of the two discs (the former by hammering, the latter by filing) while at the same time testing the cymbals by playing them every so often. The hammering and filing continues until the craftsmen are satisfied with the sound produced. The degree of thinness of the periphery of each disc *(zili)* depends —as the cymbal-makers claim— on its thickness and the depth of the original concavity. However, one should not leap to the conclusion that a specific thickness and concavity necessitate a corresponding thinness at the periphery. There is no rule, nor do the cymbal-makers follow specific proportions as regards size, thickness, or concavity in the course of their work. It is while working on the cymbals that the blacksmith and bronze-worker discover how much they need hammer or file the discs in order to obtain the desired sound. Their essential guides are aural sensitivity, experience and skill in working the metal.

Playing technique

The two *zília* are struck lightly against each other, without any violence, the wrist always free and flexible. The striking of the cymbals is not always a frontal clash, however, especially during the playing of fast, lively melodies. It can be in the nature of a very rapid rubbing of one disc against the other, carried out by a movement of the hands in opposite directions. Because of their concavity, the two cymbals do not make contact over their entire surfaces, but only at the narrow zone of their peripheries, the rims that have been hammered or filed. Thus the sound they produce does not depend solely on the quality of their manufacture, but also on the way they are played. The cymbals —a rhythmical accompanying instrument *par excellence*— in the hands of a skillful player may very well produce expressive nuances of sound; soft and gentle as a caress when accompanying the lyrical melodies of the islands, or austere and abrupt in the dance-tunes of mainland Greece.

Until the advent of the Second World War, cymbals were occasionally played together with other popular musical instruments: for instance, the island bagpipe and cymbals (*askomadoúra* and *zília*) in western Crete, the mainland bagpipe and cymbals *(gáida* and *zília)* in Macedonia, the violin and cymbals *(violí* and *zília)* in certain islands. But for the most part, whether or not played together with the triangle *(tríghono)*, cymbals were the instrument with which children —until a few years ago— accompanied the carols *(kálanda)* sung in many parts of Greece at Christmastide, the New Year and Epiphany. Today, however, there are few places in the country where children are still to be found accompanying carols with cymbals on feast-days.[62]

Finger-cymbals

Besides the type of cymbals already described, another —finger-cymbals— was common until the period between the two World Wars. These were very small (3-4 cm in diameter), were usually made of bronze, and were very fine. These finger-cymbals, long familiar in the East,[63] whence they were introduced to Greece, were played in this country —albeit to a much lesser extent— by women singers and dancers, especially at the so-called café-amán.[64] A pair of finger-cymbals held in each hand (the loop was of a size that enabled the cymbals to be worn on the terminal phalange of the thumb and that of the middle finger) beat the rhythm; the right hand marked the strong beats, the left the weak beats (figs. 1a, 1b). A number of factors contribute to the distinctive colour of the rhythmic accompaniment of the finger-cymbals, such as the movement of the hand, especially the wrist; the quick or 'lazy', strong or weak striking together of the cymbals (in this instance the cymbals are not rubbed against each other but are simply struck together); the ornamentation of the beat with intermediate strokes on the strong, and more especially, the weak beats.

Small finger-cymbals or larger cymbals, held in the hand, were used until only a few years ago in certain traditional rituals (*dhrómena*) in Thrace, such as the *Köpék-Bey* (Turkish, Lord of the Dogs) and the *Kalóyeros* (Monk). Apart from their musical function, the rhythmical accompaniment to processions and dancing,[65] the significance of these instruments as sound-producers intended to drive off evil spirits and purify the sites of the rituals is perfectly evident.

The zília in the Greek world

The origin of cymbals can be traced back to the period of antiquity in Greece.[66] A great deal of information, both from literary and iconographic sources, confirms the part they played as musical instruments in the Byzantine era. The Church, we know, condemned the old pagan music as far back as the earliest centuries of Christianity. Among the instruments proscribed, first by Clement of Alexandria (2nd century A.D.)[67] and later by the other Fathers of the Church, cymbals are also mentioned. "With perfumes, laughter and concerts of songs, for which they require cymbals (*kýmvala*) and the crashing of feet...", wrote Gregory the Divine in the fourth century A.D.[68] Information regarding the use of cymbals is also found in the works, among others, of John Chrysostom[69] and Gregory of Nyssa,[70] and in certain canons of the Ecumenical Councils.[71]

Despite the opposition of the Church, cymbals, as well as musical instruments in general, continued to be played by the Byzantines to accompany songs and dances at weddings, fairs and various entertainments. In his *De Ceremoniis,* the Emperor Constantine VII Porphyrogennetus (10th century) refers to tambourines *(défia)* and hand-cymbals *(cheirokýmvala)* being played together with other instruments at imperial weddings.[72] Nikitas Choniatis (12th-13th century) also refers to the playing of cymbals *(kýmvala)* and drums *(týmbana)* at a wedding: "Cymbals were clashing all that night, and drums were beating...".[73] Before their wedding, Digenis and "the maiden" were acclaimed with songs and hand-cymbals:

> *And comely handmaidens, brilliantly adorned,*
> *Some bearing flowers, roses, myrtle boughs,*
> *Perfuming the air with balmy scents;*
> *Others were beating cymbals (kýmvala) as they sang*
> *A song exceedingly sweet, praising the young man,*
> *The maiden with him, and the parents of both.*

Cymbals, here referred to as *zília* (their present name), are mentioned in the following lines of a Cypriot folk song:

> *What does the king want with me, why has he summoned me to go to him?*
> *If he wants me to dance, I must also take my cymbals (zília).*[74]

From Leo Deacon (10th century) we learn that cymbals, as well as other instruments, were played in the course of the performance of martial exploits: "After ordering the army drawn up in deep ranks, he then gave the order that the trumpets sound the war song repeatedly, that the cymbals clash, and the drums loudly roll".[75] Further evidence —this time culled from a Byzantine Book of dreams— underlines the part played by cymbals in the everyday life of the Byzantine people: "To see cymbals clashed or held, or dancers with cymbals, means battle and lamentation".[76]

Cymbals are also one of the most frequently represented musical instruments in Byzantine and post-Byzantine art. Both types of cymbals, large and small, are encountered over and over again in numerous miniatures and wall-paintings.[77] A study of these representations suggests that the present day cymbals *(zília)* are morphologically identical to the cymbals of the Byzantine era *(kýmvala).* They have the same dimensions, and are played in the same manner. A comparison between these cymbals and ancient Greek archaeological finds leads to a similar conclusion.[78]

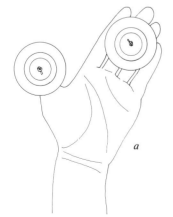 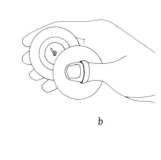

a   b

Fig. 1.

KOUDHOUNI (Bell)

Terminology

The word *kódhon* (bell), *koudhoúni* in modern Greek, is to be found in the writings of ancient Greece as early as the 5th century B.C.[79] In our time, *koudhoúni* is a generic term applied to all kinds of bells, regardless of their shape, weight, and the materials used in their construction. Nevertheless, in certain regions of Greece where animal husbandry is highly developed —the pastoral world of shepherds and sheep-folds— we encounter a host of other names which are indicative of shape, size, weight, material of construction, sound produced (onomatopoeic), the kind of animal to which they are attached, the place of manufacture, etc.[80] However, among this plethora of names, we can easily distinguish four basic types of bells, found principally on the Greek mainland, especially among the Sarakatsani.[81] These are the *'koudhoúni'*, the *tsokáni*, the *kýpros,* and the pellet-bell *(spherikó koudhoúni)*.

According to the method of construction and materials used, bells in Greece are forged *(sfyristá),* made from copper-plated sheet-iron, or cast in brass or bronze *(chytá)*. Of the four basic types, the first two and their variants (figs. 2-14) are forged bells, whereas the latter two types and their variants (figs. 15-20) are cast-bells. All types of bells are made in various sizes. Forged bells are made by bell-makers or blacksmiths, and cast-bells by the so-called *kyprádhes* (kypros-makers), bronze-casters or makers of weighing scales.

The 'Koudhoúni'

Apart from its generic sense, the term *'koudhoúni'* is also used to describe a particular type of bell (when so used it will appear in the text inside inverted commas). This kind of bell is encountered more frequently than any other throughout Greece (fig. 2); it is to be found in many different regions, with slight variations of shape or simply under different names, such as the *boúka* (Naxos), *poungí* or *poúngos* (Karpathos), *trakaliéro* (onomatopoeic) (Kalymnos), and *lighnotsámbalo* (Rhodes); in the Dodecanese, besides the panhellenic, generic term *koudhoúni*, bells of a similar type are also called *tsambália*. The large, heavy *'koudhoúni'* is also called *koudhoúna, koúna* (Cyprus), *bíba, bíbisa, bímtsa, pípa, bibína* (onomatopoeic), *batáliko, batáli,* etc.

There are also several important variations of the *'koudhoúni'* type of bell: the *'koudhoúni'* with its two edges slightly bulging at the widest part, used in bygone times by the Sarakatsani (fig. 3); another model having both sides sharply bent to a point at the widest part —the so-called *yanniótiko koudhoúni me aftiá* (bell of Ioannina with 'ears') (fig. 4); the *dhimitsaniótiko koudhoúni,* (bell of Dimitsana), which is long and narrow with a small triangular opening on the lips (fig. 5); the *chondrotsámbalo* or *kourkoúta* or *tsambalás* of Rhodes (fig. 6); and the bell most often used for the flokcs of Roumeli in the past— a large *'koudhoúni'* with a small *kýpros* (see below) in place of the usual clapper (fig. 7 and 8).

The Tsokáni

The second type of bell, an isosceles trapezion in form, is the *tsokáni* or *tsoukáni, tsoukána, tsiokáni, tsókanos, tsakári, tráka, trokári, trokáni, troungáni, tsiakárka, tsiakaroudháki,* etc. (fig. 9). The same type of bell is also called the *platikéfalo koudhoúni* (wide-headed bell) in Macedonia, and *charcháli* or *charchála* in the Fourni islands of Ikaria.

Variants of the *tsokáni*[82] include the *tsokáni* with its large surfaces slightly curved (fig. 10); the *fouchtokoúni* or *chouchtokoúni* or *chochtokoúni*, a long narrow *tsokáni* found in Cyprus (fig. 11); the same variant, with a wider upper part and slightly bent at the two edges is called *tsambáli* in Kos (fig. 12); the *léri* (fig. 13) and the *sklavéri* (fig. 14), made and used on the island of Crete,[83] are also known as the *tsáfara*.[84]

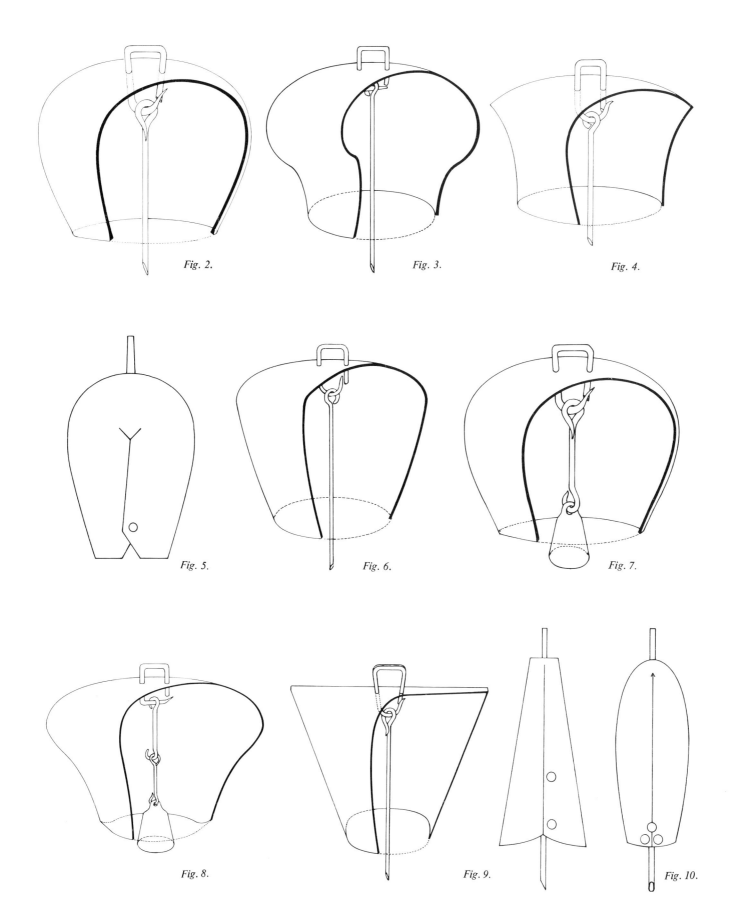

Fig. 2.

Fig. 3.

Fig. 4.

Fig. 5.

Fig. 6.

Fig. 7.

Fig. 8.

Fig. 9.

Fig. 10.

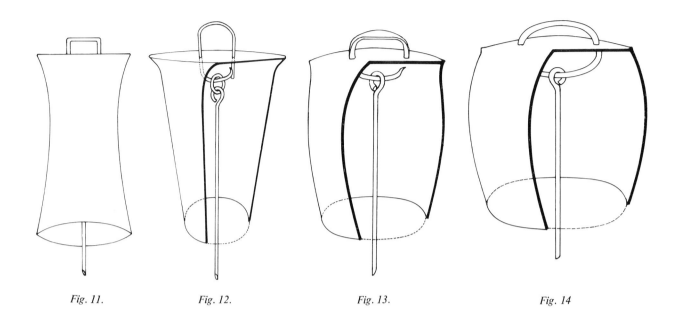

Fig. 11.   *Fig. 12.*   *Fig. 13.*   *Fig. 14*

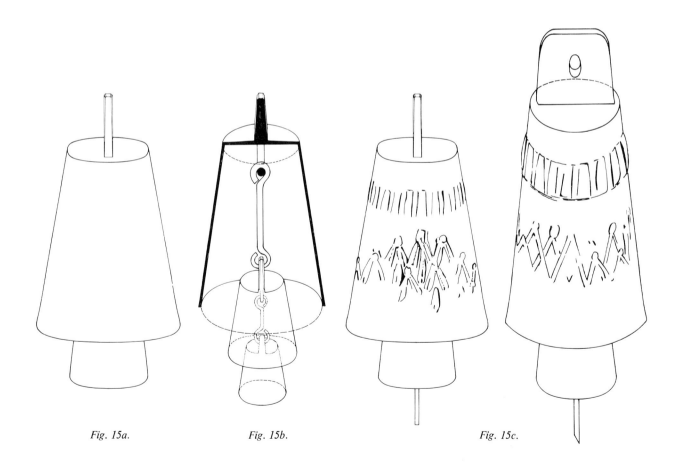

Fig. 15a.   *Fig. 15b.*   *Fig. 15c.*

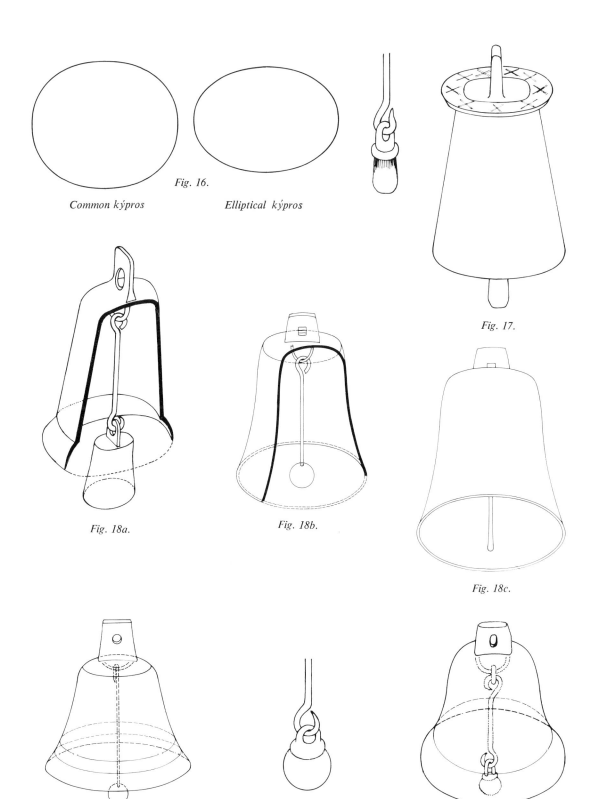

Fig. 16.

Common kýpros

Elliptical kýpros

Fig. 17.

Fig. 18a.

Fig. 18b.

Fig. 18c.

Fig. 19a.

Fig. 19b.

The Kýpros

The third type of bell has the shape of a truncated cone with two elliptical bases, and is called *kýpros, kyprí* (sing.), *kyprokoúdhouno* (fig. 15a, 15b, 15c); In Epirus the large *kýpros* is known as *kambanéli;* elsewhere (Crete, Cyprus, Kos, Karpathos, Naxos, etc.), the term *kambanéli* is used for any kind of *kýpros*. In Cyprus, the small *kambanéli* is called *psilárin*. The *kýpros* having a smaller *kýpros* as a clapper *(parákypros* or *parakoúdhouno)* is also known as the *dhiplókypros* (double kypros) (fig. 15a, 15c). When two smaller *kýpri* (pl.) are hung in side a larger *kýpros,* one inside the other, it is called *triplókypros* (triple kypros) (fig. 15b). In the district of Elis, the *dhiplókypros* is called *dhighónia*.[85]

Fig. 20a.

Variant forms of the *kýpros:* The *plakerós kýpros* or *plakoúla,* or *encháraktos kýpros* (engraved kypros), whose two bases are more elliptical (fig. 16); in Naxos, the small *plakerós kýpros* is called *chlividháki*. The *monós kýpros* or *monókypros* (single kypros) having a protruding upper base (fig. 17). The *kýpros* with slightly upward turned lips and a curved upper base (fig. 18a, 18b, 18c); the latter variant of *kýpros* is encountered in Epirus and occasionally in other regions of Greece; in Rhodes it is called *rabaoúni* or *rabáouna*. The *kambanéli* or *kambanítsa* or *vlangári,* whose base is always circular in shape (fig. 19a, 19b).

The Pellet-bell

The fourth type of bell, the pellet-bell *(spherikó koudhoúni)* is known under the following names: *gringarídhi* or *ghreveláki* (Sarakatsani), *vrondíli* (Rhodes), *drouganéli* (Epirus), *soussounári* (Cyprus), *ghargh'áli* or *foúska* and *foúka* (Thessaloniki area), *koudhoúni* (Karpathos), *zíli* (Paramythia area), *roghovíli* (mainland Greece), *yerakokoúdhouno* (Roumeli, Crete and other islands) (fig. 20a, 20b).[86] One should also note the *acheloniá* on the island of Kos,[87] a bell of primitive manufacture, made from tortoise shell, with a small stone hung inside instead of a clapper (fig. 21).

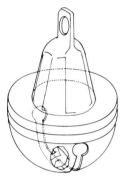

Fig. 20b.

Construction of forged bells

In the construction of forged bells, the *'koudhoúni'* and the *tsokáni,* sheet-iron approximately 1-1.5 mm thick is worked by the bell-makers. Formerly, copper was also used in the making of these bells, but today only sheet-iron is used. (See Pl. 17, 1-8).

Stages of conctruction and tools: The sheet-metal is cut into various shapes and sizes using special models or forms for each type of bell or variant; e.g. the *'koudhoúni'* (fig. 22), the *tsokáni* (fig. 23), the *léri* (fig. 24), and the *sklavéri* (fig. 25). The *pósta* is then prepared; this consists of five or six precut pieces of sheet-metal sandwiched together, and held in place by a thin rivet fixed at the very tip of one corner (fig. 26). The *pósta* is then heated over a furnace —in earlier times, charcoal and a bellows were used; nowadays coke and an electric motor are used— and the several sheets of metal making up the *pósta* are hammered, thus being hollowed for the first time. Each resulting hollowed sheet of metal is known as a 'cap' *(skoúfia)* (fig. 27). The hammering out is done with a special long hammer, the *ghouviastíras* (hollower) (fig. 28). Several hammerings of the 'cap' follow, both while it is red-hot and after it has cooled, on the anvil-mould *(kaloúpi)* (fig. 29). This anvil-mould, today made of cast-iron, was formerly made from hard stone or a hollowed piece of wood. In the Cretan smithies the sheet-metal forms are hammered without having been previously heated in the crude furnaces there.

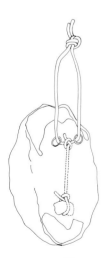

Fig. 21.

Then after the lateral edges of the 'cap' have been joined together, the *zoumbás* or *zombás* (fig. 30a) is used to punch out one or more holes according to the size of the 'cap' on both sides, low down where the lips of the 'cap' are joined; the two lateral edges are then riveted together (fig. 31, also see figs. 5, 9, and 10). With this joining and riveting of its lateral edges, the 'cap' takes on a bell-shape (fig. 32). In earlier times, other methods were used to join the two lateral edges, by clasping *(thilíkoma)* (fig. 33), or by bending them at their edges (fig. 34). In the smithies of Crete, in addition to the rivet, they also use the *thiliá* or *psallídha* to join the two edges — this is a small rectangular metal clip which is folded over and pinches the lateral edges where they join (fig. 35).

58

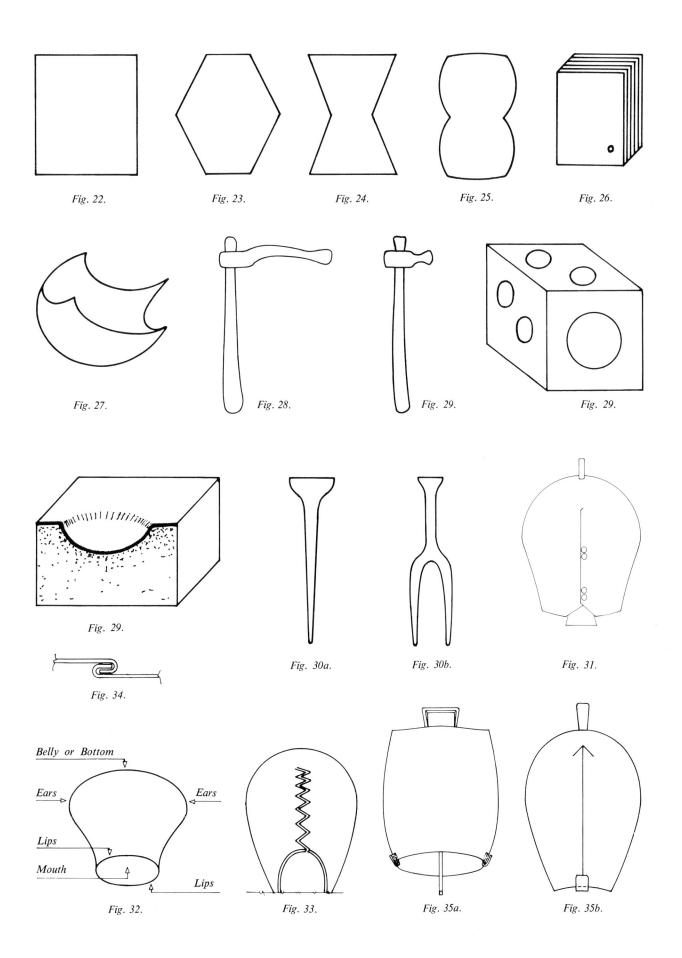

Fig. 22.

Fig. 23.

Fig. 24.

Fig. 25.

Fig. 26.

Fig. 27.

Fig. 28.

Fig. 29.

Fig. 29.

Fig. 29.

Fig. 34.

Fig. 30a.

Fig. 30b.

Fig. 31.

Belly or Bottom

Ears

Ears

Lips

Mouth

Lips

Fig. 32.

Fig. 33.

Fig. 35a.

Fig. 35b.

Next follows the final hammering on the anvil-mould *(kókoras* or *zoúmbos)* (fig. 36a, 36b, 36c). Then two holes are punched in the 'belly' of the bell with a double punch *(zoumbás)* *(fig. 30b)*; through these holes the staple *(thiliá* or *vastáki* or *ambeliá)* from which the clapper will be hung is inserted (this is done over a ring-shaped base, fig. 37). Finally, a special pair of shears or a simple, large pair of metal cutters *(sidheropsállidho)* is used to make even the lips of the bell around its mouth (fig. 38).

Fig. 36a.

The clapper, *ghlossídhi* or *ghlóssa* (tongue), or *avdhéla,* or *sístros, sístro,* apart from the single exception mentioned (fig. 7, 8), is a thin iron rod which causes the bell to sound when it strikes against the lips. Its size and thickness are in proportion to the size of the bell. In good workshops, the clapper is never suspended directly from the staple, but from a small leather thong passed through the staple (fig. 39). This thong prevents the two metal parts, the staple and the clapper, from rubbing against each other, thus avoiding damaging the bell while at the same time contributing to the quality of its sound. It should be noted that the finished bell is copper-plated —on both its internal and external surfaces— in order to protect it from oxidation, and to close the holes made for the insertion of the staple and the slots made at the points where the two lateral edges are joined. (The bells are copper-plated with an alloy of earth, copper, water and salt which is prepared in a furnace).

The 'tuning' of forged bells

Fig. 36b.

Finally, a special hammering of the bell is carried out to 'tune' it; this hammering leaves what look like small scratches all around the circumference of the bell, from the middle of the body downwards (fig. 40). In Crete this process consists of a slight hollowing of the bell's surface, called *kordhonáki* or *siríti* (cord, thong); this is accomplished by hammering the bell a little above the lips (fig. 41), or by simply hammering thin the lips around the mouth of the bell.

The pitch of the note produced depends on the weight and size of the bell, as well as on this final 'tuning' process, the so-called *skáliasma.* The larger and heavier the bell, the deeper its sound. The reverse also holds true: the smaller and lighter the bell, the higher the pitch of the note it produces. During the 'tuning' process the craftsman gives each bell the sound most appropriate to its size and weight. While hammering the bell, he tests it every so often by listening to the sound it produces when lightly struck against his anvil. As a guide —one could say as a tuning-fork— he uses a bell of the same size and weight which has previously been subjected to the same treatment. In many workshops, however, even though bells of approximately the same size and weight are to be found, they nevertheless differ in pitch: two bells of the same size and weight often vary in pitch from workshop to workshop. Until the Second World War, one could also find bells with different weights but the same pitch. Those craftsmen good at 'tuning' bells were always few and far between; apart from love of the work and the need of many years of experience, the bell 'tuner' was also required to have a good musical ear.

Fig. 36c.

Nowadays, specialists of this kind are becoming even more difficult to find. This is due to a combination of factors, such as the decline of animal husbandry and the closure of most smithies; the invasion of the music of the West, which reaches the most isolated Greek villages via radio, television and the cinema; the alienation of the villagers themselves from the roots of their musical traditions; and generally, indifference to the fate of traditional music in Greece.

Until the first decades of this century, the notes produced by the 'tuning' process were a tetrachord, covering a perfect fourth (e.g. C-D-E-F). In other words, the notes C-D-E-F were 'tuned' to four bells, with a corresponding difference in size — the first bell giving C, the second D, and so on. The same four notes were then repeated, either one octave higher or one octave lower; that is, they were 'tuned' to smaller or larger bells. The choice of the notes of the perfect fourth was not, of course, fortuitous. They represent tradition, the sequence of intervals on which old folk melody is based (see *Introduction*). As for the repetition of this same sequence of intervals an octave higher or lower, this may be attributed to the fact that the shepherd —for whom bells are a source of both pleasure and assistance in his hard work— and the bell-maker alike carry this sequence of intervals inside themselves; they are familiar with it through the playing of the pastoral flute *(floyéra)*, which can repeat a melody one octave higher by overblowing.

With the passing of time and the insidious influences of Western music, the craftsmen bell-makers began to make use of the notes G-A-B as well. In this way, they came to 'tune' their bells to seven instead of just four notes —to C-D-E-F-G-A-B— in other words, to the diatonic scale of seven notes. Until the advent of the Second World War, the tonal range within the reach of those bell-smiths who made bells of the *'koudhoúni'* type, shown in fig. 2, was approximately two octaves, or sixteen notes, beginning below the stave in the treble clef (depending on the workshops and the size of the bells made). The *kýpros* type of bell was also 'tuned' to cover much the same range of notes (fig. 15).

At that time, shepherds who really loved bells would sometimes add intermediate 'voices' to those they owned. Apparently they acted under the influence of the ornamental style of the free-rhythm type of melody found in the *klephtic* songs — a decorative idiom practiced both by players and singers,[88] especially since the days when the clarinet ousted the shawm to become the leading instrument in the *companía*.[89] The shepherds thus added C sharp and D sharp in order to achieve a 'richer harmony'. In this manner the diatonic tetrachord C-D-E-F was transformed into the chromatic C - C sharp - D - D sharp - E - F.[90]

Here one should note that the craftsmen bell-makers who carried out the 'tuning' process on the bells they made, actually 'heard' intervals; in other words, they perceived notes in terms of their tonal relativity and not as isolated notes of absolute pitch. In addition, these intervals were of the *natural scale,* and not of the tempered scale (see *Introduction*). Moreover, the notes 'tuned' to a series of bells were not pitched with perfect accuracy. Essentially, it was only the low, basic tetrachord (e.g., C-D-E-F, beginning with middle C) that was accurately pitched. In contrast, the absence of accurate pitch was evident in the higher notes; the higher pitched the notes, the more apparent was this defect. This observation also applies to the cast type of bell, the *kýpros* (fig. 15). The latter however, due to the materials used and the method of construction, generally had a more clearly determined pitch. In any event, although one can easily distinguish that the pitch is progressively higher the smaller the bell, in small bells of both types —those with the highest pitch, for example— it is impossible to accurately determine the pitch of the sounds produced; therefore, it is also impossible to determine the intervals between those notes.

Nowadays, 'tuned' bells with a range of two octaves are not to be found in any Greek workshop. In the greater centres of bell manufacture —Amphissa (forged bells of sheet-metal), and Ioannina (brass or bronze cast-bells)— no more than eight or ten sizes of bell are made for the simple reason that shepherds no longer request more than that number. What is more, it is only rarely that even these ten sizes of bells are accurately 'tuned'.

The second type of forged bell, the *tsokáni* (fig. 9), is made in very much the same way, although a few of the details of construction differ. In general, the *tsokánia* are considered to be bells of inferior quality; they are made of thicker sheet-metal, and in most workshops they are not copper-plated. Series of *tsokánia* that were 'tuned' could be found in Greece until the advent of the Second World War, chiefly in Amphissa. Nowadays, *tsokánia* are made only in small and medium sizes, and are not 'tuned'.

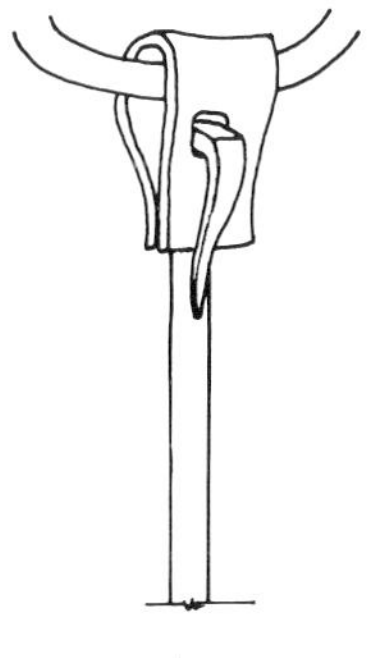

Construction of cast-bells

Cast-bells —the *kýpros* and its variants, together with the pellet-bell— are made of brass and bronze; the smaller sized bells are made of brass (an alloy of copper and zinc), while the larger bells are made of bronze (an alloy of copper and tin). The latter alloy is the stronger, and better withstands humidity and constant use.

Every size of the *kýpros* and the pellet-bell has its bell-shaped model or form. This is used to construct the mould *(kaloúpi),* into which is poured molten brass or bronze, previously heated to its liquid state in a furnace. The concave mould is constructed of damp, clean earth, placed in a pair of bronze containers *(pandéflia)* — the uppermost container is known as the 'male', and the lower is referred to as the 'female'. The 'female' container serves to form

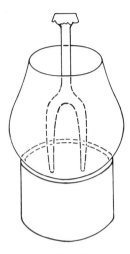

Fig. 37.

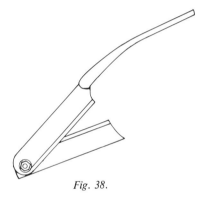

Fig. 38.

Fig. 39.

61

the external surface of the mould, while the 'male' container is used to make the internal surface. (See Pl. 18, 1-14).

Stages of casting and implements used: The bell-shaped model is placed inside the 'female' container (fig. 42); the latter is then filled with earth, thoroughly pounded so that it will hold firm (fig. 43). The container with the compacted earth and the bell-shaped model inside is then inverted, and the model is removed. Thus the earth remains in the container, holding the impression of the external surface of the model, as well as a path *(dhrómos)* —a groove which has been opened in the earth through which the molten metal will later be poured (fig. 44). An iron staple is then placed in the small base of the model, from which the clapper or the *parákypros* will later be hung. The bell-shaped model is then filled with earth, and an iron rod is placed inside to avoid scattering the earth and disturbing the position of the iron staple when the model is removed (fig. 45). The model, still full of earth, together with staple and rod is returned to its original position in the lower section of the mould (fig. 46). The upper section of the mould is then placed on top of the lower section, and is then filled with earth (fig. 47). The two united sections of the mould are then turned upside down, the lower section is removed (fig. 48), and the model is taken out. The upper section of the mould retains the impression in relief of the internal surface of the bell-shaped model— this is the so-called 'heart' of the model (fig. 49). The two sections of the mould are once again joined together, the lower section retaining the impression of the external surface of the model and the upper section retaining the impression of the internal surface of the model; in other words, the two sections together contain a complete earthen replica of the bell to be cast. They are now ready to receive the molten alloy of brass or bronze (fig. 50). Such moulds are made in great numbers, according to the demands of each casting, and they are squeezed together in a vice, thus ensuring that the upper and lower sections are tightly joined before the molten metal alloy is poured into them.

After its removal from the mould, the ready-cast *kýpros* is then cleaned by filing and grinding with an emery wheel so as to remove any irregularities and smooth any sharp angles or corners. Holes for the suspension of the *kýpros* from an animal's neck are made in the handle, it is 'tuned', and a clapper is suspended inside the finished bell.

The clapper hung inside the *kýpros* is generally a smaller *kýpros* —known as a *parákypros* or *parakoúdhouno* (fig. 15a). Sometimes a second *parákypros* is suspended inside the larger *kýpros* (fig. 15b); more rarely an iron clapper similar to that hung in the 'koudhoúni' and *tsokáni* is used (fig. 15c). A long, thin clapper— not of iron, however, but of bronze— is suspended inside the single *kýpros* (fig. 17), and a spherical clapper is attached to the *kambanéli* (fig. 19). A similar long and thin, or circular clapper is also sometimes hung inside ordinary *kýpros*, as well as in the *plakerós kýpros* (fig. 18). In recent years, and especially since the Second World War, whenever the need to replace the *parákypros* or bronze clapper has arisen —either because of loss or damage —it has become common practice to suspend different objects in its place: a screw, a nail, a piece of thin tubing, etc.

The pellet-bell is cast in a comparable manner, with one important difference; in place of a clapper, one or more small metal balls or pellets are placed in its hollow interior.

'Tuning' of cast-bells

The *kýpros* is 'tuned', or given its 'voice', with a file —through the filing down of the external surface of the bell, especially around the lips. The remarks made earlier regarding the 'tuning' of the 'koudhoúni'— the skill required for the task, as well as the musical interval employed in the 'tuning' process — equally hold true for the *kýpros*. Compared to that of the 'koudhoúni', the sound produced by the *kýpros* is clearer and more intense, which allows for its carrying farther. The 'koudhoúni', on the other hand, produces a more unobtrusive, less penetrating sound.

Among the different bells made in Greece today, only those cast in brass or bronze are decorated with incised motifs in relief (schematic shapes, abstract designs, geometrical designs).[91] For examples of the characteristic designs on *kýpri* and pellet-bells, see fig. 51 and 52.

Fig. 40.

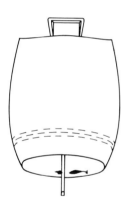

Fig. 41.

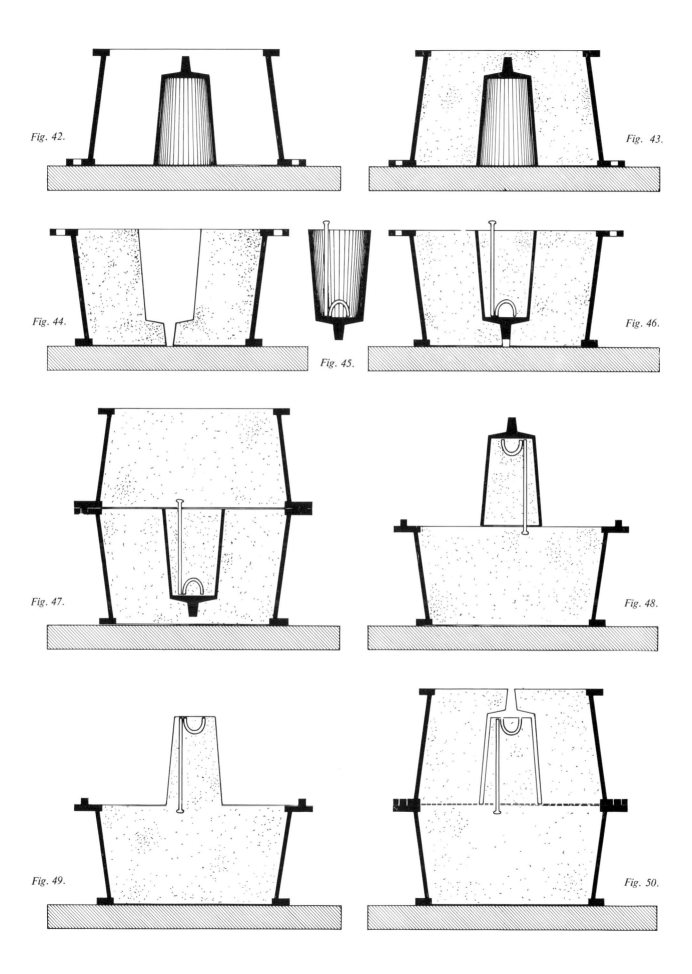

Fig. 42.

Fig. 43.

Fig. 44.

Fig. 45.

Fig. 46.

Fig. 47.

Fig. 48.

Fig. 49.

Fig. 50.

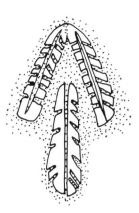

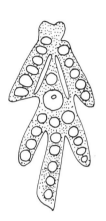

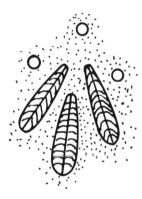

Centres of bell-making

Apart from the two most important bell-making centres —Ioannina for the production of cast-bells and Amphissa for the production of forged bells— the two bell-making processes were also to be found in several other towns in Greece, until the advent of the Second World War. Among these, the most noteworthy were Larissa, Karditsa, Trikala, Messolonghi, Karpenissi, Nafpaktos, Drama, Komotini, Xanthi, Patras, Pyrgos, Dimitsana, Stemnitsa, Crete, Mytilene et alia. Their production satisfied not only the requirements of domestic trade and consumption, but also those of the export trade, significant quantities of bells being sent abroad.[92]

Nowadays, bell-smithies in Greece have become very rare indeed, and few bell-makers are to be found in towns other than Ioannina and Amphissa. Of these exceptions, the most notable are Katerini, Kozani, Thessaloniki, Ayiassos (Mytilene), Chania and Armeni (Crete), and others. A characteristic feature of the changing times is the way in which, in recent years, a good number of the remaining Greek bell-smiths haved turned to production for the tourist trade. Ever increasing quantities of small forged and cast-bells leave Greece for Switzerland, Germany, America, Canada, and elsewhere— to be sold as tourist items.

Original use of bells

Before examining where and how the bell is used, we would do well to recapitulate certain of the conclusions reached by ethnomusicologists regarding its original functions. Curt Sachs, who has collated the results of world-wide research on the bell in his *History of Musical Instruments,* writes that we are still ignorant of its early beginnings, and that we do not know whether the bell was first made of organic materials (nuts, crab claws, shells, wood, etc.) or of metal, nor whether it was originally a form of amulet. Bells were suspended from the necks of animals, not to mark their ownership more clearly, nor yet again for the music the bells made, but to protect the animals from evil spirits. In the same way, the original use of bells in holy places was aimed at protecting such places with the magical power attributed to their sound, and not the summoning of the faithful to worship.[93] It was only much later, with the passage of time, that the bell began to be used by shepherds to aid them in their arduous labour, while at the same time pleasing them with their music; to summon the faithful to church; to warn of the advent of a visitor or customer (when hung over the entrance of a house or shop), etc. It was only then that the apotropaic character and function of the bell lost ground and came to be forgotten; it was only then that the bell became nothing more than a simple sound-producer. The bell as an apotropaic device, sound-producer, or musical instrument, has been chiefly used in Greece for flocks of sheep and herds of goats and other animals, for single animals, in the observance of traditional rituals, in the Church, and so forth.[94]

'Equipment' of flocks

The belling of flocks —'koudhoúnia' for sheep, *kýpri* for goats— first of all serves practical purposes; on the one hand, the bells "protect the animals", while on the other hand they "guide the shepherd and help him in his work".[95] All the same, one should not forget the magical power attributed to their sound, a power which can avert evil —a remnant of pre-Christian paganism. In time, however, the sound of bells —their 'voices'— came to satisfy the shepherd emotionally as well. They gave him pleasure — a pleasure quite free of any profitable valuation. Together with the pastoral flute *(floyéra)* they became his personal music. The extent to which the shepherds regard their bells as a source of joy and music is evident in their traditions of mourning; in earlier times, when a Sarakatsanos leading shepherd *(tsélingas)* died, the heavier bells were removed from his flocks for the period of mourning, and nobody played the *floyéra* during that time.

The shepherd who wishes to equip his flock of sheep or herd of goats with a set of bells must have the same aural sensitivity as the craftsman, or bell-smith, who 'tunes' the bells. The quality of a flock's equipment of bells depends upon the shepherd's love of bells, his ability

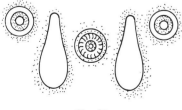

Fig. 51.

64

17.   *Construction of forged bells in the workshop of Theodoros Stamatelos and Ilias Flokos, Amfissa:*

1. Heating of metal sheets in crude furnace.

2   3   4

2. *Hammering of red-hot metal sheets over mould.*
3. *Making of holes for riveting of lateral edges of hollowed metal sheet (skoúfia = cap).*
4. *Hammering on anvil of hollowed metal sheet, the cap.*
5. *Final hammering of cap-bell.*
6. *Insertion of staple for hanging of bell: from this staple the clapper is suspended inside.*
7. *Cutting of bell lips with guillotine to straighten them.*

5

6

7

8. Copperplating of bell over furnace.

18. *Casting of bells in the workshop of G. K. Papanikolaou, Ioannina:*

1. *Bell-shapes, moulds (upper and lower sections), earth and tools for making cast-bells.*

2

3

4

2. Bell-shapes placed in lower section of mould, filled with earth.

3. Bell-shapes removed from upturned lower section. The earth holds the impression of the external surface of the bell-shapes.

4. An iron staple is placed in the small base of the bell-shape, through which the clapper will later be hung; the bell-shape is filled with earth; an iron rod is placed to avoid scattering the earth which would disturb the position of the iron staple when the bell-shape is removed. The bell-shape, still full of earth, together with staple and rod, is returned to its original position.

5. 6. 7. The mould's upper section is placed on the top of the lower and the former is also filled with earth which is then beaten flat.

8. 9. Once closed, the mould is turned upside down, the lower section is lifted off and the bell-shapes are removed. The upper section keeps the imprint – in relief – of the internal surface of the bell-shapes.

10. The fluid metal alloy held over the furnace.

11. Pouring the molten metal alloy into the mould.

12. 13. Cleaning the finished cast-bell by filing and grinding with an emery wheel.

8

9

10

5

6

7

11

12

13

14. *Seals for decoration of cast-bells.*

to choose and harmonise bells, and his economic strength. A study of the belling of flocks of sheep and herds of goats, when animal husbandry was flourishing in Greece, leads to the conclusion that there was no single guiding rule. Each flock of animals had its own characteristic sound, to such a degree that one could distinguish one flock of animals from another, even if they were made up of the same number of goats or sheep. One shepherd might prefer bells with deep 'voices', for instance, while another preferred those sounding in the middle and upper registers. The former would equip his flock with a greater proportion of heavy bells, whereas the latter would use more bells of a relatively lighter weight. Some of the wealthier shepherds had bells hung on half the animals of their flocks; others, perhaps less fortunate, would bell one animal in three, one in five, or yet an even smaller proportion of his animals.

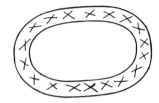

Nevertheless, the choise and matching of the bells does follow a certain procedure, even to this day. If a shepherd has a flock of two hundred sheep, for instance, he will begin by choosing a basic set of bells with deep 'voices', the notes of which constitute a sequence of intervals (e.g., a perfect fourth of C-D-E-F, beginning with middle C). These four bells are hung on four of his largest rams — the animals that have been distinguished as leaders of the flock *(brostáridhes)*. On the other animals in the flock, depending on the means and wishes of the shepherd, bells are hung on half, a third or an even smaller fraction of the animals. These bells have been 'tuned' to the same sequence of intervals as the first four bells (i.e., a perfect fourth), but are pitched differently, and are an octave or even two octaves higher than the basic set. His doing so naturally depends on the shepherd's being able to find correctly 'tuned' bells in the higher registers. The combination of 'tuned' bells makes-up the equipment of the flock, the so-called *armáta,*[96] *takími,* or *douzína.*[97]

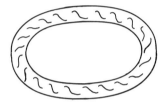

This characteristic, basic combination of bells is only one of many different groups that may be made-up for flocks with the same number of sheep. Instead of the four deep-voiced bells, the shepherd may choose eight, thus doubling his basic *armáta.* Thus the aural character of the flock becomes "richer in deep-voiced bells". Occasionally, in order to achieve a variety of timbres, one set of four bells is made-up of *'koudhoúnia',* while the second set of four bells are *kýpri* of an equivalent pitch; both sets are 'tuned' to the same perfect fourth (C-D-E-F). Alternatively, one may have six *kýpri* and two *'koudhoúnia'* — all of which are 'tuned' to the same pitch. Then again, intermediate 'voices' can be inserted between those of the heavy or medium bells, or both. In this manner, the diatonic perfect fourth (C-D-E-F) is transformed into a chromatic sequence (C - C sharp - D - D sharp - E - F); this is described as being an *armáta* with 'rich harmony'. Similar combinations arise from the shepherd's initial choice, made from the seven notes of the diatonic scale (C-D-E-F-G-A-B); in this case, the tonal range of the basic *armáta* begins with a single octave, and can be extended to approximately sixteen notes.

Fig. 51.

Of greater complexity is the belling of large flocks of 500 or more animals. The reason for this is that 500, 1000, or 1500 animals do not constitute a single large flock but are divided into smaller groups, the sheep flock and the herd of goats. These two broad divisions are themselves sub-divided, the sheep flock into *ghalária* (milch-ewes), *zighoúria* (yearlings), and *stérfa* (sterile sheep), and the goat-herds into *ghaláres ghídhes* (milch-goats), *rífia* (yearlings), and *stérfa.* The head-shepherd *(architsélingas),* who knows just how many sheep and goats his flock contains in all, and into how many smaller flocks it has been divided, will bell his smaller flocks in such a way as to give each of these its characteristic sound — its own 'voices'— as well as maintaining one 'harmony' in the flock as a whole. Each such smaller 'sub-flock' has its own attendant shepherd, as well as its distinctive 'voices' that separate it from the others. Each shepherd knows his flock's 'voices' well. The 'voices' of their bells tell him at every turn where his animals are and what they are doing; in this way, he is able to maintain control over the animals.

The head-shepherd will equip his flock with bells by following the procedure we have described earlier. He will first select the basic *armáta:* four heavy bells making-up a sequence of intervals, e.g. a perfect fourth (C-D-E-F), or eight heavy bells comprising the intervals of an octave (C-D-E-F-G-A-B-C), or twelve bells making-up one octave and five notes, or whatever combination accords both to his fancy and the amount of money he is prepared to spend. He will not, however, limit himself to buying only one basic *armáta,* but will acquire as many as he needs to bell as many animals leading the 'sub-flocks' as he desires. Because his flock in its entirety is made-up of both sheep and goats, he will differentiate between the two; the *armáta* for his sheep will be composed of *'koudhoúnia',* while the goats will be assigned an *armáta* of *kýpri.* All of the *armáta* will naturally be 'tuned' to the same pitch.

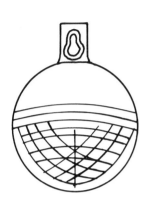

Afterwards, the shepherd will equip the remaining animals of his flock with bells having the same 'voices', but pitched an octave higher than the eight notes of the basic *armáta* (provided the basic armata is made-up of eight bells). The number of sheep and goats he will bell depends upon the shepherds love and understanding of bells and his inventiveness in matching them. Of primary importance to him is that the belling process will enable him to distinguish each of his 'sub-flocks' from the other, as well as from those belonging to another shepherd. He will thus make certain that he uses a variety of bells to equip his flock, bells differing in size and weight and hence in pitch, and bells of different types, hence differing in timbre. By combining these two elements —pitch and timbre— the shepherd can equip all of his smaller 'sub-flocks' in such a way as to give each its distinctive 'voices' without disrupting the 'harmony' of the whole.

Fig. 52.

The variety of 'voices' resulting from the combination of pitch and timbre is almost unlimited. It should suffice to recall the number of combinations which could be from the wide range of notes to which the different bells were 'tuned' in the heyday of animal husbandry in Greece, as well as the timbre of the different bells and their variants. The fact that certain kinds of bells cannot be 'tuned' to a specific pitch — among them the *gringarídhi,* the *tsokáni,* and the smaller bells in general— did not prevent the Greek shepherd from using these as well in equipping his flock. Such diverse smaller bells provided marvellous results in the formation of the aural character of the flock.

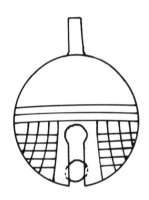

The difficulty of matching these two elements —pitch and timbre— lies in the number of bells that must be used each time from one or the other element in order to attain a good, novel combination of sounds. A 'good' combination of sound in this context means one that is unambiguous and easily recognised. For this matching of bells there is no guiding rule; once again, the measure is in the individual shepherd's experience and his sensitivity of ear.

From among the many sound combinations in the belling of a large flock, we give the following example. In a flock of one thousand animals —for example 600 sheep and 400 goats— it is usual to bell some 400 or 450 animals, in addition with the leaders of the flock. Such a flock can be divided into smaller flocks:

Sheep			Goats		
350 milch-ewes	200 yearlings	50 sterile sheep	250 milch-goats	100 yearlings	50 sterile goats
150 milch-ewes	100 yearlings and sterile sheep		100 milch-goats	50 yearlings and sterile goats	
150 'koudhoúnia' giving: 75, c″ 75, d″	50 small 'koudhoúnia' giving f″ or g″ and 50 small pellet-bells		100 kýpri giving: 50, c″ 50, d″	50 small kýpri giving: 25, f″ 25, g″	
or	or		or	or	
150 'koudhoúnia' giving c″	50 small 'koudhoúnia' giving d″, 10 c″ and 40 pellet-bells		10 kýpri giving c″, 10 d″ and so on until up f″	20 very small kýpri of indeterminate pitch, 20 pellet-bells, and	
or	or		or g″;	10 kýpri giving f″	

80 *'koudhoúnia'* giving:	90 pellet-bells	the remaining goats are			
10, c″	5 *'koudhoúnia'*	equipped with			
10, d″	giving c″ and	untuned		or	
10, e″ etc.	5 d″	*tsokánia*		40 pellet-bells, and	
until the octave				10 very small *kýpri*	
is covered; and					
70 untuned *tsokánia*				or	
of medium size				50 very small	
and weight				*tsokánia*	

(Designations of different octaves according to Harvard Dictionary
of Music, Willi Apel, Second Edition, 5th printing, 1972, p. 679).

Formerly, the wealthier shepherds also used bells of different weight but identical pitch in order to achieve a yet greater differentiation in sound between their flocks. For example, two *'koudhoúnia'* or two *kýpri,* respectively weighing 400 and 200 drams (see note 97), could be 'tuned' to middle C. The opposite also held true; they would use *'koudhoúnia'* or *kýpri* identical in weight and size, but sounding two, or sometimes even three different notes. For instance, of three *kýpri* weighing 400 drams each, one would give c′, one d′, and the third e′ (see The 'tuning' of forgedbells, p. 60 f.). These large *kýpri* were primarily suspended from the necks of the leading animals. For example, a 200 drams *kýpros* 'tuned' to middle C would be hung from a sheep-ram's neck, while a goat-ram would wear a 400 drams *kýpros* 'tuned' to the same note. Thus, the shepherd in charge of the flock could tell whether he was hearing a sheep-ram or a goat-ram —because of the different sound quality produced by bells of different weights. In former times, it was customary for the shepherd to attach the largest *triplókypros* to the largest leading animal, the leader of the entire flock. This bell would weigh five or six kilos, and sometimes as much as seven kilos. Matched to the 'tuned' bells of the flock's *armáta,* this bell usually gave an interval of a perfect fourth— e.g., the notes of C and F, with the C given by the large *kýpros* and the F by the large *parákypros* an octave higher, i.e. an interval of an eleventh; or the notes C and D, the D being given an octave higher, i.e. an interval of a ninth.

Yiannis Yiannikoulis, for thirty years a master bell-smith in Amphissa, has recorded for this author a belling that was used very often following the Second World War; it gives some indication of the decline of animal husbandry in Greece. Out of approximately 200 sheep only 50 were belled —one quarter of the entire flock. Eight *'koudhoúnia'* 'tuned' to the octave C-D-E-F-G-A-B-C were suspended from so many well-fed sheep, beginning with the flock leaders. The remaining 42 sheep each wore a *'koudhoúni'* sounding the note middle C. In this example of the belling of a flock, one sees what a small proportion of the animals were belled, as well as the simplicity of the *armáta.* This simple bell-series was nevertheless always present in Greece, even during the golden age of animal husbandry, with one essential difference, however. In those days, this simple series of bells was just one of many; these would inspire the shepherd to invent new, ever-original, even daring combinations of sounds in an age when the belling of one's flocks was a labour of love and an incentive to compete. Today, however, these combinations of sounds, whether simple or complex, have ceased to function as a lively, personal means of self-expression and have taken on the guise of cold rigid rule— a ready made impersonal formula to be followed by one and all.

Today, the belling of small flocks of from 50 to 100 animals is done on the basis of an even simpler *armáta;* this consists at the most of two, three or four heavy bells all 'tuned' to the same note, middle C for example, and ten or twenty bells of medium weight, half of which are 'tuned' to C, and half to D, an octave higher. In other words, this *armáta* is limited to only two 'voices', the notes of C and D, and lacks any other means of differentiating sound.

Bells and other animals

In addition to sheep and goats, mules were also formerly equipped with bells; in the days when mules were extensively used in Greece for transportation of persons and cargo. Nor was the belling of mules due to chance. In a train of ten or fifteen mules, three or four would wear *kýpri*—so that the animals would hear the sound and not wander off— which were invariably matching in sound and arranged in any one of a number of possible combinations, as mentioned above. Here we should like to note some of the combinations used in Greece: one *kýpros* might give c″, and the remaining three would be 'tuned' to d″; sometimes the three or four *kýpri* gave, respectively, c″, d″, e″, or c″, d″, e″, f″; again one *kýpros* might be of determinate pitch —c″ for example— while the other three very small bells would be of indeterminate pitch. Older people in Greece recall from the Second World War that mules with "beautiful, matched bells" would carry the bridal party from one village to the other (Macedonia), with a *gáida*-player leading the procession. A passage from the *Epic of Digenis Akritas* gives the following descriptive account of horse-bells:[98]

> *He saddled a horse as white as a dove,*
> *Whose forelock was embroidered with precious stones,*
> *And little golden bells among the stones;*
> *So many little bells they made a noise*
> *that was delightful and astounded all.*

Bells and the shepherd's flute (floyéra)

The shepherd whose work is to him a labour of love goes further still, and matches his flute (*floyéra*) to the bells of his flock. In his endless hours of solitude, his flute does more than provide him pleasure, but is also a means of communication with the animals he is tending, a valuable tool of his trade. Generally, the shepherd himself makes the flute he plays — usually from cane, a piece of wood or metal or, best of all, from the bone of a bird of prey (see *floyéra*).

In order to match his flute to the bells of his flock's *armáta,* the shepherd must know the 'voices' of his animals' bells well —they must be a part of himself— and he must be able to distinguish them clearly. If this be the case, after many unsuccessful efforts he can make a flute 'attuned' to the bells of the *armáta*. For instance, if the bells of the *armáta* are based on the perfect fourth C-D-E-F, the tonic of the scale of his flute must be C. Thus his improvisations on the flute will correspond tonically with the notes sounded by the bells of the *armáta*. Quite often other kinds of correspondence are encountered, however. For example, the first note of the flute can be as much as an interval of a fourth or a fifth of the lower note of the 'tuned' bells of the *armáta;* in such a case, if the *armáta* is 'tuned' to give C-D-E-F, the tonic of the *floyéra* need not be C, but can be F or even G. As we know, after unison and the octave, the fourth and fifth are the closest intervals. The shepherd's improvisations on his flute —"dirges" (*miróloyia*) as they are called in Epirus, "shepherd's songs" (*vláchika, tsopanárika*) elsewhere— are usually slow melodies of the free-rhythmic type, almost invariably beginning in the low register, and repeated one octave higher. Their deep and, in the lower register, somewhat hoarse quality of sound changes colour in the higher octave, becoming bright and clear.[99]

There is still something further the shepherd can do. As we have said, a shepherd's flock may be rich in heavy and medium-weight bells and have few or no light-weight bells, or it may have only medium and light-weight bells, or it may have few medium-weight bells and many light-weight bells, etc., etc. In the first case cited above, the shepherd who has a sensitive musical ear and who is a skillful flutist, will improvise on his instrument, using for the most part the low and middle range notes of his flute, although use of the upper register notes is not precluded. In the case of the second example given above, the shepherd will generally play his instrument in the middle, and secondarily, in the upper register. If the third case be true, the shepherd will play in the upper register, although the use of a few of the notes from the middle and low range are not precluded.

With the passage of time and their constant repetition, improvisions on the *floyéra* gradually acquired a somewhat more concrete form. They began to express more directly the personality of their creator, without, however, losing their improvisational character. When the piping of a flute is heard in a shepherd's encampment, people know that the player is he who has the milch-ewes, or the shepherd with the yearlings. What is more important, however, is that by degrees the animals themselves come to recognise these melodies. For instance, when the flock is led out to graze at night, the animals finally become accustomed to the particular melody the shepherd plays on his flute, and associate it with night grazing *(skáros);* later, whenever they hear this particular playing, the animals follow the shepherd to the night grazing fields without any further urging. The same thing happens when the flock leaves its noon-tide resting place; hearing the familiar melody piped by their shepherd, the animals know it is time to leave. We would also like to note that some shepherds have managed to train their flocks to distinguish between particular melodies, and to respond accordingly. Thus there will be one particular melody played to signal night-time grazing, another to call the animals to leave their resting place, and yet another —or several others— to signal the time for ordinary day-time grazing.[100]

Choosing bells

The shepherd's interest in belling his flock is evident when he selects and buys the bells that will make-up his flock's *armáta*. The patience with which he chooses them, as well as the number of trials he makes to ensure that their sound is clear and accurate are proof of this. With one bell in his right hand and another in his left, he tests them over and over again, for many hours, and in many workshops, until he finds what he has been looking for — the combination of bells that suits him most. He takes several measures to be certain before he buys, including the following:

a) He listens to the bells, striking them gently near his ear; or he may lower them to the distance from the ground they would be when hung from the neck of an animal before checking their sound.

b) He listens to them from a distance of ten or twenty metres or more, to see whether they sound the same.

c) He tests them again, after having wetted them, to see whether they produce the same sound as before. Thus he can check whether the sound the same under rainy conditions as under dry weather conditions.

d) He lightly touches with a pointed object, such as a nail, the external surface of a *kýpros* while it is still sounding; if the bell does not stop sounding immediately, but the sound merely alters in pitch or in quality, the *kýpros* in question is not well-made, and he will not buy it.

In the same manner as the master bell-maker, so too, the shepherd, when choosing bells to equip his flock, 'hears' the intervals of the bells sounded. Such intervals, moreover, were of the *natural* and not of the tempered scale among the shepherds of old, as has been established. In addition, one should not forget that as far as the tonal accuracy of the intervals of bells is concerned, what has been noted above regarding the 'tuning' of bells applies here as well.

The use of the bell in customs and rituals

As we have mentioned beforehand, the bell in Greece is to be found performing three functions by virtue of its properties: as an apotropaic device, as a sound-producer, and as a musical instrument. We recapitulate this in an effort to underline just how difficult it sometimes can be to clearly define the limits of these three functions, to determine where one ends and the other begins. When does a bell function as an apotropaic device, when is it merely a sound-producer, and when is it more of a musical instrument. If one is dealing with only a few bells distributed among the animals of a small flock of thirty sheep, the answer is simple; for the shepherd in this case, the bells serve as simple sound-producers which help him in his work. However, from the moment the shepherd chooses bells and matches them in sound they are no longer mere sound-producers; they continue to aid him in his shepherding, of course, but at the same time their combined and well matched notes are a source of pleasure and joy to their 'arranger', the shepherd — they are his 'music'. In such a case the bell as exceeded the limits of the definition of a simple sound-producer, and has moved into the domain of the musical instrument, even though at this point it cannot in fact be regarded as such. The bell is more truly a musical instrument when the shepherd matches the playing of his flute with the sounds produced by the 'tuned' bells of his flock's *armáta,* sounds which serve as an 'accompaniment' and which 'harmonise' with his playing.[101] One encounters many similar examples, in which one function overlaps another, is atrophied and replaced by another, or coincides with other functions and properties of the bell.

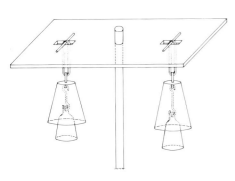

Fig. 53.

The very ancient apotropaic properties attributed to the bell, even though they have gradually been forgotten, can be recognised today in popular worship, in the church, as well as in other rituals. At the *Anastenária,*[102] for example, which is a popular celebration held on May 21, and which includes ritual animal sacrifice, ecstatic trances on the part of initiates, walking over live coals, etc., small pellet-bells are suspended from the icons carried by the entranced participants known as *anastenáridhes.* With the movements of the dancers, these pellet-bells —together with gold or silver votive offerings also attached to the bell-bedecked icons— give out a thin, piercing sound, which is indeterminate in pitch. The timbre of this 'bodiless' sound clearly has no connection, tonal or otherwise, with the musical instruments that accompany the peculiar dance of the *anastenáridhes;* today the music is made by a combination of drum *(daoúli)* and *líra;* formerly, the drum, shawm *(zournás),* and mainland bagpipe *(gáida)* were played.

In different parts of Greece, children singing the "Swallow Song" (a kind of carol) on the first of March carry with them the wooden effigy of a swallow; in earlier times they used to suspend small pellet-bells from its neck (fig. 55).[103] The women of Astypalea (Dodecanese) decorate their local costumes with small pellet-bells of silver along with other ornaments.[104] Similar small bells, or small bells of another type, were once hung from the sickles used for reaping in Cyprus. In the town of Tripoli, in the Peloponnese, small children once went around with bells in their hands or suspended from their waists on the last day of February; they did so to chase away the *koutscflévaros* (literally, 'lame February'), in other words, to drive away winter and its accompanying bad weather.[105] The children of the Vlachs of Pindos would also wear bells on the 25th of March, the Annunciation, in order to chase away snakes and lizards from the fields and the surrounding hills.[106] On the island of Paxi, the local inhabitants would "place beneath the bridal bed the clapper of a bell, representing the penis, naturally", in order to ward off the 'binding' of the bridal pair. According to the islanders' beliefs, the 'binding' *(ambódhema* or *dhéssimo)* was an evil spell inducing sexual impotence.[107]

In the Greek Orthodox Church, the censer is equipped with twelve small pellet-bells. The *katsí,* or incense boat, is still used to this day in monasteries in Greece, especially on Mount Athos, and is also equipped with the same kind of bells. Small silver or even golden pellet-bells are also attached to the vestments worn by the prelates and bishops of the Church.[108] Similarly, small bells were attached to anyone 'promised' to saint by a religious vow in exchange for good health, etc. The bell, symbol of his 'enslavement' to the saint, remained attached to his person until the terms of his vow expired and he was free from his pledge.[109] As further evidence of popular Greek belief in the magical, apotropaic power of sound, we cite John Chrysostom, who condemned the practice of attaching bells to small children, allegedly to protect them from evil.[110] Another graphic account of the use of bells in traditional rituals is provided by J. Doubdan (1651), who describes the ritual of the "miraculous descent of the Holy Light from Heaven", on the night of Holy Saturday, at the canopy of the Holy Tomb. Besides the Patriarch, wrote the French cleric, stood four deacons, each holding a shining 'sun' decked out with numerous little bells and fastened to a staff. These 'suns', which were slightly inclined over

78

the head of the Patriarch, were frequently shaken, causing the bells to sound.[111]

A similar survival of the apotropaic properties attributed to the bell can be recognised in the use of bells in many traditional rituals *(dhrómena)* observed for beneficial effects. In such cases, however, the bells function simultaneously as musical instruments. The most significant traditional *dhrómena* in Greece are those of the *Kalóyeros* (on Cheese-Monday),[112] and the *Karnavália* (Carnivals) which take place in Monastiraki, Xiropotamos, Kali Vryssi,[113] Petroussa, and Volakas (region of Drama in Macedonia, 5-8 January), and Nikissiani (region of Pangeon, January 7); at Sochos and Nea Volvi of Langadas (Macedonia); on the island of Skyros;[114] and Ayiassos (in Mytilene) (the last days of the Carnival). In the observance of these traditional rituals, the bell is an indispensable accessory in the zoomorphic (animalistic), among others, disguises of the mummers. The number of bells they hang around the waist varies; in some traditional rituals they hang three bells, in others, four or five bells. These bells are either *'koudhoúnia'* or *kýpri*, but the latter are the type used most commonly. When the mummers wear three bells, they can be either three *'koudhoúnia'* or three *kýpri*, or sometimes two *kýpri* and one large *'koudhoúni'*. When four bells are used, they are generally three *kýpri* and one large *'koudhoúni';* when five bells are used, they are almost always four *kýpri* and one large *'koudhoúni'*. In all of these cases, the large *'koudhoúni'*, with its distinctive timbre and often indeterminate pitch, acts as a bass, while the other bells, the *kýpri*, when matched in sound (a rare phenomenon nowadays), give the same intervals found in the *armáta* of flocks of sheep and goats — tone or semitone, third or minor third, and perfect fourth. In the traditional rituals mentioned above, the bells also function as rhythmical musical instruments; they accompany the sing and dancing when the mummers sing traditional songs and dance local dances in company with their fellow-celebrants.

The same observations also hold true for the bells used in the following traditional rituals or customs: The *Bey* (on Cheese-Monday) in Mavroklissi, Didymotichon (Thrace)[115] and Ortakioee (Adrianopolis); bells were once suspended from the knees at this same traditional ritual at Lititsa;[116] the *Rogátsia* or *Rogatsária* (January 1-6), at Megas Palamas, Karditsa (Thessaly);[117] at The Wedding of Karagiozi (*O Gámos tou Karagíozi*) celebrated during Carnival in Gonoussa near Corinth, *'koudhoúnia'* or *tsokánia* are suspended under the celebrants' petticoats or dresses;[118] on the island of Samothrace at Carnival time, people hold bells in their hands and imitate animals;[119] at the Ayiassos' Carnival (last days of Carnival including Clean-Monday) in Mytilene the bell was often used as part of the participants' costuming;[120] during the days of Carnival on Crete, one also encounters the *lerás* wearing a masque of hare-skin, as well as flaxen moustaches, a long-sleeved shepherds' cloak with bells *(léria)* suspended from the waist or hung across the breast.[121]

The shepherds' children in Epirus use bells to accompany a kind of carol sung on Lazarus Saturday.[122] To this end they carry two or four *kýpri* suspended from a rectangular or square piece of planking, which is fixed atop a pole (fig. 53). Formerly, when the *kýpri* were two, they were held in the hands or they were hung from the arms of the shepherd youths, each having one bell. When the two *kýpri* are matched, they give an interval of a major or minor second, while if four matched *kýpri* are used, they give the notes of the perfect fourth. In these Lazarus carols the *kýpros* functions as a musical instrument, providing a free rhythmical accompaniment that does not coincide with the measures of the song; they are also part of a combination of two different timbres, that of the *kýpros* and of the human voice.

The bell, both as an apotropaic device and musical instrument, is to be found accompanying other carols as well. In the villages of Caesarea (Cappadocia in Asia Minor), Misti, Tarikli, Axos, Trochos, Koltzic, etc., each company of carollers would split up into two smaller groups. One group would enter the houses to sing the carols, while the children in the other party scrambled up onto the roof and lowered down one or two bells —a variant of the *monókypros* or *dhiplókypros* used for camels— attached to a long cord through the *kapín*, a kind of sky-light. The rope was then jiggled up and down to make the bells sound, in time with the melody sung by the carollers within; they themselves would quietly murmur the carol the better to keep

Fig. 54.

79

the rhythmical sounding of the bell in time with the singing.[123]

On the island of Skyros, children once sang carols on New Year's Eve "in groups carrying a deafening drum with snares and little bells on its heads..."[124] At Didymotichon, until quite recently carols were sung to the accompaniment of a *taraboúka* (pottery drum) by people dressed as black men, wearing bells suspended from their waists.[125]

The bell and musical instruments

Small pellet-bells are also attached to certain popular musical instruments, as, for example, to the bow of the pear-shaped *líra* of Crete, the Dodecanese, Macedonia, etc. With the movement of the bow across the strings, the bells sound a rhythmic accompaniment to the melody, as well as an *ison* or drone of indeterminate pitch. Bells are also attached to the pottery drum *(toumbeléki)*, encircling the instrument at the place where the hide is tied on, or just beneath the skin (fig. 54); this is to be found in the Kassandra region of Chalkidiki, on the island of Mytilene, together with the drum *(daoúli)* on the island of Skyros, etc.[126] In such cases, once again the small pellet-bells serve to accompany the rhythmic patterns of the instrument with an *ison* (drone); nor should one forget the primitive and now all but forgotten apotropaic qualities attributed to the bell in the past.

Today in Greece the bell continues to be closely bound up with the life of the rural Greek. Day by day, however, the craftsmen who know how to make and 'tune' bells are becoming fewer in number, as are the shepherds skilled in the belling of their flocks of sheep and herds of goats. The same also holds true for the different traditional rituals still observed in Greece, where the participants still use the same number and types of bells determined by tradition, rarely, however, matching them in sound. As has happened to so many other aspects of the traditional life of Greece, so also the bell has been forced to adapt to the demands of the age of technology. One such demand —perhaps the most regrettable— stems from the ravages and exploitation of tourism.[127]

In days now long past, during the winter months, shepherds in Greece used to hang bells outside their huts, so that they would ring when the wind blew. During the freezing nights, the sound of the bells kept evil spirits and demons away, and at the same time told of the coming of spring and the joys of living high in the mountains.[128] Today, those hung at the entrance of workmen's cafe-bars, where skewers of meat are sold *(souvlákia)*, advertise the business of the shop, and their sound attracts clients.[129]

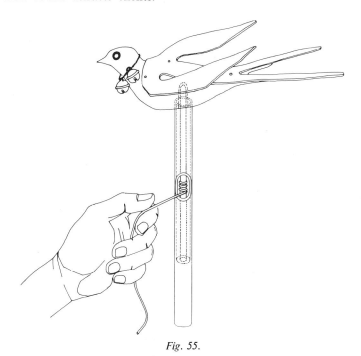

Fig. 55.

19. *Bronze double cast-bell (dhiplókypros) on leader he-goat, 36 cm. high. Region of Arta.*

20. *Bronze bell (rabaoúni), 8.5 cm. high.*

21. *Bronze pellet-bells, 11-12 cm. high.*

22. *Bronze double cast-bells (dhiplókypri), 28, 25, 22 cm. high.*

23.   *Small silver pellet-bells hung around the sacred icon. Anastenaria, Aghia Eleni, Serres (1970).*

24. *Small pellet-bells on censers.*

25. *Silver pellet-bell on woman's costume. Astypalea, Dodecanese. Greek Folk Art Museum, Athens.*

26. *Cast-bells and forged bells hung at the waist of men in costume (karnavália). Popular painting (c. 1950). Carnival, Sokhos, Macedonia.*

27. *Pellet-bells on swallow-shaped sound-producer (khelidhóna), 22 cm. high. Agriani, Serres.*

$\longrightarrow$

26

27

MASSA (Tongs with Cymbals)

The *massá* or *massiá* is shaped like a simple pair of fire-tongs, the two arms of which end in branches having a small spring-mounted cymbal (*zíli*) at their terminal points (fig. 56). The two branches are directly opposed to each other; accordingly, when the two arms of the *massá* are brought together, the attached cymbals strike one another. The instrument consists of one, or more commonly, several pair of cymbals attached to a simple strip of iron, thus enabling a single person to play them all together without difficulty. In much the same form, the instrument was known in ancient Egypt.[130] It was also to be encountered during the Middle Ages,[131] and is to be found today throughout a wide range of countries, extending to the Far East.[132]

Fig. 56.

In Greece, the *massá* is made of iron and consists of a trunk, branches, and cymbals. Its dimensions vary from about 30-50 cm in height to approximately 20-30 cm at its greatest breadth. It is made by blacksmiths, usually Gypsies, who often adorn the trunk, and sometimes the branches as well, with simple incised designs. The number of branches and pairs of cymbals of the instrument invariably depends on the individual wishes of the blacksmith or the person who has commissioned it.

The *massá,* clearly a rhythmical instrument, is still played (only by children however) in Thrace, in the region of Orestiada (at Kastanies, Marassia, and Nea Vyssa among other places) and in the Didymotichon region. The instrument is used by children to accompany the playing of carols at Christmastide, the New Year, and Epiphany, either as a solo instrument or together with a large tambourine *(dacharés)*. Formerly, however, it was played by adults at their social gatherings and entertainments. On those occasions, the *massá* accompanied the mainland bagpipe *(gáida)* or other melodic instruments, such as the violin and the clarinet, as well as instruments of the lute family; the *tambourás, laghoúto* (lute), *bouzoúki,* and even the barrel-organ *(latérna)*. The older inhabitants of Didymotichon remember having heard the *toumbeléki* (pottery drum), *massá,* and *boulgharí* (a plucked instrument of the lute family) being played at the beginning of this century.

During carol-singing, the *massá* is always played by one of the children in the group. Holding it in his right hand, the child strikes it with force against the open palm of his left hand, or against his thigh, bringing the two arms of the instrument together in such a manner that the cymbals clash between them. The sound produced by the cymbals is of an indeterminate pitch; it is harsh and abrupt, and lacks any variations of dynamics. Adults used to play the instrument in the same way when accompanying their dances and songs —either alone or together with other instruments— at feasts and fairs.

Those skilled players who had yet another method of playing the *massá* were much sought after at feasts. They held the instrument almost closed in the left hand; its branches were thus brought very close to each other and the cymbals could be played with the fingers of the right hand. When played in this manner, the cymbals clashed very lightly, thus emitting a soft sound with various dynamics and rhythmic ornamentation, according to the sensitivity and dexterity of the player. These instrumentalists often combined the two ways of playing the *massá*.

In bygone times, the *massá* was played instead of the cymbals at the traditional mummers' ritual *(dhrómeno)* at Didymotichon, the so-called *Köpék-Bey* (Turkish, Lord of the Dogs, cf. *zília*). Two or four youths, members of the festive company, dressed as girls, walked in front of the leading actor, the Bey, each holding a *massá*. This they struck as they danced to the accompaniment of other popular instruments, drums *(daoúli),* shawm *(zournás)* and mainland bagpipe *(gáida)*. In this case, the *massá* obviously did not have a solely rhythmical function, but also served as a sound-producer intended to drive off evil spirits.[133]

TZAMALA (Wooden clapper)

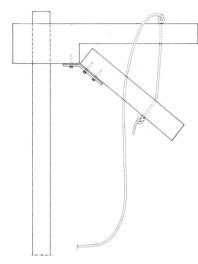

Fig. 57.

The carols of Christmastide, New Year and Epiphany are also accompanied by the *tzamála*,[134] a kind of wooden clapper that is found in the village of Kastanies and its environs, in Thrace (fig. 57).

The *tzamála* consists of two long and narrow tongues joined at two ends by a piece of leather. At the opposite ends are two holes — one in each tongue — through which passes a string knotted at one end.

The *tzamála* is held in the left hand, from the stick or branch to which it is fastened, while the right hand pulls the string, thus causing the two tongues to strike against each other.

The *tzamála* is a rhythmic instrument, and is of indeterminate pitch. It is usually played by children, together with the *massá*. The *tzamála* is often decorated with flowers.

TRIGHONO (Triangle)

The *tríghono* (triangle), often called *kambanáki* (little bell), *simandíri, símandro* (semanterion) and *skára* (grill), is an iron triangle, equilateral or isosceles, one angle of which is not closed.[135] Made by city and gypsy blacksmiths in urban and rural areas respectively, the instrument varies in size, each side ranging from approximately 15-20 cm. Suspended on a short cord attached to the players left hand, it is struck with a cylindrical iron rod held in the right hand. Its sound when struck is of indeterminate pitch.

A purely rhythmical instrument used solely as an accompaniment, the triangle is played by children who sing traditional carols at Christmastide, the New Year, and Epiphany. In each group of two or three carollers, only one child plays the triangle, at the same time singing together with his companions.[136] The accompaniment played on the triangle is generally restricted to a trill of greater or lesser frequency. Sensitive children, however, manage to vary the dynamics and timbre of the sound produced, according to the point where the instrument is struck and the speed of the movement of the hand, which actually produces the trill.[137]

Formerly, until the Second World War, children accompanied the carols with the triangle and cymbals *(zília)*. Adults played yet other instruments in conjunction with the triangle; e.g., the lute and triangle; the pottery drum *(toumbeléki)* and triangle (in the case of those Greeks from the region of Smyrna in Asia Minor);[138] violin, cymbals and triangle; etc.

The sound produced by the triangle includes many high-pitched dissonant partials. Therefore, when the triangle is played together with different melodic instruments, it creates the impression that it has the same tonality as these, despite the fact that the sound produced is of indeterminate pitch.[139]

The appearance of the triangle in Greece is relatively recent.[140] As far as we know, there is no mention of it in literary sources, nor is it encountered anywhere in Byzantine or post-Byzantine iconography.

HAND-CLAPPING (Palamákia)
SNAPPING OF THE FINGERS (Strákes)
STRIKING THE LEGS WITH THE HANDS
STAMPING THE GROUND WITH ONE'S FOOT

In this section we consider several of the musical phenomena still to be found among so-called 'primitive' peoples and in the folk music of various nations, and in which ethnomusicology today recognises the earliest manifestations of man in the sector of instrumental music. These phenomena include the beating of the ground with the feet or the palms of the hands, hand-clapping and the snapping of the fingers, and the striking of the body with the hands, on the chest, thighs or belly.[141]

Since earliest times, the Greek people have been accustomed to provide rhythmical accompaniment to their singing and dancing by the means of hand-clapping (*palamákia*, also called *koúrtala, kourtalísmata,* derived from *krótala*) and the snapping of their fingers *(strákes)* (fig. 58).[142] However, in addition to providing a simple form of accompaniment, these two means of producing a rhythmical sound may, in accordance with the mood of the moment at some gathering or wedding celebration, be used to stimulate a livelier rhythm or a heavier and stricter tempo of dance and song. In such cases, the hand-clapping and finger-snapping can be made to sound soft or hard, gentle and caressing or abrupt, whatever is deemed appropriate. The sound produced by a good dancer's finger-snapping in face-to-face dancing (faint and sharp, or loud and with a dry timbre —like castanets made of hardwood, having deliberate, slight nuances of rhythm) especially impose itself as the main musical regulator in a unique organic unity of movement (dance) and sound (rhythm and timbre).

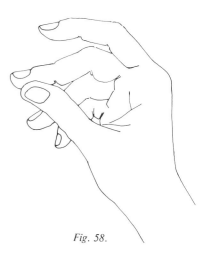

Fig. 58.

Hand-clapping during the course of funeral processions is also a characteristic case. There comes a point when, as the intensity of emotion increases, the dirges turn from musical expression into a verbal recitative, which often borders on shouting. Then, the lamenting women not only tear their hair and beat their breasts, but also lift their hand high and clap. Hand-clapping in this instance can be considered a kind of punctuation, helping the mourners give vent to excess emotion, to return to a calmer state of mind, and to move again into new outbursts of emotion, and so on.

Hand-clapping and the snapping of the fingers are not the only means through which men especially, but occasionally women as well, can emphasise musical rhythm. They also can slap a leg with one hand, as, for instance, in the *pendozális* and *chaniótikos* dances of Crete, in the face-to-face women's dance *onimá-onimá* of Pharassa in Cappadocia, in the face-to-face dances of Cyprus, et alia. Again the ground can be struck with the knee or the sole of the foot, as in one of the *zonarádhiki* dances of Thrace, in the *tripáti* dance, also of Thrace, and in certain dances of the Greeks of the Black Sea area (Pontos) etc. We should also note that the player of the pear-shaped *líra* emphasises the rhythm by beating the ground strongly with the heel or sole of his foot, usually his right foot.

Many literary sources attest to the popularity of hand-clapping among the Greek people. In the fourth century we hear from John Chrysostom that "those who concerned with the theatre and banqueting play *krótala* and clap their hands".[143] In the same century Gregory the Divine rails against hand-clapping: "Do not the sound of the *bárbitos* and the clapping of hands goad one to madness?"[144] Similarly, Canon N.D. 54 of the Ecumenical Synod of Laodicea prohibited this: "neither dance, nor jump about, nor clap your hands to make noise".[145] Later, in the ninth century, the Patriarch Photius wrote of "troupes of maidens dancing to celebrate the victory, and bands of men clapping their hands..."[146]

A Byzantine illuminated manuscript of the eleventh century depicts one of the corybants (priest of Cybele) clapping his hands. The illustration in question shows the baby Zeus, and the corybants playing different instruments, hand-cymbals, a bowed stringed-instrument, a small drum *(daoúli)*, a flute, and one of them clapping his hands, so that Cronus, in accordance with the myth, would not hear the baby's crying.[147] Vitsentzos Kornaros' *Erotocritos* contains the characteristic line

they clap their hands to show their delight . . . [148]

A decapentesyllable line from the poem of Markos Depharanas *Words of advice from a father to his son* (1543):

if it is applause (koúrtala) you want, you can have it any day.[149]

Finally, the Englishman Edward Daniel Clarke. in his *Travels,* gives us an extremely vivid picture of a women's face-to-face dance accompanied by singing and hand-clapping.[150]

The following proverbs also deserve mention here: "The big wedding must have hand-clapping *(koúrtala)*, and the little wedding must have some hand-clapping *(kourtalísmata)* as well"; "Here there is hand-clapping *(koúrtala)*, the wedding is elsewhere".[151]

In the chapter dealing with idiophones we should include certain objects that function incidentally as sound-producers, and sometimes even as 'musical instruments'.

NOMISMATA (Coins)

Metallic coins *(nomísmata)* of every description, both Greek and foreign, have long been a constituent element of Greek costume decoration, particularly that of women.[152] When the wearer moves, walks, or runs, the coins and other decorative accessories jangle against each other, producing a distinctive sound. Thus, they function as a sound-producer.

In dancing, the periodical rhythmical movements of the dancer's body incidentally transforms the coins, together with the other ornaments of the costume, into a sensitive 'musical instrument', which accompanies the dance steps rhythmically. This is especially noticeable when the dance is accompanied only by singing, and when no instruments are available. Such a dance was observed by Jacob Spon and George Wheeler at Arachova, towards the end of the eighteenth century. As the authors relate in their *Voyage,* when the villagers began to dance, the coins suspended from their clothes produced a sound much like that of the tambourine.[153] A similar picture is presented today during the traditional ritual *(dhrómeno)* of *Boúles,* celebrated during the last days of Carnival at Naoussa, in northern Greece. Every male member of the mummer's group wears suspended from the breast of his kilted costume *(foustanélla)* some five kilograms of coins. The rhythmical movements of the dance transforms these into a resonant, rhythmical 'musical instrument'.

"The habit, well-nigh panhellenic, of wearing coins dangling on chains, stems from an old Greek tradition and has undergone repeated changes both in character and function. We know that throughout the Byzantine era people wore coins as talismans and that the most common of these were called —right up to the present day— *constantináta.* Difficult times followed the fall of Constantinople, and the Greek people, conquered and oppressed, found a means of preserving and bequeathing legacies by making and wearing chains strung with coins of different currencies. Although the custom's origins may be rooted in superstition, it gradually acquired a purely practical significance. After the War of Independence, when the danger from oppression and extortion had passed, the wearing of coins came to be regarded as a mere adornment, with no practical significance other than that it marked the wearer, always a woman, as a person of wealth and rank. In the years that followed —the virtual swan song of Greek national dress— the coins that were strung on chains were false".[154]

The same can be said for the *massoúr-plexídhes* and the *sourghoút* as well as for other similar ornaments of feminine head-dress or braided hair, which are found even today —although more and more rarely— function as 'musical instruments' and accompany dance rhythmically (Monastiraki and Xiropotamos near Drama, and other regions).

MASSOUR PLEXIDHES (Spool-bound braids)

Fig. 59.

Massoúr-plexídhes (spool-bound braids) are one of the feminine costume ornaments found in Attica, Salamina, and elsewhere.[155] They consist of silver 'knots' and 'spools' *(massoúria)* hooked onto cords which are suspended from the traditional plaited hair-braids of Greek women, or are intertwined with hair so braided (fig. 59). In the walking and dancing of the wearer the knots and spools strike against each other, thus producing sound. In other words, they func-

92

tion as a sound-producer in the case of walking, and as a rhythmical 'musical instrument' in dancing. With the advent of the Second World War, reasons of economy led to the substitution of glass knots and spools for the silver ones; following the war, these were replaced in turn by plastic ones. As a consequence of this, the *massoúr-plexídhes* ceased to function either as a sound-producer or as a 'musical instrument'.

SOURGHOUT (Headband ornament)

The so-called *sourghoút,* or *serghoútsa,* most commonly found in the form of a flower, is another costume ornament — it was attached to the headband of the traditional female costume of Kapoutzides (Thessaloniki). Whenever its wearer walked or danced, the leaf-shaped or geometric pendants of the *sourghoút* would jangle against one another, and in so doing would emit a delicate, silvery sound.[156] (See Pl. 31.)

KOUTALIA (Spoons)

Spoons *(koutália)* are usually made of wood, and are of a type still used for cooking and eating in some places in Greece. They are made of different kinds of wood, although hardwoods are considered superior, as they produce a clear and penetrating sound.

The spoons are used to accompany rhythmically the face-to-face dances of the Greeks of Asia Minor,[157] and Greek islanders, especially those inhabiting the islands off the coast of Turkey.[158] They are played by the dancers themselves, particularly by women. The dancers hold two spoons in each hand, with the hollow bowls of the spoons facing outwards, so that they will strike against each other with the opening and closing of the fingers. The right hand strikes the strong beats and the left the weak ones.

Spoons are also played to accompany circular dances and singing at different feasts. One member of the company holds two spoons in his right hand, hollow part outwards, and strikes them rhythmically against the palm of his left hand, or against his thigh. When his spirits rise, he may start beating them on his head, his chest, or other parts of his body. In bygone times convicts used spoons to accompany their singing, in the manner described above.[159]

The playing of the spoons is not as simple as it looks. The fingers of the hand holding the spoons must be supple and free, and not too tightly pressed against each other. They must nevertheless still hold the two spoons firmly in position. The difficulty does not lie so much in striking one spoon against the other, as in bringing the spoons apart again quickly, without their shifting position, so that they are ready for the next beat. One spoon always remains firmly fixed, while the other strikes against it. In the first method of playing, the movement is created by the opening and closing of the fingers holding the spoons; in the second, it results from the resistence the spoon meets when it strikes against the palm, or thigh of the player.

In the hands of real enthusiasts the spoons are not merely a simple, monotonous rhythmic instrument. In accordance with the nature of the song or dance, the rhythm, tempo and character of the melody, the sound produced by the spoons varies in nuances and dynamics. Sometimes it is soft and gentle, while at other times it can be abrupt and hard; it may be muffled, or bright, etc. The spoons are either played alone or together with a tambourine *(défi),* or in conjunction with such melodic instruments as the *tambourás, oúti,* Cretan *líra,* Cretan bagpipe *(askomadoúra),* etc.

The wooden spoon, whether simple or decorated with engraved designs or bas-relief, has long been one of the most treasured items of wood-working among the shepherds[160] and monks of Greece.[161]

MAYIRIKA SKEVI (Kitchen utensils)

Kitchen utensils *(mayiriká skévi)* —baking-pans, frying-pans, sauce-pans, etc.— were customarily beaten by housewives and children so as to drive out fleas, bed-bugs, and other troublesome household pests. This was traditionally done on the first of March. The kitchen utensils were beaten rhythmically, as 'improvised musical instruments' that is, while the women and children sang: "Out with fleas and bed-bugs, in with March and joy...". This custom, still remembered by many older people in Greece, was observed in Mytilene in 1671, and was described clearly and vividly by the French traveller Grelot.[162]

Of all the kitchen utensils used as 'musical instruments' in Greece, the copper baking-pan *(tapsí)*, known in many parts of the country as the *lingéri,* was the one most commonly made use of. "During the days of Carnival, on the island of Kos, girls and young men gather in the houses of friends and sing the *lingéri* songs. A single girl, wearing a ring, turns the *lingéri* around and around again on the surface of a low round table *(sofrás)* with her fingers, beating out the rhythm of the song with her finger-ring all the while".[163]

In the villages of Koskinou and Trianda on the island of Rhodes, "a baking-pan is turned round and round with the tips of the fingers, and the buzzing sound thus made by the pan accompanies the voice of the singer" in the singing of Carnival songs.[164] In Drymos (Elassona), a copper baking-pan was struck on its sides with a spoon in order to provide a rhythmical accompaniment for the dances and songs of Lazarus Saturday, after church services were over. These were performed almost exclusively by women, and without any investments whatsoever. This pan, into which coins were thrown, was held by a single woman who stood singing in the middle of the circular dance. With each beat, the coins would leap high into the air —some higher and other lower, according to their weight— and on falling back into the pan would produce an additional set of sounds of varying intensity and pitch. This custom, the so-called *Lazarínes,* was maintained until quite recently. Similarly, in Katirli (Bithynia), a large metal tray known as the *siní* was formerly used as a rhythmical 'musical instrument'; it was "supported on all five fingers of the hand, and was struck with flat pieces of wood".[165]

POTIRAKIA (Wine glasses)

A simple, improvised rhythmical instrument is provided by the thick, stemless small glasses *(potirákia)* used in Greece for wine or ouzo. When no musical instruments are available, two such glasses held in each hand can be clashed against each other by the opening and closing of one's fingers — thus providing rhythmical accompaniment for singing. The right hand marks the strong beats of the measure, the left hand the weak ones. Wine glasses are usually played alone, although they sometimes accompany such melodic instruments as the violin, the Cretan *líra,* the *tambourás,* etc. (see *kombolói).*

KOMBOLOI (Rosary, 'worry-beads')

Attached by a button to the waistcoat, the chain of 'worry-beads' *(kombolói)* was held extended in the left hand, while the right hand would brush the lips of a small, somewhat thick wineglass against the beads. This was once a popular way of accompanying songs —especially when, at certain gatherings, there were no musical instruments available— or accompanying instruments of the lute family, such as the *tambourás,* the *baghlamás,* and others. Only those having a good sense of rhythm and skill at rubbing the beads with movements appropriate to every possible rhythmical pattern used the *kombolói* in this manner. Nowadays, this mode of rhythmical accompaniment is to be met with in Greece more and more rarely.

The *kombolói* also functions as a sound-producer. It is "a means of passing the time during rest hours", or, as Elias Petropoulos writes in his *Rebetica Songs,* "with the *kombolói* a fine and slow splitting up of time is achieved which makes life last forever".

The beads that make up the *kombolói* differ in number and size from one *kombolói* to another, and are made of various materials, such as amber, mother-of-pearl, glass, wood, fruit-stones, dried seeds, and occasionally precious metals. The intensity and the timbre of the sound produced by a *kombolói* depends upon the size of the beads and the material of which they are made, as well as the manner in which it is played.

SIMANDRO (Semanterion)

Terminology

The *símandro* (semanterion) is a long and narrow piece of planking or sheet-metal which is sometimes used instead of the bell in monasteries and chapels. Apart from the generic name *símandron, simandírion,* or *simandíri,* there are many other descriptive names indicating the material from which the semanterion is made, the way it is held, its size, etc. Among these are: *xilosímandro* (wooden semanterion), *xílo* (wood), *hieró xílo* (sacred wood), *xíla athríssima* (wood for gathering people together), *cheirosímandro* (hand semanterion), *mikrón símandro* (small semanterion), *mikrón xílo* (small wood), *meghasímandron* or *símandron mégha* (large semanterion), *kópanos* (beater), *tálandon* (wobbler), *símandron sidhiroún* (iron semanterion), or *aghiosídheron* (sacred iron), or *sídheron* (iron). Sometimes the name refers to the purpose for which the semanterion is employed, as the following: *afipnistírion símandron* (awakening semanterion) or *exipniastikón sfiríon* (awakening hammer, the name used to describe the striking of the semanterion with which the monks were awakened); *sinaktírion símandron* (summoning semanterion, struck to call the monks together for prayer); *trapezikón xílon* (table wood) or *xílon tis vrósseos* (wood of refreshment, used to summon monks to a meal). Nowadays, *símandro, kópanos* and *tálando* are most commonly used.

Construction

Wooden semanteria, both the portable and suspended or fixed types, are made in different sizes and from a wide variety of woods. The portable hand-held semanterion *(cheirosímandro)* is narrowed in the middle so that the monk who operates it may manage it more comfortably. At its two edges there are usually bored three, four, or five holes, and the wood is thinner there. The holes symbolise the Holy Trinity and the Cross; in both cases their apotropaic significance is evident (fig. 60). The *kópanos,* the type of wooden semanterion that is permanent suspended, is made from the same kinds of wood as the portable hand-held semanterion, and often resembles it in form (fig. 61). Its weight, as well as its often unusually large dimensions necessitate its being hung in such a manner as not to hinder its vibrating when it is struck (fig. 63). Certain features contribute to the quality of the sound of the semanterion; the kind of wood it is made of (maple and linden are considered the best); the cleanness of the wood used (it should be dry and free of knots); the skill and dedication of the craftsmen who make it (it should be of equal thickness throughout); the positioning of the holes and the thinness of the two edges — these factors assist vibration.

The iron semanteria —long and narrow, ellipsoid, oval, semi-circular or circular— are always permanently suspended from a fixed point. They are always thinner at the two ends, usually have three holes (occasionally four), and are made in many different sizes (fig. 62). Formerly, it appears, copper semanteria were also made in Greece.[166] The small wooden or iron mallet with which the semanteria are struck is also called a *kópanos* (fig. 64).

In addition, Curt Sachs notes that at one church on the island of Chios a "sonorous stone" was used in place of a semanterion.[167] A village on the island of Ikaria used a hollowed-out

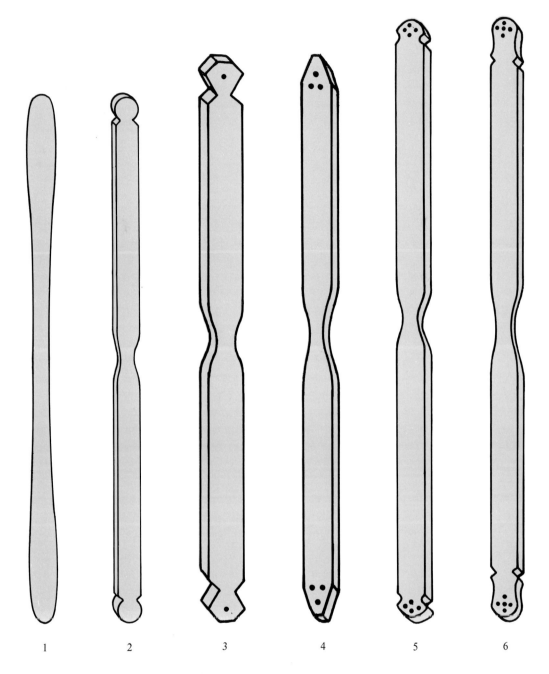

1   2   3   4   5   6

Fig. 60.

Fig. 60. Wooden hand-semanteria in Monasteries of Mount Athos: 1. L. 195 cm., W. 9 cm., Karakalou, Aghii Apostoli. 2. L. 195 cm., W. 4 cm., Th. 2 cm., Protato, Karyes. 3. L. 156 cm., W. 10 cm., Th. 4 cm. and 4. L. 132 cm., W. 7 cm., Th. 3 cm., Grigoriou, Aghios Nicolaos. 5. L. 200 cm., W. 6.5 cm., Th. 2 cm., Chilandariou. 6. L.c. 200 cm.

Fig. 61. Hung wooden semanteria in Monasteries of Mount Athos: 1. L. 376 cm., W. 25 cm., Th. 8 cm., and 2. L. 325 cm.,W. 60 cm., Th. 8 cm., Chilandariou. 3. L. 275 cm.,W. 29 cm.,Th. 11 cm. and 4 L. 370 cm.,W. 36 cm., Th. 10 cm., Great Lavra. 5. Stavronikita. 6. L. 195 cm., W. 23 cm., Th. 7 cm., Protato, Karyes. 7. L. 365 cm., W. 35 cm., Th. 13 cm., Koutloumoussiou. In Monasteries of Meteora: 8. L. 160 cm., Th. 4.5 cm., and 9. L. 125 cm., Th. 3 cm., Aghiou Stephanou. 10. L. 205 cm., Th. 6 cm., Varlaam. 11. L. 360 cm., W. 45 cm., Th. 6 cm., Transfiguration (from the large hole the beater is suspended) and 12. L. 120 cm., W. 8.5 cm., Church "Naos Tou Taxiarchou", Kastoria.

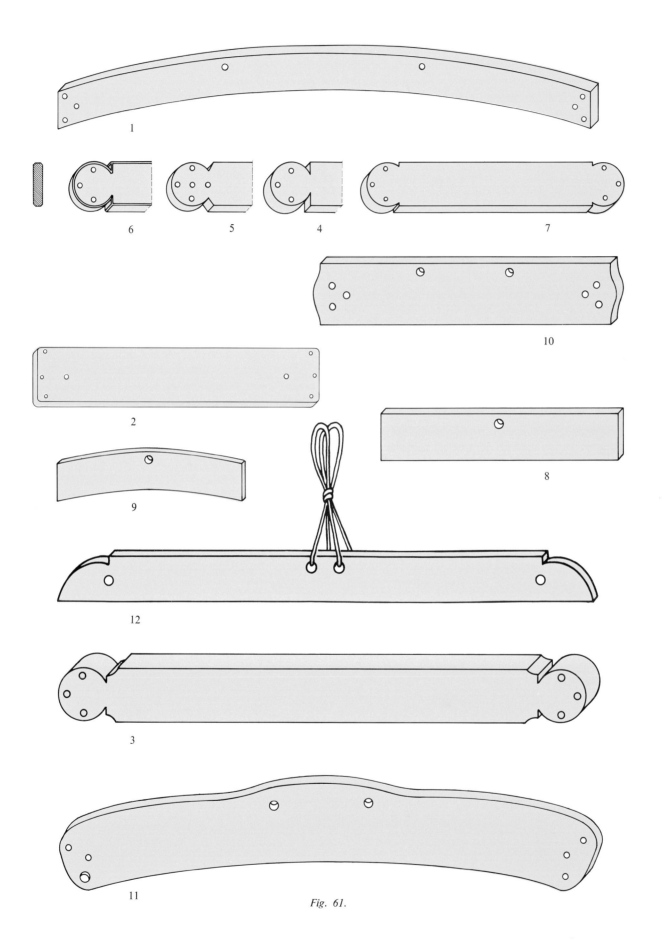

Fig. 61.

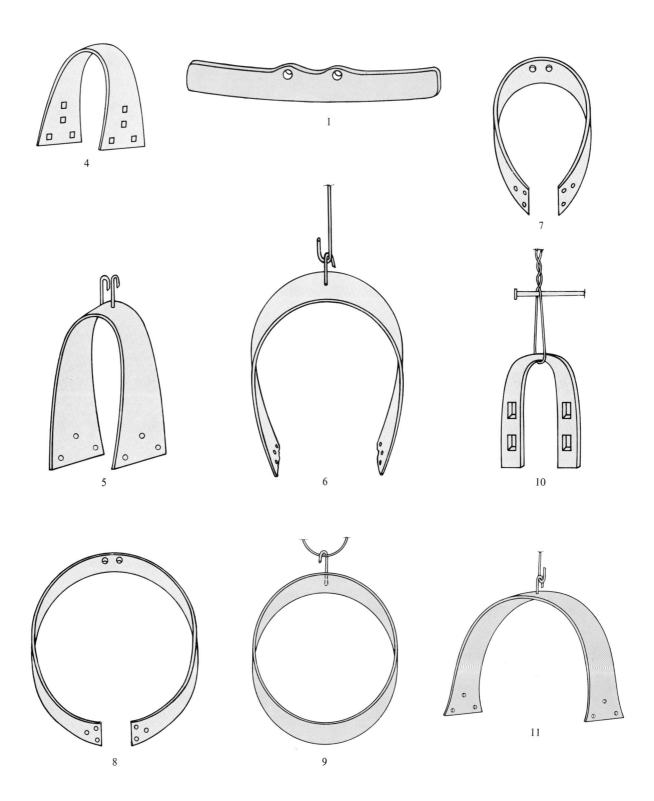

Fig. 62. Hung iron semanteria in Monasteries of Mount Athos: 1. L. 142 cm., W. 15 cm., Th. 2 cm., Great Lavra. 2. (decorated), Dionyssiou. 3. L. 166 cm., W. 6 cm. in the middle and 19 cm. at each end, Th. 2.5 cm., Dochiariou. 4. Opening 17 cm., W. 6 and 12 cm., Th. 6 cm., Height 28 cm., Philotheou. 5. Opening 18 cm., W. 15 cm., Th. 8 cm., Height 41 cm., Xiropotamou. 6. Lower opening 30 and largest op. 42 cm., W. 15 and 17 cm., Height 50 cm., Chilandariou. 7. Karakalou. 8. Iviron. 9. Diameter c. 100 cm., Panteleimonos. 10. Opening 10 cm., Th. 1-2 cm., Height 30 cm., Chapel Dormition of the Virgin (Molyvoklissia), Karyes.

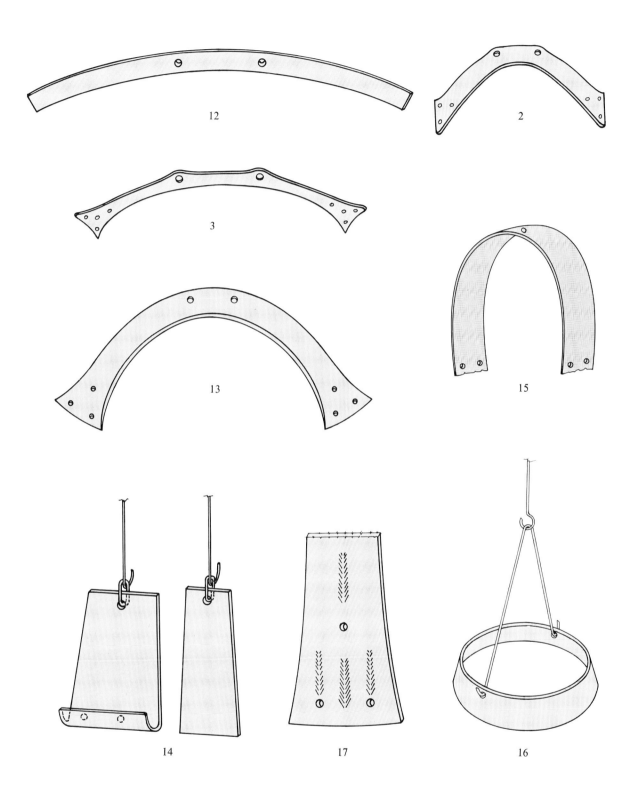

11. Opening 63 cm., W. 13 cm., Th. 1.5 cm., Height 53 cm., Protato, Karyes. In Monasteries of Meteora:
12. L. 100 cm., W. 5 cm., Th. c. 1 cm., Roussanou. 13. Opening 60 cm., W. 7 cm., Aghiou Stephanou.
And: 14. Height c. 50 cm., Aghios Athanassios Kouvaras, Attica. 15. Opening 35 cm., W. 10 cm., Height
45 cm., Byzantine Church of the Savour ("Tou Sotiros"), Amphissa. 16. Monastery "Tou Stavrou", Samos.
17. Decorative motif on the iron semanterion No 2, Dionyssiou Monastery, Mount Athos.

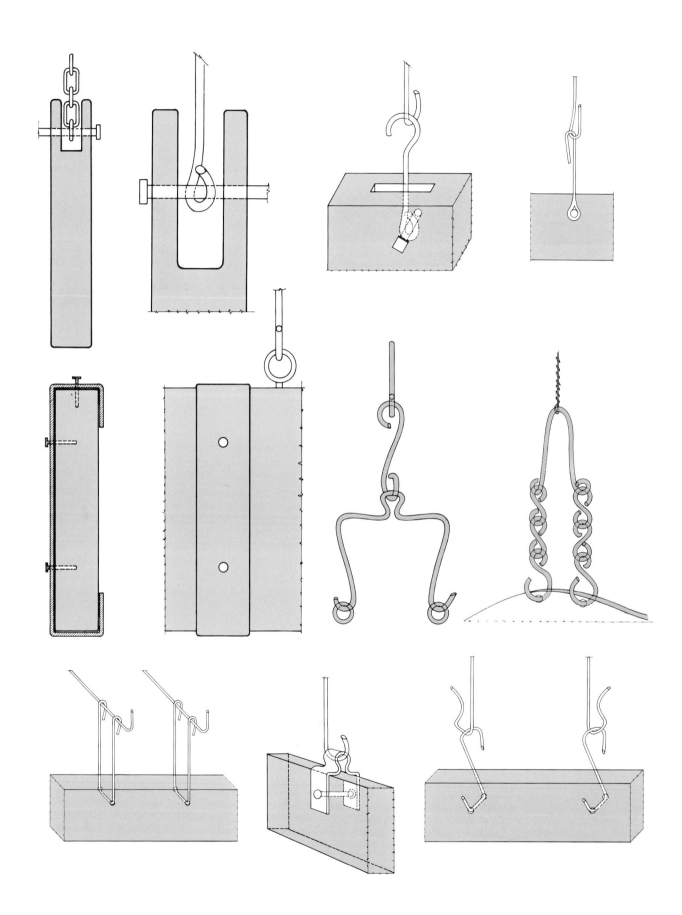

Fig. 63. How the wooden semanteria are hung.

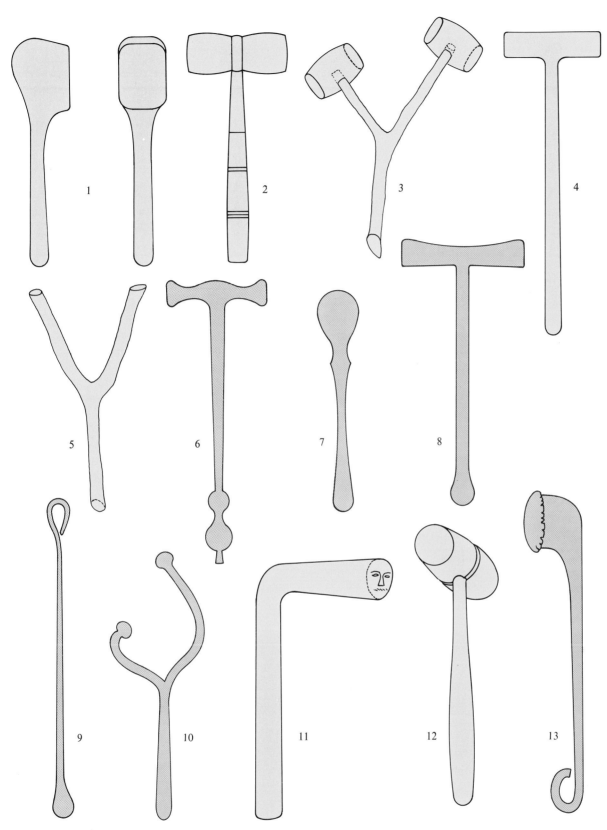

Fig. 64. Beaters used with the semanteria. In Monasteries of Mount Athos: (Wooden) 1. Height 31 cm., W. 7 cm., Grigoriou, Aghios Nicolaos. 2. Height 19 cm., and 3. Height 20-22 cm., W. 8 cm., Protato Karyes. 4. Iviron. 5. Beater made from a forked branch, Xenophontos. (Iron) 6. Height 20 cm., Great Lavra. 7. Stavronikita, 8. Chilandariou. 9. Height 30 cm., Chapel Dormition of the Virgin (Molyvoklissia), Karyes. 10. Xeno-phontos. In Monasteries of Meteora: (Wooden) 11. Height 22 cm., Th. 2.5 cm., Transfiguration. 12. Height 20 cm. (Iron) 13. Height 20 cm., Roussanou.

101

tree-trunk for the same purpose; the tree-trunk was covered with a tightly hide. This was struck with a wooden mallet *(kópanos)*, producing a deep and dull sound resembling that of the large wooden semanterion, the also called *kópanos*.[168]

Nowadays, for reasons of economy, as well as the rarity of those craftsmen having the requisite knowledge and skill for the making of iron semanteria, certain small monasteries make use of different metal objects instead. Examples of such makeshift substitutions are the toothed flywheel of an old machine at the monastery of Hosios Meletios (Kitheron), two iron trapezoidal plates at the monastery of St. Athanasios Kouvaras (Attica) (fig. 62), shell-casings, etc.

Place and manner of use—Sound potential

Semanteria —both wooden portable ones as well as those of wood or iron that are permanently suspended— to this day continue to be used in monasteries throughout Greece (Mount Athos, Meteora, et alia). They are used alongside the regular church bells to call the monks to their various services at different times of the day and night — in accordance with the rules of the monasteries. Only at Easter are all the semanteria played together. The iron semanterion is also normally used to summon the faithful to services held in those country churches which have no bells.[169]

The sound produced by the semanterion when struck is generally indeterminate in pitch. Of the three types of semanteria mentioned above, the iron semanterion and the wooden hand-held semanterion produce a clearer and more distinct sound than the large wooden semanterion *(kópanos);* the sound produced by the latter can be described as dull and dark in comparison to the other semanteria. Nevertheless, it is easy to distinguish the lower and higher sound produced by two hand-held semanteria of different sizes, even though it may not be possible to determine the pitch of the two sounds with any accuracy. It is known that formerly the semanterion was struck "at times in the centre and at times at various points around the centre, so that various sounds might emanate from the different blows"; in other words, the sounds produced thus varied in pitch. Good musicians continue to follow this mode of striking certain percussion instruments, such as the tambourine, the pottery drum, and the drum; however, we find that the semanterion is no longer played in this manner.

The rhythm beaten out on the semanterion is simple, and is usually a trochee or an iambus. Adapted to words that are repeated over and over again, these rhythms are easily conceived and learned by the monks. (Macheras Monastery, Cyprus):[170]

The rhythmic beating of the semanterion is described by Alexandros Papadiamantis with all the incomparable charm of his artistry in the short story "The Easter Chanter" (1893), as follows: "...Papa-Dianellos came out for a moment, and, taking a piece of old planking and a mallet-shaped piece of wood, improvised a semanterion, because, alas, there had been no bell for considerable while... With this semanterion the priest began to beat out, first in trochaei (Adám, Adám, Adám) and then in iambi (to tálandon, to tálandon) so as to awaken the midnight echoes".[171]

During the week following Easter Sunday, those days of joy in the wake of the Resurrection, all the semanteria, wooden and iron alike, as well as the bells of a monastery are beaten simultaneously and with a complete freedom of rhythm; this is an old custom in Greece. The different sizes and variety of these sound-producers produce sounds varying in pitch and timbre inside a poly-rhythmic sonorous framework. In certain of the monasteries of Mount Athos, among them Xenophondos, Karies, et alia, during this festive period mallets with twin heads (fig. 64) are used to beat the semanteria. These enable the monks to strike the iron and hand-held semanteria with greater rapidity, thus enhancing the festive atmosphere all the more.[172] At the Monastery of St. John the Divine on the island of Patmos, on certain feast days, two monks use four mallets to strike the permanently suspended wooden semanterion there — the largest to be found in Greece (approximate dimensions: length, 8m; width, 16 cm; breadth 5.5 cm).

We may note two further instances of the use of the semanterion in Greece. In the first instance, the villagers of the agricultural region of Neon Souli (Serres), in the procession they make on the feast-day of St. George, beat a rhythmical accompaniment on the semanterion to the song they sing in the hope of having a good, rich harvest. They sing the following: "Christ is risen / in truth he is risen / milk in the fields / honey in the vineyards / over flowing baskets". In this case, the semanterion functions simultaneously as an apotropaic sound-producer and as a rhythmical musical instrument.[173]

In the second noteworthy instance, the older monks of the Karakalou Monastery on Mount Athos recall the use of the semanterion to summon the monastery's cats at feeding-time. A simple rhythm was beaten out on the large wooden semanterion there —always the same rhythm, and always at the same time of day— and in a few seconds all the cats within hearing would have gathered.

Literary and iconographical sources

From literary sources we learn that the semanterion was already in use around the fifth and sixth centuries A.D. in the Eastern Orthodox Church. We also discover that from then until the present day, the semanterion and church-bell[174] have both been the principal sound-producers used for the summoning of the faithful to the Church's holy services. "Sound the wood *(to xýlon)* on time as it should be!", wrote Theodore the Studite in the ninth century.[175] Constantine Porphyrogennetus (10th century) also mentions the wooden semanterion in his work *De Ceremoniis*.[176] Theodore Balsamon (12th century) concerned himself with all three types of semanterion in his "Study of the summons to the divine chapels of the monasteries effected by the three semanteria".[177]

The careful study of Byzantine and post-Byzantine iconography reveals to us the similarity of the modern semanteria with their historical counterparts. In an eleventh century miniature, the body of a monk and a parallellogrammic semanterion, without holes at the two edges, form an initial capital 'T'.[178] A wooden hand-held semanterion is also represented in a twelfth century icon of the Sinai Monastery: "The children beating the semanterion inside the church on the holy feast-day".[179] Again, a monk is pictured beating a hand-held semanterion with a mallet in a twelfth century miniature.[180] Many post-Byzantine wall-paintings on Mount Athos, in· Meteora, and elsewhere, depict hand-held semanteria and semanteria of the large, wooden, suspended type.[181]

Interesting information has also been culled from the accounts of those travellers who, from the Middle Ages until as late as the nineteenth century, have visited Greece and the Near East, and who encountered the semanterion in their journeys.[182] Finally, the popular muse uses the semanterion and the church-bell to underline the dramatic intensity of the first images in the lament for the fall of Constantinople:

> *They have taken Constantinople, they have taken her!*
> *They have taken Thessaloniki! They have taken Aghia Sophia too;*
> *The great monastery, which had*
> *Three hundred semanteria, and sixty-two bells.*[183]

Mention of the semanterion is also to be found in love-songs in Greece, such as that given below:

> *The sun has set, the semanterion is struck,*
> *A girl and a youth are talking through a window.*[184]

Semanteria are also encountered in old books interpreting dreams, as the following:

"If a woman dreams she is beating a semanterion, it means she will soon be exposed to public shame and ridicule."[185]

"If one dreams of an iron semanterion being beaten, troubles lie ahead."[186]

Also noteworthy is a traditional custom practiced in Gournaki (Neochorion, Grevena): When the Easter service has concluded, and after all the red, dyed eggs of the congregation have been blessed by the officiating priest, the members of the congregation leave the church and one by one they break their eggs on the semanterion hung outside the church.[187]

Also of interest are the surnames derived from the semanterion, such as Simandiris, Simandirakis, etc.[188]

KONDIO (Struck bell)

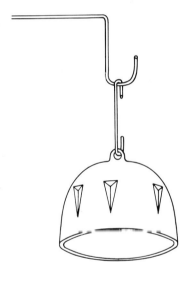

The *kóndio* or *kóndi* is shaped like a bowl and made of bronze, iron, or some other alloy.[189] It is preserved in the sanctuary of the church, usually suspended, and is sounded by the gentle tapping of a thin metal rod or hammer (fig. 65). The sound of the *kóndio* cues the psalmodist to cease his chanting when the officiating priest is ready to resume the liturgy, having concluded a series of sotto voce blessings inside the sanctuary.

Once, it was also sounded when the Gospel or other sacred texts were read; one or several *kóndia* would be struck at each verse-ending, at the end of each paragraph, or at each break in the liturgical text. The sounding of the *kóndio* could be described as a form of sonorous punctuation — which rhythmically accompanied the readings: "During the liturgy of the Resurrection, while the Gospel was being read verse by verse... boys holding the *kóndia* —a type of bell with a handle in the centre, struck by a small hammer— accompany each verse-ending right up to the conclusion of the Gospel. In this manner they continue to strike the *kóndia* while the "Christos Anesti" (Christ is risen) text is read, every day until that of the Ascension... Others do this only during the week after Easter. At the end of each verse or paragraph they strike the *kóndia* to coincide with the appropriate pauses of the psalmodist, another singer beginning at the point where the liturgy is chanted by many persons. However, when the liturgy is sung in the villages by a single priest, the *kóndia* are struck at each verse-end, phrase termination, or break in the text".[190] The *kóndio* was also used for litanies: "The litany procession started from the Kastro, finishing at Exambela amidst the wafting of incense, bell-ringing, and chanting, led by the talented person who struck the celebrated *kóndi*. What kind of instrument the *kóndi* was, I failed to ascertain, because in over eighty years it has not made a single appearance. According to one story, while the *kóndio* was being transported, it fell into the sea and 'drowned' (was lost)". Thus writes Theodosios Sperantzas in his "Cycladic Stories".[191]

Kóndia are to be found even in the present day in Greece, although the churches that possess them are few, and are located far from the great urban centres. Some exist in such monasteries as those of Patmos and Mount Athos (Esphigmenou, Koutloumoussiou, St. Paul's, et alia) as

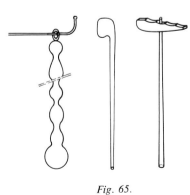

Fig. 65.

28. Cast-bells (kypriá) and forged bells (koudhoúnia) hung at the waist of men in costume (karnavália). Carnival, Nikissiani, Region of Pangheon, Kavala (1972).
←

29. Coins hung on chests of men in "foustanella" (Boúles). Carnival, Naoussa, Macedonia (1972).

30. Coins on bridal costume of Attica.

31. Ornament on headscarf of a woman's costume (sourghoút). Drymos, Thessaloniki.
→

33. *Wooden ratchet, 27 cm. high, 31 cm. wide. Stavronikita Monastery, Mount Athos.*

32. *Iron tongs (massá) with finger-cymbals (zília), 37 cm. high. Didymotikhon, Thrace.*

←

34.   *Wooden spoons (koutália), 21 and 24 cm. long.*

35.   *1. Nickelled brass cymbals (zilia), 6 cm. diam.   2. Bronze cymbals, 10.5 cm. diam.*

→

well. In some churches, a small bell (of the *kýpros* type, which is usually hung on the necks of sheep and goats)[192] or an *asterískos,* a liturgical implement used to keep the cover of the Communion plate from touching the sacred Communion bread, is struck in place of the *kóndio.*[193]

ROKANA *(Ratchet)*

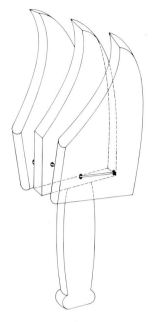

The *rokána,* also known as the *roukána* or *trokána,* is a kind of wooden ratchet; a thin strip of wood hits against a toothed wooden wheel, which revolves around its axis. The sound thus produced is dry and penetrating. In Greece today, the *rokána* is a favourite toy of children and adults alike, especially during the days of the Carnival. However, according to the writer Pouqueville, the *rokána* was once used in Greek towns to announce church services.[194] In Rhodes as well, up until the time of the Second World War, the children in the various quarters of the town "would announce the Resurrection ceremony by sounding *roukánes* and singing in the streets".[195]

Curt Sachs maintains that "during Holy Week, the *rokána* was used in Catholic churches as well as in Orthodox monasteries",[196] apparently not, however, to call the monks to the various services.[197] The monks of Mount Áthos claim that with the *rokána* they "frightened the wild beasts". Its dry but penetrating sound was ideal for chasing away the birds or beasts of prey, the foxes, jackals and wild boars, that used to raid the monasteries and eat the fruit and vegetables in the gardens and the grapes from the vineyards.

Fig. 66.

RENDELA *(Wooden clapper)*

The *réndela,* or *rendila* is a three-tongued wooden clapper that was used in the days of sailing-ships to signal the changing of watches at the helm (fig. 66).[198]

VOLACHTIRA *('Beater')*

The *volachtíra, volastíra,* or *volatíri* is a pierced stone suspended from a cord. It is used to strike the surface of the sea or the gunwhale of the boat during fishing, in order to drive the fish into the nets.

In many places in Greece the gunwhale is also kicked with the feet for the same purpose. Skillful fishermen strike the sea or the boat's gunwhale at regular intervals, and each time with the same number of beats.[199]

ANEMODHIKTIS — SKIACHTRO *(Wind-blown scarecrow)*

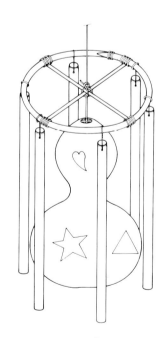

The *anemodhíktis-skiáchtro* (wind-blown scarecrow) is used to chase marauding birds away from the villagers' vegetable gardens, melon-beds, and vincyards. It is usually in the form of a man wearing the traditional kilt *(foustanélla)* or baggy trousers *(vráka),* or of a bird, and is made of some light-weight material, so that the wind can easily make it revolve around its axis. In addition, some simple mechanism is fitted to this sound-producer —such as the cogwheel and the sheet-metal of a ratchet, two small suspended counterweights, bells, etc.— which allow the figure to revolve more easily, and which at the same time produce a sound that frightens and chases the birds away.

Another device used to this same end is the sound-producer (fig. 67) from the collection of the folklorist Kitsos Makris in Volos. This idiophone consists of a dried, empty gourd,

Fig. 67.

113

suspended from the centre of a wooden hoop; six dried reeds are hung from the hoop all around its circumference, so that when the wind blows they strike against the hollow gourd, thus producing a rather dry and penetrating sound. The gourd (25 cm long) is open at both ends, more so at the bottom, and is decorated with etched designs — a cross, rosettes, a heart, a triangle, and a pentangle. The reeds (26 cm long) are open at the lower end and are blocked at the ends from which they are suspended.

This sound-producer, the name of which is unknown, was formerly in use on the property of farmer Athanassios Kapravelos, of the village of Lafkos in southern Pelion.[200]

PYROVOLISMI (Gunshots)

Apotropaic properties were attributed to gunshots *(pyrovolismí)*, originally; they were widely used in different traditional customs throughout Greece until quite recently — weddings, festivities, etc. The inhabitants of 'old Greece' (see note 30)[201] used gundshots at Easter and during the Carnival season in order to "drive away the evil demon". In Argyrades, on the island of Corfu, german measles (rubella) was exorcised by the expedient of having a left-handed man fire a gun, at the same time he would repeat an apotropaic verse three times: "Go away, go away *alofrostiá* (rubella), or I will burn you with my firing. I am a left-handed huntsman, and wherever I find you I will strike you".[202] The 'evil demon' was chased away with gunshots whenever the mother of a new-born child was stricken with eclampsy.[203] Friends and relatives would also fire their guns to salute anyone who was leaving for foreign parts.[204] In Arcadia, "guns are fired into the air for a wedding, and into the ground for the death of a child" — into the air for a wedding, because then the "menacing spirits are up in the air".[205]

Nowadays, the original apotropaic properties attributed to gunshots have been forgotten. All that remains of these traditional customs has been transformed into noisy expressions of joy; such, for instance, are the underlying reasons for the use of firecrackers and fireworks during the last days of Holy Week, especially on Saturday, the eve of the Resurrection.

Children imitate those gunshots once fired by adults in Greece with a number of toys. One such toy is made by placing two or three match-heads inside the 'bore' of a 'female' key, after which the hole is blocked with a nail; both the key and the nail are tied respectively at either end of a single piece of string. Holding the string in the middle, the children then violently strike the nail against a wall or a fixed stone; when struck in this manner, the match-heads inside the 'hollow' key are detonated.

A similar toy of the same nature is the *chtipáres* (strikers), which is made from a twig of elder by the children of Chryssi in Kastoria. In the same village, the children are accustomed to play with yet another sound-producing toy, especially at Christmastide. They place burning coals on a stone upon which they have first spit, then strike them with a kind of pestle *(tzioumáka)*, or with the flat end of a hammer, axe or similar implement, thereby detonating the burning coals.[206]

HARTAKIA (Strips of paper)

We may also note the children's custom of attaching long, thin strips of paper *(hartákia)* to the tail of a kite; these rub against one another when the kite is flying, thus producing a distinctive rustling noise. A similar sound, resembling that made by the ratchet *(rokána)*, although it is less dry in quality, is obtained when small, somewhat thick pieces of paper (e.g. playing-cards) are placed in the wheel of a child's windmill (toy), or in the spokes of a bicycle wheel.

Fig. 67.

114

MEMBRANOPHONES

DAOULI (Drum)

Terminology

The drum is known throughout Greece as *daoúli, tavoúli, davoúli, toúmbano, týmbanos,* and *toúmbanos.* In Mytilene it is also called the *toumbanéli* or *gbanéli;* in western Roumeli it is known as the *tsokáni.*[207] It is also called *árghano*[208] and *tamboúrlo.*

The *daoúli* —a wooden cylinder, covered at both parallel ends with skin held taut by rope— is principally a rhythmic instrument. It is played by striking the drum-head with two specially made drumsticks *(daoulóxyla)*. The *daoúli* is made in various sizes: the diameter of each skin surface or drum-head varies from approximately 25 cm to one metre, and its height (i.e., the distance between the two skin surfaces) ranges from approximately 20 to 60 cm. The size of the *daoúli* is primarily determined by two factors: tradition (this varies from region to region —in some areas large *daoúlia* are made, in others, smaller *daoúlia* are more common), and the *daoúli*-player himself *(daouliéris)*, who "makes the *daoúli* according to his measure"— to suit his height and girth, the length of his arms, etc. In recent years, especially since the Second World War, progressively smaller *daoúlia* have been made in Greece, even in those regions where the instruments had traditionally been large in size.

Fig. 68.

Construction

In order to make a drum, the first step is the construction of a cylindrical frame or skeleton of the desired size (fig. 68). A cylindrical wooden surface is then cut to the dimensions of the framework, and nailed to the latter. Today, the wooden surface, the drum-shell, is made of a single piece of layered wood — beech, walnut, or others. In the past, such shells were made by joining two or three pieces of wood from the inside, with bars fastened with pins or glue or with tacks (fig. 69a, 69b). In order to acquire its cylindrical form, the wood is first soaked in water, or worked into shape by means of fire. Two iron rings are attached to this wooden shell when once it is ready; subsequently, when the instrument has been completely finished, a sling is passed through these so that the drum can be suspended from the shoulder of the drummer. Finally, an 'air-hole', usually circular in shape, is cut at some point in the surface of the cylindrical shell so that the air inside the drum can 'leak-out' — so that the skins do not burst as a result of the strong vibrational movement of the air inside the drum when it is beaten. This 'air-hole' also affects the sound produced by the instrument; a very small opening makes for a sombre and dull sound, whereas a very large hole makes for a hollow sound. The usual diameter of the 'air-hole' ranges from approximately 1.0 to 1.5 to 2 cm, according to the overall size of the drum. On large drums, one occasionally meets with two or sometimes even three such 'air-holes'.

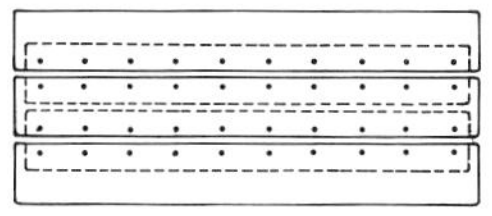

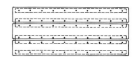

Fig. 69a.

Fig. 69b.

To make the two heads of the *daoúli,* goatskin, or, more rarely, sheepskin is treated and used. The hides of the wolf, the dog (used only for small drums), and the donkey are also considered suitable material, because, according to older drummers, "they are strong and do not have many pores". There are two principal methods of preparing the hides; either the skin is left in the sun to dry, or it is salted by the addition of alum, and kept rolled up for from three to five days, after which it is soaked in slaked lime and water, again for from three to five days. Then it is cleaned and made as thin as desired with a piece of glass; and many tanners grease it with oil so that it will remain soft when it has dried out. Today, ready-made commercially produced hides are also used to make drum-heads. After it has been tanned the skin is then stretched and fastened to two wooden hoops, which are fitted to the two parallel ends of the cylindrical shell of the drum. Finally, evenly spaced holes are cut around the circumference of the skins. A rope is then passed through the holes of the two skins, bracing them together, and is tightened by being bound in different ways (fig. 70).

In some regions where small drums are commonly used, as in eastern Crete, two 'snares'

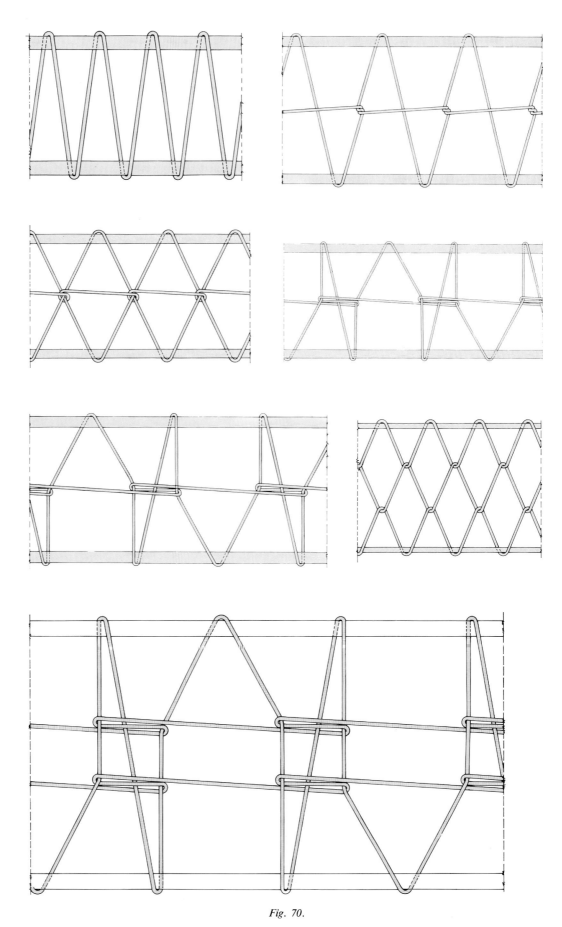

Fig. 70.

of sheep-gut are diametrically stretched over either one or both of the drum-heads, and are fastened to the wooden hoop or hoops, as the case may be. These 'snares' add sharpness and a distinctive timbre to the sound of the drum.[209]

Playing technique

The *daoúli* is played with two wooden beaters *(daoulóxyla, toumbanóxyla, daoulóverghes)*, held one in each hand. The drum-beater held in the left hand *(vérgha, vítsa)* is very thin and light, and resembles a switch; that which is held in the right hand is thicker and heavier, resembles a club *(kópanos)*, and is made in different shapes and sizes (fig. 71). The length of the *kópanos* and the weight and mass of the end that strikes the batter-head of the *daoúli* depend on the size of the drum and the build of the drummer.

When a *daoúli* is constructed, the drummer, who is usually the maker of the instrument as well, takes especial care that one of the two drum-heads is from approximately one to two centimetres bigger than the other, and that its skin is thicker in comparison to that of the opposite drum-head. By so doing he ensures that the bigger and thicker head, the batter-head— which the beater strikes to mark the strong beats of the measure— produces a heavier sound than the other drum-head. By contrast, the smaller and thinner-skinned drum-head, the switch-head —on which the switch marks the weak beats of the measure— produces a sharper sound. Nowadays, however, it is only rarely that one finds drums with one drum-head differing from the other in this way. Those *daoúli*-players who still take pride in the sound of their instrument, achieve a difference in the sharpness of the sounds produced by the two drum-heads by an appropriate tightening of the bracing and linking of the two drum-heads together. They tighten the bracing near the switch-head, taking care not to tighten the part attached to the batter-head.

The *daoúli*-player *(daouliéris, daoultzís, tymbanáris, tambourlís, tambourliéris)* 'tunes' his instrument by tightening the bracing. Although there is a clear difference in pitch between the two drum-heads of a good *daoúli*-player's instrument, one cannot, however, speak of a definite tonal relationship between the two drum-heads. Nevertheless, in certain *ziyiés* of one *daoúli* and one or two shawms (see *Introduction*, *ziyiá*, p. 27),[210] the *daoúli* does have some kind of 'tonal' relationship with the shawm or shawms it accompanies. Despite the difficulty of recognition, this relationship is sometimes an interval of an octave and sometimes an interval of a perfect fourth or fifth between the tonic of the scale played by the shawm and the 'note' given by the batter-head of the *daoúli*.

This tonal relationship is to be found in those *ziyiés* whose members have been playing together for years. Through a musical partnership of many years, often of a lifetime's duration, the *daoúli*-player gradually becomes accustomed to the key in which the shawm *(zournás)* plays its melodies — always the same key, insofar as it is the same instrument that is played. He grows used to it, or, in other words, he 'hears' it and it becomes a part of himself. This happens to such an extent that when he stretches tight the bracing of his *daoúli*, thus 'tuning' his instrument, the batter-head struck by the *kópanos* produces a sound which, as the musicians say, "flirts with the 'voice' of the *zournás*" i.e. with the tonic, the dominant, or the subdominant of the scale played by the *zournás*, as noted above. Thus, the *daoúli* —whenever this effect is achieved in certain *ziyiés*— has a further function, parallel to its principal function of producing the contrapuntal rhythmical accompaniment to the other melodic instrument or instruments. One might say that in this case the *daoúli* functions as an 'harmonic' instrument. It accompanies the *zournás* with a scarcely discernible and imperfect 'harmony', actually an *íson* (drone) of the kind so well known to the Greek musician from Byzantine song, as well as from the manner in which other popular instruments such as the mainland bagpipe *(gáida)*, the *líra*, etc. are played.

The *daoúli*-player beats his instrument while standing upright, his drum slung from his left shoulder. In hanging his instrument in this manner, he takes care that the batter-head should be to his right. On the batter-head he beats out the strong beats of the measure with

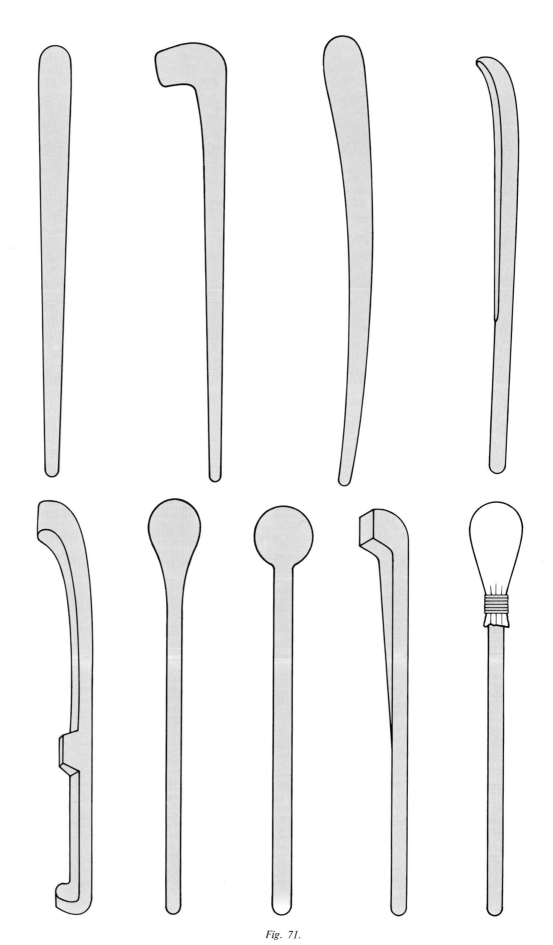

Fig. 71.

36.
Tambourine. Wall-painting by Theophilos (detail), early 20th cent. Greek Folk Art Museum, Athens.
←

37.
Small drum. Wall-painting: Jesus is mocked (detail), 16th cent. Stavronikita Monastery, Katholikon, Mount Athos.

38. Drum. Wall-painting: Parable of Dives and Lazarus (detail), 16th-17th cent. Loukous Monastery, Astros, Kynouria.

40.   *Small drum and shawm. Wall-painting: Praise ye the Lord (?) (detail), 17th cent. Monastery of St. John the Baptist (Timiou Prodromou), Serres.*

39.   *Bowed stringed-instrument, shawm (?), triangular harp (psaltery ?), hooked trumpet, bowed stringed-instrument, drums, shawm (?), hooked trumpet, ornament (sound-producer) on the plait of the last dancer. Wall-painting: Praise ye the Lord, first half of 18th cent. Chapel of Koukouzelissa, Great Lavra Monastery, Mount Athos.*

←

41.   *Trumpet and drum. Wall-painting: Jesus is mocked (detail), 16th cent. Varlaam Monastery, Katholikon, Meteora.*

42. *Mirlitons (made of shell: nounoúra; made of carton: ghourghoúra).*

43. *Small drum. Wall-painting: Parable of Dives and Lazarus (detail), 17th cent. Church of St. Demetrios, Chryssafa, Lakonia.*

the thicker drumstick, the *kópanos,* held in his right hand. On the switch-head he either lightly beats out the weak beats of the measure with the switch, the *vérgha,* held in his left hand, or else he "holds the *íson*", according to the customary expression referring to a kind of rhythmical drone.

On certain islands, that of Mytilene for instance, the *daoúli* (usually small in size) is played in two ways, one of which is the technique described above. When, however, he performs for a gathering in a closed space, the drummer is seated. He holds the *daoúli* on his left thigh and strikes it on one side only, using the palms and fingers of both hands; he marks the strong beats of the measure with his right hand, the weak beats with his left, which rests on the drum and thus assures that the *daoúli* stays in position on the player's leg. The small *daoúli* of eastern Crete is played in the same fashion. Here, there is but one difference: instead of using their hands, the drummers gently strike the *daoúli* with two small drumsticks, again on the one side only, using the right hand drumstick for the heavy beats and the left hand drumstick to mark the weak beats of the measure. Thus we see that in certain instances —to be found only in the islands— the *daoúli* is played in the same manner as the islander's *toubí* (q.v.).

In its role as an accompanying instrument one can distinguish two ways of playing the *daoúli,* according to the dictates of the kind of musical rhythm in each case. When the melody to be accompanied is of the *periodic rhythmical type* —the melodies of dance-tunes, for example— the drummer strikes the strong beats of the measure with the *kópanos* held in his right hand, and the weak beats with the *vérgha,* held in his left hand. Periodicity, however, does not always mean exactly the same pattern; in other words, the right and left hands do not necessarily repeat identical sequences of strokes. The good *daoúli*-player will continually embroider his performance with interstitial beats — secondary to the strong and weak beats of the time signature. For a few moments, when playing he will reverse the functions of his two hands by striking the strong beats with the *vérgha* and the weak beats with the *kópanos;* or, he will turn the *daoúli* over so that the *kópanos* strikes the higher-pitched switch-head; or, again, he will strike, now the hoop, now the ground at his feet, instead of either drum-head; and so on. At the same time he will vary the manner in which he strikes the drum-head — strongly or gently, with a clean, hard stroke or with a soft, light stroke. He also varies the point of contact, striking the centre of the drum-head, the area near the edge of the drum-head, the area nearest the hoop — all of which give each a different musical timbre to the sound produced.

On the other hand, when the melody to be accompanied is of *free rhythmical type* —such as convivial table-songs *(traghoúdhia tis távlas),* or a great many slow *klephtic songs*— the *daoúli* is then confined to widely spaced strokes of the *kópanos,* to which the left hand provides an echo-like tremolo accompaniment with the *vérgha.* The tremolo can also be produced by means of a simultaneous or separate application of the *kópanos* and *vérgha.* Such widely-spaced beats and the tremolo effect are a means of rhythmical punctuation in melodies belonging to the *free rhythmical type.*

The daoúli in the ziyiá

As an instrument intended to provide rhythm, the *daoúli* is never played on its own, but is always heard in combination with at least one melodic instrument. Together with the shawm *(zournás)* it makes-up the *ziyiá,* the traditional instrumental group of mainland Greece in particular, the group with which so many generations —right up to our own day— have enjoyed their folk songs; at festivities lasting many days in the wake of some marriage or baptism, village fairs, and any other occasions for general revelry. These two instruments are especially suited for open-air performances — with their strong penetrating sound, they psychologically prmie the crowds hearing them in the open. Until just after the First World War, when it replaced with ever-increasing speed by the more recent musical group, the *companía* —consisting of *klaríno, violí, laghoúto, sandoúri* (clarinet, violin, lute, dulcimer)— the *ziyiá* of *zournás* and *daoúli* was the principal bearer of the popular musical tradition in Greece. Indeed, it was the very symbol of that tradition. From the Greek countryman's point of view, the principal instrument of the *ziyiá* of *zournás* and *daoúli* is not, as one might think, the melodic instrument *(zournás)*; it is the *daoúli*, the rhythmic instrument. This is witnessed by the following expressions: "We'll take up the *toúmbana*"; "The *toúmbana* will come"; "We'll go and fetch the *daoúlia*"; "Let's go for the *daoúlia*"; "The *týmbanos* has come"; "The *daoúlia* have arrived"; etc. They also refer to the *ziyiá* as *"ta daoúlia"*, "a pair of *toúmbana*", "a pair of *daoúlia*", "they are beating the *daoúlia*", etc. In short, the melodic instrument *(zournás)* is not even mentioned in these phrases. And although everyone knows there is only one *daoúli* accompanying one or two *zournádhes* in every *ziyiá* (the second *zournás* provides the *íson*, or drone), the drum is always referred to in the plural.

The daoúli in the Greek world

The *daoúli*, one of the instruments used to perform the music for the *Anastenária* and *Kalóyeros* traditional rituals *(dhrómena)*, is considered sacred by the initiates. For this reason, the *daoúli* is kept the whole year round in the *konáki*, a private closed sanctum located beneath the iconostasis, and is used only on the days during which the *Anastenária* and *Kalóyeros* rituals are observed.[211]

Furthermore, the *daoúli* was since early times one of the instruments of 'martial music'. It was played to bolster the courage of the warriors and to instill fear in the enemy camp. And, together with the *zournás*, it spread the joy that followed a victory. The Byzantines provoked the Turkish armada to engage in battle with them by means of shouting, the beating of drums, and the blowing of trumpets, writes George Phrantzes in his *Chronicle* (1477): *As those ships were well prepared and lined-up in war formation, the men in them with trumpets (salpinx) drums (tymbana), and innumerable voices, called on the Turkish triremes and ships to do battle.*[212]

We are given the same picture in the *Romance of Belisarius* (14th-15th century), as follows:

> *And at dawn they played martial instruments, trumpets (troumbétes),*
> *viols (vióles), shawms (píffara), drums (týmbana), nakers (anakarádhes).*[213]

Makryannis, in his *Memoirs*, writes that "they beat drums" at the battle of Myli as well.[214] Panayiotis Zographos has depicted a pair of drummers, with their right arms raised in readiness to strike the *daoúlia*, on one of his paintings illustrating the Greek War of Independence of 1821, "The Battle of Vasilika", *Thoughts of Makryannis*, no. 4, 1836.[215]

Nowadays, there are not many *daoúlia* to be found in Greece. Even those which do exist do not display the variety in their dimensions, the knotting of the rope-bracing, the craftsmanship of the leather parts, and in general, the manner of their construction, as was to be found throughout the country up to the early decades of the twentieth century. The *daoúli* was known as early as Byzantine times, when it originally appears to have had smaller dimensions and was long and narrow in shape, only later developing into the form in which we know it today. That it was used extensively from then on is evidenced by a host of Byzantine and post-Byzantine miniatures and wall-paintings. In all of these —from such early examples as the miniature depicting two musicians, each beating upon a long, narrow drum (9th century illuminated manuscript from the Pantocrator Monastery, Mount Athos)[216] to the more recent miniatures and wall-paintings dating from the 14th to the 18th century[217]— one can discern basic morphological characteristics, as well as methods of playing the *daoúli* of the present day — the form, the manner in which the bracing is tied and the instrument is slung over the shoulder, the use of drumsticks or bare hands for beating the instrument, etc.

The picture pieced together from the iconographical evidence is amplified by literary sources: *To crash the cymbals (kýmvala) and beat the drums (týmbana)* (Leo Deacon, *History*, 10th century);[218] *All that night the cymbals crashed and the drums beat* (Nikitas Choniatis, *History*, 12th-13th century).[219]

> *The trumpets (salpinx) resounded and the drums (týmbana) roared*
>
> (*Epic of Digenis*, 14th century)[220]

There is such a tumult, it ascends as far as the clouds
—instruments, sistra, drums (týmbana), horns (voúkina)— melodious all
(Libistros and Rhodamne, 14th-15th century)[221]

There where the fighting is, may your ears hear
a thousand drums (tamboúrla) beating from one side to the other
(G. Chortatsis, Katzourbos, 16th century)[222]

With mute and soundless trumpets (salpinx) and broken drums (týmbana)
(V. Kornaros, Erotokritos, 17th century)[223]

To carry earth and play drums (tamboúrla)
(M. Tzanes Bounialis, The Cretan War, 17th century)[224]

Fig. 72a.

To the above literary references two further sources should be added — the folk song, and the accounts of travellers in Greece, who frequently refer to the drum *(daoúli)* in their accounts of their journies.[225]

Earlier, in Byzantine times, the *daoúli* was used as a sound-producer in the hunting of cranes; in that era, cranes' flesh was eaten and, indeed, was considered a great delicacy. A *daoúli* was beaten to scare the cranes into the air before the hunting-falcons were set loose upon them.[226]

In Byzantine and post-Byzantine times, nakers *(anakarádhes* or *niákara*, Arabic *naqqāra)* were also used: these were drums with hemispherical or ovoid sound-boxes, originally of clay and later made of metal, covered with skin. They were usually played in pairs, resting on the ground or on a horse's back, on each side of the horseman-drummer or slung over the performer's shoulder. Nowadays, the nakers are no longer to be met with. In the 14th century, we read in the *Offices of the Palace of Constantinople and Offices of the Great Church* that *when the king was ready and mounted on horseback, the drummers beat the nakers (anákara)...*[227]

Proverbs - curses - idioms:

"Beat the drums *(ta toúmbana)* softly because it's a poor man's wedding"
"Excepting the drums *(ta toúmbana)*, the wedding is costly"
"If the drums *(ta árghana)* are not beaten, if the goat is not slaughtered..."
"A wedding needs drums *(týmbana)*, a church needs a psalmodist"[228]
"May God turn you into a black drum *(taoúli)*!"[229]
"The drum *(to árghano)* calls for artistry"[230]
"I'm becoming a drum *(davoúli)*" (swelling-up)
"I am making a drum *(toúmbano)* of it" (I am broadcasting the news)[231]
"The world makes a drum *(toúmbano)* of it, and we admire it secretly"
"When you hear drums *(toúmbana)* in your neighbourhood, welcome them into your courtyard too"
"My belly has become a drum *(toúmbano)*" (I have overeaten)
"They found him drumlike *(toúmbano)*" (dead and swollen)[232]

Fig. 72b.

The following surnames are also worth noting: Davoultzís, Daoúlas, Daoúlis, Toúmbanos, Toumbanákis, etc.

TOUBI (Small drum)

Fig. 72c.

The *toubí* —diminutives *toubáki* and *toubanáki*— is a small drum, usually played in the islands.[233]

It is made in different sizes, of much the same materials and in much the same manner as the *daoúli* (q.v.) Sometimes the diameter of either of the two round bases of the shell is greater than the overall height of the *toubí*, as measured between the two drum-heads (fig. 72a,

131

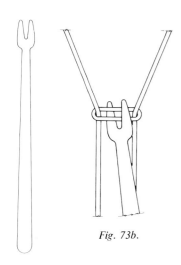

Fig. 73b.

Fig. 73a.

b, c). The differences in manufacture between the *toubí* and the *daoúli* are insignificant. Hide is stretched over the two open circular bases of the shell, either by means of bracing as in the case of the *daoúli*, or by the use of small nails. In addition, two strands of sheep-gut (snares) are always stretched diametrically over the two drum-heads, either on the outside or inside the shell of the *toubí*.

The *toubí* is played slung from the left shoulder or the neck. Alternatively, it can be held beneath the armpit or over the left thigh; or again, it can be suspended from a small, looped strap on the left arm, just above the wrist. The *toubí* is always beaten on one of its drum-heads, with the player using either the palms and fingers of his bare hands or two small, wooden drumsticks, *toubóxyla*, (or *laoúdhia* as they are called on the island of Santorini). The drumstick often has a triangular notch cut at one end. With the aid of the notched end of his drumstick, the player *(toubakáris)* tightens the bracing of his instrument: in this manner, he "tunes the *toubí*", as the younger players say (fig. 73).

When struck, the *toubí* produces a sound of indeterminate pitch. As a rhythmical instrument, it is usually played in combination with at least one melodic instrument. Usually encountered in the islands, the *toubí* is there played together with the island bagpipe *(tsaboúna)* or *líra*: *tsaboúna* and *toubí*, or *líra* and *toubí*. It is sometimes also encountered in combination with the island *ziyiá*: *violí* (violin), *laghoúto* (lute), and *toubí*. However, whenever there is merrymaking and other musical instruments are not available, the *toubí* accompanies the songs and dances on its own. It is also played by children performing Christmas and New Year carols *(kálanda)*.

The presence of the *toubí* in Greece since as early as Byzantine times is proved by the same iconographical sources as those bearing upon the *daoúli*. Further confirmation is provided by literary references:

> *They play trumpets (troumbétes), drums (órghana), toubiá and nakers (anakarádhes)*[234]

we read in the *Most Beautiful Tale of the Marvellous Man Called Belisarius* (14th-15th century).

Also, the family name Toubakáris is old.[235] Today, there are many Greeks with the surnames Toubakáris and Toubís.[236]

It should be noted that formerly the *toubí*[237] was also used as a sound-producer for other than musical purposes: "During the years of Turkish rule, the man responsible for calling the Christians to church would awaken them by beating a drum *(toubí)*. For this reason he was called *toubakáris* (drummer), as the dialect of Skyros shows us, and where the word has been preserved with this meaning".[238]

DEFI (Frame drum)

Terminilogy

The panhellenic name of the tambourine is *défi* or, more rarely, *délfi*. Especially in the regions of Macedonia and Thrace, it is also called *dairés (daerés, dacharés)* or *tagharáki*.

The *défi* —a single-skin frame drum— consists of a wooden cylinder whose diameter invariably exceeds its height, which is covered on one end only with skin. It is a rhythmic instrument of indeterminate pitch, and is played with the bare hands.

Construction

Its construction resembles that of the *daoúli* in its general lines; it is made in different sizes, the diameter of the head ranging from approximately 20-50 cm, although it is sometimes larger. The hide —usually the skin of a goat, sheep or hare— is affixed to the edge of the cylindrical frame with glue or small nails, or both. To ensure the head's greater firmness, a wooden hoop is often fixed over it. Many *défia* have small bronze cymbals *(zília)* attached to them, placed at regular intervals around the frame. In earlier days, the cylindrical shell was decorated with

132

engraved patterns, or, when inlay was used, with such geometrical designs as rhombi, squares, triangles, etc. In Thrace, the *dairés* is still adorned with many-coloured ribbons, and various colourful designs are painted on the skin of the head.

Playing technique

When played, the *défi* is usually held in the left hand and struck with the right. The strong beats are obtained by striking the centre of the head with force, the weak beats by lighter strokes along the edge of the head. By striking the head of the *défi* near the centre one obtains a deeper and fuller sound, whereas the peripheral area produces a sharp and dry sound. Again, at times the *défi* is struck with the fingers of both hands, in different rhythmical combinations. In such cases, the *défi* is held in both hands. By forefully rubbing the thumb or middle finger against the skin of the head of the *défi*, using a circular motion and keeping to the edge of the head near the shell, a good player varies his performance — sometimes employing hissing or whistling sounds, at other times discontinuous, broken ones. In addition, due to the rapid movements of the *défi*, the attached cymbals give out a metallic, bell-like sound.

The *défi* is usually played in conjunction with other musical instruments: *líra* and *défi;* *gáida* (mainland bag-pipe) and *défi; violí* (violin), *laghoúto* (lute), and *défi; massá* (q.v.) and *défi; violí, klaríno* (clarinet), *laghoúto, sandoúri* (dulcimer) and *défi;* and other combinations. Nevertheless, it is also played on its own —when no other musical instruments are available— to accompany songs, or, in conjunction with song, to accompany dances, especially women's and men's face-to-face dances.

In the Greek world, the *défi* is known to us from ancient times by the name *týmbanon*.[239]

The name *taghári,* encountered today in northern Greece in the region of Florina,[240] is used by the poet Antonis Achelis in his verses *The Siege of Malta* (1565):

> *They played nakers (anakarádhes), trumpets (voúkina),*
> *drums (taoúlia) and tambourines (taghária)*
> *and raised banners bedecked with moons.*[241]

Among the other instruments with which the Greek people entertain themselves, the *défi* is noted in the chronicles of those travellers who from time to time visited Greece or passed through the country on their way east.[242] I. M. Konsolopoulos, in his *Mykoniatika Chronika,* describes the skill of a *défi*-player *(defitzís)*[243] towards the end of the nineteenth century: "The gathering was enriched by the barrel-organ that played at the door of the theatre, where, with great mastery, a real enthusiast *(meraklís)* struck a *défi* with little bells;[244] sometimes he struck it against his knees, sometimes on his elbow, and, for fortissimo, against his forehead. This was really something original".[245]

Nowadays, only two of the names for the *défi* mentioned here continue to live on in the mouths of the Greek people — *défi* and *dairés*.

TAMBOUTSA — TOUMBANAS (Frame drums)

The *tamboutsá,* or *tamboutsiá,* is a large sieve with an unpierced skin stretched over the hoop, which in Cyprus is used as a musical instrument in addition to its other functions. It is a simple household item, one that circumstances can transform at times into a rhythmical musical instrument of indeterminate pitch (fig. 74).

The skin of the head of the *tamboutsá* is usually that of the goat, and covers an area of approximately 50-55 cm in diameter, although at times it can be smaller. It is mainly brought in to accompany the violin in the absence of the lute *(laghoúto)*. It is also played to accompany singing and dancing when no other musical instruments are to be found. It is played with the palms and fingers of both hands, or with two small drumsticks, and is held against the left thigh

Fig. 74

of the seated player. In other words, it is played in much the same manner as the *toubí* and the *toumbeléki* (q.v.).

"'Boil' the *tamboutsá* so we can play a little", say the musicians when the skin of the head —which is nailed or glued to the wooden frame of the sieve— has slackened due to atmospheric humidity and must be heated over a fire to become tight once again. This is essential if the sieve is to be used for musical purposes.

The *toumbanás* (diminutive *toumbanidháki*) is likewise a sieve. The inhabitants of Chrysomilia (Fourni, Ikaria) use this as a tambourine *(défi)* to accompany their singing and dancing when no other musical instruments are available. It is played just as one plays the *défi*.

When a *défi* was not to be had, a sieve was also used by the children of Megara, in Attica, to provide accompaniment for their Christmas and New Year carols *(kálanda)*, either in conjunction with the triangle and cymbals *(zília)* or on its own.

TOUMBELEKI *(Pottery drum)*

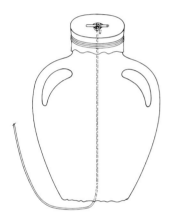

Fig. 75.

Fig. 76.

The *toumbeléki* (pottery drum),[246] which is also called *taraboúka*[247] and *stámna*[248] (jar), is a rhythmical instrument, principally to be found in northern Greece (Macedonia and Thrace) and the islands of the eastern Aegean (Mytilene, Chios, etc.).[249]

Its earthenware shell is usually shaped like a handleless jar, open at one end with a skin stretched and glued or bound over the other end.[250] If the skin is bound, this can either be done very simply with a thin cord, or with more complex knotting of various kinds towards the neck of the instrument — much like the bracing of the drum *(daoúli)* (see fig. 70). This depends upon the particular manner in which the folk musician wants his *toumbeléki* prepared. It is made in different sizes — children use small ones for singing carols, while professional instrumentalists use larger *toumbelékia*. In earlier times it was customary for the pottery drum to be decorated with various designs, and small mirrors were frequently attached. Another tradition, persisting to this day, is the suspension of small pellet-bells either immediately under the skin of the drum-head or around the neck of the jar to which the skin was bound

The *toumbeléki* or *taraboúka* is played with both hands, or, more rarely, with a pair of small drumsticks; it is usually held under the player's left armpit or suspended from his left shoulder. Alternatively, if the player is seated, it may be gripped between his two thighs. The right hand is used to strike the strong beats of the measure, the left hand the weak beats. The strong beats are obtained by striking the circular skin of the drum-head somewhere near the centre, which can be relied upon to produce a lower pitched and fuller tone than the edge, on which weak beats are produced — these are higher pitched and less rounded in tone.

A good player will never accompany singing or dancing with a simple repetition of the strong and weak beats of the measure, but will constantly variate his performance with a wide range of secondary beats in order to break up the basic rhythmic components of the measure. He may play a syncopated rhythmic pattern, or a kind of tremolo in which the skin of the drum-head is gently struck by both hands, in a rapid, even, alternating motion. At other times, he may strike the strong beats of the measure on the drum-head and the weak beats on the edge of the earthenware soundbox near the head where the skin is fastened to the shell, or, vice versa, he may beat out the rhythm with one hand only, using the other to interrupt the vibrations of the skin by touching the drum-head with palm of his hand or his elbow.

An able performer can vary the pitch of the sound he produces by pressing the skin of the drum-head in the appropriate place. Let us also not forget the special timbre the sound of the little pellet-bells (see above) adds to that of the reverberating skin. Also, by varying the size of the bells, a range of different 'notes' is brought to the listener's attention — even though he would find it difficult to determine the exact pitch of these.

The *toumbeléki* is played in conjunction with at least one melodic instrument — usually the mainland bagpipe *(gáida)*. It may, however, be encountered as a part of other combinations of instruments, such as the *líra* and *toumbeléki,* and, in former times, "the *tzourá* (a small *klaríno*), two *ivghiliá* (violins) and a *stámna*"; "a *floyéra,* two *violiá* (violins) and a *stámna*"; and so forth.[251] It can nevertheless be heard on its own, when it accompanies children's Christmas and New Year carolling, as well as song and dance at those gatherings where no other musical instruments are available. Like so many other popular instruments, the *toumbeléki* once used to accompany its owner into the hazards of battle. In one of his letters, Odysseas Androutsos refers among other matters to the booty captured at the battle of Vasilika on the 22nd of September in 1822; he writes: "We captured their 'bouyiouk bairaki', (Turkish, large banner), as well as everything else, including their toumbelékia".[252]

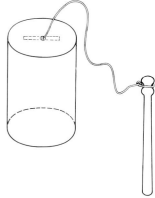

MOUGRINARA — GHOURGHOURA (Friction drums)

The *mougrinára* (derived from *mougrízo,* to roar) was formerly used in central and western Crete,[253] to frighten away marauding birds and beasts (foxes, badgers, etc.) from melon-patches and vineyards (see *rokána*). The *mougrinára* is a sound-producer consisting of a bottomless jar, the mouth of which is covered with a taut skin. A leather thong, waxed string, or even a rush is passed through the interior of the jar and is affixed to the external surface of the skin by means of a knot or small piece of wood — using prepunched holes in the skin of the 'head' (fig. 75).

The player of the *mougrinára* is seated; with wet hands he pulls the waxed string or rush, in a continuous pulling motion, holding the body of the 'instrument' between his legs. The sound produced in this fashion resembles a loud bellowing or roaring. The same sound-producer was once made in the monasteries of Mount Athos as well — not using a jar, however, but using half of the shell of a well dried calabash, which was covered with the skin of a hare, rabbit, or other animal (fig. 76).

The same method is used today to make the *ghourghoúra* (onomatopoeic) or *troumbéta* (trumpet) — a sound producing toy sold at village feasts throughout Greece (fig. 77). In place of the jar or calabash, the shell of the *ghourghoúra* is made of a cardboard cylinder, open at one end and covered with paper (formerly with skin) at the other end. A string is then tied to a simple wooden handle. When the *ghourghoúra* is whirled around, the string tightens as a result of centrifugal force, rubs against the wood of the handle to which it is tied, thus setting up vibrations. These vibrations are transmitted to the opposite side of the cylinder, thus producing the sound.

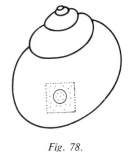

NOUNOURA (Mirliton)

The panhellenic name for this sound-producer is *nounoúra,* or, *niounioúra*. It is also known by other names, however, including *chochlionounoúra, chochlidhonounoúra,* and *chochlobádouro* on the island of Crete; *karáolos* in Cyprus; *karívolas* in Chrysomilia in the Fourni islands off Ikaria. Rarely, it is called *mourmoúra,*[254] which in Greek literally means 'murmur'. This sound-producer is very easily made. A hole is pierced in a snail-shell, on which is affixed a spider's cobweb *(tsípa),* cigarette paper, or even an onion skin (fig. 78). The *nounoúra* is essentially a children's toy, which is nevertheless used by adults as well when there are no instruments available for their merrymaking. The *nounoúra* is held with the open end of the shell against the mouth and a song is either sung or hummed. With the player's breathing, the air within the shell vibrates, together with the membrane of cobweb, cigarette paper, etc. — this gives the sound produced a distinctive nasal timbre.

Children also make the *nounoúra* from other material. They stick or bind a spider's web or cigarette paper to one or both of the open ends of a reed. If cigarette paper is used, a hole is cut in the reed (fig. 79). Another method is to open a hole —called 'a little window'— in

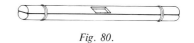

a piece of asphodel, which is then cut through the centre. Cigarette paper or cobweb is then placed over the hole, and the two pieces of asphodel are joined and bound together at their ends (fig. 80).

COMB AND CIGARETTE PAPER *(Mirliton)*

A piece of cigarette paper is affixed to the flat side of a comb, at the end where the teeth of the comb are densest. With this simple sound-producer, a skillful player can imitate the sound of the shawm *(zournás)*, 'playing' different popular tunes.

1   2   3

44.   *Drums (daoúlia): 1. Diam. 38 cm., cylindrical frame 20 cm. high, Sitia, Crete. 2. Diam. 50 cm., cyl. fr. 39 cm. high, Naoussa, Macedonia. 3. Diam. 26 cm., cyl. fr. 23 cm. high, Messolonghi.*
        ←

47.   *Drum (daoúli) and beaters, diam. 38 cm., cylindrical frame 20 cm. high. Sitia, Crete.*
                                                                                    →

45.   *Drum (daoúli), diam. 32 cm., cylindrical frame 25 cm. high. Amfissa.*   46.   *Drum with snares (toubí) and beaters, diam. 38 cm., cylindrical frame 25 cm. high. Kythnos.*

50. Tambourines (défia) with jingles (zilia): 1. diam. 22 cm., cylindrical frame 6 cm. high. 2. (Dakharés) diam. 47 cm., cyl. fr. 9 cm. high, Macedonia. 3. Diam. 35 cm., cyl. fr. 6 cm. high, Epirus. →

48. Tambourine (défi) with jingles (zília), diam. 33 cm., cylindrical frame 5.5 cm. high. Thrace.

49. Tambourine (toumbanás), diam. 37 cm., cylindrical frame 8 cm. high. Chryssomilia, Fourni, Ikaria.

53. *Pottery drums (toumbelékia): 1. with geometrical design, 13.5 cm. diam. skin surface, 52 cm. high, Mytilene. 2. 15 cm. diam. skin surf., 26 cm. high. 3. with floral decoration, 20 cm. diam. skin surf., 42 cm. high, Macedonia.*

→

51. *Pottery drum (toumbeléki), decorated with small mirrors, 20 cm. diam. skin surface, 33 cm. high. Mytilene.*

52. *Pottery drum (toumbeléki) with floral decoration, 13.5 cm. diam. skin surface, 26 cm. high. Sifnos.*

54.   *Pottery drum (toumbeléki) with pellet-bells hanging from skin surface, 24 cm. diam., 51 cm. high. Didymotikhon, Thrace.*

AEROPHONES

FLOYERA — SOURAVLI — MADOURA (Pipes)

Three kinds of pipes are particularly associated with the life of the Greek shepherd: the *flo-yéra* (an end-blown ductless flute), the *sourávli* (a ducted flute), and the *madoúra* (a clarinet-type instrument). All of these three instruments have two morphological characteristics in common: a hollow cylindrical soundbox with holes along the entire length of its body — the holes can be round, oval, or, more rarely, square. Where they differ radically from one another, however, is in that part of the instrument which produces the sound. It is this element which enables us to differentiate organological and classify these three pastoral instruments.

The floyéra: Construction — Playing technique — Types— Terminology

The *floyéra,* an end-blown flute, is a long, narrow, hollow cylindrical tube open at both ends (fig. 81). It is made in various sizes, between 15 or 20 cm to approximately 85 cm in length, and of various materials — cane, wood, bronze, iron, bone, and, following the Second World War, of plastic.[255]

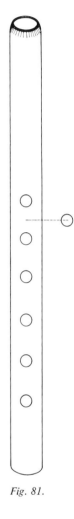

The construction of a *floyéra* calls for patience and love of the work for its own sake, as well as experience. From the moment a shepherd decides to search for the cane, wood, or whatever material he will use in the making of his *floyéra,* to the opening of the holes in the cylinder and its possible final touches of ornamentation, he must pay attention to many points of construction, and must proceed by trial and error.

When the instrument is to be made of cane, the latter must be dry, free of protuberances, and as straight as possible; the walling must be consistent in thickness, and the internal diameter of the bore must not vary throughout the length of the *floyéra.* One end of the cylindrical tube is cut so as to include a knot, while the other so as not to have one at all. The point at which the player blows, the 'mouthpiece', is cut, not just below the knot, where the cane is not of the same thickness and internal diameter as the rest of its length, but slightly further along the cylinder. This point is made thinner all around, by paring the external surface of the cylinder. The opposite end, the end from which the air is expelled, is initially cut with the knot still attached; this is opened afterwards, just enough to ensure that the air does not escape too freely. In this manner blowing into the cylinder becomes less tiring, while at the same time the quality of the note given by the lower hole as well as that of all the high notes is improved. The inner surface of the hollow cane must be smooth; the holes are usually all circular, and must all be of equal diameter and equidistant from one another.

The shepherd opens the first hole approximately in the middle part of the *floyéra.* Then, stopping this hole with his left forefinger, he places the fingers of both hands on the cylinder as though he were actually playing the instrument; the points where they make contact with the cylindrical tube are where he opens the remaining fingerholes. The fingerholes are usually made through the application of a red-hot nail to the cylindrical soundbox at the appropriate places.

As for the wooden *floyéra,* made from different kinds of wood,[256] everything mentioned above applies here as well, with the obvious exceptions that necessarily arise due to the different nature of the material used in construction. In the case of the wooden *floyéra,* the shepherd must also cope with the delicate task of boring and carving the wood. Formerly done with a red-hot iron skewer, which called for great patience, the boring is now done with a drill. Similarly, the carving of the exterior of the instrument must be carefully executed, so that the walls of the cylindrical tube are as consistently thin as possible. When a narrower vent is re-

Fig. 81.

147

quired for the expulsion of air from the *floyéra,* the internal diameter of the lower end of the cylinder is made smaller by affixing wax or a thin wooden ring or a piece of cardboard around the inside. This is also done for other types of *floyéra* — those made from other material, such as bronze, iron, or bone.

It was once customary to slide large, single-piece wooden *floyéra* into the intestine of a sheep or goat before the fingerholes were opened. The sheep-gut, which in time would dry out and become inseparable from the wood, served to keep the wood soft and to prevent its breaking. The same function is performed by the oil or butter with which the wooden *floyéra,* regardless of size, is greased with, both inside and outside, to this very day. The fingerholes of the iron or bronze *floyéra,* which is usually an ordinary piece of pipe or tubing or the barrel of an old gun, are opened by the village blacksmith, under the guidance of the shepherd.

The bone *floyéra,* made from the medial wing-bone of an eagle or other bird of prey, needs special preparation. After the wing has been plucked, the bone is buried in the ground in order to clean it; this, through the natural decomposition of the flesh and narrow. The bone is then taken to church, where it is left to be 'sanctified' through its presence at the liturgy over a period of several days. "The bird of prey belongs to the devil and is unwholesome: it must be purified".[257] Finally, holes are opened in the bone, which is polished smooth with ashes or boiled together with ashes to bleach it; it is decorated with various designs if so desired.

The *floyéra,* which can be up to 50 cm in length, usually has 6 equidistant frontal fingerholes and 1 rear thumbhole — or simply 6 frontal holes. The thumbhole, should there be one, is usually positioned midway between the first and second frontal fingerholes, or slightly higher than the first frontal fingerhole.

The *long floyéra* — always made of wood or metal — which ranges in length from between approximately 60 to 85 cm, is known as the *tzamára* in Epirus and the *kaváli* in Thrace. This instrument has 7 frontal fingerholes, or 7 frontal fingerholes and 1 rear thumbhole. Apart from these fingerholes, however, the *tzamára* has several additional holes (vent-holes) on the lower part of the cylindrical tube.[258] The short version of the *tzamára,* which is approximately 60 cm long, has one such vent-hole, whereas the somewhat longer instruments have two. The long *tzamára* is between 75 and 85 cm in length, and has four vent-holes, three frontal and one rear. These holes are never stopped with the fingers, but remain open always, and serve to modulate the pitch and quality of the sound produced by the instrument. Should these holes be stopped, the key in which the *tzamára* is 'tuned' is lowered, and the timbre of the sound its emit is altered.

Due to the length of the instrument, the shepherd always plays the *tzamára* sitting on the ground, cross-legged, and with the lower end of the instrument resting on the ground or on the shepherd's shoe. In this manner, the 'mouthpiece' stays more firmly between the lips of the player, which makes for easier playing, and his fingers are allowed more freedom of movement. When not in use, the cylindrical tube of the *tzamára* is stuffed with a long thin twig. As is said: "That way it is filled up, and doesn't break if it falls down". The twig is also used to clean the interior of the *tzamára,* a piece of wool dipped in oil being attached to one end of the twig for this purpose. Lubricated during cleaning, the wood of the instrument thus remains soft, and is thereby proof against splitting. In Thrace and Mytilene, the long wooden flute, there called *kaváli,* is usually constructed in three separate parts which can be fitted together.

The *floyéra* is held at a slight oblic angle, towards the right, so that the player's breath will strike the sharply-angled lip of the instrument on the opposite side, thus producing sound. When the player is right-handed, as in this description, the fingers of his right hand (forefinger, middle finger and ring-finger) stop the holes on the lower part of the *floyéra,* while the fingers of his left hand stop those fingerholes nearest the 'mouthpiece'. The reverse of this holds true for the left-handed player.

When blown into gently, the *floyéra* produces a series of low notes. Overblowing, together with the same fingering, produces the same notes as before, but one octave higher. More intense overblowing produces a few still higher notes. The tonic of the scale which these notes constitute depends upon the length of the *floyéra:* the longer the instrument, the lower the tonic. The reverse holds true as well. An adept musician playing a well-made *floyéra* should be able to cover a range of two octaves and a fifth, although the sound quality is not consistent from one end of this range to the other. The lower notes, those produced by gentle blowing, are somewhat dull and a little hoarse. The notes of the next octave higher, which require overblowing, are bright and penetrating. Still sharper and yet more piercing are the few notes to be obtained over the second octave.

The *short floyéra,* approximately 50 cm in length, with 6 frontal fingerholes and 1 rear thumbhole, gives the intervals of the diatonic scale (C-D-E-F-G-A-B-C). The *long floyéra* —the *tzamára* and the *kaváli*— approximately between 60 and 85 cm long, with 7 or 7+1 holes, gives the following sequences of intervals: one tone and six semitones, or one tone and seven semitones. The sound it produces are generally hoarse; the longer the instrument, the hoarser the sound.

Another *long floyéra* is the *darvíra* or *skipitára;*[259] it is still to be found in Euboea, although once it was to be heard in Roumeli and the Peloponnese as well. Some 60 cm in length or more, the *darvíra* has only 5 frontal fingerholes, or 5 frontal fingerholes and 1 rear thumbhole, and usually has no vent-holes like those of the *tzamára.* It produces intervals of one tone and four semitones, or one tone and five semitones, respectively. Like the *tzamára,* it is characterised by a deep and somewhat hoarse sound, and like it also, it too gives a series of intervals in which a tone is followed by a series of semitones.[260]

In performance, the player continually embellishes the notes of the melodic line with different kinds of ornamentation, including appoggiaturas, trills, and tremolos, and these —as with monophonic music— add verve and expression to the single monophonic melody played on the *floyéra.* This verve derives from the internal complexity these ornaments impose upon the rhythmical structure of the music, while such embellishments invariably add a distinctive colour to the melody and hence make for greater depth of expression. They are the personal hallmark of each player, and serve to distinguish him from every other shepherd who plays the identical tune on the *floyéra.*

The *floyéra* is primarily an instrument of mainland Greece. Apart from the generic terms *floyéra* and *kalámi,* found throughout the country, one also encounters the following regional names for this instrument: *floéra, flouyiéra, flouéra, fióra* (used by the Greeks of the Kavakli region in northern Thrace); *flióros* (Nikissiani, region of Pangeon); *fráouro* (Pelion); *makrofloyéra* (Kassandra, Chalkidiki); *tzourlás, tsourlás, zourlás, and sourlás* (Peloponnese); *tzamára,*[261] *tzourás, tzourái, tzirádhi* (principally in Epirus); *varvánga* (in the regions of Karditsa and Trikala); *kaváli, kavála* (Thrace and Macedonia); *ghavál* (among the Greeks of the Black Sea area); *payiávli* (Mytilene and Chios);[262] *tsafári, tsafliár(i)* (in northern Greece and the Peloponnese); *darvíra, dilivíra, skipitára* (found in Roumeli, the Peloponnese and Euboea); *virvíra, svírka* and *pistoúlka* (nome of Serres); *doudoúka, toutoúkin* (region of Komotini); *soupélka* (region of Ardea, nome of Pella); *violí* (Dorion, region of Trifylia, nome of Messinia); *laghoúto* (Amorgos); *nái* or *néi* (older names that are no longer in use).

Universally considered a pastoral instrument, the *floyéra* is usually played solo by shepherds as they watch over their grazing flocks. A skilled player, however, on occasion —at some gathering of friends or village festival— may perform on his *floyéra* together with other instruments. Co-operation of this nature, with such recognised instrumental combinations as the *ziyiá* of violin and lute, *(violí* and *laghoúto)* or even with single instruments, is never more than a transient phenomenon, however, the result of particular circumstances in each given case.

We discuss elsewhere (p. 76-77), in connection with the use of bells in Greece, how the *floyéra* features in the life of the Greek shepherd as both a sound-producer and as a musical instrument.[263]

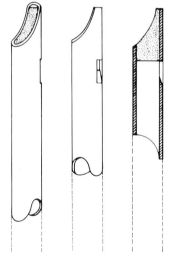

Fig. 82a   Fig. 82b.   Fig. 82c.

The sourávli: Construction — Playing technique — Types — Terminology

The *sourávli* is a ducted flute, i.e. not blown from a completely open hole; its 'mouthpiece' is usually cut diagonally and stopped with a plug *(tápa),* which leaves only a narrow slit open,

149

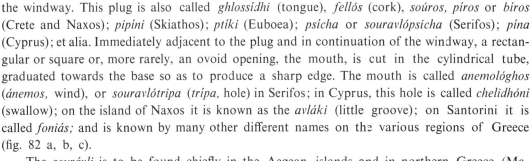

Fig. 83.

Fig. 84.

Fig. 85.

the windway. This plug is also called *ghlossídhi* (tongue), *fellós* (cork), *soúros, píros* or *bíros* (Crete and Naxos); *pipíni* (Skiathos); *ptíki* (Euboea); *psícha* or *souravlópsicha* (Serifos); *pína* (Cyprus); et alia. Immediately adjacent to the plug and in continuation of the windway, a rectangular or square or, more rarely, an ovoid opening, the mouth, is cut in the cylindrical tube, graduated towards the base so as to produce a sharp edge. The mouth is called *anemолóghos* (*ánemos,* wind), or *souravlótripa* (*trípa,* hole) in Serifos; in Cyprus, this hole is called *chelidhóni* (swallow); on the island of Naxos it is known as the *avláki* (little groove); on Santorini it is called *foniás;* and is known by many other different names on the various regions of Greece (fig. 82 a, b, c).

The *souravli* is to be found chiefly in the Aegean islands and in northern Greece (Macedonia and Thrace). It is made in much the same way as the *floyéra,* in different sizes ranging from 15-20 cm to around 65 cm, and is constructed of various materials — principally of cane and wood, and sometimes of bone and bronze. Different kinds of wood are used to make the *souravli,* (see note 256). Soft woods, such as oleander, sage, and fig are used to make the plug, which must fit snugly if the instrument is to 'confess'. The larger wooden *souravli* consists of two or more wooden sections which are fitted together for playing. In Cyprus, the cane *souravli,* known locally as the *pithkiávli,* is often pushed into a snakeskin or a case of the bark of the oleander. These two materials fuse with the cane upon drying out, and thus serve to protect the latter from splitting or breaking.

The *souravli* usually has 6 frontal fingerholes spaced at equal intervals from one another; or 6 frontal fingerholes and 1 rear thumbhole. Some *souravlia,* however, including those made in former times, have fewer fingerholes — specifically, 5 frontal fingerholes, with or without a rear thumbhole. Such *souravlia* are to be found in Crete, on Santorini, Naxos, Paros and elsewhere. Since the Second World War, *souravlia* with 7 or 7+1 holes have also appeared in the country.

When it is played, the *souravli* is held perpendicular to the mouth of the player *(souravliéris),* who blows through the windway left open after the insertion of the plug, and the sound is produced by the 'striking' of his breath —it "breaks", as the players themselves say— against the sharp edge, the lip, on the opposite side of the mouth. The *souravli,* like the *floyéra,* produces a series of low notes when it is blown into gently. The same fingering, in conjunction with overblowing, produces the same notes raised an octave higher. The lower notes produced by gentle blowing are of rather dull quality, whereas the higher notes are bright and piercing. The *souravli,* when it is approximately 50 cm long, gives the intervals of the diatonic scale. The longer *souravli* gives intervals of one tone and six semitones.

Apart from those *souravlia* with a diagonally cut mouthpiece and plug, there also exist similar instruments with straight cut 'mouthpiece' and plug (fig. 83). The shorter *souravli,* principally encountered in the islands, is usually diagonally cut, whereas the longer *souravli* of northern Greece has a straight cut 'mouthpiece'. In the latter instrument, the windway and the rectangular or square mouth are positioned on the underside of the cylindrical tube, opposite the fingerholes. This enables the player to hold the instrument relatively low, which means he will not tire very easily. In this kind of *souravli* the fingerholes are not always equidistant from each other, with a larger space being left between the third and fourth fingerholes than between the other fingerholes.

A diagonally cut *souravli* without a plug used to be played in certain villages in the nome of Messinia (Dorio, Psari), etc. (fig. 84). In place of the artificial stopper, a player of such a *souravli* would use his lower lip — a 'living' plug in other words, that enabled him to create the sound and to control the accuracy of the intervals given by the instrument.

On the island of Naxos, a double ducted flute *(dhisávli)* consisting of two cane *souravlia* bound together, was once to be heard. One of these, with 6 frontal fingerholes and 1 rear thumbhole, carried the melody. The second *souravli* of the pair was shorter and narrower, and had no fingerholes at all; this *souravli* accompanied the melody with a kind of *ison,* an uninterrupted drone, consisting of a single, piercing note (fig. 85). Formerly, in Epirus and Macedonia, one could also find the *boulboúl*, also k(n)own as the *vourghára* or *ghorghára*. This was another kind of double ducted flute, but was fashioned from a single piece of wood. One of the two tubes was equipped with 6 fingerholes, while the other had a single hole placed on its side — so as to remain unobstructed by the player's fingers stopping the other six fingerholes (fig. 86a, b). Yet another double ducted flute, the so-called *glousnítsa* of the Serres district, was constructed of two single cane or wooden *sourávlia* bound together with string.

Two *pithkiávlia (sourávlia)* together, each one have either 6 or 6+1 holes, are still to be found in Cyprus, though rarely. The two instruments are not bound together, but are held in the mouth in such a way that they form an acute angle. The playing of these two *pithkiávlia* in this manner results in an increase of volume of sound produced; the two instruments in unison play a melody instead of a single instrument. It is nevertheless possible for a skilled musician to vary the melody by short drones, or by means of momentary consonances or dissonances. To achieve these effects, he stops or opens certain fingerholes on only one of the two *pithkiávlia*. None of the above mentioned effects in any way alters the monophonic character of the instrument.

In addition to the common term *sourávli*, the instrument is also known by the people of Greece as the following: *siliávri* (on Lemnos and among the Greeks of the Black Sea region); *souriáli* (Santorini); *souvliári* or *soughliári* (Naxos); *souvriáli* (Mykonos); *souliávri* (Chalki); *sourghál(i)*, *sournávli; pinávli, piniávli, piliávli* (Fourni islands, Samos, Kos); *pithkiávli, pidhkiávli* or *pidhiávlin* (Cyprus); *pirávli* or *pidhávli* (Ikaria); *perniávli* (Karpathos); *payiávli* (Serifos, Chios); *flevoúra* (Chios); *oliávri, oliavír* (Imvros); *kavál* or *kaváli* (Macedonia, Thrace); *sfyríkla* (Nikissiani, region of Pangeon); *sfírighla* (Kallithea, region of Drama); *thiabóli, thiambóli, fthiabóli, ftiabóli, fiabóli, pabióli, babióli, chabióli, sfyrochábiolo, sfyrochábouolo, pyrochábiolo, ghlossochábouolo* (Crete); *zourtás* (Greeks from Pharassa in Cappadocia); *makrofloyéra* (nome of Katerini); *pistiálka* (Pyrgi, region of Drama); *et alia*.

Although the terms *floyéra* and *sourávli* refer organologically to two different instruments, they are used indiscriminately throughout Greece. In mainland Greece, the name *floyéra* is used to designate the instrument we have discussed above under that heading (q.v.); however, the term *floyéra* is not infrequently applied to the *sourávli* with diagonally cut 'mouthpiece' and plug. The same holds true with a number of regional names for the two instruments. For instance, in northern Greece *kaváli* denotes both the end-blown ductless flute *(floyéra)* and the ducted flute with plug *(sourávli)*. The same thing happens again with such names as *payiávli, zourtás*, and *makrofloyéra*, to give but a few; these are used interchangeably for both the *floyéra* and the *sourávli*.

The *sourávli*, like the *floyéra*, is principally a solo instrument. Nevertheless, upon occasion it is combined with other local instruments when circumstances necessitate this — the only requirement in such cases is that the *souravliéris* must be an adept performer. This author recalls hearing a combination of *líra, toubí* (small drum) and *souriáli* on the island of Santorini. On Serifos, the *sourávli* and the *toubí* are often played together — indeed, this particular combination has acquired the status of a true island *ziyiá*, and is now considered a *sine qua non* for all celebrations and weddings on the island. The same is true of Naxos, where one can hear the *souvliári* and the *doubáki* (small drum) played together in a combination known locally as the *doubakosoúvliara*. Scores of similar instances could be cited.

In comparison with the *floyéra*, the *sourávli* is held by the player far more steadily than the former. It rests between the lips of the player, whose fingers are relatively free to move. The sound is easily produced, and has a soft quality. The *floyéra*, on the other hand, is not held nearly as firmly; the slightest movement causes the instrument's open 'mouthpiece' to slip from its correct position against the lips of the player, with the result that the quality of the sound may be altered or interrupted in mid-song. The fingers of the *floyéra*-player have far less freedom of movement than those of the *sourávli*-player, and it is far more difficult to produce sound on the former instrument than on the latter.

Shortcomings in the manufacture of either of the two instruments can be dealt with and compensated for during performance; the player must either adjust his blowing accordingly

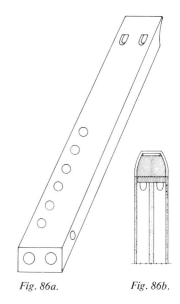

Fig. 86a.   *Fig. 86b.*

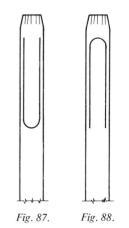

Fig. 87.   *Fig. 88.*

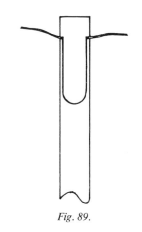

Fig. 89.

or make certain alterations in his fingering, opening or closing the fingerholes of the instrument only partially, in order to correct such faults. In the same manner, those performers who still adhere to the traditional monophonic popular melodies play their instruments within the *natural scale* rather than in the *tempered scale* (see *Introduction*).

The madoúra: Construction — Playing technique — Types

The *madoúra*, or *padoúra, badoúra,*[264] is a clarinet-type instrument with a single-beating reed,[265] which is played mainly in Crete. The reed is made by the cutting of a thin wedge into the walling of the upper end of the cylindrical tube of the instrument, the end itself being completely closed by a knot in the cane. This closed end bearing the reed is placed in the player's mouth so that the entire reed is enclosed; the breathing of the player causes the reed to vibrate, thus producing sound.

Although the reed is usually up-cut so as to open away from the player's mouth (fig. 87), the opposite, the down-cut reed, is also to be found — in the latter case the reed opens in the direction of the knot closing the end of the cylindrical tube held in the player's mouth (fig. 88). In the latter kind of *madoúra,* the player's breath control is greatly facilitated, with the result that a softer tone is produced, and the slight muffling to which the other version of the *madoúra* (fig. 87) is somewhat prone is avoided. In the *madoúra* with up-cut reed, a thin thread such as a plant fibre, or even a human hair, is placed underneath the reed at the very point where it is bent away from the walling of the cylindrical tube of the instrument (fig. 89). This effectively prevents the reed from closing completely and adhering to the wall of the cylinder, by keeping it slightly elevated and separate from the latter. The reed is thus left to vibrate freely when blown upon, without any interference towards the production of sound.

The *madoúra* is made of narrow cane, in sizes ranging from approximately 20 to 30 cm in length, and usually has 4 or 5 fingerholes (more rarely, 6 fingerholes). In some instances, however, a *madoúra* is made from wider cane, in which case the end bearing the reed enclosed by the player's mouth is usually made thinner. Sometimes two pieces of cane are used: the longer piece, open at both ends, carries the fingerholes, while the second piece of cane, narrower and considerably shorter, bears the reed. This kind of *madoúra* is assembled by fitting the shorter piece into the longer piece of cane (fig. 90). The incorporation of a separate reed-bearing section makes it easier for the player *(madouráris)*[266] to change a damaged or broken reed. Otherwise, were the instrument made of a single piece of cane, the player would be obliged to throw away the entire *madoúra* for the sake of a broken reed alone, and to begin all over again the process of making a new instrument.

Fig. 90.

The *madoúra* —constructed either of a single piece of cane or of two interlocking sections— is also to be found throughout the islands of the Aegean under the names *monotsábouno, mono-bíbiko (monós,* single; *bibíki* or *tsaboúni,* reed), or simply *tsaboúna.* In the islands, however, it is never used to accompany either singing or dancing, and, indeed, in Crete where it is most commonly played, it is confined to a few musical figures of limited melodic span *(kondyliés)*[267]. The making and playing of the *madoúra* there is simply a preparatory exercise, leading to the more complex demands of the island bagpipe *(tsaboúna)* and the mainland bagpipe *(gáida)*; the two Greek bagpipes possess a single-beating reed similar to that of the *madoúra.*

In Crete, in the region around Prine Milopotamou (nome of Rethymnon), the *tzybrayiá madoúra*[268] or *dhiplopadoúra* (double *madoúra*) was still made and played until the period between the two World Wars. This instrument consisted of two *madoúres* bound together with plant fibres or string, and producing identically pitched notes (fig. 91). To achieve this tonal identity, the two *madoúres* were constructed so as to be equal in length and width, with corresponding reeds and fingerholes. When the craftsmen/players failed to achieve the desired tonal 'agreement', despite their painstaking efforts, they would then employ various methods of 'tuning' one *madoúra* to the pitch of the other. The methods they used differed according to the particular faults causing the disparity between the two instruments' production of sound. For instance, they would scrape one of the two reeds with a knife until the desired result was achieved; or they

Fig. 91.

152

55.   Long flute. Wall-painting: Nativity (detail), 16th cent. Varlaam Monastery, Katholikon, Meteora.
←

56.   Bowed stringed-instrument, lute, pan-pipe, psaltery, tambourine, shawm, bagpipe with drone. Wall-painting: The
       Ark carried to Jerusalem (detail), 16th cent. Varlaam Monastery, Sanctuary of the Katholikon, Meteora.

58. *Long flute. Wall-painting: Nativity (detail), 16th cent. Great Lavra Monastery, Katholikon, Mount Athos.*

59. *Straight trumpet and hooked trumpet. Wall-painting: The Last Judgment (detail), 18th cent. Church of St. George, Panitsa, Gythion.*

60. *Shawm, tambourine. Carved wooden iconostasis (1803). Monastery of St. John the Baptist (Timiou Prodromou), Serres.*

61. *Horn, small drum, bowed stringed-instrument, trumpet, lute. Wall-painting: The Ark carried to Jerusalem (detail), 16th cent. Stavronikita Monastery, Sanctuary of the Katholikon, Mount Athos.* →

57. *Pan-pipe and flute. Miniature, 11th cent., Codex Taphou 14, f. 33 v. Patriarchal Library of Jerusalem.*

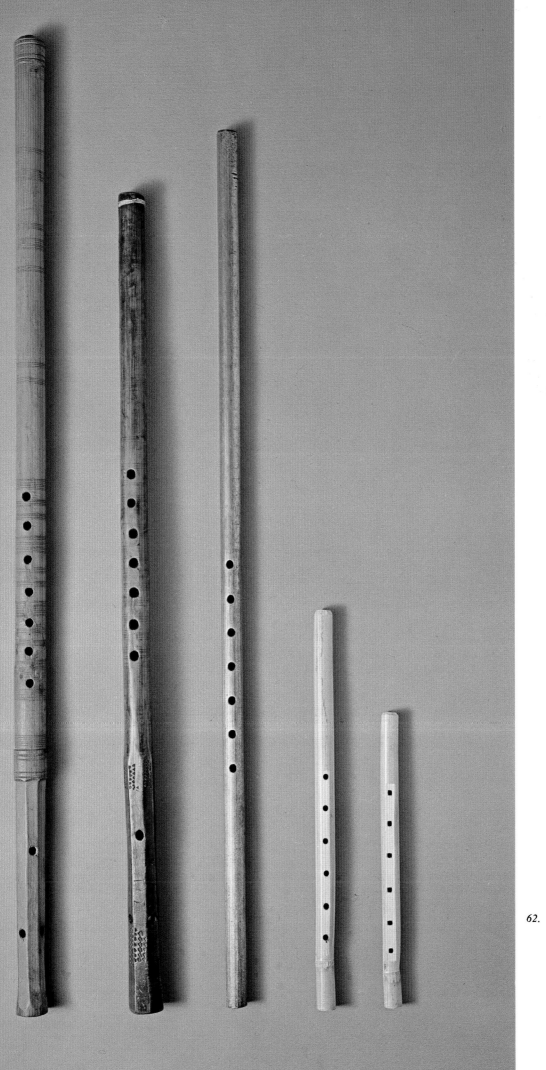

62. Flutes: 1.2. Wooden long flutes (tzamáres), 82.5 and 69 cm. long, Epirus. 3. Bronze long flute (tzamára), 74.5 cm. long, Epirus. 4.5. Cane flutes, 34 and 25 cm. long.

1   2   3   4   5

would place a thread underneath the reed of one of the two instruments, as described above. Sometimes a thin thread was wound three or four times around the base of the reed, where it was attached to the wall of the cylindrical tube; this thread was then knotted (fig. 92). (The two methods were most effective, as the rate of vibration of the reed was affected, and hence the pitch of the sound produced by the instrument could be adjusted to correspond to that of the second *madoúra.*) Another approach was the widening or partially blocking (with wax of those holes on the first instrument that did not produce the same sound as the corresponding fingerholes of the second instrument. Other adjustments could be made as the need arose. The only advantage afforded by the *dhiplopadoúra* was the increased volume of sound produced, as the two constituent *madoúres* played the same melody in unison.

The decoration of the *floyéra,* the *sourávli* and, more rarely, the *madoúra,* is usually limited to engraved designs. These incised patterns sometimes consist of geometric figures, such as rhombi, triangles, circles, etc., and sometimes of designs derived from the natural world of plants and animals. The *floyéra* and the *sourávli* generally bear designs carved in bas relief, or, less commonly, carved in the round.

Fig. 92.

The floyéra, the sourávli, and the madoúra in the Greek world

It is important that a clear distinction be made between the *floyéra* —an end-blown ductless flute— and the classical Greek *aulos (avlós),* a clarinet- or oboe-type instrument with a single or double reed (see note 265). There is often considerable confusion on this point. Similar care must be taken with regard to the literary and iconographical data dealing with the *aulos;* this applies as much to the references made by the Church Fathers in the early years of Christianity as it does to the use of the word *aulos* in classical writings. For example, let us consider the following two references: When John Chrysostom writes of "*auloi, syringes, kymvala* and wine",[269] and when Basil, Bishop of Caesarea, refers to "*auloi, kitharai* and *tymbana*",[270] we are certainly in no position to maintain that *aulos* refers to some pastoral instrument of the time, resembling the present day *floyéra* in function and construction.

Despite this reservation, however, there does exist considerable evidence that instruments similar to those discussed in this section were played in early times. The *sourávli,* for instance, is noted among other musical instruments that were played at the Palace in Constantinople during the Christmas Eve service, during the first half of the fourteenth century: "There stand all the so-called *paigniótai* (musicians), namely trumpeters *(salpingtai),* (nakers-players) *(anakaristai),* and pipers *(souroulistai)* ..."[271]

The unknown author of a folk song from the Dodecanesian island of Chalki refers to a *sourávli* (ducted flute):

> *Up the mountain I did ascend*
> *and a thin reed did I find,*
> *then I cut a souliavráki*
> *and went my way, playing upon it.*[272]

In the following examples of folk and literary verse the *sourávli* and the *madoúra* were encountered yet again — under their regional Cretan names, of course (*padoúra* and *madoúra* for the clarinet-type instrument; *fiabóli* for the ducted flute):

> *Let me play neither padoúra nor fiabóli,*
> *let me enter neither field nor garden.*[273]

> *I am afraid we haven't accomplished anything, master Loura,*
> *without money the blind wan't play the madoúra.*[274]

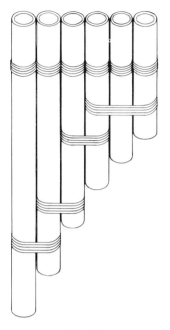

Fig. 93.

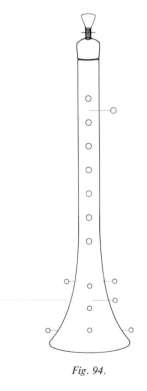

Fig. 94.

Like the *sourávli*, the end-blown flute *(floyéra, kalámi)* is also mentioned in many a line of literary and popular verse:

> *The Vlachs take to the mountains,*
> *their women-folk as well,*
> *their children follow*
> *playing flutes (floyéres).*[275]

> *...I see a shepherd grazing his flock,*
> *holding in one hand a pastoral flute (kalámin)...*[276]

> *Nakers (anakarádhes), trumpets (voúkina)...*
> *flutes (syrládhes) and shawms (bífara)...*[277]

From among the foreign travellers who have written of the folk songs, the dances, and the popular musical instruments of the Greeks —and there were many who did so— one may here single out John Covel, who refers to the manufacture of the bone *floyéra* as early as 1670. His observations are of especial value, for we learn that in the Greek islands at that time "small pipes" were made not only from the wings of birds of prey (see above), but also from the bones "of the wings and thigh bones of Crowes, Bustards, Pelicanes, etc.".[278] No less interesting is the account of a *floyéra* preserved for us by the Englishman Edward Daniel Clarke. In his *Travels...* he recounts how he purchased it, in 1802, from a shepherd at Corinth. His detailed description enables us to reconstruct the instrument as a small and conical goat's horn, pierced with five fingerholes and having "a small aperture at the end for the mouth", like that of the *floyéra*, i.e. without a reed.[279] No such pastoral instrument with a curved, conical pipe made of animal horn is to be found in present day Greece. However, its existence in the past is attested to by its appearance in a number of representations of the Nativity, chiefly in post-Byzantine wall-paintings and icons.

Generally speaking, Byzantine and post-Byzantine iconography —wall-paintings and miniatures— bears witness to the existence of the pastoral flute throughout the Greek world, from the first centuries of the Byzantine era up until the present day. These same sources are also useful for the considerable information they furnish regarding the dimensions of the different flutes (whether they were long or short), their shape (cylindrical or slightly conical), and whether they were played perpendicularly, or laterally in relation to the player's lips (the *sourávli* and the *floyéra* respectively). From paintings in the rock-hewn churches at Göreme, Cappadocia, to those of the Monasteries of Mount Athos and Meteora and the yet more recent religious wall-paintings of the eighteenth century, only exceptionally is the Nativity of Christ depicted without the presence of a *floyéra*. Likewise, it is significant that a great proportion of manuscript illuminations portraying the Nativity also represent a shepherd playing the pastoral flute.[280]

In these illuminated manuscripts we also meet with three other related instruments, the *playíavlos* (transverse flute),[281] the *polykálamos avlós* (many-pipes flute, the Pan-pipe), and the *dhiplós avlós* (double flute).[282] Only the last of these instruments is still played, and that ever more rarely; now surviving only in Cyprus, it could once be heard in Epirus, Macedonia and Crete (see above, under *boulboúl, glousnítsa, tzybrayiá madoúra*, as well as the pair of Cypriot *pithkiávlia* played together while held at acute angles to each other). The *playíavlos*, played in the same manner as the modern transverse flute, and the *polykálamos avlós*, better known as the *syrinx* of the cloven-hoofed Pan (fig. 93),[283] lasted into the Byzantine epoch, but have not survived up to the present day in Greece.

There is a page in M. Chourmouzis' *Antigone Isle* which colourfully illustrates the longing with which shepherds once used to desire the ownership of a fine *floyéra*, as well as their disappointment whenever the instruments they had proved unsatisfactory: "Karypis' goatherd in 1867 was called Fotis, a youth of some twenty or twenty-two years from Epirus, and of mid-

162

dling height... he spoke but little, having indeed little knowledge to expound; his mouth rarely strayed from his *floyéra,* and he seems to have played it even in his dreams, since even when he lay down to sleep he had by him his *floyéra* in his leather belt. I bought him two *floyéres,* and he accepted them as though there were some great gift. On the very next day, however, he returned them to me, saying: 'A pity to have spent money for them, as to me they are worthless."[284]

Nowadays, the *floyéra* has begun that gradual descent into oblivion that has overtaken so many other traditional popular musical instruments in Greece, yielding pride of place to the transistor radios that many young shepherds have taken to carrying around with them as they work during the last few years. As for the *floyéres* now sold in tourists' souvenir stalls alongside the traditional Greek shepherd's foot-wear *(tsaroúchia)* and a motley collection of 'national costumes' designed for tourists' consumption, such 'instruments' are turned out by the dozen with identical, lifeless decorative motifs, much as any other mass produced consumer item.

Popular expressions and proverbs

— "His brains are a *floyéra",* said of one who has a awelled head and is pumped up with selfesteem.
— "Have you begun your *madoúra* again?" and
— "Oh, not that *madoúra* once again", said of grumbling and complaining.
— "Everyone's mind is like a *pidhikiávlin,* to be played however he wishes".[285]

Related surnames

Among common surnames to be found today throughout Greece, the following deserve mention: Floeroúlas, Sourávlas, Sourlás, Sourlatzís, Tsiafarás, Tsiafliarás, etc.

ZOURNAS (Shawm)

Terminology

The *zournás* (shawm), or *karamoúza* or *pípiza* is an oboe-type instrument with a double reed (fig. 94). The name *zournás* is employed primarily in Macedonia, Thrace, western Roumeli and Mytilene, while throughout the rest of Greece the instrument is generally called *karamoúza* and *karamoútza,* or *pípiza* and *pípitza.* Apart from variants of these names —*zornés* (Cyprus), *zornás* (Kozani region), *tzournás* (Lefkada), *pípeza, pípitza, pípitsa, píptsa, pípa* etc.— it is also known as *niákaro* or *niákara* on the islands of Zakynthos and Cephalonia, and *kalámi* (cane) in western Roumeli. One should also note the older literary term *avlós:* G.N. Vizyinos wrote in 1897: "Let us henceforward leave the sweetsounding *avloi* and the thundering drums far behind us..."[286]

Construction

The *zournás* varies in length from approximately 22 to 60 cm, and is constructed from different kinds of wood — beech, cherry, walnut, olive, black mulberry, apricot, arbutus, medlar, maple, and, in rare instances, ebony. It is also made of thin brass sheeting, which has the advantage of being less fragile than wood, although popular musicians themselves confess that the quality of sound produced by such instruments is inferior to that produced by the wooden *zournás.*[287] The smallest shawms are found today in western Roumeli; these are the famed *psilá zournádhia* (highpitched shawms) of Messolonghi.[288] The largest instruments, which produce a deeper sound, come from Macedonia. Throughout the rest of the country, the shawm, usually known as *karamoúza* or *pípiza,* is to be found varying in length from approximately 30 to 40 cm.

The *zournás* consists of three principal sections: the *zournás* itself (fig. 95), the forked clothespeg-like insert *(kléftis,* thief) (fig. 96), and the staple *(kanéli,* channel) with the attached double-

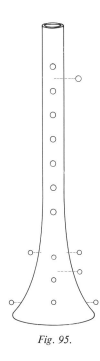

Fig. 95.

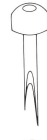

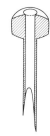

Fig. 96.

Fig. 97.

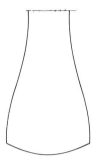

Fig. 98a.

Fig. 98b.

Fig. 98c.

reed (fig. 97). The tube of the *zournás* —usually slightly conical, but occasionally cylindrical in shape— terminates in a bell (*choní,* funnel), also known as *kambána* (bell), or *tatára,* which is more or less open-ended (fig. 98a, b, c). This section of the instrument must be made of dry and knot-free wood, to withstand usage and the vagaries of climate; the walls must be thin and of consistent thickness throughout. This serves to contribute to the purity, intensity and clarity of the sound produced. Nowadays, a drill is used to bore the tube; formerly, this was done by means of a thin iron rod, previously heated in a fire until red-hot. In those days, the wood used in the construction of the *zournás* was boiled, to ensure against its cracking easily. Today, should the tube of a *zournás* crack it is tightly bound with the bladder of a slaughtered animal; in time this bladder dries out and fuses with the wood, thus serving as a sealer and preventing further cracking.

The *kléftis* (fig. 96) is attached to the upper end of the conical or cylindrical tube; this must be tightly fitted to prevent any air from escaping when the instrument is played. The *kléftis* also goes by the names *mána* (mother), *kefalári* (head), *pistómio* or *pistómi* (mouthpiece) in Macedonia, *fásoulas* in western Roumeli, etc. This section of the *zournás* is usually made from boxwood, although other woods such as cedar, bitter orange, olive, etc. may be used as well.

The staple *(kanéli)* bearing the double-reed *(tsaboúna)* (fig. 97) is attached to the *kléftis;* the *kanéli, kanoúli,* or *karnéli* is a small, thin-walled cylindrical tube made of brass sheeting, to which the *tsaboúna,* a double-reed made from cane, is bound. This double-reed is also known as the *tsimbón* (Black Sea area), *tsapoúni* or *tsaboúni* (Peloponnese), *pipíni* (Volos, Livadia), *pipíngi* (Roumeli), *pipinári* (Gidas), *píska* (Asvestochori, region of Thessaloniki), etc.

The double-reed is the *zournás*-player's unending source of concern. At the proper season he must search for the cane from which he will fashion his instrument's reed; he must painstakingly choose those individual canes best suited to his needs, and he must carefully prepare the final double-reed, drawing upon a long tradition, however such tradition may vary from region to region within the country. The double-reed of the *zournás* is made from the wild cane *phragmites communis,* which, thin-walled and approximately 5-9 mm in diameter, is cut from lake and river areas. This 'harvesting' takes place in many regions in Greece in the months of July and August: in Asvestochori (Thessaloniki) on the Feast of the Assumption (15th August); in Agoriani (Parnassida) in May; in Gidas (Thessaloniki) during the last few days of October, etc. Those canes gather from Lake Kopais were especially sought after, at least until 1931, when the lake was drained. Double-reeds made from the Kopais plants stood up to long hours of playing, and produced a full, bright sound. Theophrastus informs us that the same high esteem was also accorded the reeds from this Boeotian lake in the ancient Greek era.[289]

The gathered cane is first cut into smaller sections, of from approximately 15-20 cm, which are then cleaned by scraping with a knife or piece of glass lightly around their external surfaces. The pieces so treated are then left, either in the sun or in the shade, to dry out, or, according to the popular expression, "to draw their water". The length of time required for this operation depends upon the cane as well as upon the *zournás*-player himself. Depending upon the degree of maturity of the canes —and this depends upon when they are cut or gathered— they are left for shorter or longer periods to dry out. They are also left to dry for a short time whenever the *zournás*-player may desire a particularly soft double-reed.

To prepare the double-reed, the 15-20 cm long sections of cane are further cut into smaller pieces of equal length, ranging from approximately 1.5-2.5 cm each. The exact size of these pieces is determined by what dimensions each *zournás*-player desires his instrument's double-reed to be; generally the shorter instruments are fitted with smaller double-reeds —in length as well as width— as compared to the longer instruments. After they have been cut, each of these small pieces of cane is cleaned on the inside by means of a thin, wooden dowel; in this manner the pith attached to the interior walls of the cane is removed (fig. 99). The cane, thus cleaned both on the outside and on the inside, is then soaked in water and carefully fitted to a cylindrical wooden form, to which it is firmly bound (fig. 100). This wooden form is of the

164

same diameter as the staple to which the reed is ultimately destined to be attached. The upper, free-standing part of the cane is then pressed with the fingers, thus producing a double-reed (fig. 101). In order to make the reed retain its shape, it is 'ironed' while still moist by means of a small knife that has previously been heated in a fire. Many *zournás*-players, having rounded the reed or having cut it slightly at its two corners, lightly burn its edges to prevent the absorption of liquid and so become stuck together during a performance. Again, other players burn the edges of the double-reed with a cigarette when they are to perform, claiming that "such burning strengthens the *tsaboúna*". Finally, when the double-reed has been prepared as described above (fig. 102), it is bound to the staple (*kanéli*) (fig. 97).

Another accessory of the *zournás* is the *foúrla*, a disc made of bone, metal (often a silver coin is used), or even wood. With a hole bored in its centre, the disc is passed over the double-reed and positioned so as to 'sit on the *kléftis*'. When the *zournás* is played, the shawmist *(zournatzís)* rests his lips upon the disc, and this aids him in blowing more easily. Though differing in shape and form, the *foúrla* functions in the same manner as the *phorviá* of the ancient Greek *aulos*.[290]

In former days, when weddings and saints' day festivities lasted for many days, players were wont to suspend from the disc a chain, to which they had tied several staples complete with their double-reeds. These were 'spare parts', enabling the performers to replace reeds made useless by long hours of playing without wasting time. Today, for the same reason, the *zournás*-player always has a few reeds at hand, which they keep in a metal box. During the summer months, in order to keep the sensitive double-reeds somewhat cool, a few leaves from one tree or another are also placed in the box. In addition to a wide variety of ornaments, small silver coins, small blue beads to ward off the evil eye, etc., the *zournás*-player also used to hang from the disc a 'form' made of bone or hardwood, or, upon occasion, of silver (fig. 103). This was used to refashion the staple and, especially, the double-reed, whenever these were damaged or blocked. In different regions of Greece the *foúrla* is also known as the *fourlídha* (Makrynitsa, region of Volos); *forlídha* (Agoriani, region of Parnassos); the *péna* (Gidas, region of Thessaloniki); *pína* (Asvestochori, near Thessaloniki, and Naoussa); *boúzlia* (Kriekouki, nome of Attica); *dhachtylídhi*, or ring (Naoussa); *dhískos;* etc.

On the foremost section of the *zournás, karamoúza* or *pípiza* are located seven fingerholes, usually circular in shape, spaced at equidistant intervals; there is also one hole underneath for the thumb. (The latter opening is usually positioned between the first and second uppermost fingerholes or above the first fingerhole). In addition to this 7+1 configuration of fingerholes, the *zournás* has several vent-holes on the underside of the bell. These holes, which are not covered by the player's fingers but always remain open, affect the tonality of the instrument and the quality of the sound it produces. Stopping these holes results in a lowering of the instrument's pitch, and alters the accuracy of its intervals and its timbre. These vent-holes vary in number from one to as many as ten, according to regional tradition and the aural sensitivity of the instrument's craftsman/player. The number of openings on the bell of the shawm does not vary in proportion to the length of the instrument. Indeed, there exist shawms without any such openings whatsoever, as well as others with only 6 frontal fingerholes or 6 frontal fingerholes and 1 rear thumbhole.

Playing technique —Musical possibilities

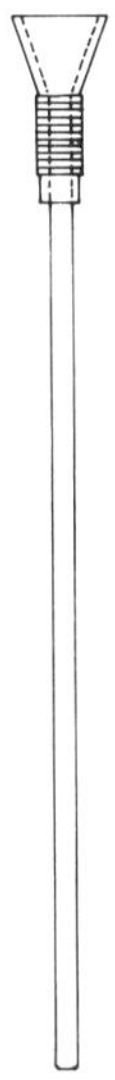

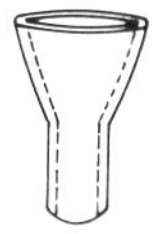

When the *zournás* is played, the entire double-reed is kept inside the performer's mouth. When he blows, the two lips of the double-reed vibrate; in other words, they open and close, striking rapidly against each other, thus producing sound. Skilled *zournás*-players adopt the characteristic technique of simultaneously inhaling and exhaling their breath. The player inhales air through his nostrils while continuing to play; the air, retained in the cavity of the mouth, is used shortly thereafter, in turn being replaced by a new supply of 'wind', which enables the performer to continue blowing on his instrument without a moment's pause. Before he begins

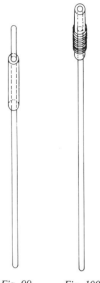

Fig. 99.   Fig. 100.

Fig. 102.

Fig. 101.

Fig. 103.

a performance, the *zournás*-player first keeps the reed in his mouth for a short while, so as to moisten it; alternatively, he may moisten it with a little water or wine.

The range of the diatonic scale of the *zournás* extends over one octave and two notes. A skilled performer, however, can achieve a much wider range by overblowing in conjunction with the appropriate tightening of the lips. These extra notes are not often employed, as the effort required to produce them is very tiring for the performer. The exact pitch of the tonic depends, as in the case of the *floyéra*, on the overall length of the *zournás*, as well as upon the dimensions of the reed. A skilled performer, by dint of suitable fingering and blowing, can neutralise in playing whatever defects of manufacture his instrument may suffer from, and provided he be well steeped in the traditions of folk melody, he can produce the intervals of the *natural scale* rather than those of the *tempered scale* (see *Introduction*, p. 26).

With its sharp, penetrating sound, the *zournás* is an instrument well suited to open-air performances. On religious feast-days or during merrymaking in the village square, its wild charm, as one might describe it, together with the sweetness of its sound, perhaps expresses more than any other popular instrument the style and character *(ethos)* of mainland Greece's folk music. The *zournás* is limited in the sense that it has no varying degree of intensity. He who performs on the *zournás*, monophonic instrument that it is, adorns the melody with trills, appoggiaturas, and other musical ornaments: accentuations achieved each time by the appropriate breathing, glissandi effected by the player passing one of his fingers across all the fingerholes in rapid succession when his excitement flares up, etc.

Furthermore, one should note that in certain regions of the country —in Carpenissi, for instance, in several Macedonian villages, and in Perachora, near Loutraki— *zournás*-players were wont to keep and make use of two instruments. One of these, the shorter of the two, was used to play the lighter melodies, while the longer *zournás* was used to perform the so-called "heavy songs". In Perachora, moreover, the *zournás*-player George Koliakos —locally famous in the period between the two World Wars and himself the son and grandson of shawmists— used to attach a particularly wide-lipped double-reed to his instrument when he accompanied merrymakers who sang the older "heavy songs". The same musician would speak of three sizes of *zournás;* as he himself explained, he did not differentiate in terms of the size of the instrument alone, but of the longer and wider-lipped reeds as well. He would stress that only an experienced and well-tried player could manage a "size one *zournás*". Does this perhaps reflect the ancient Greeks' division of the *aulos* into four categories, *parthénioi, paidhikoí, téleioi,* and *hypertéleioi*? This statement itself is consistent with other similar claims made by aged musicians throughout the country.[291]

The shawm *(zournás)* is always played together with the drum *(daoúli);* these two instruments constitute the traditional instrumental grouping of mainland Greece (see *daoúli*). The usual combinations to be met with include one drum and either one or two shawms. When two shawms are played together, the leading performer —playing the melody— is known as the *mástoras* or *primadhóros*, while the second performer, maintaining a drone *(íson)*, usually the tonic of the scale in which the lead-player performs the melody, is known as the *bassadhóros* or *passadhóros*. In addition to maintaining the drone, a 'good' *bassadhóros* will also play some phrases of the melody along with the *mástoras*. In order to complement each other —to match the tonal pitch of the two shawms— the players shorten or lengthen one of the two instruments by either pushing the reed or even the *kléftis* further into the body of the shawm or by pulling the same part or parts outwards.

Occasionally, in the past, when village festivals and such major religious holidays as Easter and the Assumption of the Virgin called for the entire village to participate in the dancing, the music was provided by three or four shawms in conjunction with two or three drums. Although it does sometime transpire that the *zournás* and *daoúli* are joined by yet another instrument, such as the mainland bagpipe *(gáida)* in Macedonia, such combinations are exceptional, and have in no way influenced the traditional composition, style or technique of the *ziyiá* of *zournás* and *daoúli*.

166

The zournás in the Greek world

The oboe family of instruments, characterised by the use of a double-reed and including, as has been noted above, the neo-hellenic *zournás,* existed in the Greek world as early as the Homeric era, as is borne out by the presence of the *aulos,* the primary wind-instrument of ancient Greek music. The extent to which the *aulos* remained bound-up with the life of the people well into Byzantine times is witnessed by the writings of the Church Fathers, in which the latter bitterly inveigh against its corrupting effect on the character and morals of Christian men and women.[292]

Literary and iconographical sources attest to the role of the shawm in the Greek world in more recent times as well. It was among the instruments Baron de Salignac saw played on the island of Chios in 1604.[293] The Reverend Father R. de Dreux wrote of drums and shawms accompanying the *battue* made by some four thousand men for a hunting expedition of Mehmet IV near Larissa in 1669.[294] R. Chandler in 1817,[295] Pouqueville in 1820,[296] and other travellers all refer to the *zournás* in the accounts they wrote of their journeys.

Apart from these witnesses —invaluable for the history of the instrument with which we are here concerned— the impression made on the foreign travellers when they heard the shawm is of especial interest. Their own musical training was so far removed from the Greek tradition as to make it impossible for them to come to terms with the melodic and rhythmic idiom of Greek folk music, or, indeed, with any of its acoustic characteristics. Pouqueville found the *zournás* to be a "shrieking flute" (flute criarde). Lord Byron, again, remarked of the *zournás* he heard at Arachova in 1809: "The music was a large drum, which, in our cottage, was louder than thunder, and was beaten without any regard to time, or the motion of the dancers. A squeaking pipe was also added to the entertainment; it sounded like the most unharmonious bagpipe, and the person who played on it, either from the quantity of wind required for the instrument, or for effect, made the most frightful contortions".[297]

Such comments run directly counter to the modern ethnomusicologist's obervations on the performance of the *ziyiá* of shawm and drum *(zournás* and *daoúli).* However, it must not be believed that this *ziyiá* was any more fully appreciated by the educated Greeks of the nineteenth century. On an excursion from Patras to Messolonghi in 1842, the Heptanesian composer Pavlos Karrer wrote in his *Memoirs* that he saw villagers "dancing and singing, playing national *floyé-res,* (by which he meant *zournádhes*) and *daoúlia".* He continues, claiming that "the sight was most original, and all the more so for us in that we were seeing it for the first time".[298]

It is also noteworthy that certain literary sources of the sixteenth and seventeenth centuries refer to the *zournás* under the names *pífera* or *bífera,* originating from the Italian *píffero,* an oboe-like instrument:

> *...then drums (tamboúrla), shawms (pífera) and trumpets (voúkina) sounded...*[299]

> *All night long they heard shawms (bíferes), nakers (nakarádhes),*
> *drums (týmbana) and singing, and the thunder of the bombards.*[300]

There is a great variety and number of iconographical sources depicting the *zournás;* painted vessels and other objects, wall-paintings, miniatures, woodcuts and copper engravings illustrating the chronicles of the great travellers, et alia. An excellent example of such is the scene of a musician playing a *zournás* executed on the lid of a Byzantine silver vessel (12th century, Hermitage Museum, Leningrad),[301] as well as wall-paintings from the monasteries of Hosios Nicanor, Zavordas, (Grevena) (Jesus is mocked, 16th century),[302] Varlaam (Meteora) (Jesus is mocked, 16th century),[303] Loukous (Astros) (Parable of the Dives and Lazarus, late 16th or early 17th century).[304]

Popular expressions and proverbs

— Stop the *zournás!* (Stop grumbling).
— Maro is fond of dancing and so found a *zournás*-player for her husband.

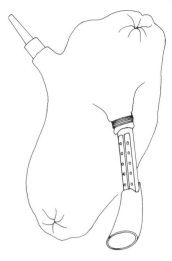

Fig. 104.

— They raised him to be a psalter and he ended up a *zournás*-player.
— The *zournás* can crack a nut.
— Man's mind is a *zournás;* as you play upon it he dances.[305]
— If you have no wind, by no means become a *zournás*-player.[306]

Related surnames

Zournás, Zournatzís, Zournatzídis, Karamoúzas, Karamoúzis, Karamouzáris.[307]

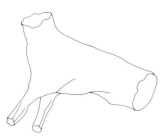

Fig. 105.

TSABOUNA (Island bagpipe)

Two kinds of bagpipe *(ásklavlos)* exist in Greece, the *tsaboúna* and the *gáida*. The *tsaboúna*, a drone-less bagpipe, is to be found throughout the Greek islands, while the *gáida,* a bagpipe with drone, is encountered on the Greek mainland, especially in Macedonia and Thrace.

Terminology

The island bagpipe, the *tsaboúna*, has many regional names, of which the following are the principal ones in use: *saboúna* or *tsamoúnda* (Andros, Tinos, Mykonos); *tsabounáskio* (Naxos); *tsabounofyláka* (Ikaria); *askotsábouno, skortsábouno* and *klotsotsábouno* (Cephalonia); *moskotsábouno* or *dhiplotsábouno* (Mani); *askomadoúra, askobadoúra* or *flaskomadoúra* (Crete);[308] *angíon,* or *angopón, touloúm zournás* and *gáida* (among the Greeks from the Black Sea region); *káida* (Sifnos); *gáida* (Kythnos); *saboúnia* (Syros, Kymi); *askozaboúna* (Ainos); *askávli, askotsábouno, touloúmi, askáki, tzaboúrna, askotzaboúrna;* et alia.[309]

Fig. 106.

Construction

The *tsaboúna* is almost always made by the player himself (known as the *tsabounistís, tsabounáris, tsabouniáris*), and is to be found in a wide range of sizes. It consists of a bag *(askí),* a mouthpipe, and a sound producing device, the double-chanter (fig. 104). The bag is usually made from goatskin or kidskin, or, more rarely, from sheepskin.[310] It is also known as the *touloúmi, angíon* or *póst* (among the Greeks from the Black Sea region), *dhermáti* (Ikaria, Samos), *fyláki* (Kythnos), *thylakoúri,* etc. Regardless of whatever animal skin used in the making of the bag, it is important that it be sound and undamaged, and not cut at the throat or any other place as is usually the case when the animal has been slaughtered primarily as a source of meat. The fresh, untreated skin, the so-called *výrsa,* is cured by special treatment so as to resist spoiling, and to ensure that it remains soft and white when it finally dries out. In its original, uncured state, the skin is first given a cursory cleaning with ordinary water (this stage is omitted on several islands), after which the inner side of the skin is rubbed with salt, which has been ground neither too fine nor too coarse. The skin so treated is then rooled up and left for from three or four to as many as fifteen days, "so that it will seak in the salt and thus be baked (i.e. cured)", as they say in the Fourni islands off the coast of Ikaria. Or, in the words of the villagers of Aghii Deka, near Iraklion, Crete: "thus it drinks the salt and does not stink". Furthermore, bagpipers (players/craftsmen) maintain that "very coarse grained salt doesn't dissolve easily, while finely ground salt dissolves immediately and is poured away" with the surplus fluid that is drained from the hide during the tanning process. Many bagpipers are accustomed to add alum to the salt, which tightens the skin in addition to bleaching it and preserving its softness. On Kythnos, instead of rolling the skin up and letting it cure with the passage of time, they "work it with their hands"; in other words, they knead the treated skin with their hands until it "drinks the salt and alum".

On certain islands, other methods of treating the skin apart from the salting process described above are to be found. On Karpathos, for example, the skin is covered with ashes for

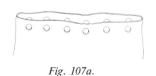

Fig. 107a.

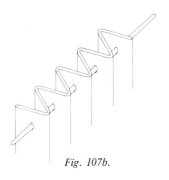

Fig. 107b.

168

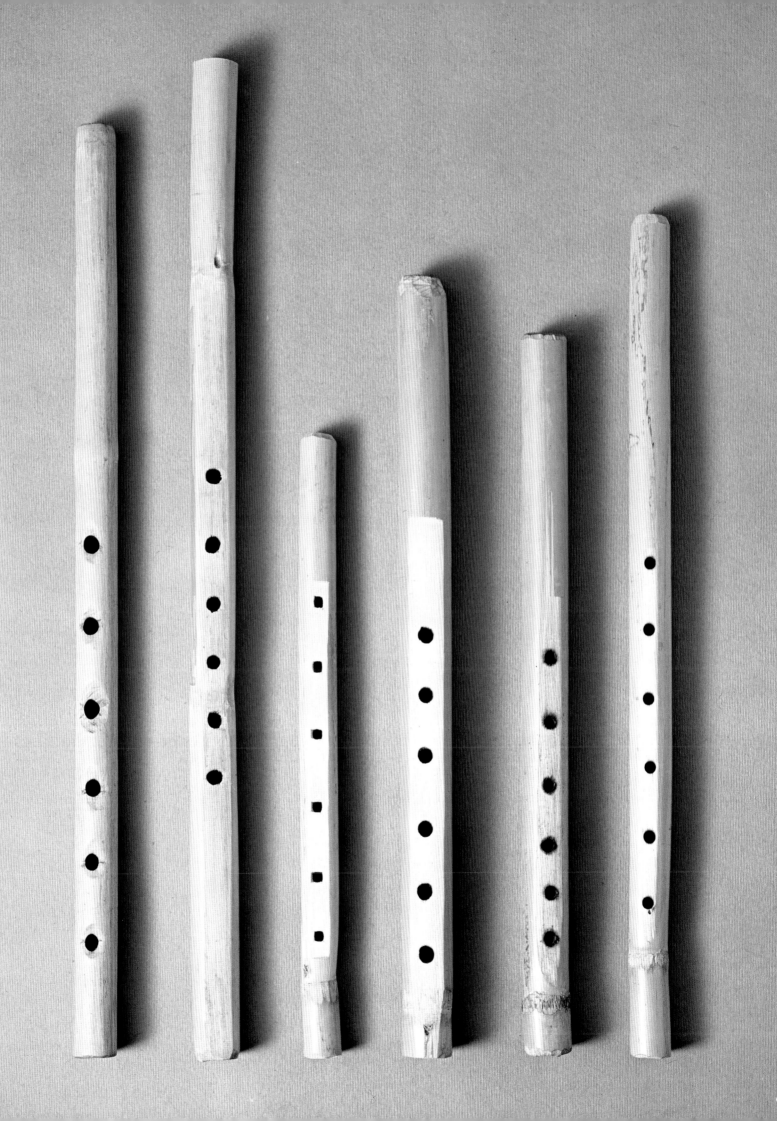

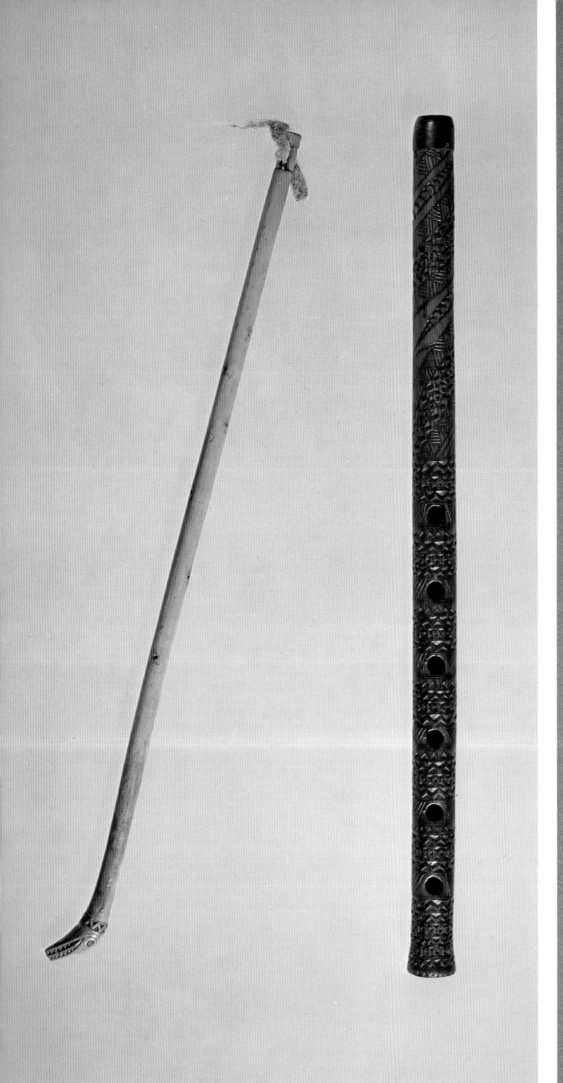

64

65

1   2   3   4

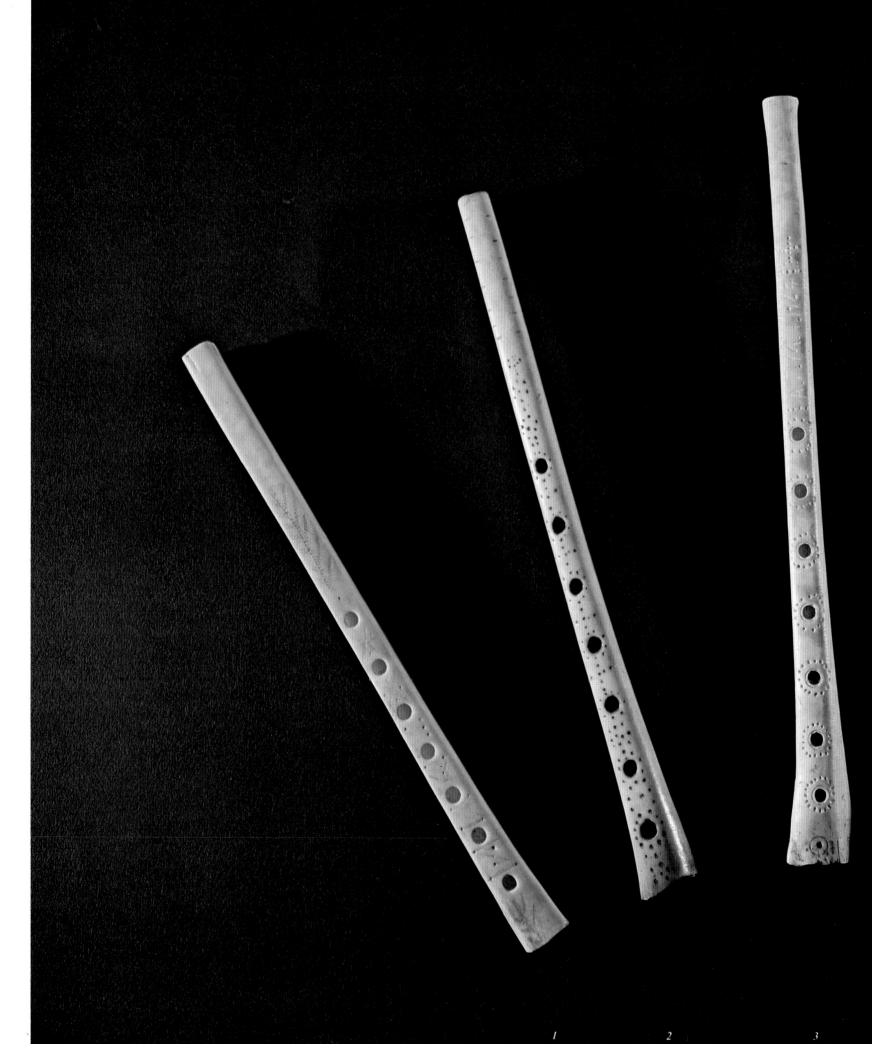

1   *2*   *3*

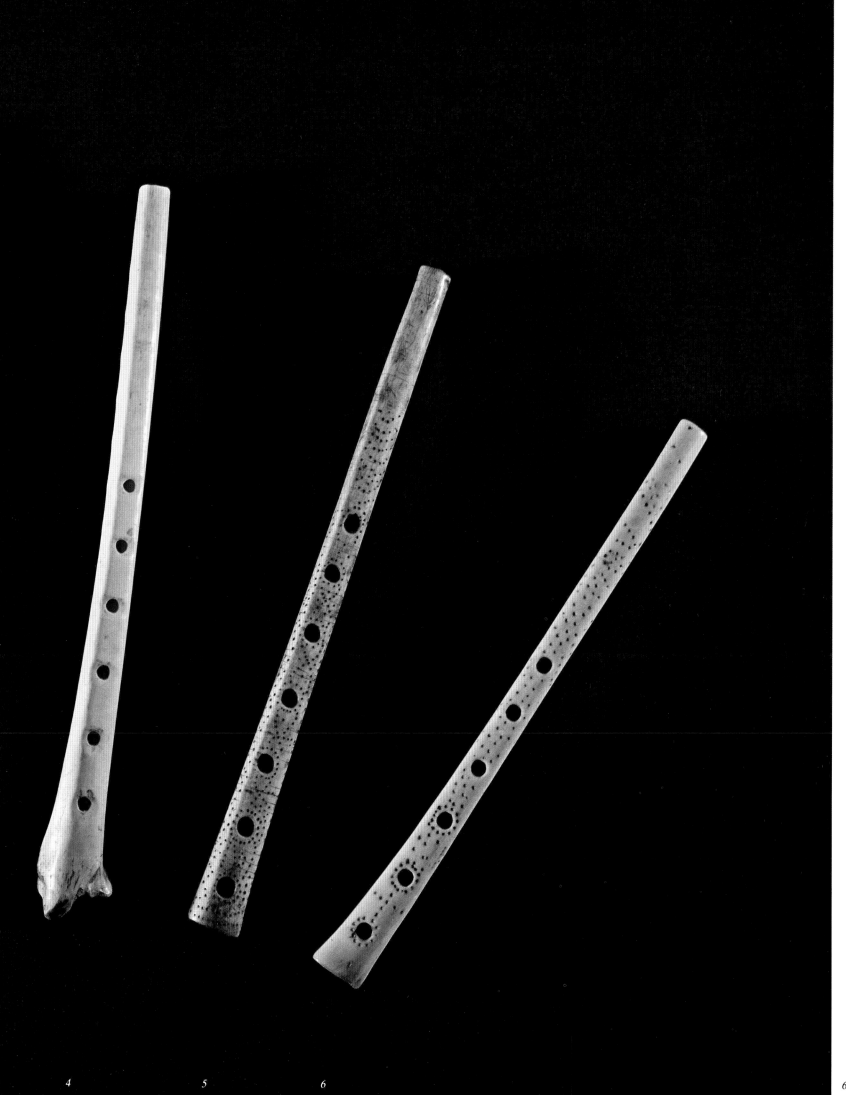

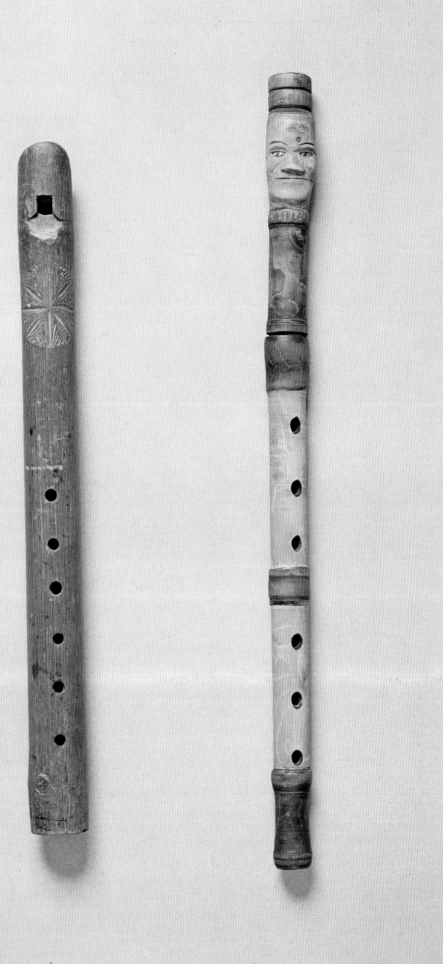

68. 1. Cane flute (thiambóli), 44.5 cm. long, Rethymnon area, Crete. 2. Wooden ducted flute (kaváli), 51 cm. long, Skopia, Florina.

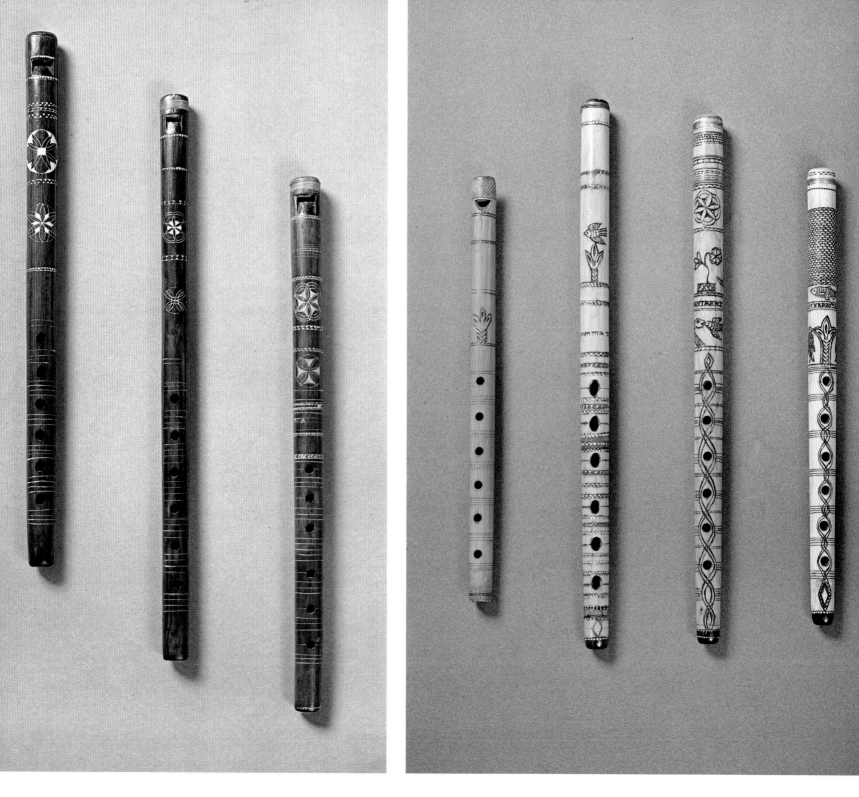

69.70. Wooden and cane ducted flutes (sourávlia) 32-41.5 cm. long. Doumbia, Chalkidiki.

63. Cane flutes (floyéres) from various regions of Greece, 25-40 cm. long.

64. Wooden carved flute (floyéra) with serpent-like stick for cleaning, 34 cm long. Maker: Theodoros Chronis, Ligourio, Argolid.

65. Bronze flute (floyéra), 32 cm. long. Aghali, Tripolis.

66. Cane ducted flutes (sourávlia): 1. (pithkiávli) in snake-skin, 33.5 cm. long, Cyprus. 2. (pithkiávli) with engraved designs, 32 cm. long, Cyprus. 3. with engraved geometrical designs, 28 cm. long, Santorini. 4. 32 cm. long.

67. Flutes made from wingbones of birds of prey, 24.5-28.5 cm. long: 1. Eressos, Mytilene (c. 1910). 2. Delphi area. 3.4. Agoriani, Parnassos region (1967). 5. Epirus. 6. Epirus (?).

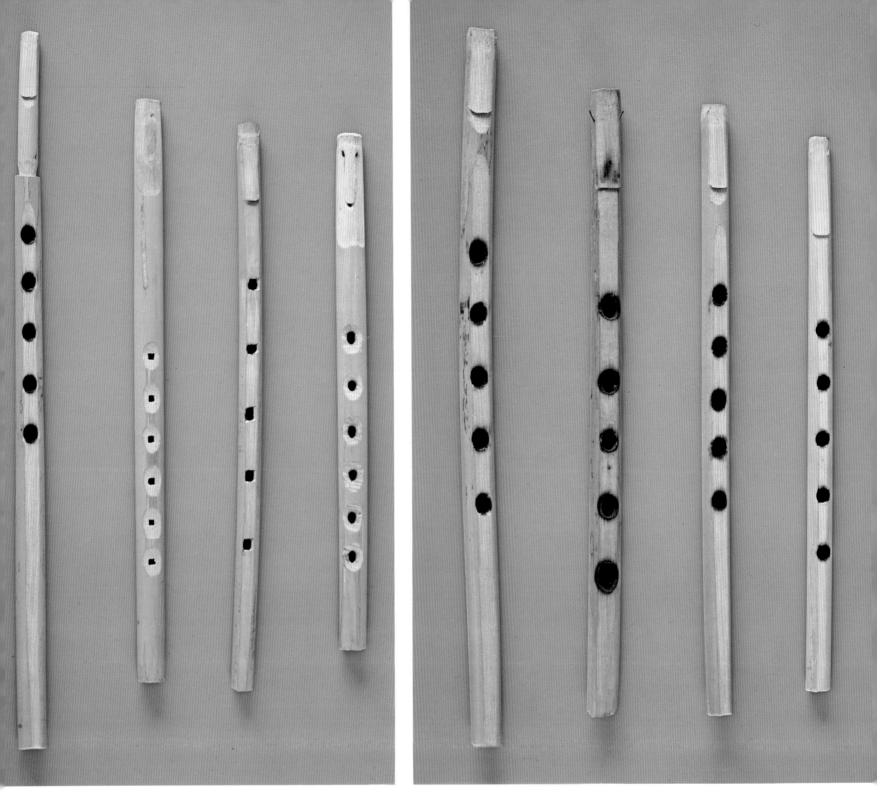

71.   Cane folk-clarinets, 24-32 cm. long: madoúra from Crete or monotsábouno from other Aegean islands.

several days, and then covered with flour for an additional day or two. Many Greeks from the Black Sea region treat the skins first with water and ashes, and then with alum. On Kos and Mykonos, as well as on other islands, certain of the bagpipers place the skins in sea-water, and then leave them to dry in the wind. On some islands, others simply leave the skins to dry in the wind, after their having been washed, without any other treatment. In the last instance, the treated skin does not last for a great period of time, even though it may not begin to rot, as it will readily burst or puncture with the slightest provocation, and requires constant softening.

The hair of the skin is cut with scissors, not down to the roots, but so as to allow approximately 1-1.5 cm of hair to remain. The short bristles aid in keeping the pores of the skin closed, for when all the hair has been shaved down to the skin, the pores stretch and open too easily during playing, with the result that the bag deflates much more rapidly. In addition, the short bristles also serve to hold moisture and saliva, which accumulate gradually inside the bag with the player's breathing. Thus, the moisture is prevented from spreading and damaging the reeds by means of which the instrument is made to produce sound; such moisture would otherwise soften the reeds, causing them to "go out of tune".

In order to avoid perforating the skin with their scissors when shearing the hair, many bagpipers temporarily bind up the 'holes' or natural openings at the neck, feet and elsewhere, leaving a single opening by means of which the bag is inflated prior to the cropping process. This operation may be carried out either before or after the salt-curing of the skin, custom varying in this respect from island to island. Those bagpipers who prefer that all the hair be completely removed from the skin of their instrument accomplish this by placing the skin in slaked lime. They justify this treatment on the grounds that, in performance, any hairs that become detached from the skin tend to accumulate against the reeds of the instrument, thus blocking them.

After the skin has been treated with salt and alum, and when the skin has dried —usually in the open air, with the hair-covered side folded inwards— the skin is then soaked in sea-water or patiently kneaded on a round, smooth piece of wood "in order to be worked and softened". Following this process, the skin is rearranged so that the hairy side is outermost, when the legs, buttocks and tail are cut off and thrown away (fig. 105). The nether region is closed, tightly bound with waxed string or a leather strap, so that "when it dries and shrinks it won't lose air and the player's breath won't leave". Finally, the skin is turned completely inside out, so that the hair-covered side is on the inside. The neck is then pulled through one of the leg-holes and is firmly tied in the same manner as the nether part of the skin; it is then pulled inside once again.

Another method of tying together the neck and nether part of skin is even more secure; holes are punched at regular intervals around the edge of each opening in the skin (fig. 106). Through these holes a small, thin wooden rod is passed; the latter is then tightly bound to the skin (fig. 107 a, b). Following this, one of the legs is pulled through the opening of the second leg and the mouthpipe is attached. The entire leg with the mouthpipe is then returned to its former position, and the sound-producing device, the double-chanter, is attached to the exterior of the second leg.

The mouthpipe of the *tsaboúna* is a cylindrical or conical tube made of cane, different kinds of wood, or even occasionally from the bone of the leg of a bird. To the end of the tube, inside the bag, is bound a round piece of leather —onion peel was used in former times— which functions as a valve and prevents the escape of air from the bag (fig. 108).

On certain Greek islands, as the Fourni islands (Ikaria) and Samos, among others, the mouthpipe of the *tsaboúna* is fashioned in a special manner. A short, thin piece of cane is forced into an oleander twig from which the pith has previously been extracted. This composite tube are then fitted to a small spool or round piece of wood analogous in shape and size; this assembly is finally attached to one of the legs of the skin. The leather valve is usually affixed with wooden pegs, as these are proof against rusting (fig. 109).

When the *tsaboúna* is not equipped with a valve and the player wishes to stop blowing and

177

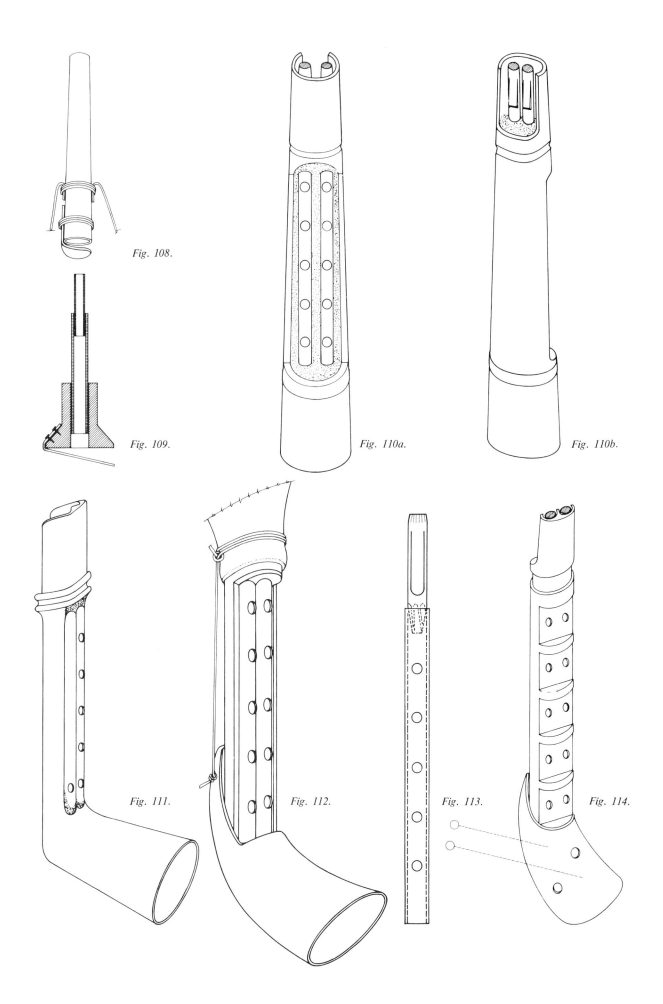

Fig. 108.

Fig. 109.

Fig. 110a.

Fig. 110b.

Fig. 111.

Fig. 112.

Fig. 113.

Fig. 114.

take a rest, he closes the mouthpipe by pressing it against his tongue or his cheek, thus preventing the bag from deflating. Another solution to this particular problem is as follows: the feet of the skin are cut to different lengths, and the mouthpipe is attached to the longer of the two. The player is thus enabled to keep the air from escaping from the bag by temporarily bending this leg, with a simple movement of his hand.

The mouthpipe of the *tsaboúna* is made in different lengths, ranging in size from 6 to as many as 18 cm on occasion. While this part of the instrument is most commonly called the *fysitíri* or *fysitári* (*fysáo*, to blow), it is also known as the *fyseró* or *pibóli* (Ikaria), *fouskotári* (region of Lassithi, Crete), *stomotíra* (among the Greeks from the Black Sea region), *masoúri* (Kythnos), *boúzounas* (region of Sitia, Crete), *kókkalo* (Mykonos), *flómos* or *karélli* (Leros), *sifoúni* (Samos), etc. The leather valve also goes under a variety of names, including: *tápa* (stopper), *alepú* (fox) or *kofterídhi* (among the Greeks of the Black Sea region), *petsí* (skin) (Kos), *valvídha* or *tsifoúski* (Karpathos), *soústa* (Kalymnos), *petsáki* or *flómos* (Leros), *kléftis* (Symi), *anapniá* (*anapnéo*, to breathe) (Tzermiadho, region of Lassithi, Crete), *anemológhos* (*ánemos*, wind) (Mykonos and neighbouring islands).

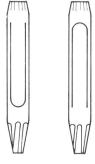

Fig. 115.   Fig. 116.

The sound-producing device itself consists of a grooved base into which are placed two cane pipes; these have single-beating reeds similar to that of the clarinet (fig. 110 a, b), and are positioned parallel to one another. This grooved base terminates in a funnel-shaped bell, which varies in size according to local tradition and the personal preference of the craftsman/player (fig. 111). This part of the instrument is not always of one piece with the grooved base, nor is it necessarily constructed of the same material. Often it is an extension; for example, it could be the horn of some animal, fixed at one end and bound with string at the other, where the grooved base of the pipes is joined to the bag (fig. 112).

The horn (*kérato*), the name by which this funnel is usually known, "is like the cone of the gramophone", as this author was informed on the island of Kythnos. Yet another *tsaboúna*-player, this time from the Fourni islands, claims that "if it is very short, the horn is of no assistance, while a very long horn dulls the sound". An aged *tsaboúna*-player from Evdilo (Ikaria) adds: "We take a long animal horn and shorten it by degrees, testing it continually until it produces a clean, sweet sound. This requires patience".

The grooved base is open on top, while the sides are low so as to allow the bagpiper ready access to the fingerholes of the two pipes. It is closed at the rear, excepting the uppermost section containing the two reeds. The latter section is always inside the wind-bag; when the bag is squeezed, the resultant wind-pressure causes the reeds to vibrate, thereby producing the desired sound (see fig. 110). The grooved base is constructed from different woods, both hardwoods and softwoods, among them asphodel, oleander, sage, fig, olive, walnut, mulberry, cedar, plum, boxtree, etc. This section of the *tsaboúna* is called *márta* or *mártha* (Kalymnos, Leros, and other islands of the Dodecanese); *áfouklas* and *afouklári* (Naxos, Paros); *agathós* (Syros, Kythnos, Kea); *potamós* and *váthra* (Ikaria); *madouróxylo*, *thikári*, and *skáfi* (Crete); *tsabounokáfkalo* (Karpathos); *angóxylo* and *náv* (among the Greeks of the Black Sea region); etc. On many of the islands, should the wood chosen for the grooved base be green, it is covered with animal dung (usually that of the goat) and left in a shady place to dry out before it is worked into shape. The overall length of the grooved base ranges from approximately twenty to thirty centimetres. Occasionally, the grooved base of some island bagpipes is fashioned out of cane.

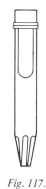

Fig. 117.

Neither of the two pipes of the *tsaboúna*, each with a single-beating reed, is made of a single, integral unit; instead, each pipe is made of two separate, interlocking sections of cane. The longer of the two sections —open at both ends— has the fingerholes. The second section, much shorter and smaller in diameter, is open at one end only; the reed is located at the closed end (fig. 113) (see also *madoúra*). The two cylindrical tubes with the fingerholes are made first; they must be perfectly straight and must have the same diameter bore. Greeks from the Black Sea region have their own particular method of ensuring that the diameter of the two tubes will be the same: they fill one of the two tubes with gunpowder or small shot, keeping the lower end of the tube closed with one finger. They then check to ascertain whether the same quantity of powder or shot fills the second tube to the same level as that of the first. Some *tsaboúna*-players, prior to opening the fingerholes, use a small knife to pare down the surface of the cane tube "so that the player's fingers fit more easily" — i.e., to facilitate the player's stopping the fingerholes more easily and firmly during performance. The fingerholes, usually round in shape (in rare cases they are square), are opened by the application of a red-hot nail or similar pointed implement to the cane tube; they must all be of the same size and spaced at equal intervals from one another. The measure governing the size of the fingerholes is provided by the fingers of the player himself; his fingers must not rub against each other, as that impedes his playing. Usually, each pipe has a configuration of 5 fingerholes. On certain of the islands, however, it is usually the pipe on the left side of the *tsaboúna* that has 5 fingerholes; the right pipe may have either 1 fingerhole (Patmos, Kos, Karpathos, Andros, Symi, Samos, et alia) or 3 fingerholes (Fourni islands, Kalymnos, Astypalea, et alia). There also exist isolated instances of *tsaboúnes* having 5 fingerholes on the left pipe and 2 fingerholes on the right pipe (Fourni islands, Ikaria); *tsaboúnes* with each of the two pipes having six fingerholes (Aghii Deka near Iraklion, Crete, and Fourni islands, Ikaria); and even rare instances of *tsaboúnes* having grooved bases carrying three pipes. In the last instances, the third pipe has no fingerholes whatsoever, and serves to carry the drone, *(íson)*, emitting only one note, identical in pitch to the lowest note provided by the other two pipes (Aghii Deka, Crete). There are even *tsaboúnes*, rarer yet, the sound-producing device (double-chanter) of which has both the grooved base and the two pipes with fingerholes made of a single piece of wood (fig. 114).

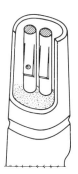

Fig. 118.

Once the cane pipes have been affixed to the grooved base, the bagpipers seal any spaces that may have been left with pure wax or with propolis,[311] especially at the point where the device enters the bag. The wax or propolis serves to keep the pipes firmly in place and prevent "the wind from leaking". The longer sections of the pipes, generally known as *bibikománes*, are also called by the following regional names: *chabiólia, kalámia* and *stimónia* (Crete), *mánes* (Symi), and *lámnes* (Kalymnos). They range in length from 15 to 22 cm.

The reeds of the two pipes of the *tsaboúna* are always of paramount interest and concern to every bagpiper. Crafting them calls for patience, experience and a love of the task at hand. The performance of the instrument depends upon the proper functioning of these reeds. The small sections of the pipes, the reed-bearers, range from 4 to 6.5 cm in length; their bores range from 7 to 10 mm in diameter. On most of the Greek islands they are known as *bibíkia* or *tsaboúnia;* apart from those two common names, they are also called *pirpíngia* (Symi), *chabiolákia, madourákia,* and *madoúres* (Crete), *tsaboúnes* and *tsambiá* (Kythnos), *tsibónia* and *tsoubónia* (among the Greeks of the Black Sea region), etc.

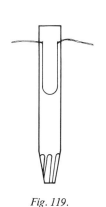

Fig. 119.

The reed (*ghlossídi,* tongue; or *fteroúla* or *tsambí*) is usually up-cut, i.e. with the base of the reed adjacent to the knot of the cane (fig. 115). On several of the islands, however, among them Leros, Karpathos, Kalymnos, Patmos, Kos, Ikaria (Fourni), and Crete (Zaro, region of Iraklion), as well as among the Greeks of the Black Sea region, we also encounter the down-cut reed, i.e. with its base near the open end of the cane (fig. 116). According to skilled bagpipers, the down-cut reeds give "a sweeter voice". And they are far from mistaken, for indeed, having the opening of the reed —one might say its 'mouth'— opposed to the current of air coming from the instrument's bag enables the reed to function far more easily in comparison with the up-cut reed (fig. 115), which is positioned in the same direction as the flow of escaping air from the bag of the *tsaboúna*. At Zaro (Iraklion, Crete), the author has encountered *bibíkia* equipped with down-cut reeds made of cane that had previously had the knot removed, the openings thus created being filled with wax. Such *bibíkia* are termed 'female' — the other *bibíkia*, with the knots intact and with the up-cut reeds are called 'male'. The 'female' *bibíkia* are easily matched, for, having cut off the knot, the player (*askomadouráris,* as the bagpiper is called in Crete) is enabled to exercise more control over the internal diameter of the pipe along its entire length.

Fig. 120.

The reed-bearers *(bibíkia)* are 'fried' in a small quantity of oil; it is claimed that "baking them enhances their tone". They are left over a fire inside a small frying-pan, until they assume

180

a slightly reddish tint. In this manner, the *bibíkia* are thoroughly dried out; as a result they are not affected by atmospheric humidity or by the accumulation of the player's spittle in the bag. In addition, they are rendered proof against natural decay. On Mykonos and a number of other Greek islands, the *bibíkia* are treated with vinegar rather than with oil when they are placed over the fire; the vinegar is said to 'strengthen' the cane. On yet other islands, such as Kythnos and Leros, they are simply roasted, much as coffee beans are prepared. The Greeks of the Black Sea region follow another procedure: they first boil them in milk, and after they cut the reeds. The milk softens the cane, thus enabling the reed to be cut with ease, once the *bibíkia* treated in this fashion have dried, they are durable and "have a steady voice".

In order to 'match' the two reeds of the bagpipe —in other words, to make them produce notes of the same pitch— the reed-bearers must be the same length and have identical interior diameters; the reeds must be identical in length, breadth and thickness. For all practical purposes, such perfection is impossible; the slight differences involved are not visible to the naked eye, and the technical equipment for precision cutting and measuring is not available. For this reason Greek bagpipers have recourse to different, convenient measures whereby it is possible to "give the same note" to the two reeds. The most common of these is the winding of a piece of thread three or four times around the root of the reed; this is then tied in a knot (fig. 117). Whenever they wish to give the reed a higher-pitched voice, they push the thread closer towards its opening (the mouth); should they wish to produce a lower-pitched voice, they push the thread in the opposite direction, away from the mouth of the reed. Many bagpipers have both the reeds of their instruments permanently bound with thread, so as to be able to 'match' them quickly and accurately. According to the position of the thread, the reed is either lengthened or shortened, thus making more or fewer beating movements respectively. These two factors, in accordance with well-known principles of physics, are decisive in raising and lowering the pitch of the sound produced by the two pipes of the island bagpipe.

Fig. 121.

The bagpiper from the Black Sea region *(gaidatzís* or *angitzís)* deals with the same problem in another manner. He pushes the wax —which has been spread on the upper part of the grooved base to prevent the escape of wind from the instrument (see above)— so as to cover either one of the roots of the two reeds of his bagpipe. In other words, he shortens the length of the reed with wax instead of thread, thus changing the tonic pitch of the instrument's voice. This method only serves for an approximate 'tuning' of the two pipes; to make any necessary finer adjustments he applies small bits of wax to either one or both of the reeds of the instrument, closer or further away from their openings or mouths as the case may be (fig. 118). Despite the small quantity of wax used in this operation, its weight affects the rate of vibration of the reeds, and consequently their pitch.

The pitch is also affected by the thin thread or strand of hair pushed underneath the reed at its root; this has the effect of lowering the pitch (fig. 119). It is also common for the reed to be scraped slightly with a small knife; when the reed is made thinner in this manner, it also becomes lighter, and the subsequent increased rate of vibration produces a change in pitch. Once the two reeds have been matched in pitch, the reed-bearers *(bibíkia)* are fitted to the long sections of the pipes with the fingerholes.

When the two pipes of the *tsaboúna* have finally been readied, they are then tested to check whether "their voices sing well". Should the matching of their voices require adjustments, these are made in any of the following ways. "The *bibíkia* are interchanged" — they are changed one with the other, or their position in regard to the pipe-tubes is altered; either one or the other of the two *bibíkia* is pushed further into the cane pipe-tube with the fingerholes, or pulled out slightly until the desired effect is achieved. Those fingerholes that 'complain' —in other words, those fingerholes that do not match the pitch of the corresponding holes of the other pipe— are either widened or made smaller by stopping them with a small quantity of wax. Finally, they will take a rush-stem or a broom-straw and push it in through the open end of the pipe until it reaches the particular fingerhole which continues "to bear no witness" — an expression indicating dissonance between the corresponding fingerholes of the two pipes. The

181

pipe on the left side of the grooved base of the bagpipe is usually considered the more important of the two. The second pipe, on the right, with 1, 3, or 5 fingerholes, supports the other. It is this supportive pipe which is invariably 'matched' to the principal pipe.

Just how well the *tsaboúna* bears up to use depends not only upon the quality of its manufacture, but also upon the player's maintenance of his instrument. As the passage of time and continual playing cause the bag to shrink slightly and to lose wind at the places where it is tied, a 'good' bagpiper upon observing the first signs of this process, will detach the bag from the other components of the instrument. He will then turn the bag inside out and will wash it thoroughly in the sea, after which he will patiently wait for the bag to dry completely. He will then turn it right side in again, scrape the outer surface of the skin so that it whitens, carefully clean the mouthpipe and sound-producing device and re-assemble all of the components until the *tsaboúna* has been completely restored. In order to maintain the suppleness of the bag, its exterior surface is sprinkled with spirits (*oúzo* in Leros and *tsikoudhiá* in Crete), or with sea-water (Kythnos, Rhodes, Fourni islands, etc.) — elsewhere, towards the same end, a small quantity of milk (among the Greeks of the Black Sea region), water or wine is poured into the bag through the instrument's mouthpipe; the bag is then shaken vigorously until it has been thoroughly soaked.

The manner in which the bag is mended when it has been punctured is worthy of note. If the puncture is very extensive, the bag is discarded; otherwise, the player disassembles the bagpipe. He turns the bag inside out, so that the hair-covered side of the skin is now on the outside. He then places a small pebble over the puncture, on the outside; this pebble is then bound tightly to the skin with waxed string, thus effectively closing the hole (fig. 120). The skin is then turned right side in again, with the hair-covered side of the skin on the inside, the neck and hind-quarters are tied once again, the mouthpipe and sound-producing device are attached, and the bagpipe is again ready to be played.

When the *tsaboúna* is not in use, the sound-producing device is detached from the instrument, wrapped in a piece of clean cloth, and stored in the family linen-chest. The bag, with the mouthpipe still attached, is hung on the wall with a piece of string provisionally tied to the mouthpipe. Wind and the natural humidity of the island atmosphere serve to keep the bag soft.

Decoration of the *tsaboúna* is largely restricted to incised geometric patterns on the grooved base and funnel of the instrument. More rarely, one may also encounter instances of stylised designs derived from the plant and animal worlds. It was formerly the custom to suspend different ornaments in front of the bag by means of delicate chains — small gold coins, pellet-bells, little tassels and beads to ward off the evil-eye, as well as tiny mirrors in some instances.

On certain of the islands, in addition to the animal-skin bagpipe as has been dealt with in the preceeding passages, there exist small bagpipes having only one pipe instead of two and lacking the grooved base; these are made from the bladders of oxen, pigs, goats, or some other animal rather than from a true skin. This type of *tsaboúna* —usually called a 'single-pipe bagpipe' *(monotsábouno)*— is first taken up by those children who wish to learn to play the instrument. It is made easily, and the children themselves can construct it in a relatively short time. On the island of Kythnos, in former times, when the children were engaged in rubbing salt into the animal bladder to preserve it from rotting they accompanied this task with a rhythmical chant: "Become, become, o my bladder, like the head of a pig!"

It is also noteworthy that even though *hornpipes* (a type of *tsaboúna* in which a dried gourd takes the place of the skin-bag (fig. 121)[312] are no longer to be found in Greece, there is every indication that they were once known and played in the country. At least two *hornpipes* of Greek provenance have been preserved to this day, one from the island of Tinos in the Pitt-Rivers Museum of Oxford University[313] and the other in the Boston Museum of Fine Arts.[314] The presence of this most ancient type of musical instrument in the islands of the Greek archipelago is taken by Curt Sachs as a confirmation of its distribution along a sea-route leading from the Indian Ocean, through the Mediterranean, to as far north as the Atlantic Ocean.[315]

Playing technique — Musical possibilities

The *tsaboúna* is played with the bag generally held under the player's left armpit. The bag-piper, should he be a skilled performer, breathes from his diaphragm rather than from his chest; this enables him to blow into his instrument for hours on end without tiring. The bagpiper breathes through the mouthpipe of his instrument while at the same time he squeezes the bag with his left arm, thus forcing the air to create pressure on the reeds of the two pipes. When the bagpiper temporarily desists from blowing into the mouthpipe, he squeezes the bag somewhat more tightly with his left forearm in order to avoid a reduction of pressure; he relaxes again as soon as he resumes his blowing into the instrument. As a result of the balance obtained through his simultaneously blowing into the mouthpipe and squeezing the bag, the bagpiper is able to maintain a steady wind-pressure on his instrument's reeds, and consequently produce notes of a constant pitch. The customary position of the player's fingers on the instrument's pipes is as follows: counting from top towards the bottom, the index-finger and the middle-finger of the player's left hand cover the first two fingerholes, and the index-finger, middle-finger, and fourth-finger of the player's right hand cover the remaining three fingerholes. Each of the player's fingers stops the fingerholes of the two parallel pipes, i.e. the corresponding, opposed fingerholes. When he is playing his instrument, the *tsabounáris* wets the two pipes with saliva on the tip of his finger every so often; this ensures that his fingers adhere closely to the fingerholes so that "the *tsaboúna* will not grumble".

The playing of the *tsaboúna*, as indeed that of any other monophonic melodic instrument, derives its character from the embellishments with which the bagpiper continually adorns the melody. As for the bagpipe, such ornamentation usually consists of grace notes —the appogiatura of Western music— and the mordent, where one note of the melody is repeated rapidly immediately after the next highest or lowest note has been played first.

In addition to such melodic ornamentation, the skilled bagpiper stopping only one of the two opposing holes, first of one and then of the other parallel pipes, achieves a very distinctive polyphonic effect. The simultneous sounding of intervals of a second, third, fourth, and even a sixth, sometimes no more than a fleeting effect, at other times held for an appreciable amount of time, does not, of course, detract from the essentially monophonic character of the instrument. However, in conjunction with the timbre of the sound produced by the *tsaboúna*, it contributes to the character of the sound of the island bagpipe.[316]

Yet another factor contributes to the overall character of the sound produced by the island bagpipes. Those instruments having two parallel pipes, each pipe with 5 fingerholes, often present slight differences in pitch in the high range when the two opposing fingerholes are stopped, giving the same notes; this is true even in the case of those instruments that have been most carefully 'matched'. Such a difference in pitch would be unthinkable in the 'serious' music of the West; in the case of a popular instrument such as the *tsaboúna*, however, it constitutes an additional element of the overall acoustic effect.

The intervals of the scale given by the *tsaboúna* —intervals of the *natural scale*, and not the *tempered scale*, of the old master bagpipers— are as follows: two tones, one semitone, two tones. The pitch of the tonic of the scale given by these six notes is not fixed, as it depends upon the size of the *bibíkia* of any given bagpipe. It generally ranges between the notes G and B (above middle C). In performance, the second-lowest note, and not the lowest note, usually serves as the tonic. The lowest note is employed as a sub-tonic, which is a characteristic of the modal style of Greek folk music.

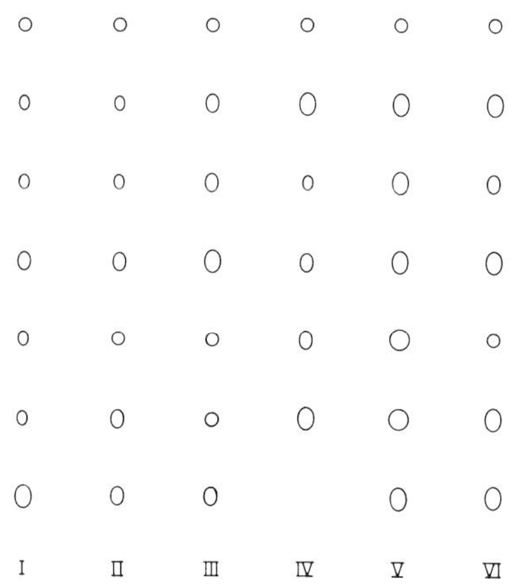

The performance of the *tsaboúna* is greatly affected by prevailing weather conditions. Atmospheric humidity and southern winds, as well as the player's spittle and air inside the bag, all serve to moisten the reeds excessively; the result is that sometimes the quality of sound produced by the instrument alters, and even stifled upon occasion. Northerly winds, on the other hand, are the most favorable weather conditions for the *tsaboúna*-player. The same problem arises when the bagpipe has been played continuously for several hours; the reeds, especially

I	II	III	IV	V	VI
○	○	○	○	○	○
○	○	○	○	○	○
○	○	○	○	○	○
○	○	○	○	○	○
○	○	○	○	○	○
○	○	○	○	○	○
○	○	○		○	○

Fig. 127.

those which have not been prepared with great care, become saturated and heavy, and the tone of the instrument is lowered.

The *tsaboúna* is to the Greek islands what the shawm *(zournás)* and the drum *(daoúli)* are to mainland Greece: the popular musical instrument which, more than any other, has long been played to accompany the dancing and singing at weddings, baptisms, and village festivities. On several islands, the *tsaboúna* is also played to accompany the traditional Christmas carols *(kálanda)*.

Whereas the musicians of the *ziyiá* of *daoúli* and *zournás* are generally professional performers, most often Gypsies, the *tsaboúna*-players are for the most part amateurs; they are often local shepherds, farmers, or even fishermen, who happen to play the *tsaboúna* in addition to their regular occupation.

Although the *tsaboúna* is played as a solo instrument, it is also played in conjunction with other popular musical instruments; the most common of these is the *toubáki* (see *toubí*), which is "the bass" of the *tsaboúna,* as the people of Mykonos describe this combination. On the island of Naxos, the *ziyiá* of *tsaboúna* and *toubáki* is known as the *tsabounodoúbaka* or *doubákia*. In Pyrgi (Chios), the *tsaboúna* —also known locally as *gáida* or *káida*— is played together with a *toubí* or with a small drum *(daoúli)*. On several other islands —among them Crete, Kasos and Kalymnos— the *tsaboúna* and the *líra* are played together; this combination is known throughout the Dodecanese as the *lirotsábouna*. In Zaro (Iraklion, Crete) there is to be found the combination of bagpipe (known there as *askomadoúra*) and *kombolói* (q.v.). On the island of Kythnos, the lute *(laghoúto)* provides accompaniment for the bagpipe. On the same island, the small, children's bagpipe is accompanied by a broom played in the manner of the lute. The broom is rubbed with a makeshift wooden plectrum in accordance to the rhythm of the melody, much as the strings of the lute are strummed. In this manner a simple everyday object is transformed into a rhythmical 'musical instrument'.

Laboring to the accompaniment of music (musique fonctionnelle) is a practice to be found throughout many lands, in factories, shops, and other places of work. As a result of the broadcasting of carefully chosen musical programmes —tailored to suit the educational level of the workers and the job at hand— the laborer feels less tired and does not lose his disposition to work, while at the same time he is more effective at his tasks, suffers fewer accidents, and increases production.[317] Something of the kind, albeit differing both in the motivation and the social organisation of the workers, was to be found at the end of the nineteenth century and into the early twentieth century at Tzermiado (region of Lassithi, Crete). Together with the stones they carried on their shoulders from afar in order to build the mills at Ambelos (on the border separating the nomes of Lassithi and Iraklion), the labourers also bore upon their shoulders a huge stone *(peléki),* upon which sat the renowned bagpiper Andonis Tzermias, who played his instrument *(askomadoúra)* the entire way. A little *tsikoudhiá* and the music of the bagpipe went a long way towards alleviating the burden of the heavy stones, which were carried with ease and with high spirits.[318]

Such is the *tsaboúna*. "Like a sheepskin flask, it was made from a kid. In front it had a horn, pardon the expression, like an ox. And inside there were cane pipes; they made holes in these, and that is where they would find the notes with their hands". This graphic description of the *tsaboúna* comes from Manolis Loukataris, a native of the island of Sifnos.

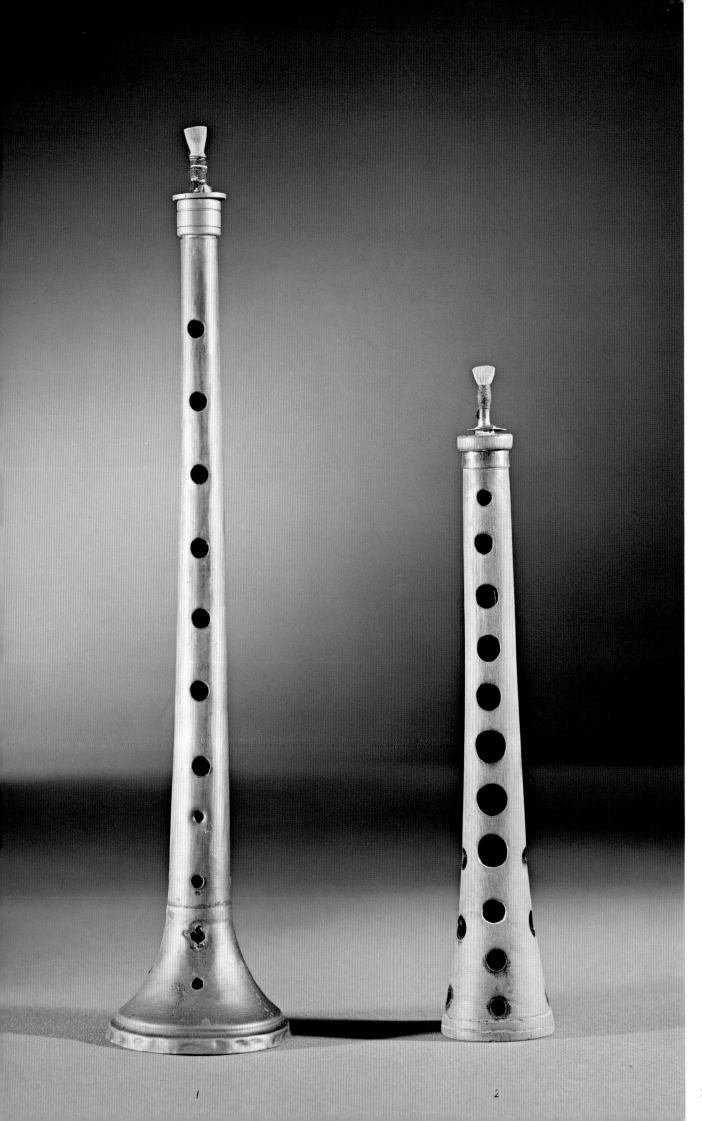

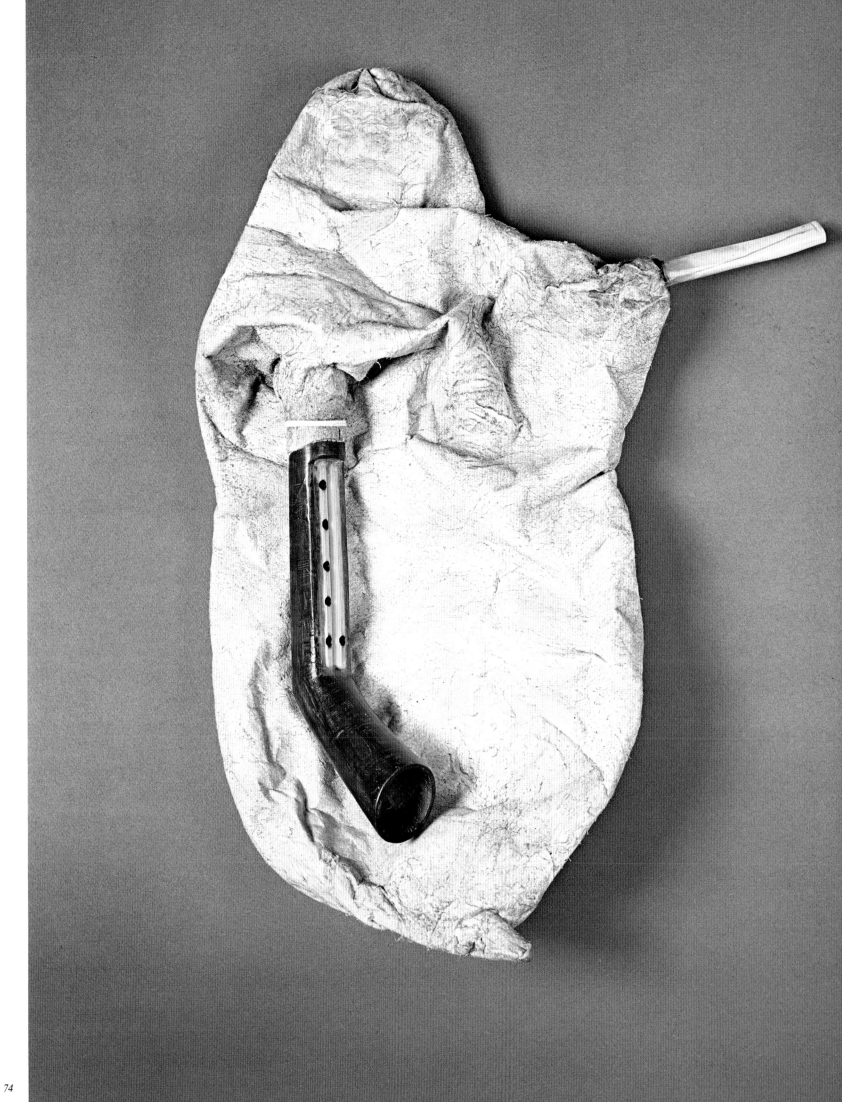

72. Shawms: 1. (zournás), 59 cm. high, Macedonia.
2. (karamoúza), 34 cm. high, Attica.

73. Shawms: 1. (karamoúza), brass, 31.5 cm. high, Attica.
2. (zournádhi), wood, 22 cm. high, Messolonghi.

74. Bagpipe (tsaboúna), bag c. 51 cm. long. Symi, Dodecanese (1954).

75. 1. Two up-cut and 3. Two down-cut, single reeds (bibíkia or tsaboúnia)
of an island bagpipe (tsaboúna) or a bagpipe of Mainland Greece (gáida).
2. Three shawm staples (kanélia) with double reeds (tsaboúnia).
4. Cane from which shawm (zournás) double reeds are made.
5. Stages of making of a shawm double reed.

78. Bagpipe with drone (gáida), bag c. 60 cm. long. Macedonia. Inter-War years.

75

77. Bagpipe with drone (gáida), bag c. 59 cm. long. Maker: K. Zapartas
(c. 1950), Soufli, Thrace.

76. Bagpipe (tsaboúna), bag c. 57 cm. long. Naxos (c. 1960).

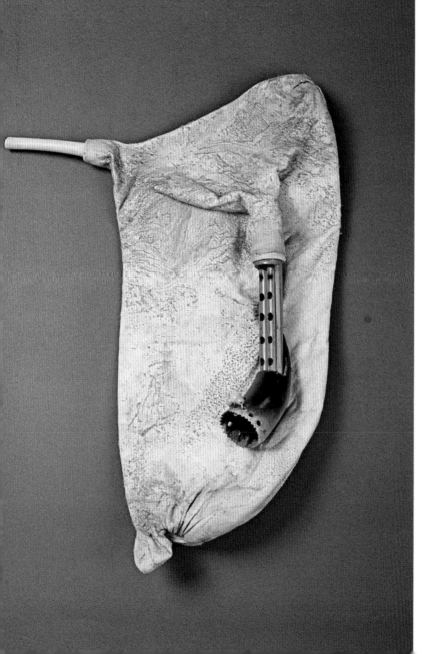

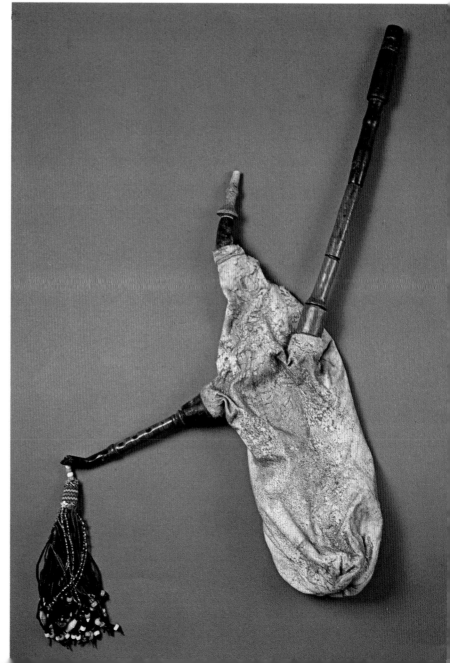

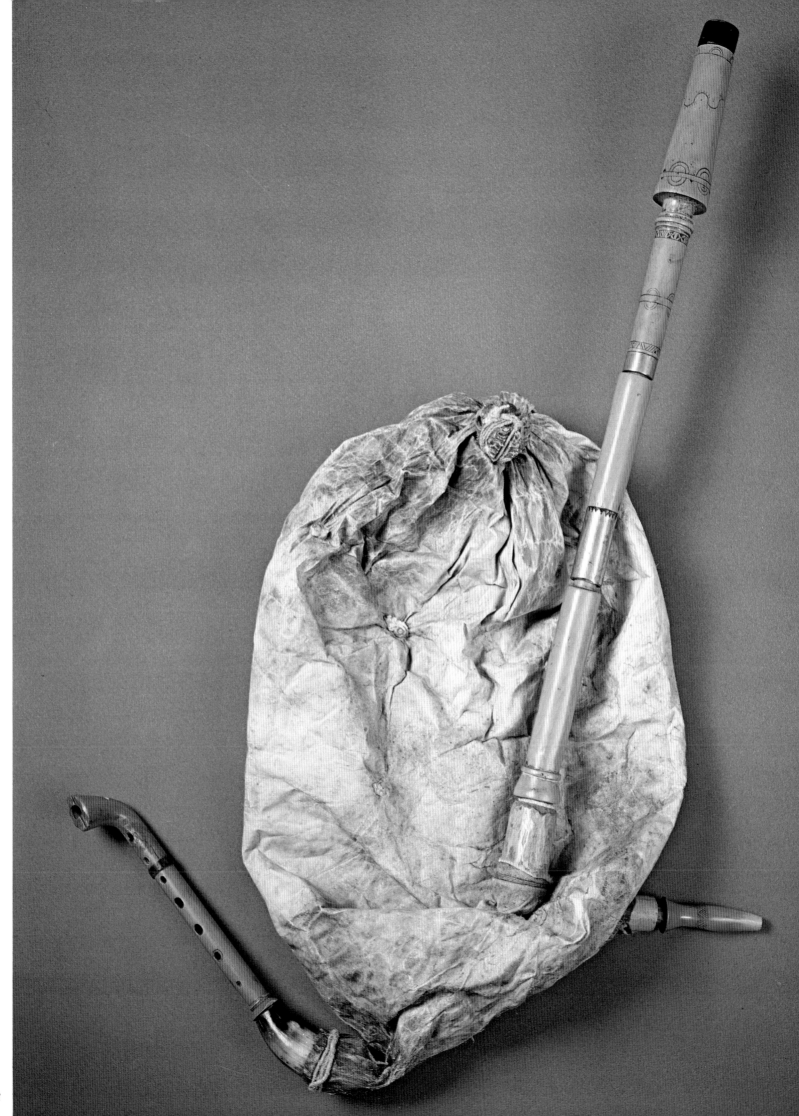

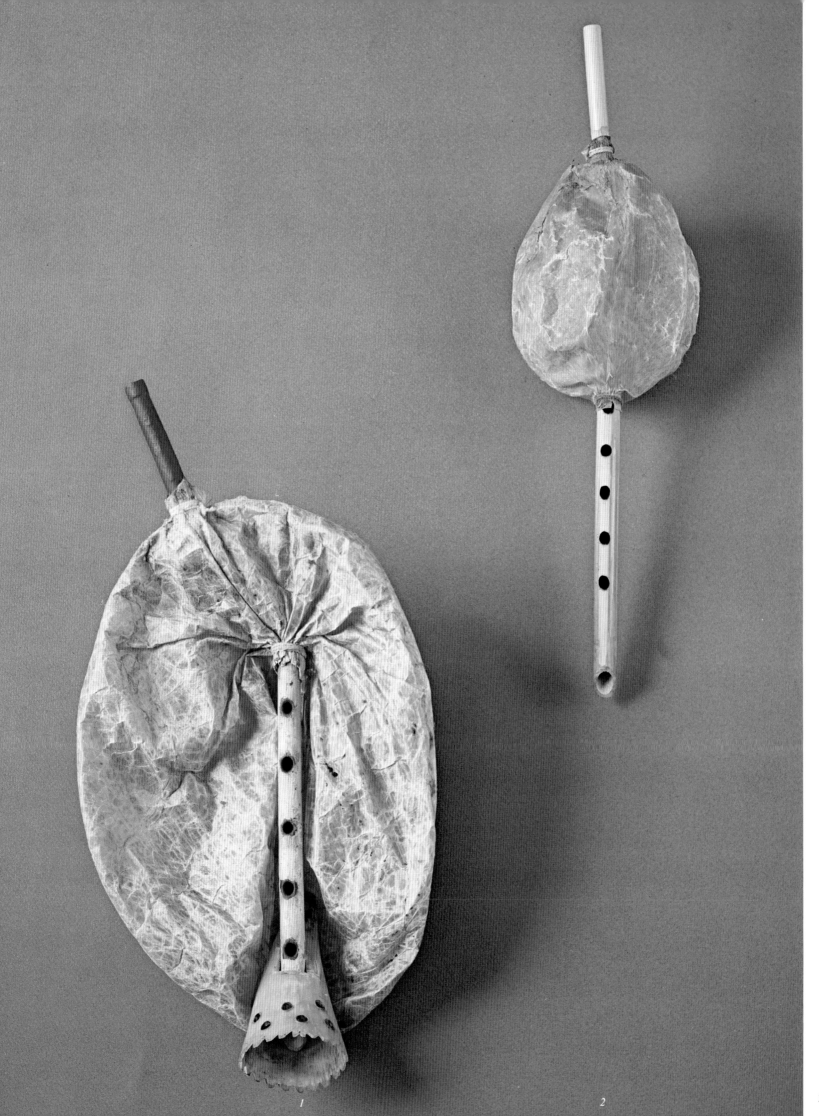

79. *1. Bagpipe (monotsábouno), bladder c. 31 cm. long. Maker: Andreas Chalas (ca. 1960), Batsi, Andros. 2. Children's bagpipe (tsabounáki), bladder c. 14 cm. long, Kythnos (1963).*
←

80. *Sound-producing devices of island-bagpipe (tsaboúna), 24-28 cm long: 1. Karpathos. 2. Kalymnos. 3. Cephalonia. 4. Fourni, Ikaria.*

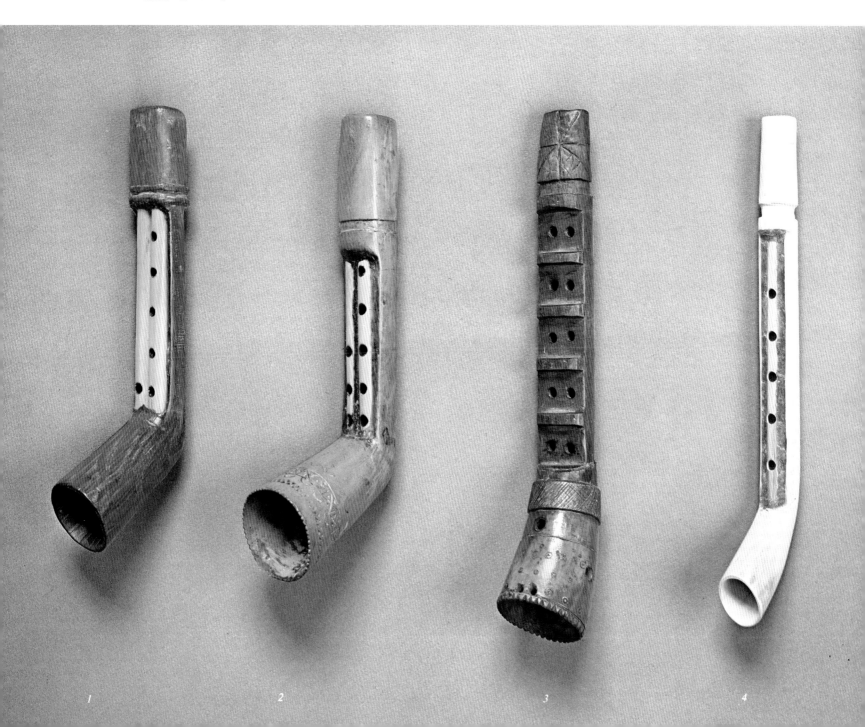

1   2   3   4

81. *Trough-like yoke of a sound-producing device of a Cretan bagpipe (askomadoúra) with engraved verses (1938).*

82.   1. Trumpet made of horn (voúkino), 23.5 cm. long. 2. Brass trumpet (troumbéta), 20 cm. long.

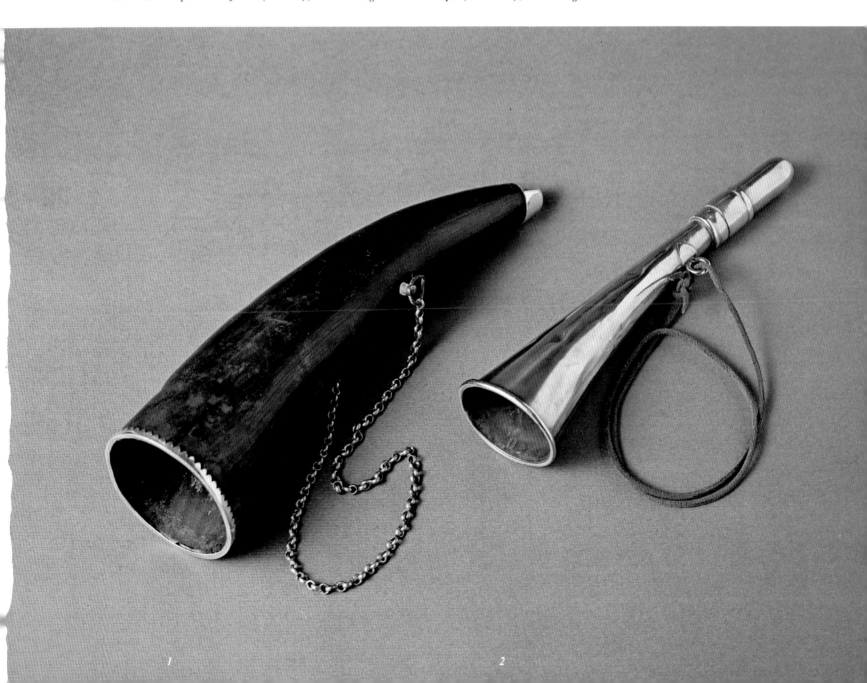

1

2

84. *Whistling water-pots (lalítses), 10 and 8.5 cm. high.*

85. *Whistle on animal-shape handle of a shepherd's crook.*
→

83. *Conch (bouroú), 26 cm. long.*

84

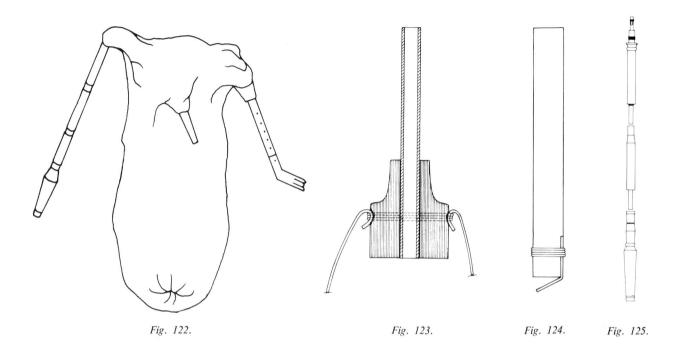

Fig. 122.　　　　　　Fig. 123.　　　Fig. 124.　Fig. 125.

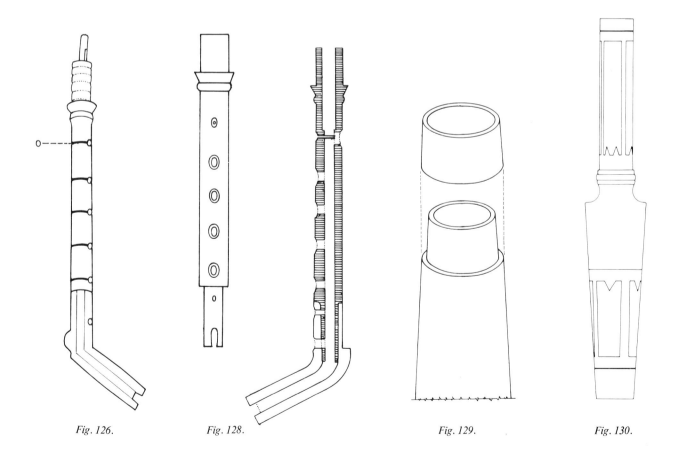

Fig. 126.　　　Fig. 128.　　　　Fig. 129.　　　Fig. 130.

GAIDA (Mainland bagpipe)

Terminology — Construction

The *gáida*, a bagpipe with drone, nowadays played mainly in Macedonia and Thrace, was once to be heard throughout the Greek mainland. It is also known as the *gáidha*, *ghâidha* or, more rarely, the *káida*. It is usually constructed by the player himself; of different sizes, the instrument consists of a wind-bag, a mouthpipe, and two pipes, the drone and the chanter (fig. 122). The player of the *gáida* is known as the *gaidiéris*, *gaidhiéris*, *gaidháris*, *gáidatzis* and *káidatzis*.

The bag *(askí)*, generally called *touloúmi*, *tomári*, *dhermáti* or *kóza*, is made of the same kinds of skin and is treated, tied, maintained and repaired in the same fashion as that of the *tsaboúna* (island bagpipe). It should be noted that before the Second World War the skin of the donkey was also used whenever it was available, being particularly suited to this end because of its size and durability. The *gáida* is generally larger than its near relative, the droneless island bagpipe.

The other components of the *gáida* —the mouthpipe and the two pipes— are not directly attached to the bag, but are each fitted to the *kefalári*, a wooden or bone socket permanently tied to the bag (fig. 123). The mouthpipe —a cylindrical or conical tube made of wood, bone, or, occasionally, of cane, and blown into by the player to fill the bag with air— ranges in length from approximately 12-20 cm (fig. 124). The overall length of the mouthpipe is calculated so as to include that section of the wooden or bone socket which protrudes from the bag. Among the names most commonly used to for this mouthpipe are the following: *fysári (fysáo*, to blow), *fyseró*, *fysolátis*, *fouskotári*, *fýtsi*, *douyiálo*, *douálo*, *pipíni*, etc. As in the case of the island bagpipe, the small valve that prevents the air from escaping when the bagpiper pauses for breath, is known as the *petsáki* (small piece of skin), *stop* (sic), *lipálo* or *lépka*, *kapátse*, *zaletoúch*, etc.

In addition to the mouthpipe, the two pipes of the *gáida* are also made of wood, usually almond, cornet, apricot, jujube, et alia. The longer of the two pipes, the drone, is usually constructed in three interlocking sections, and ranges in length from approximately 50-70 cm, although occasionally longer examples are to be found (fig. 125). This pipe lacks finger holes, and is fitted with a clarinet-type single-beating reed; this is attached to the end of the pipe where it is joined to the bag. This produces a single note. The internal cylindrical opening or bore of the drone is not necessarily consistent from end to end; the last of the three sections often swells to a funnel-shaped bell, or may narrow to a point "so that its 'voice' will not scatter". The drone is known as the *bourí*, *básso* or *pásso*, *zoumár* or *zamári*, *karamoúza*, *zournás*, *taragóxylo*, *garóxylo* or *garózi*, *angará*, *boutsálo*, *bourtsálo*, *boúkalos*, *bertsálo*, *birtsiálo*, *rigáts*, *tsirílo*, etc.

The shorter of the two pipes, the chanter, provides the melody, and is usually equipped with 7 frontal fingerholes and 1 rear thumbhole underneath, although occasionally there will be a configuration of only 6+1 holes. The chanter is cylindrical and straight, or it may terminate in a funnel —smaller or larger as the case may be— which forms an obtuse angle with the tube of the pipe. At the uppermost part of the chanter, where it is joined to the bag, the reed-bearer *(bibíki)* with a clarinet-type single-beating reed is attached (fig. 126). The fingerholes on the chanter are relatively equidistantly spaced. They vary in size, however, and often differ in shape as well; the larger fingerholes are oval, while the smaller ones tend to be circular. The chart in fig. 127, I-VI, indicates the various sizes and shapes of the fingerholes of six different *gáides*: I Didymóticho; II Soufli; III Palatitsia (Imathia); IV Serres region; V Didymoticho; VI Orestiada.

Paschalis Christidis (b. 1926), one of the skilled *gáida*-players from the village of Didymoticho in Thrace, says of these fingerholes: "The first hole from the upper end of the instrument is the smallest; the second and third are the same shape, and slightly larger than the first; the fourth is the largest of all; the fifth is slightly smaller than the second and third fingerholes; the sixth is slightly larger than the fifth; and the seventh is somewhat larger than the sixth. The thumbhole underneath the first fingerhole is approximately the same size as the fourth fingerhole". He further describes how, with a small, sharp piece of metal, hooked liked a bird's talon, he hollows out the holes from the inside of the pipe, "so that the *gáida* will have a clear voice." One or two additional small vent-holes are often cut into the sides of the bent funnel-like bell or on the lower end of the straight cylindrical tube of the chanter; as in the case of the *tzamára* and the *zournás* (q.v.), these holes are never stopped with the fingers, but are made to enhance the 'voice' of the instrument. In addition, a small circular vent-hole is often made between the second and third fingerholes from the lower end of the chanter, on the underside. The *gaidiéris* partially blocks this hole with wax in order to regulate the pitch of the note given by the first fingerhole from the lower end of the chanter.[319] Finally, the first hole from the upper end of the chanter —usually the smallest of the series— is fitted with a small tube, usually fashioned from the quill of a chicken's feather, thrust tightly through to the inside of the instrument's tube (fig. 128). Among other names, the chanter is known in Thrace, as the *gaidanítsa, divridína, zamarofloyéra, gaidofloyéra, zamára;* in Macedonia it is called the *gaidanáki, gaidanoúla, tzaboúna, gaidhoúrka, tsab(ou)nári, douinítsa, píska, klepársa, soúrla,* et alia.

The small cylindrical tube *(bibíki)* bearing the single-beating reed, which is fitted inside the chanter, is generally made of cane. Should a thin tree-branch be used instead, it must be pithy, straight-grained, and free of knots or irregularities; cut in the winter, it must be left to dry until the summer months before it can be used. After the pith has been removed from the cut branch, the latter is cleaned both inside and outside; the interior walls are smoothed by means of a thin, red-hot iron rod. Following this, one of the open ends is then carefully sealed with a wooden stopper and some wax. The reed is then cut —up-cut or down-cut— and is scraped with a small knife and tested repeatedly until it produces the desired 'voice'. The tube bearing the single reed is known as the *zaboúna, ghlossídhi, piskoúni, píska, fíta,* etc.

In the case of the *gáida,* as in that of the *tsaboúna,* the reeds are 'reddened' in the flames of a fire; they are 'fried' or 'roasted' in this manner to ensure that they function well without 'sticking'. Furthermore, a thread or a strand of hair is used to keep the lips of the reed open, a thread is wound around the root of the reed, or, should it prove necessary, the reed is thinned by means of a small knife. Also noteworthy are the so-called *kókkala* (bones) or *dhachtylídhia* (rings) which are fixed over the ends of the principal components of the *gáida* — the mouthpipe and the two pipes. These fittings are pieces of goat or dear horn, cut to size with a saw. After they have been boiled over a strong fire in order to soften them, they are pressed into wooden moulds with the same measurements as the components to which they are ultimately to be attached. When they have been hammered into their final shape they are ready to be fitted to the instrument by means of appropriate notches cut into the ends of the mouthpipe and the two pipes. The bone rings are then filed down until they are flush with the outer surfaces of the latter (fig. 129). These rings serve to protect the mouthpipe and the two pipes from splitting, while at the same time they decorate the instrument. For the same purpose molten lead, and, in former times, silver, was used (fig. 130). In addition, incised designs and, before the Second World War, basrelief in the form of geometric patterns and rare representations from the plant and animal worlds were used to decorate the *gáida.*

Playing technique —Musical possibilities

In regard to playing the *gáida,* apart from those features shared with the island bagpipe, the *tsaboúna,* and which have already been discussed under that heading —the position of the bag, the technique of breathing, the types of melodic ornamentation— it is necessary to treat separately with certain features of the instrument dictated by the different construction of the *gáida.* The longer of the two pipes, the drone, is usually held under the player's armpit or allowed to rest on his shoulder or forearm; more rarely, it is simply left to hang free. As has been pointed out earlier, the drone has no fingerholes and thus produces a single note, which invariably is 'tuned' to the tonic of the chanter which carries the melody. Thus, while the *gáida* is played, the melody is accompanied throughout by a kind of drone on the key note, usually an octave below the tonic. Thus, the drone *(íson)*, one of the most ancient forms of polyphony, is maintained.

The 6+1 or 7+1 configuration of fingerholes of the *gáida* give the intervals of the **natural diatonic scale**. The tonic of the scale is usually given by the fourth fingerhole from the lower end of the chanter, with the subtonic provided by the preceding fingerhole. The pitch of the tonic depends, as in the case of the island bagpipe, upon the size of the chanter and its reed.

The *gáida* is customarily played alone, although it may also be played in combination with the pottery drum *(toumbeléki)*, the tambourine *(dairés)*, the drum *(daoúli)*, or, in the Evros river area, together with the *líra* or *massá* (q.v.) (The latter combination ceased to exist before the Second World War).

Although it has been claimed that in former times the *gáida* was constructed in Greece with an oboe-type double-reed, to date we have been unable to discover any evidence on this score in the course of our researches.

The tsaboúna and the gáida in the Greek world

Like so many other instruments, the bagpipe was introduced to Greece from Asia, approximately during the first or second century A.D., according to the reliable and unambiguous evidence given by Suetonius, Dion Chrysostom, et alii.[320] From then on, the presence of the bagpipe in Greece and among the Greeks of the Near East can be traced through many literary and iconographical sources, of which the following are among the most significant: bagpipes of the *tsaboúna* type are to be found in a miniature from a Greek manuscript of the eleventh century,[321] and the same instrument is mentioned in the writings of the Persian philosopher, Avicenna (Ibn Siná), of the same century.[322]

Fig. 131

The same type of bagpipe can be found in wall-paintings —in St. Nicholas, near Kakopetria, Cyprus, in a representation of the Nativity, fourteenth century;[323] in the Monastery of St. Fanourios, Valsamonero (Iraklion, Crete) in a fifteenth century Nativity;[324] and in the Karakalou Monastery on Mount Athos, depicting the transport of the Ark, eighteenth century. The second type of bagpipe, the *gáida*, appears in the Great Lavra Monastery on Mount Athos and in the Monastery of Varlaam, Meteora, in a representation of the Transport of the Ark, sixteenth century. Again, Nicolas de Nicolay illustrates his journal with a "Greek Villager" playing the *gáida*, also in the sixteenth century.[325] These representations of the *gáida* are of especial interest; inasmuch as they give evidence of the existence of the instrument at that time, the three *gáides* are depicted as having conical pipes.

Such a type of *gáida*, which is played in many parts of Europe in the present day —Southern Italy, Sicily, France, Spain, Scotland, and elsewhere— yet is no longer to be found in Greece. In addition to the above-mentioned iconographical evidence, information to the effect that formerly the double-beating reed was used for the Greek *gáida* —the very kind of reed which today is part of European bagpipes with conical pipes— lead us to assume that *gáides* with conical pipes were conceivably once made in Greece as well.

Of the different travellers who passed through Greece and recorded the use of the bagpipe in their chronicles — after seeing and hearing them played at weddings and country fairs— Jean de Gontaut Biron (1604),[326] Robert Sauger (1698)[327] and Pouqueville (early 19th century)[328] are particularly noteworthy.

The following verses are also relevent here; we hear that "there speaks a nun, whose former dignified restraint was disturbed by the sweet voice of a passerby":

> *Farewell, dear cross; go, my nun's robes, to the Holy Mountain!*
> *And, you, my rosary, off to the Holy Sepulchre!*
> *And I will go and marry, take myself a fine young man,*
> *I'll marry this singer, this first among tsaboúna-players.*[329]

In the following we meet the verb *tsabounízo* (literally, to play the *tsaboúna*, metaphorically,

200

to talk nonsense) in the freely translated decapentesyllable lines rendered below:

— What is it, Dog, that you are whining *(tsabounízis)* about?
— Nonsensical Hare, why are you carrying on *(tsabounízis)* so?
— And even were he king, as he boasts *(tsabounízi)*...[330]
— Why are you braying *(tzabounízis)*, Ass, and what are you making wind about?[331]

Related surnames: Gáidatzis,[332] Tsabouniáris,[333] Kaidatzís, Tsabounáris.

KLARINO *(Clarinet)*

The clarinet *(klaríno)*, as a popular musical instrument, arrived in Greece from Turkey with the Turkish Gypsies *(Tourkogýfti)*, around 1835. It first appeared in northern Greece —in Epirus and western Macedonia— whence it gradually spread southwards. Initially played together with the violin and lute *(laghoúto)*, and later with the dulcimer *(sandoúri)*, it made up the *companía*, or *coumpanía*, the Greek popular musical combination *par excellence* which in time came to replace the traditional *ziyiá* of drum and shawm *(daoúli* and *zournás)* (see *zournás)*. The clarinets played by Greek popular musicians today are usually in C. In the past, however, clarinets in Eb as well as instruments in Bb were played. Clarinets were also manufactured in different parts of the country, but these were relatively unsophisticated, having few keys. Today, all clarinets played in Greece come from abroad.

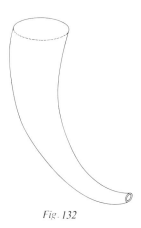

Fig. 132

The history of the clarinet in Greece, as well as its especial function as a popular instrument, has been recorded by Despina Mazaraki in *The Popular Clarinet in Greece,*[334] a unique work of its kind. The information given above has been culled from this study, to which we refer for every particular connected with the popular clarinet in Greece.

The clarinet constitutes the last great stage in the development of instrumental music for modern Greek wind-instruments. The young shepherd lad begins with the pastoral flutes, either the *floyéra* or the *sourávli*— the simplest of the wind-instruments in construction and, relatively speaking, the easiest to master. After this introduction, should he have the desire and patience, he takes up the bagpipe —the *gáida* in mainland Greece, the *tsaboúna* in the islands— or the shawm *(zournás)*. Finally, he will turn to the clarinet. At the time when the clarinet made its first appearance in Greece (c. 1835), Greek folksong had essentially completed its creative cycle. Because of its great technical and expressive potential —as compared to the shawm, which, as has been pointed out above, gradually gave way to the newcomer— the clarinet rapidly assumed pride of place among the Greek melodic instruments. It was recognised as a 'national' instrument, and in the hands of skilled musicians it became the most outstandingly expressive musical instrument throughout mainland Greece.[335] With the introduction of the clarinet Greek folk song lived through a new —and final— brilliant period in the sphere of instrumental music. This, because what most characterised folk song for the last one hundred and fifty years was not the creation of new melodies, but the reworking of the old ones.[336] And here the role of the clarinet proved decisive.

The aim of every skilled clarinettist *(klaritzís)* is the elaboration or 're-working' of the folk melody, i.e. to embellish the notes of a folk song with the greatest possible melodic ornamentation. And the ensuing 'harvest' is indeed plentiful; an unbelievable variety of melodic and rhythmic ornaments, side by side with an impressive virtuosity of fingering techniques. It is to this wealth of ornamentation and the skillful virtuosity with which the clarinet was played that the above-mentioned final period owes its brilliance. To this selfsame ornamentation, however, folk melody owes its change of face. With the embellishment of its notes, with ever increasing numbers of 'intrusive notes' in different rhythmic patterns, the true dimensions of the folk melody are distorted. The rhythmic skeleton of the folk melody is transformed, and the principal notes of the original melody are slurred and become unrecognisable, with the end result that the character of the melody is altered in its entirety.

The clarinet constitutes one of the most representative contributors to and bearers of the spirit that has characterised folk song in Greece throughout the last one hundred and fifty years of its development.

TO PHYLLO DHENDROU (The tree-leaf)

In the past, when there were no musical instruments at hand to accompany entertainments held in the open-air or in enclosed areas, certain revellers would 'play' different songs and dance airs with the leaf of a tree; held between the lips and the teeth of the player, this would serve as a primitive reed. This leaf —acacia, walnut, maple, pear, etc.— in order to achieve the desired effect must be large, moist, and mature. The 'playing' of this leaf served not only to accompany and help group-singing, but also accompanied the dancing. Today, this make-shift 'musical instrument' —in Macedonia it is known as the *sfyrí*— is to be encountered mainly in popular taverns.

BOUROU (Conch)

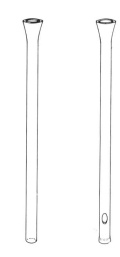

Fig. 133.   Fig. 134.

The *bouroú* is a large conch —usually belonging to the buccinum and allied genera— from which the top has been removed by patiently scraping it against a hard stone; this is done in order to open a hole, which serves as a 'mouthpiece' (fig. 131). The *bouroú* has been used since the distant past as a sound-producer —much as the trumpet— to broadcast messages, especially among seafaring people in coastal areas and on islands. It may announce the arrival of a cargo-laden caique in the harbour: "Sound the *bouroú* for them to come down", says the captain to his deck-boy. Again, it may be blown to signal the passengers to prepare for the boat's departure. A continuous uninterrupted, held note *(boúrisma)* means preparation for sailing; a series of shorter blasts signifies urgency or haste. The latter signal is also used when the ship is endangered in the open sea, when aid is needed, or when the ship is surrounded by fog.

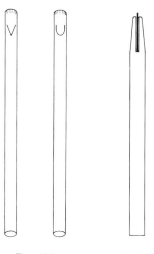

Fig. 135.   Fig 136.

In Crete, the *bouroú* was used until only one generation ago — by postmen and shepherds, who sounded the *bouroú* to warn of their approach and to summon their flocks.[337] The *bouroú* was also used in the past by the field-wardens of the Aghii Deka (region of Iraklion, Crete), as well as by the Greek camel-drivers of Cyprus whenever one of their laden animals strayed away from the trade-caravan. Again, the *bouroú* "could be heard in the fields like a steamboat whistle", as thus was used in former times to chase away hungry wolves when, in exceptionally cold winters, they descended as far as the settlement of Agoriani (region of Parnassos).

The *bouroú* was once sounded to announce a death by the shepherds who used the barren islets around Crete as their winter pasturage. Isolated there throughout the winter, writes Nikos Angelis, whenever one of their number died they would attempt to notify the villages lying across the water by whatever means they could. "If it is night-time and the stars are out they light fires and make signals with burning tree-branches. During the day, however, or when there is mist, they search for large conches on the seashore and blow into them as though they were trumpets. These produce a deep, hoarse sound, like a death-rattle, a lowing plaint, which passes over the sea and reaches the careworn ears of the mothers of those whose death it heralds".[338] The *bouroú* is also blown by the 'Frank' at the Skyros Carnival, according to the archaeologist Dawkins — one of the first to conduct research on that most ancient, traditional ritual *(dhrómeno)*.[339]

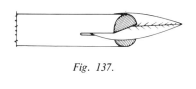

Fig. 137.

Fig. 138.

The *bouroú* has been familiar throughout the Greek world —as a sound-producer— from the classical era, as two verses of the poet Theognis of Megara (6th-5th century B.C.) demonstrate: "For already, one who died at sea calls for me to return home; although he is dead, he speaks with a living mouth".[340] The following verses of Euripides also refer to the conch:

Blowing upon conches (kóchloi) and summoning the natives.[341]

Also, the following by Theocritus:

Taking a hollow conch shell, (kóchlos), he bellowed.[342]

As an example from modern Greek poetry, these lyrical lines from Odysseas Elytis' *Sailor Boy of the Garden* come to mind:

Dawn breathes into her conch (kochýla)
a foaming prow draws near.
Angels: ship your oars
that the Evangelistria
*   might anchor here!*[343]

The *bouroú* is also known as *kóchylas, kóchlos* (conch shell), *kírykas* (herald), *tsaboúna, bouroús,*[344] *pouroú* (Cyprus), *kouryialós* and *kochliós tis thálassas* (snail of the sea) (Crete), et alia.

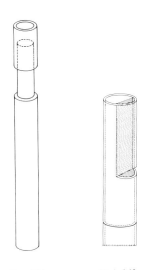

Fig. 139.   Fig. 140

TROUMBETA or VOUKINO (Horn)

The animal horn *(kéras)* has been used in Greece as sound-producer since early times (fig. 132). From a decree of the Venetian Republic issued in 1360 it is learned that the refuse collectors of that time in the region of Candia (Crete) used a horn to notify the inhabitants of their presence and to call upon them to bring their refuse to the carts.[345] The horn was also used by those Greek camel-drivers who used to carry merchandise in Cyprus. Moreover, until the advent of the Second World War, the horn was also used by Greek field-wardens and postmen in many regions of the country, and was known as the trumpet *(troumbéta* or *voúkino)*. The *shofar* —used in their worship by Greek Jews, as well as by their co-religionists all over the region of the diaspora— is also an animal horn.[346] This type of sound-producer —known as the *natural horn*— open at both ends without any additional holes on its conical body, is one of the most ancient surviving aerophones.

One kind of 'trumpet' *(troumbéta)* which was used until 1964 —and which is still used today, albeit only during emergency— belongs to the Athens-Piraeus electric railway stations. This instrument, although superficially it resembles the natural horn, does not however come under the same category; instead, it is a sound-producer of the clarinet-type, and is equipped with a metallic single-beating reed.

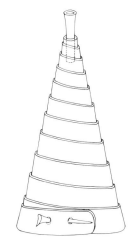

Fig. 141.

WHISTLES AND WHISTLING

Whistling is a practical aid in his daily life to every rural Greek, be he shepherd, farmer, huntsman, or whatever. Various manners of whistling are to be found throughout Greece. The best known of these are the pursing of the lips; the placing of the thumb and forefinger of either hand or the forefingers and middle-fingers of both hands in the mouth; the forming of a hollow resonator with the palms of both hands and the placing of the cupped hands against the mouth, rapidly moving one or more fingers up and down, etc. By means of the latter method, which is rather more than a simple form of whistling, different bird calls, the hooting of an owl or the cooing of a dove, can be imitated. A shepherd who is skilled in woodcarving will sometimes shape one end of his crook in such a manner that it can be blown into as a whistle.[347] The section that produces the sound is fashioned with a stopper, as is the corresponding section of the ducted flute *(sourávli)* (q.v.).

Foreign travellers have reported some interesting observations on whistling and the use of whistles in Greece and among the Greeks of the Levant. It has been noted by H. Castela (1612) that a whistle was blown to call the Greek Christians to service in an Orthodox church

Fig. 142.

Fig. 143.

in Gaza (Palestine).[348] Similar information —from the 16th-18th centuries —, is also available for these Chiotes who bred and raised partridges in the island. The partridges were released every morning and allowed to range with wild partridges in the neighbouring mountains. When night fell, they were called home, some by means of a song, others by means of a whistle or by simple whistling, according to how the fowls had been trained.[349]

Fig. 144.

CHILDREN'S WHISTLES

I was a child just oustside Glarentsa
and wore 'katákopa' and played with whistles (sfyrístria).

These two lines from the *Poulologos* bear witness to the fact that children were wont to play with whistles —as they do today— from as far in the past as the Byzantine era.[350]

Children's sound-producing devices are made by the children themselves, as a pastime, especially during the spring and the summer months. Of these, the best known throughout Greece are the whistles *(sfyríchtres)*, some of which are simply constructed, and others which are more sophisticated. The simpler whistles are generally made by the smaller children, while the more complex whistles are made by the older children, with the supervision of adults.

The most simple whistle (approximately 5-7 cm in length) is fashioned from a green barley or oat stalk, or even from a pumpkin stalk; by squeezing the lips of the stalk together with the fingers, the teeth, or against the forehead, they thus create a 'double-beating reed', upon which they blow. The opposite end is either left open (fig. 133), or is closed by a knot in the stalk; in the latter case, a small hole is left near the knot (fig. 134).

Fig. 145.

Another type of whistle is to be found, having the lower end open and the upper end closed by the knot of the stalk. The 'single-beating reed' of this variation of whistle is cut close to the knot, like that of the *madoúra* (fig. 135). This whistle is known as the *bisbíka* in Chrysi (region of Kastoria).

Children also fashion whistles from the twigs of different trees and bushes. After such twigs have been whittled down at one end, the children then make an incision near the middle, into which they insert a laurel leaf. The whistle is played held perpendicular to the mouth (fig. 136). The same whistle is also made without whittling down one end; in the latter case, it is held flute-fashion, lengthwise against the mouth (fig. 137). In the Elassona region this variant of the whistle is called the *sfíka* (wasp). Another kind of whistle is fashioned from a piece of woody vine-stem, sliced lengthwise into two pieces by means of a small knife. Between the two halves is placed bark from the same vine; these are then lined up and bound together at both ends with thread, which is held in position by the knots of the vine-stem. This whistle is blown into from the side (fig. 138), and is generally known as the *klimatosfyríchtra* (vine-whistle). On the island of Crete it is also called the *tsitsíra, skliríthra* and *klimatopadoúra*. A similar type of whistle is also fashioned from the stem of the asphodel. In the case of the latter, cigarette paper is substituted for bark, although in the past, spider's cobweb *(tsípa)* was used for this purpose.

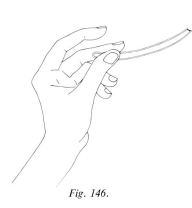

Fig. 146.

Those whistles fashioned from the twigs of trees and bushes range in size from approximately 5-10 cm long, and are generally known as *sfyríchtres*. In addition, however, they are also known regionally as *pipíngia* (Roumeli and Thessaly), *pipiríngia* or *peperíngia* (region of Nafpaktos), *birbília* (Chrysi, Kastoria),[351] *karamoúzes* or *tsaboúnes* (Laconia), *sourávlia* (Mytilene), and *katsaboúnes* (Cyprus).

Another type of whistle, slightly more difficult to construct, is made by children from a green twig of the oleander, fig, mulberry, willow, walnut, or some other tree. To fashion such whistles, first the bark is removed from one end of the twig —a strip approximately 1-2 cm long— care being taken that it does not break in the process. The inner, cylindrical core of the twig is then whittled down slightly, the ringlet of bark is replaced, and the child blows as he would on a 'female' key; he holds the ringlet of bark down upon his lower lip with his left hand and supports the twig with his right, moving the latter up and down rhythmically (fig. 139). In much the same manner children fashion a *sourávli*-like whistle (ducted) (fig. 140).

Another kind of whistle is known as the *karamoútza* or *troumbéta:* this is made in different sizes, from the bark peeled from the branch of the willow, walnut, chestnut, or some other tree. After incising a spiralling pattern around a green twig from one of these trees, the children peel off the bark and twist it so as to form a cone. The base is secured by means of a thorn, while over the top another piece of bark is affixed; this piece of bark is shaped like a ring, and is approximately 1.5-2.5 cm long. This section of bark is peeled from another twig —very small in diameter— and is lightly pressed into place at the top of the cone, so as to form a kind of 'double-beating reed'. The strong, penetrating sound of the *troumbéta* or *karamoútza* recalls that of the shawm *(zournás)* (fig. 141).

In all of the cases described in the foregoing, the twig is lightly tapped all around in order to facilitate the removal of the bark. This was done by the children of Bithynia when they desired to make such whistles, according to George Pachtikos: "While this rhythmical tapping proceeds, the melody... (he gives the score, in his *Collection*) is sung; by means of it, the child's mind believes that the separation of the bark from the twig is more easily achieved".[352]

Apricot stones are also used by children to make whistles. In such cases, the fruit-stone is pierced by scraping it upon a stone; the kernel is removed, and the hollow stone is blown like a 'female' key (fig. 142). Sometimes a small pebble is placed inside the emptied stone; when the whistle is blown, the pebble is set in motion, striking the walls of the fruit-stone. This simultaneously serves to increase the volume of the sound and alter its timbre. Until the advent of the Second World War, for those whistles fashioned from the stones of fruit, the kernals contained within the fruit-stones were allowed to dry to such a degree that they resembled small pebbles. The same type of whistle —albeit without a pebble inside— is made from the acorn, from which the cup has been removed beforehand. The acorn is cut at the base with a small knife, and its content are removed, care being taken to keep the shell intact (fig. 143).

Yet another sound-producing toy is fashioned by children from the shell of the crab. After the body has been boiled, a hole is cut in the head at some point between the eyes; the content are then carefully extracted in such a way as to avoid puncturing the internal membrane. This device is made to produce sound in two ways: either the children blow upon it as they do in the case of those whistles made from fruit-stones, or they hum a tune into the hole in the shell, so that as it passes through the interior of the shell its timbre is altered. In this case it functions as a membranophone. This variant of the whistle is known as the *niounioúki* or *nounoúra*.

LALITSA (Water-whistle)

The *lalítsa* —also known as *nerosfyríchtra* (water-whistle), *aïdhonáki* (little nightingale), or *koúkkos* (cuckoo)— is another type of whistle, made of clay. It is generally a small, hollow, clay figure, shaped like a bird, fish, cock, crock, or other familiar form, and is made in popular potteries. With a 'mouthpiece' resembling that of the ducted flute *(sourávli),* and usually half filled with water, such items are used by small children as whistles. When it is blown into, "the *lalítsa* gurgles". This kind of whistle was once a particularly beloved children's toy throughout Greece, although it is becoming more and more rare in the present day (fig. 144). According to an address made in 1845 by Koletis, then Prime Minister of Greece, such a whistle was used to send the proclamation of the Revolution of 1821 to Ioannina: "I was in Ioannina when the Revolution began, when our fellow countrymen in Corfu sent me certain items, among which I noticed a *koúkkos* (whistle) —two whistles, three whistles, four whistles, five whistles! I looked at them, asking myself what so many whistles could be doing there— and what did I find inside them? This very proclamation!" And he held up the famous proclamation of Petrobeis Mavromichalis, dated March 25th, 1821 — the date upon which the liberation of Greece is considered to have begun.[353]

It is also noteworthy that children also make use of cartridge cases, 'female' keys, and whatever other hollow objects can be made to sound like a whistle.

VOUGA (Bull-roarer)

Another children's sound-producing toy is the bull-roarer known as the *voúga*, or *vourvoúna*, *vrondára*, *vrondalídha* (onomatopoeic). This device consists of a thin, triangular or long and narrow piece of wood —suspended from a string— which the children twirl around their heads as fast as they can, holding it by one end of the string. The *voúga* is fashioned in different sizes, and the wood from which it is made is chosen for its weight. The friction created by the rushing of the wood through the air produces a sound, the sharpness of which depends upon the dimensions of the piece of wood and the speed at which it revolves (fig. 145).[354]

SEED-PODS

The same principle as that governing the bull-roarer *(voúga)* is also the basis for yet another sound-producing toy with which the children of Crete amuse themselves. They separate the seed-pods of the oleander lengthwise into two halves; then, taking one of the two halves between the thumb and middle finger, they squeeze it tightly, at the same time hurling it violently into the air with a sudden, twisting movement. As it spins about its axis, the half of the seed-pod hums like a bee as it pursues its course through the air (fig. 146).

ANIMAL BLADDERS

In the past, even the bladder of the pig was transformed into a sound-producing toy by Greek children. During the slaughtering of swine at Carnival in the Cretan village of Mourne (Aghios Vassilios, nome of Rethymnon), up until the advent of the Second World War, the village children were wont to take the discarded bladders and clean them. After the bladders were inflated with air, the children would deflate them rapidly by squeezing them between their hands. Forced violently from the bladder in this manner, the rushing air caused the bladder to produce a characteristic stuttering sound, sharp or dull according to the dimensions of the bladder opening.

CHORDOPHONES

TAMBOURAS (Tamboura)

The people of Greece have long used the term *tambourás* to denote a series of plucked instruments of the lute family, irrespective of the dimensions of the instruments or the number and tuning of their strings. These instruments share the following common morphological features: a small and usually pear-shaped soundbox; a long, narrow and perfectly straight neck (*chéri*, handle; also known as the *kotsáni*, stalk, or *ourá*, tail) which is an extension of the body of the instrument, although it cannot be clearly distinguished from the soundbox; moveable or fixed frets; lateral and front pegs, usually T-shaped; strings resting on a moveable bridge and attached to one or more buttons *(koumbiá)* affixed to the body, on the rear edge of the soundboard; with or without soundholes on the table or/and the body. These instruments are played with a plectrum *(pénna)*, or, as was the custom in the past with the smaller sized instruments, with the fingers. The best plectra are made from the dried bark of the cherry, morello, and other trees. Instances have been recorded where certain *tambourádhes* have 'broken' necks — in other words, where the uppermost part of the instrument's neck is bent backwards, as in the case of the lute *(laghoúto)*, and can be easily distinguished from the soundbox when the latter is made of staves.

Terminology

Apart from the generic name *tambourás (tamboúri*,[355] *támbouro, támbouras, tambrás, tsambourás)*, these instruments also appear under the following names according to their size and the number and tuning of their strings: *sázi, bouzoúki, baghlamás, yiongári, boulgarí, kíteli, kavónto, tzivoúri, karadouzéni*, etc. Today, however, these names do not correspond throughout Greece to a specific type of instrument with strictly defined dimensions, number of strings, and tuning. In Iraklion (Crete) for example, the oldest living manufacturer of lute-type instruments, Manolis Vlachakis or Malliotis (b. 1894), used to use the terms *boulgarí* or *baghlamás* to denote a pear-shaped *tambourás* 55-65 cm long, having three double strings tuned to intervals of a perfect fifth and fourth. The same instrument was called *boulgarí* or *baghlamás* in Messenia, whereas in Pyrgos (Elis) it was called *yiongári* or *baghlamás*. It is noteworthy that the term *tambourás* is also used for the lute in certain mountainous regions and other areas far removed from the larger urban centres: Ierisso (Chalkidiki), Epirus (in mountain villages), Nikissiani (in the region of Pangeon), Agoriani (Parnassida), villages of the Tyrnavos region (Thessaly), etc.

Construction

With regard to the manufacture of these instruments, what is described in connection with the construction of the lute applies here as well (see *laghoúto*). It should be added, however, that the body of the *tambourás* is either hollowed-out like that of the pear-shaped *líra*, or made with staves, and that, while retaining in general outline its pear-shaped form, it is nevertheless to be encountered in a great number of morphological variations (fig. 147, mould of a small *tambourás*; fig. 148, mould of a small *tambourás* with block and stave). Soundboxes are to be found that are longer than they are wide, or short and wide at the base; shallow soundboxes with a slightly curved body, and yet others with deep and hemispherical bodies, etc. In former times, such soundboxes were made from a tortoise's carapace, from half of a dried gourd, and occasionally from such objects as water canteens; the last-named were often used by soldiers or prisoners to make makeshift *baghlamádhes*. Older Greeks also recall *tambourádhes* having soundboards made of tanned skin instead of wood. Angeliki Hadjimichali writes of the Sarakatsan *tambourás:* "It was made of a single piece of wood —walnut or oak— which was hollowed-out; a tanned skin was stretched over this".[356]

Among all of these instruments a special place is reserved for the true *tambourás,* an instrument of the lute family having an hemispherical soundbox, a neck over one metre in length, and usually two double strings tuned in fifths, or three or four double strings tuned in fourths or fifths (see Plate 108). As a result of the long neck and the moveable frets, which can be raised or lowered with ease, the *tambourás* covers the entire range of intervals required by Byzantine as well as Greek folk music: diesis, leimma, major tone, minor tone, minim-minor tone.[357] This particular *tambourás* is difficult to handle, and the technique required to play it is not easily learned; it is no longer to be found being performed on Greek soil. Smaller, more manageable *tambourádhes,* however, were commonly played up until the advent of the Second World War; these instruments had a pear-shaped soundbox and moveable frets. In the hands of those musicians who closely adhered to tradition, they gave the intervals of the *natural scale,* as well as the basic intervals of Byzantine and of Greek folk music.

Today, of all the above-mentioned kinds of *tambourás,* only the *bouzoúki* and the *baghlamás* are still played in Greece. These names arise from the long years of Greek contact with the Turks, but their wide distribution throughout the country is primarily due to the influence of those Asia Minor Greeks who fled to Greece in the aftermath of the Greco-Turkish War of 1922, and the exchange of ethnic communities in 1923. The present day *bouzoúki* consists of a body (*skáfi,* trough) made of staves, a table with a large soundhole, a neck with its uppermost part bent backwards, a head and pegs like those of the mandolin, and fixed frets. This instrument may either be three or four-stringed. The three stringed *bouzoúki* has three double strings tuned to a perfect fifth and to a perfect fourth. The four-stringed version may have either single or double strings for the two lower ones; the two upper strings are always double strings. The instrument gives the following intervals: perfect fourth, major third, and perfect fourth. The *bouzoúki* ranges in overall length from approximately 90 cm to over one metre. The *baghlamás* is a small (approximately 40-70 cm) three-stringed instrument, made in different sizes. The tuning of the *baghlamás* is similar to that of the *bouzoúki,* except that all of the strings of the former instrument are tuned an octave higher than those of the latter. The *sázi,* which is only rarely to be found, is made in different sizes, and usually has three double or triple strings; these are tuned in different arrangements based on the intervals of fifths and fourths.

The other kinds of *tambourás* no longer played today include the *yiongári* or *liongári* (three-stringed); the *boulgarí,* or *bougarí, bourgharí, bourgalí* (varying number of strings); the *kíteli* or *kintéli* (two-stringed instrument tuned to the interval of a fifth);[358] the *kavónto* (with a level body and three double strings; approximate length 95 cm); the *tzivoúri* (two double strings and one single string, tuned to a fifth and an octave); and the *karadouzéni* (a kind of large *baghlamás*).[359]

Playing technique—Musical possibilities

The *tambourás* —and all its variant forms— was formerly usually played without any other instrumental accompaniment. The instrument has a characteristic delicate and relatively subdued sound, and is emminently suited to accompany those songs or dances in which only a few people participate, especially in an enclosed area. The melody was usually played on the instrument's first and highest string, the *cantíni,* while the other open strings provided a simultaneous drone *(íson)* accompaniment of tonic or fifth, or the two together, etc. The exact nature of this accompaniment depended upon the number of the strings and the manner in which the instrument was tuned. In the course of time, this drone evolved into a harmonic accompaniment based on the tempered scale and on western music.

This is the harmonisation now played on the *bouzoúki* to accompany the *rebétiko* song. A virtuoso instrument *par excellence,* the *bouzoúki* is not only the principal melodic instrument of the *rebétiko* orchestra, but also shares the harmonic accompaniment with the other instruments of the orchestra, the guitar, piano, et alia. Its fixed frets and the tempered scale definitively mark off the *bouzoúki* of today from the distinctive feature that formerly characterised the instrument as a true *tambourás* — its monophonic character, played on a modal scale. Formerly, all the varieties of the *tambourás* were occasionally played in conjunction with other —usually other stringed— instruments, such as the combinations of *tambourás* and pear-shaped *líra, tambourás* and violin, etc. At Didymoticho (Thrace), up until the advent of the Second World War, the *tambourás* was played to the accompaniment of the *massá* (q.v.).

The tambourás in the Greek world

Instruments resembling the *tambourás* —having long necks and small soundboxes— can be traced as far back as classical times in the Greek world, where they were known as the *pandhoúra* or the *tríchordhon* (three-stringed).[360] Noteworthy examples of the archaeological evidence for the existence of such instruments include a fourth century B.C. relief from Mantineia,[361] terracottas bearing representations of similar instruments,[362] a mosaic representation of a *pandhoúra* played with a plectrum, from the palace of the Byzantine emperors,[363] and a *tambourás* that was discovered in 1961 in the course of excavations at ancient Corinth.[364] Thenceforth, the path of development followed by the *tambourás* and its variants through the Byzantine and post-Byzantine eras up until the present day is marked out by several literary and iconographical sources. Moreover, the instrument's modern name *tambourás* is derived from the ancient *pandhoúra* through known intermediate forms: *phandhoúra, thamboúra, thamboúrin, tamboúrin, tamboúra, tambourás*.[365]

In his treatise *De Ceremoniis* (10th century), Constantine Porphyrogennetus mentions the performers "with pandhoúres" at the vintage-time dinner[366]. *Pandhoúres* and other instruments are also mentioned in a chronicle of the 12th century, where it is said that they were played at an official ceremony at the Hippodrome in Constantinople.[367] In 1677, John Covel wrote that the people of the island of Chios played the *tambourás* and the violin at their gatherings.[368] Nikolaos Kasomoulis informs us that the heroes of the 1821 War of Independence played instruments of the same type *(yiongári, ikíteli, boulgarí, baghlamás, tzivoúri, bouzoúki)*.[369] One of these selfsame instruments —the *tambourás* of General Makriyannis— is today kept in the National Historical Museum of Athens. "Upon his own accompaniment he sang in a fine and manly voice, with the air of a true hero-warrior".[370]

The suitability of the *tambourás* for the accompaniment of song in an enclosed space is typically illustrated in a passage from the prose version of the akritic Epic of Digenis Akritas (1623): "And at each meal, when they had eaten, he took up his *thamboúra* (Digenis). The maiden's voice chimed in and astounded everyone. Afterwards she danced and sang with a melifluous voice, and the girl played upon the pine-needles they had strewn about. What word can describe that beauteous maiden, and the dancing and those wondrous songs?"[371]

From Chrysanthus, Archbishop of Dyrrachium, we learn that the *tambourás* was considered a great aid to the teaching of the intervals of Byzantine music. In his *Theoretikon*, the Archbishop writes: "Of all melodic instruments, the *pandhourís* lends itself most easily to teaching, and upon it one may the more clearly acquaint himself with the tones, semitones, and indeed every kind of interval. It is also known as the *pandhoúra* or *phándhouros;* among us it is called the *tamboúra* or *tamboúri*".[372]

The following verses from the Epic of Digenis Akritas and the akritic song cycle are also relevant to this study:

Why do you strike your thamboúra at the present time?

And he took his tamboúri and tuned it.

And cut the trunk of an olive tree and fashioned a tamboúra.

And his tambourás played all the world's sweetness.[373]

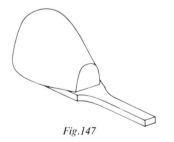

Fig.147

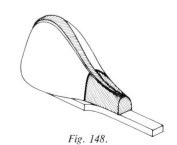

Fig. 148.

211

Greek folk songs provide us with the following:

> *He went along the roadside, he made his tambourás sound*
> *'I will not become a chattel, I do not bow to Turks'.*

> *And in his hands he holds a golden tambourás.*

> *My heavy-sounding yiongári, why do you not sound fully?*

> *Let me cut an olive leaf and play the liongári.*

> *A dervish was rushing through the market,*
> *playing the bouzoúki, striking the tambourás.*

> *And Constantine strolled, playing the tzivoúri.*

> *Bring me my támbouras and my karadouzéni.*[374]

Especially significant among the iconographical sources are several miniatures from an illuminated manuscript of the Alexander the Great Romance (14th century);[375] these depict instruments of the *tambourás* type, having an ovoid or round soundbox and two or three strings. Similar instruments, with pear-shaped, ovoid, or round soundboxes are also to be found on many wall-paintings: these include the churches of St. Demetrius at Chrysafa (Laconia), the Dormition of the Virgin at Zarafona (Kallithea, Laconia), St. Paraskevi at Sophico (Corinthia), Monasteries on Mount Athos (Koutloumousi, Xiropotamou, and Philotheou: in the representation "Praise ye the Lord" on the narthex), etc.

Also noteworthy are the illustrations of foreign travellers,[376] paintings and frescoes by modern artists (including P. Lembesis, Nikiphoros Lytras,[377] Th. Vryzakis, Theophilos, Th. Leblanc, Peter von Hess,[378] et alii), embroideries depicting 'cadis' or 'baghasákia' playing the *tambourás,* etc.[379] Just how closely interwoven with Greek tradition such *tambourás*-like instruments have been throughout the ages is amply evidenced by their representation on what Yiannis Tsarouchis calls "the 'illuminated' woven carpet".[380]

Proverbs — Adages

"My belly is playing the *tambourás*" (is rumbling).
"Your belly is playing the *tambourás* (is rumbling) about one thing or another".[381]
"He is a *bouzouki*-head".
"Now then, you *Baghlamás!*"

Surnames

Tambourás, Tambourákis, Tambouratzís, Tambouratzákis, Tambouréas, Tamboúris, Tambouriákis; Bouzoukákis, Bouzoúkas, Bouzoúkis, Bouzoúkos; Yiongarákis, Yiongarás.[382] The surnames Tambouratzís and Tambouratzákis can be traced from the middle of the eighteenth century in the Turkish Archives of the Vikelean Library, Iraklion, Crete.

LAGHOUTO (Long-necked Lute)

Terminology

The lute is known throughout Greece as the *laoúto, lavoúto,* or *laghoúto,* all of which names are derived from the Arabic *'ūd,* for wood (Sachs interprets the term as referring specifically to a "flexible stick").[383] In some regions of Greece, the instrument also goes by the names *tambourás* or *tsambourás.*[384] In former times it was also referred to as *tiflosoúrtis* ('leader of the blind'), as it served to keep the melodic instrument it accompanied —whether violin, clarinet, or *líra*— to the correct rhythm (fig. 149). The lute in Greece has a large, pear-shaped soundbox, a long, fretted neck, bent, "broken", backwards at its uppermost end, lateral pegs, and four double strings, attached to the bridge on the soundboard. The instrument is played with a plectrum *(pénna)*.

Construction

In the late nineteenth century, the lute was made in three sizes, or 'heights'. In our own time, it is the intermediate size which has become the most popular. Nevertheless, the dimensions do vary to some degree between the finished instruments of different lute-makers, although such differences are relatively slight and have no real functional significance. The lute is often made, moreover, with the bodily build of the player himself in mind —according as to whether he be tall or short, heavy or thin, or whether he has long or short fingers— as well as designed to suit his stated preferences in the purely musical sphere. The player may, for instance, request that the soundbox of his instrument be of greater or lesser depth, or that the neck be longer or shorter.

The Cretan *laghoúto* of today is longer, wider, and deeper than all other lutes made and played in Greece. At one time, lutes similar in size to those played throughout the rest of Greece were also played in Crete.[385]

The diagram (fig. 150) gives the dimensions of the intermediate-sized lute; the figures in brackets indicate the limits of the dimensions as derived from relevant measurements made of over a hundred different lutes from all the regions of Greece. From these measurements one can safely conclude that there is no fixed relationship between the dimensions of the various parts of the instrument. For example, the lengthening or shortening of the neck does not necessarily entail the increasing or decreasing in size of the instrument's soundbox. These lutes, made at various times from 1862 to the present day, constitute a living history of lute manufacture in Greece over the last one hundred and ten years.[386] They are especially valuable insofar as that period of years coincides with both the zenith and the nadir of lute-making in the country.

However, closely it may follow the lines established and preserved by centuries of tradition, the manufacture of the *laghoúto* —as holds true for so many other Greek popular musical instruments— varies both as regards the dimensions of the individual instruments and the process whereby they are crafted. Minute differences between individual instruments are apparent not only in the case of those instruments manufactured in different workshops, but even between the individual instruments manufactured by the same craftsman. Such variations constitute a living proof of the ingenuity and involvement of the lute-makers with their craft. Their search to create instruments capable of producing a finer or greater sound, increased resistance to changes in the weather, or warping, as well as the sheer beauty of their workmanship, far from acting against tradition, serves to keep it alive through a process of constant renewal.

In Greece, the *laghoúto* is crafted in the cities, in workshops with a long tradition in the making of such instruments behind them. The soundness of the instruments' construction, their satisfactory functioning and the quality of the sound they produce all depend, essentially, upon the patience, care, and loving dedication *(meráki)* with which they are made. The manufacture of each lute always proceeds in the same order of construction — body, neck, and table. Several different hardwoods are used in the making of the soundbox: ebony, palisander, asphodel, mahogany, walnut, etc.[387] Lime or some other softwood is used to construct the skeleton of the neck, while the table is usually fashioned from coniferous wood, most often pine.

The body of the *laghoúto* is made with the aid of a wooden mould (fig. 151). A triangular block *(dákos)* of some softwood, such as the linden-tree, is temporarily screwed on to the uppermost part of the mould. Upon the block, which will be left inside the soundbox as a support, and in which a groove will be incised later for the insertion of the neck, staves are affixed (fig. 152). To the middle of the block the 'mother-stave' is attached; the other staves follow, alternately attached to the right and left of the 'mother-stave', and glued to the block and to each other with fish-glue. In order to curve the staves to conform to the shape of the mould, the lute-maker 'irons' them with a special kind of hot iron (nowadays, this tool is electrically operated in several workshops in Greece), at the same time gluing them in place. Formerly, the body of the lute would be made up of as many as 23 or even 33 individual staves.[388] Nowadays, the maximum number of staves making up the body of the lute does not exceed 23, and the actual number is often even lower than that. This reduced figure is one consequence of a certain 'industrialisation' of lute manufacture. This is particularly true in the case of the *bouzoúki* as well as that of the *laghoúto* — quantities of which are sent abroad, especially to the Greek communities in the United States and Canada. In addition, it should be noted that skilled lute-makers, when cutting the staves, do not need to concern themselves overmuch with their correct length, breadth and thickness at the edges, for these measurements are maintained according to the traditions of each individual workshop. Despite the fact that the master-craftsmen work with no measuring device other than the naked eye, they never err in their efforts to achieve a balanced symmetry in their finished individual instruments.

The construction of the body of the lute is completed with the gluing of the so-called 'side-pieces' *(plaïná)* to the outermost staves, all the way around, and by adding the *kollántza* to the place where the staves meet, at the base of the instrument. The 'side-pieces' and the *kollántza (kolló,* to glue, to paste on), both of which are made of the same kind of wood as the staves, serve to keep the latter in place at the points they are affixed. When the glue has set and dried and the staves are firmly attached, the mould is removed and the interior of the body is cleaned out with a scraping tool. Small strips of a specially treated cloth *(panóharto)* are then attached to the joints where the staves of the body meet, either vertically or horizontally. Finally, at the base of the body, a thin, flat board (of any kind of wood, hard or soft) is attached to the inside 'wall' of the body in a position corresponding to that where the *kollántza* has been attached (fig. 153).

The neck of the *laghoúto,* made from a single piece of wood, usually from the linden-tree, is slotted into the groove incised for that very purpose in the triangular block affixed on to the uppermost part of the instrument's body. The neck must be precisely fitted to the block, and must be firmly glued into place; the more completely the neck and block are fitted together to form a whole, the stronger will be the construction of the overall instrument, and the less liable to warp. In the last few years, instead of making the neck of the *laghoúto* from a single piece of wood from the linden-tree, lute-makers have sometimes used pieces of wood from the linden-tree glued together with some other soft wood, such as that of the pepper tree. In such instances, the lute-maker does not have to 'dress' the neck with veneer to protect it against warping, a process that must be carried out when the neck is made of a single piece of wood. The prevention of warping, especially in the case of the neck of the instrument, is the unceasing and fundamental concern of every skilled maker of lutes.

The table of the *laghoúto* is flat or slightly curved; it is always made of coniferous wood, usually pine. A thin pine board is sliced into two layers, and these, placed side by side, together make up the table of the instrument. In order to glue these two pieces of wood together, they are placed in a mould, and then fixed from inside with seven wooden *kamária* (arches), made of coniferous wood. The slight curvature of the table, which makes it more resistant to the strain created by the tautly stretched strings, is achieved when the small pieces of wood that are the *kamária* are curved under the table (fig. 154). On the table there is a large, round soundhole with an elaborately carved rosette.

The wood to be used in the construction of the *laghoúto* is first allowed to dry out thoroughly over a period of two or three years. Older, highly skilled craftsmen with high standards continue to prefer the natural to the artificial method of seasoning and drying the wood. The natural method always allows for the retention of some moisture in the wood, which is thereby kept 'alive'; the artificial method, on the other hand, 'kills' the wood so treated, in the words of the craftsmen themselves. It is especially important that the wood to be used in the making

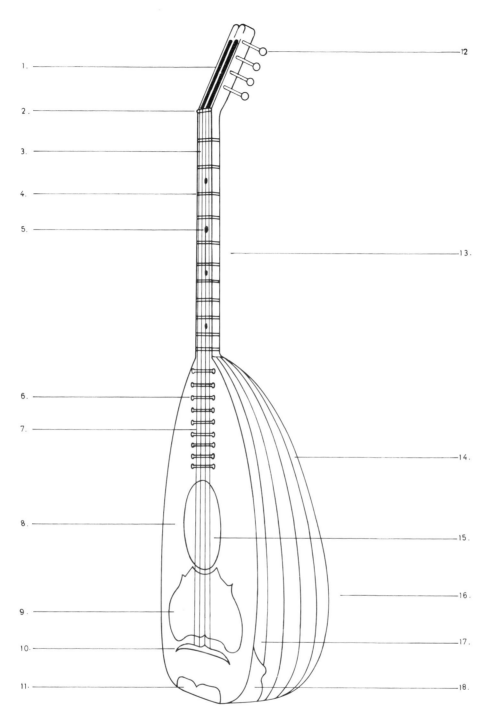

Fig. 149. Lute (laghoúto): 1. Pegbox (karávolas, karáolas, karáoulas = snail; ourá = tail; kepháli, kephalári = head, top). 2. Nut (maxilári and prosképhalo = cushion; kókkalo = bone; kavaláris = rider). 3. Fingerboard (pláka = plate). 4. Moveable frets (berdédhes = curtains, screens; thésses = positions; tásta). 5. Note-indicator (mástoris = master). 6. Fixed frets (kalamákia = small canes, cane pieces). 7. Strings (' = chordhés, córdhes; téliu = wires). 8. Table (kapáki = cover). 9. Guard (pláka = plate; tersés; penariá, piniá). 10. Bridge (kavaláris = rider; moustáki = mustache; chordhokrátis = stringholder; kaválo). 11. Thin piece of skin (= petsáki). 12. Pegs (klidhiá = keys; striftália, striftária = turners; vídhes = screws; víntsia = cranes; kopília; bouriá). 13. Neck (chéri and mánikas = hand, handle; kotsáni = stalk; ourá = tail; patoúcha). 14. Staves (= doúyes, dhoúyes). 15. Rosette (= rodhántza; ródha = wheel; kafássi = treillis, lattice work; mílos = mill; ánigma = aperture; poússoulas = sea-compass; afalós = navel; fengári = moon). 16. Soundbox (skáfi = trough; káfka, kafkí = skull). 17. Side-pieces (= plaïná; parapéta = parapets; mághoula = cheeks). 18. Kollántza, kollánda, pissinári (= back-piece).

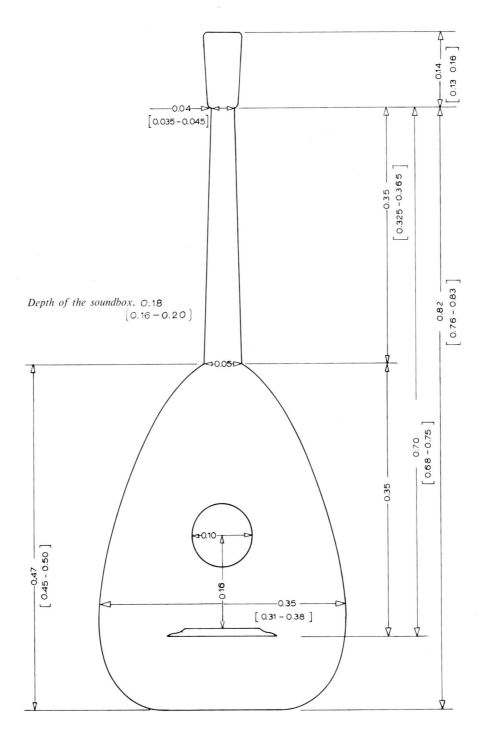

Depth of the soundbox. 0.18
[0.16 − 0.20]

0.04
[0.035 − 0.045]

0.14
[0.13   0.16]

0.35
[0.325 − 0.365]

0.82
[0.76 − 0.83]

◁0.05▷

0.35

0.70
[0.68 − 0.75]

◁0.10▷

0.47
[0.45 − 0.50]

0.16

0.35
[0.31 − 0.38]

Fig. 150

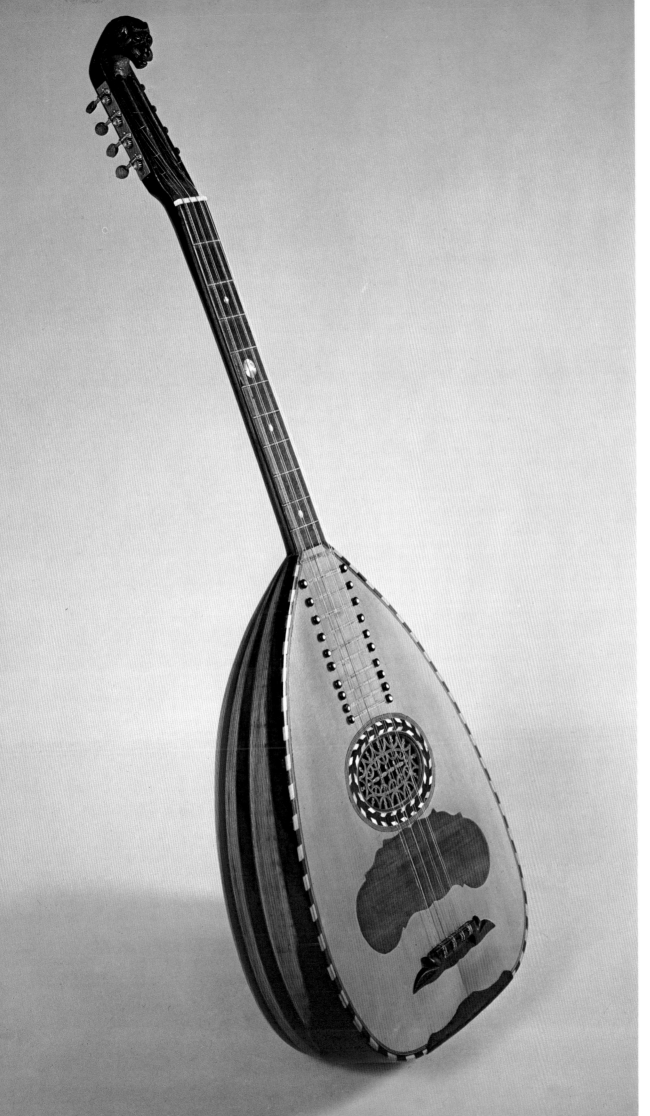

86. *Lute (laghoúto), 101 cm. long, body 35.5 cm. wide and 18.5 cm deep. Lutemaker: Ch. P. Kopeliadis, **Athens**, early 20th cent.*

←

87. *Lute (laghoúto), decorated with ivory and tortoise-shell, 90 cm. long, body 29 cm. wide and 13.5 cm. deep. Lutemaker: probably Manolis Venios, Constantinople, end 19th cent.* →

88.   Pegbox of lute   (pl. 87).

89.   Soundboard of lute   (pl. 87).

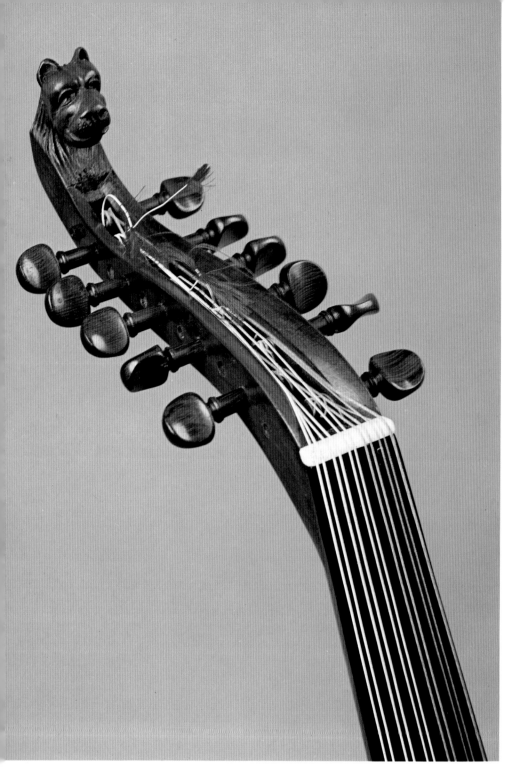

90.	*Pegbox of ʿūd (pl. 91).*

91.	*ʿŪd (oúti), 83.5 cm. long, body 35.5 cm. wide and 20.5 cm. deep. Lutemaker: Yannis Paleologos, Athens, 1971.*

92.	*Lute-guitar (laoutokithára), 96 cm. long. Inter-War years.*

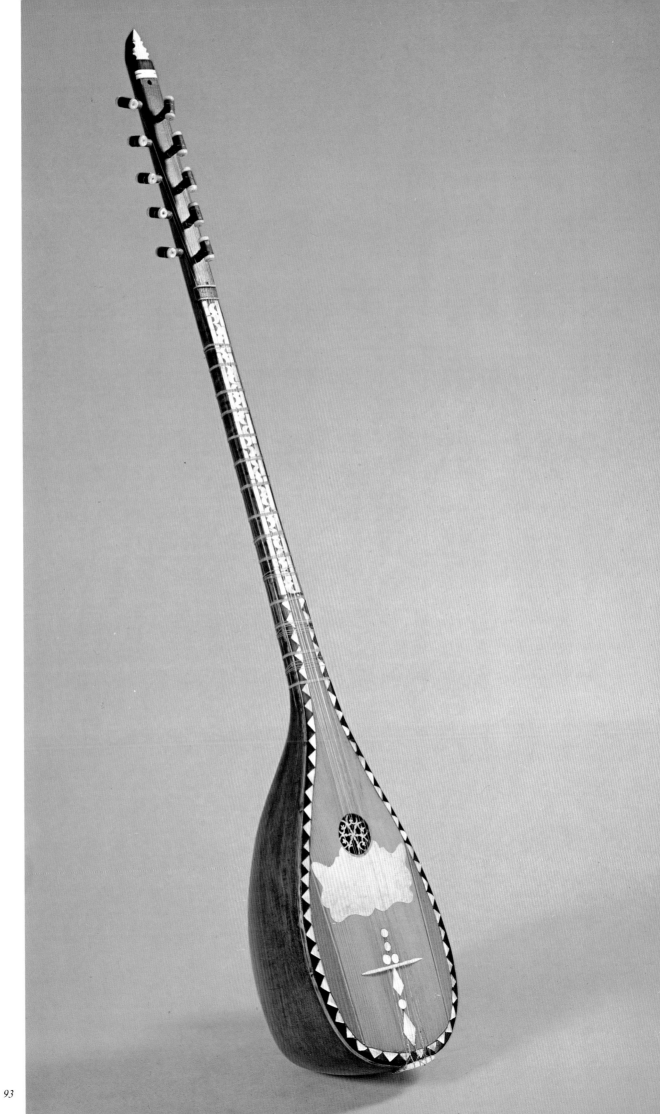

93

93. *Sázi (instrument of the lute family), 114 cm. long, body 19 cm. wide and 22 cm. deep. Lutemaker: Mikhail Skenderidis, Caesarea, Cappadocia. Early 20th cent.*

←

95. *Baglamádhes (instruments of the lute family): 1. 47.5 cm. long, body 8.5 cm. wide and 8.5 cm. deep. 2. 51 cm long, body 11 cm. wide and 8.5 cm. deep. 3. 51 cm. long, body 7.5 cm. wide and 8 cm. deep. End 19th cent.*

96. *Island Greek with tambourás, 19th cent. Benaki Museum, Athens.*

97. *Bouzoúkia (instruments of the lute family): 1. 87 cm. long, body 19.5 cm. wide and 14 cm. deep. 2. 92.5 cm. long, body 24 cm. wide and 12 cm. deep. Early 20th cent.*   →

98. *Tambourás on a Skyrian embroidery. Greek Folk Art Museum, Athens.*

94. *Tambourás. "Dames de Tine". Choiseul Gouffier, Voyage pittoresque de la Grèce (1782).*

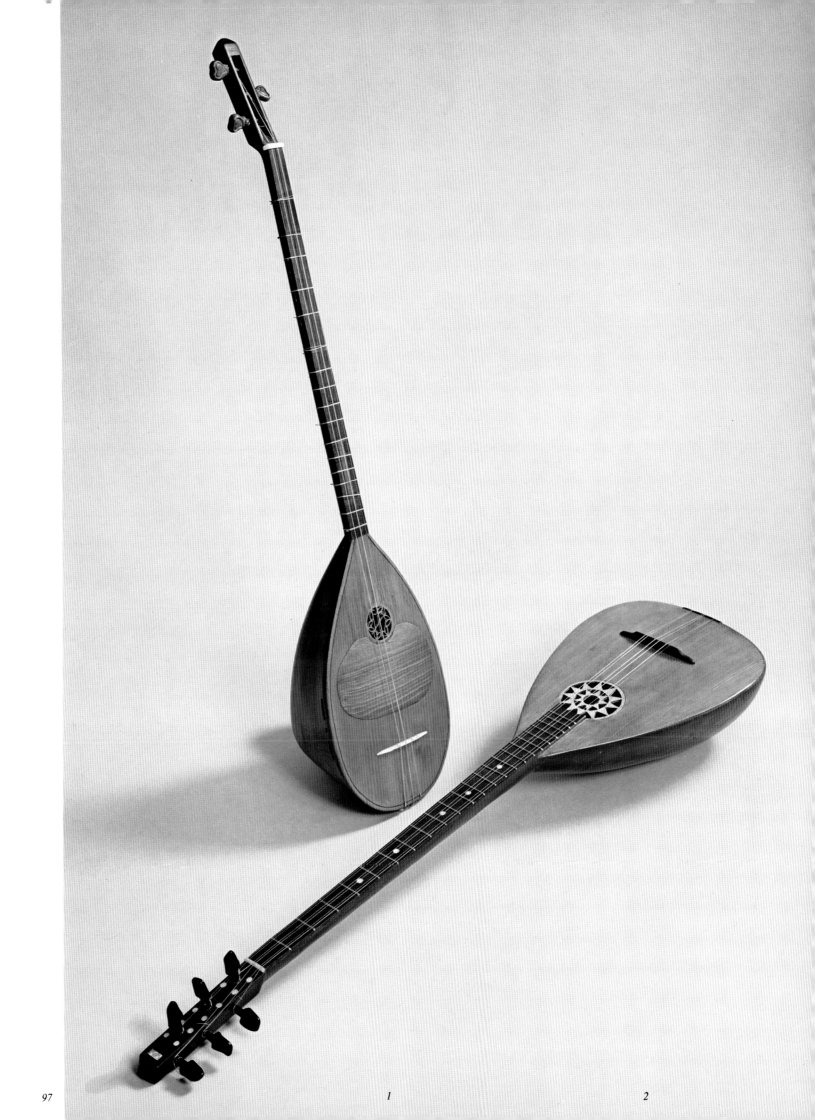

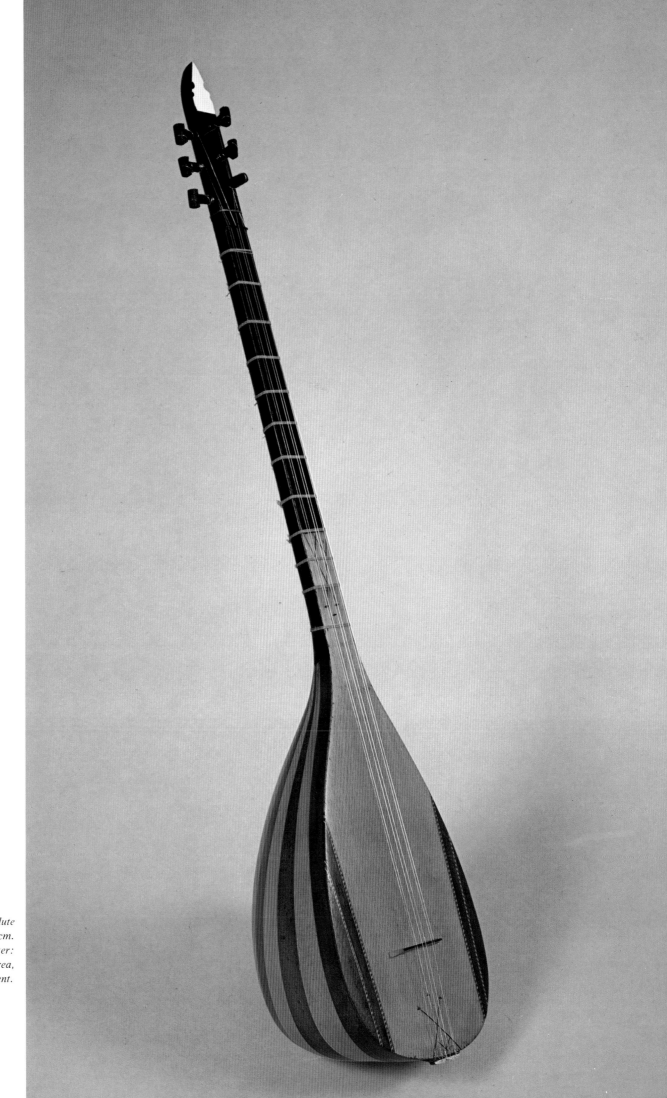

99.   *Bouzoúki (instrument of the lute family), 91 cm. long, body 18.5 cm. wide and 18 cm. deep. Lutemaker: Chr. Parassidis, Caesarea, Cappadocia. Early 20th cent.*

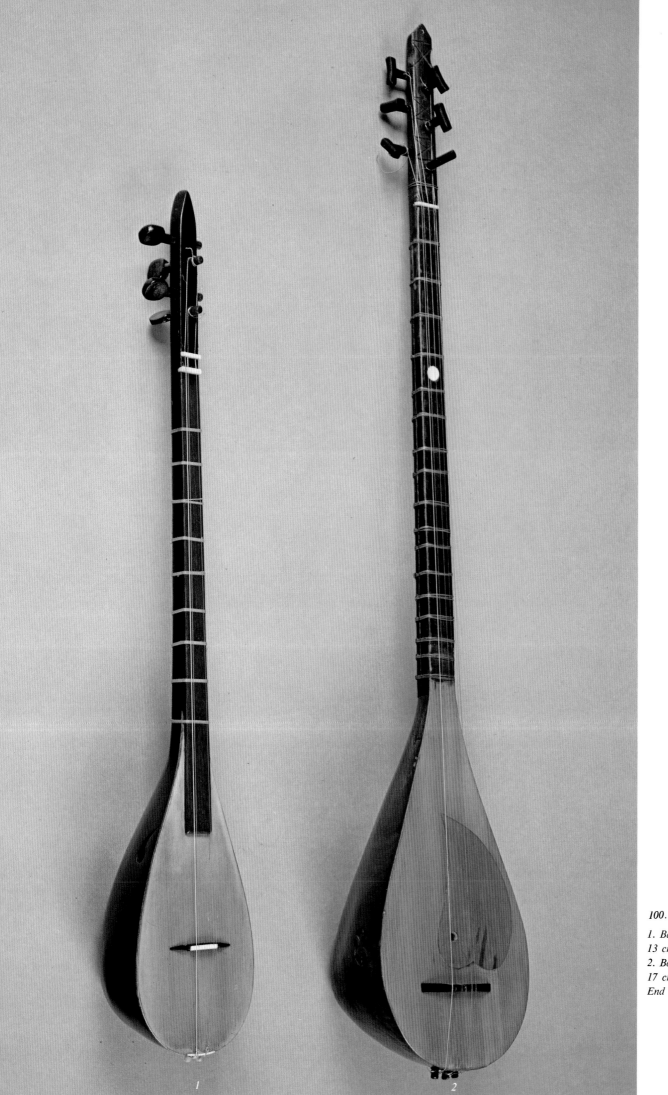

100.

1. Baghlamás, 71 cm. long, body
13 cm. wide and 11.5 cm. deep.
2. Bouzoúki, 93 cm. long, body
17 cm. wide and 15 cm. deep.
End 19th or early 20th cent.

of the *laghoúto* retain some moisture, as thus it remains pliable. This is necessary in the case of those instruments that have curved sections, and hence require 'ironing': these include the *laghoúto*, the *tambourás* (those instruments having soundboxes made of staves), and the guitar. Dry wood is used in the construction of those instruments that need no 'ironing', as they have no curved sections; these are the hollowed-out instruments, such as the pear-shaped *líra*, the hollowed-out *tambourás,* and others.

At one time, lute-makers followed a different procedure for drying out the wood instead of the natural method; the pieces of wood to be treated were boiled in brine, which, as the older makers of the instrument maintain, "prevented them from splitting". Some of the older lute-makers went so far as to purchase, at reduced prices, expensive, well-made furniture, constructed of high quality materials; they would then dismember the furniture in order to use the wood —mahogany, walnut, etc.— in order to make their instruments. This practice was adopted by one of the true masters of the craft, Manolis Venios of Constantinople, who died around the time of the First World War. The same is done today in Athens by Yiannis Paleologos (born 1904).[389]

After the table has been affixed to the body of the instrument, it is then decorated around the edges and around the rosette with inlaid fillets, or geometric figures as rhombi, triangles, squares, rectangles, diamonds, etc. Once executed in mother-of-pearl or ivory or precious woods, these decorative motifs are today carried out in ordinary wood or plastic. Such decoration as the carved arabesques of the rosette provide ample evidence of the influence of Oriental ornamental art.

Once the principal sections of the *laghoúto* (body, neck, and table) have been fitted together, the lute-maker completes the instrument with the finishing touches described below. The underside of the neck, first of all, is rounded so that the player's left hand can slide up and down more easily during performance, and the neck as a whole is cut down and trimmed to the desired length. When the neck is made of a single piece of wood, the rounded side is covered with thin strips of veneer, made of the same kind of wood as that of the staves of the body of the instrument. On the foremost part of the neck the fingerboard *(pláka),* a thin strip of ebony or another hardwood, is glued, covering the entire surface of the neck and extending to the edge of the table. The fingerboard is decorated along the edges of its entire length, with delicate wooden inlaid fillets or geometric designs. Apart from making the neck resemble more closely the body of the instrument, this wooden veneer also serves the more important function of protecting the neck from warping.

Following this, the pegbox *(karávolas)* is fitted and glued on to the uppermost part of the neck, four holes having been opened on each side to receive the eight pegs. These pegs, today similar to those of the mandolin, were formerly like those of the violin, and are generally known as the *striftária, striftália* (turners), or *kopília*. The pegbox is set at an obtuse angle to the instrument's neck; this enables the lutenist to tune his instrument with greater ease.[390]

The principal sections of the *laghoúto* are scraped with a metal rasp and smoothed with sandpaper, progressing in stages from coarse sandpaper to fine abrasive. The instrument is then ready to receive a few necessary additions to its basic state; it must be laquered with high-quality varnish, and its 'arsenal' of strings must be attached. Before either of the last two finishing touches can be made, the position on the table where the bridge is to be attached must be marked, and semitone intervals must be measured and marked off to indicate the positions of the eleven frets on the neck. The distance from the nut to the bridge should be twice that between the nut and the first cane fret, plus an additional 2-3 mm. For instance, should the distance between the nut and the first cane fret be 34 cm, then the distance between the nut and the bridge should be 0.683 m (0.34+0.34=0.003=0.683). This ensures that the instrument 'sings well' and that it doesn't give false notes. The 2 or 3 additional millimetres are a margin left when the bridge has been glued to the instrument's table. However well-constructed the instrument may be, a slight warping of the neck and table occur in time as a result of the constant tension of the strings. This invisible 'bellying' alters the correct distance between the nut

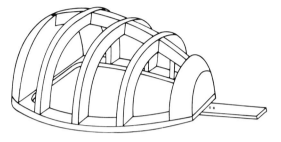

Fig. 151.

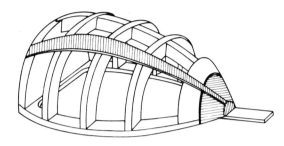

Fig. 152.

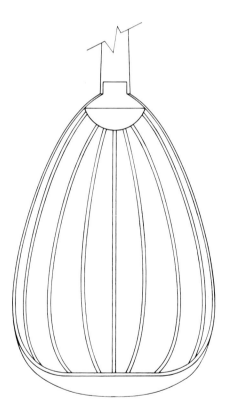

Fig. 153.

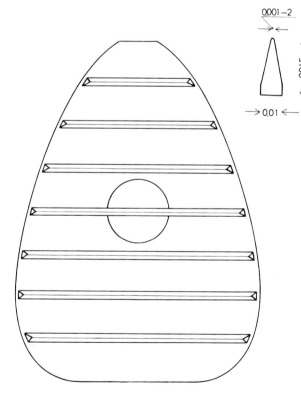

Fig. 154.

and the bridge, and consequently the accuracy of the notes emitted by the lute when the strings are plucked is lessened. In the course of the instrument's construction, the possibility of such an alteration is compensated for in advance; the bridge is attached to the table with an allowance of 2 or 3 mm from what would otherwise be its correct position.

The next step is the gluing of the so-called 'note-indicators' to the fingerboard; these are usually round in shape, and although today they made of plastic, they were formerly small pieces of ivory or mother-of-pearl. The first piece is placed between the second and third frets, the second piece between the sixth and seventh frets, and the third piece between the ninth and tenth frets. In addition, yet another 'note-indicator' is glued into position between the fourth and fifth frets: this is the so-called 'master' *(mástoris)*, and serves as an aid in the tuning of the strings. The lutenist stops the first or A-string at the 'master', thus giving D; he will tune the second string of his instrument to this D, but one octave lower. In the same manner, by stopping the D-string at the 'master' he obtains G, the note to which he will tune the third string, and so on. This method, whereby the entire set of strings is tuned, is primarily for the beginner lutenist; the instructor tells his student to "stop the *mástoris*". The experienced lutenist tunes his instrument entirely by ear alone.

Prior to varnishing the instrument, the lute-maker first cuts a small groove in the rounded underside of the neck. The ends of the frets are passed through this groove, and are tightly knotted to secure them in position. The actual varnishing of the instrument is preceded by a preparatory greasing of the body and the neck. The oil used for this "turns the wood to its proper colour", and makes it easier for the craftsman to slide the buffer —a ball of cotton wrapped in tulle— across the surfaces of the instrument. Without this initial application of oil to the wood "the ball (buffer) does not work". The actual varnish consists of a solution of gum arabic in alcohol. The correct way to apply the varnish is in stages, a little every day, so that the wood is allowed to "attract the polish" to itself. Each layer of varnish should be as thinly applied as possible. The best seasons of the year for varnishing are spring and autumn, as the lack of any moisture in the summer and the excessive humidity of the winter months is not conducive to the easy manipulation of the buffer on the part of the craftsman. Nowadays, the table of the *laghoúto* is polished with white laquer of western european manufacture, although in the past a mixture of gum arabic and alcohol was commonly used. The pegbox is painted black, the coulour consisting of aniline of alcohol mixed with varnish. The rosette is not lacquered at all, but is gilded; on older lutes it retained the natural colours of the material it was made from — tortoise-shell, bone, precious wood, etc.

After the instrument has been varnished, the bridge is glued to the table at the position previously marked out for this purpose. The guard *(tersés)* is glued into place between the rosette and the bridge. Today, the *tersés* is a thin sheet of plastic or hardwood —though it was once made of tortoise-shell, bone, or rare wood— which protects the table by preventing the plectrum from gouging out its surface during performance. At the upper end of the neck, at the point where the pegbox begins, the nut *(maxilári,* cushion) is attached. Eight grooves are made upon this accessory, which may be of ivory, bone, or hardwood, to take the strings. The nut must be high enough (2-3 mm) to prevent the strings, after they have been fitted to the instrument, from resting upon the frets. Finally, the eleven frets are positioned and then tied in place at the points previously measured and marked out for them.

The frets *(berdédhes),* nowadays made of plastic instead of the gut or silk thread *(brissími)* of bygone times, are positioned at intervals of one semitone from each other.[391] Although they are tightly fastened to the neck, they can in fact be shifted, thus compensating for the possible warping of the instrument. In the event such warping takes place, the lutenist moves them either up or down according to the nature of the deformation, and the instrument once again "sings well". In other words, it once again produces the correct intervals, which had been altered by the changing of the distances between the frets as a result of the warping of the wood. In the past, these moveable frets served another and more important function: by shifting their positions, any lutenist who was well versed in musical tradition had at his disposal the intervals of

Byzantine music, and of eastern music in general — the soft scales with minor tone (smaller than the western tone 9:10), minim-minor tone (greater than the western semitone 15:16), with the enharmonic diesis, the leimma etc.[392] All of the above are intervals that are gradually becoming an ever rarer feature of folk song today and in the playing of instruments of the lute family (see *natural* and *tempered scales, Introduction*). Heavier material is used for the first two frets than for the remaining nine; the first fret is the thickest, the second fret less so, and the others are even less thick than the second fret. Thus, when the player's finger stops a string at the first fret, the string does not touch the second fret. In the same manner, when a string is stopped at the second fret, it does not touch the third. It is not necessary for the other frets to be made of different thicknesses; because of the height of the bridge, the strings do not touch any frets lower that at which they are stopped.[393] After the frets have been fixed in position, the instrument is then 'armed' (according to a popular Greek expression) with a set of strings.

Once the strings have been attached to the *laghoúto,* in continuation of the series of moveable frets *(berdédhes)* described above, eight or more cane frets *(kalamákia)* are glued to the table, the varnish having first been scraped away from the designated areas. Like the moveable frets, the fixed frets are spaced at semitone intervals. On the A-string, the last fret on the base of the neck gives G sharp (first above middle C), and the first *kalamáki* gives the A immediately above this on the same string. The last *kalamáki* on this string gives the second E above middle C. The *kalamákia* are made from common cane, range in length from 6-7 cm and in width from 3-5 mm, and are glued to the table with their shiny surfaces upwards. The strict accuracy with which the frets and *kalamákia* are placed in position is finally tested by ear; the instrument is played, while at the same time the positions of the frets are shifted slightly should it prove necessary. A small quantity of wax or a small wooden button is glued to both ends of each *kalamáki;* this ensures that the player's fingers will not rub against them when the instrument is played.

Finally, a thin piece of skin *(petsáki),* ranging in length from approximately 15-17 cm and 3-4 cm wide, is glued to the base of the instrument at the place where the table and the body are joined together. This piece of skin prevents the perspiration of the right hand, which rests continually upon this part of the instrument, from penetrating the table, which would thereby become detached from the body.

The plectrum *(pénna)* used to play the *laghoúto* is usually made from the feather of a bird of prey — hawk, eagle, or vulture; in the event that neither of these can be found, it can be fashioned from the feather of a turkey or from plastic. Those plectra fashioned from the feathers of birds of prey are considered to be superior, as they are not only more durable, but, by virtue of their softness, they produce a sweeter sound. The quill of an eagle's feather is rather hard, and breaks the easiest. Such quills from the feathers of birds of prey have two sides, one of which is dark in colour, almost black, while the other side is white. When the plumes have been stripped and the quill is bare, the black part is separated from the white by means of a small knife; the two sections become two plectra. Each plectrum is bent double so that the lutenist, when playing his instrument, can strike the strings both on the downward and upward strokes, always with the smooth, bone-like side of the plectrum. The white plectrum is considered superior to that made from the darker side of the quill, as it is softer and more flexible, thus producing a sweeter sound. In the past, skilled lutenists would use the white plectrum when they wanted to play softly for a few revellers, and would play with the darker plectrum when long hours of hard playing at village festivals was called for. A lutenist will always keep by his side one or two plectra in reserve. Should he have other plectra, not to be used in the immediate future, he will keep them in oil to preserve their softness and flexibility. He will do the same should he have several feathers at hand, to be made into plectra at some future time. He will cut off a little of the hollow bases of the quills (the ends that are embedded in the flesh of the bird), fill the hollow quills with oil, and then hang them upside down. The oil then gradually seeps throughout the pith of the quill, which extend for a good part of its length, thus preserving the softness of the feathers.

Playing technique

The lutenist *(laoutiéris, laghoutiéris, laghouthiéris, laoutáris, lavoutáris, laghoutáris, laghoútatzis)*
is also known in Greece as the 'bass-player' *(bassadhóros, passadhóros)* as he "holds the bass".
When playing his instrument he sits with one leg crossed over the other, resting the soundbox on his chest and the uppermost part of his thighs. He also, upon occasion, plays his instrument in an upright position, as he walks, as in the case of weddings or the singing of early
morning *patinádhes* (distichs), etc. In the latter instances, the lutenist suspends his instrument
across his chest, or from his lapel, by means of a ribbon or rope, attached to a small ring nailed
to the block of wood where the neck and the body of the instrument are joined.

The *laghoúto* produces sound when its strings are struck with the plectrum, both in downward strokes and upward strokes. The lutenist holds the plectrum between his thumb and forefinger, with its tail between his forefinger and his middle finger. The skilled lutenist achieves
a good sound by never tightening his grip on the plectrum, and by allowing his wrist to move
freely and relaxedly. Should he tighten his arm or hand, the sound becomes harsh; this has the
added disadvantage of tiring the performer the more quickly.

Tuning the laghoúto

The *laghoúto* is always tuned in fifths: A, D, G, C, the first (A) string being one octave below
the A of a tuning-fork. Of the four pairs of strings, only the first pair is tuned in unison; the
other pairs are tuned to intervals of one octave each. Nevertheless, instruments with the third
pair of strings tuned in unison are frequently to be met with. In general, everything that has
already been said concerning the tuning of popular melodic instruments holds true for the *laghoúto* as well. The lutenist is invariably concerned with the relation between the intervals,
rather than with the absolute pitch of the notes given by the instruments' four double strings.
For this reason, in the past, the *laghoúto* was not tuned to the A of the tuning-fork. As a rule,
the A of the *laghoúto* was lower than that of the tuning-fork, and was determined instead by
the A of the instrument with which it was played in combination, usually a violin or *líra*. *Ziyiés*
consisting of violin and *laghoúto*, or *líra* and *laghoúto*, have been encountered in which the
tuning gave an A somewhere between a semitone and one-and-one-half tones, or even two
whole tones, lower than that of the tuning-fork.

For the popular musicians of a bygone age, the middle register of the Greek vocalist served
as a tuning-fork.[394] This was true up until the Second World War. After the war, first the *companía* of violin, clarinet, lute and dulcimer *(violí, klaríno, laghoúto, sandoúri)*, and then the
smaller instrumental groups, such as the island *ziyiá* of violin and lute *(violí, laghoúto)*, and
the pear-shaped *líra* accompanied by the *laghoúto*, gradually began to tune their instruments
higher and higher. And today, the *companíes* that work together with different recently created
'popular' dance groups all tune their instruments to the A of the tuning-fork.[395] This higher
tuning, together with the change to industrially produced metal strings, has altered the sound
of the *laghoúto*. It has now acquired a harshness, a sharp metallic tone, characteristics which
were never to be found in the case of the "sweet-voiced *laghoúto*" of yesteryear, with its low
tuning and its gut strings.

The strings of the *laghoúto* were formerly all made of gut. Gradually, however, side by
side with these, metal strings came widely into use. Such strings, the so-called *télia* (wires),
were used only for the higher strings; today, metallic strings are used exclusively for all the
instruments' strings, both *télia* and *chrysés* (strings made of metal-wrapped wire, or 'gilt'
strings).

Technical and musical possibilities

The intensity of the sound produced by his instrument depends upon the lutenist's playing.
Gentle playing of the *laghoúto* gives a sweet, but not very 'full' sound, with two principal variations of intensity, *piano* or *forte*. When the instrument is played harshly, the sound produced

is louder, only *forte*. The use of the terms *forte* and *piano* to indicate a greater or lesser volume of sound should not, however, be understood in the same sense of the dynamics of classical music, as the progressive intensity of sound from *piano* to *forte* and vice versa. The popular lutenist quite simple plays softly or loudly, gently or harshly, depending upon the singer he accompanies, whether the space he performs in is enclosed or in the open air, whether he is accompanied by another instrument, or by several instruments, etc. Skilled lutenists —those who were taught to play by renowned performers on the lute, and who closely adhere to the tradition of their instrument— are capable of varying the timbre of the sound of their instruments according to the nature of the song or dance they happen to be accompanying. Such nuances of timbre can be achieved in different manners: from the way in which the plectrum attacks the strings (angle of attack); the degree of tightness with which the plectrum is held; the sharp and rapid or gentle and relaxed plucking of the strings with the plectrum; the place at which the plectrum attacks the strings (towards the base of the body or close to the rosette); or again, when the lutenist, desiring to lend certain notes of the melody a special intensity of expression, achieves a slightly quavering effect —a kind of vibrato— by moving the left-hand finger in stopping the string behind a given fret. The last refers primarily to the older, *prima-dhóri* (see below).

The *laghoúto* encompasses a melodic range of two octaves and a sixth. The extent of the instrument's range, however, is more theoretical than real, in that today's *laghoúto* is principally played for purposes of accompaniment. It provides both rhythmical and harmonic accompaniment for the melodic instruments *par excellence —violí, líra, klaríno—* and is itself restricted at the melodic level, where it merely 'doubles' or 'replies' (in the words of the popular lutenists themselves) to a few brief phrases handed down from the principal melody, and mainly played in the middle sound range of the instrument.

When played for accompaniment, the *laghoúto* is the instrument that "keeps the rhythm"; in other words, it maintains the metre with its different rhythmical patterns. Over the framework thus provided, the periodic repetition of a single rhythmical pattern, the vocalist or violinist will freely ornament the melody with different embellishments, always, however, within the strictly defined tempo marked out by the lutenist. During performance, the lutenist is in continuous communication with the vocalist, the leading dancer, and his fellow musicians; his playing is influenced by their artistry just as it influences the latter in turn. The rich and skillfull ornamentation of the melody by the vocalist and the violinist or clarinettist or *líra*-player, the beauty and expressiveness of the vocalist's voice, the ease and daring of the leading dancer's inspired movements — all of these have a decisive effect on the lutenist, lending both vigour and effervescence to his playing. For all his strict adherence to the rhythm and tempo of each measure played, his rhythmical accompaniment does acquire a certain flexibility. The lutenist closely follows and 'participates' in the singing and dancing, and in the performance of his fellow musicians. He may play his instrument brusquely, tautly; or he may play quietly, caressingly. He might add intermediate 'pen-strokes' *(peniés)*, tremoli; he might 'double' the melody depending upon his inclinations and the mood of the moment. He might exhort the vocalist with introductory interjections, and spur on his fellow-musicians and the dancers to even more enthusiasm. All of these and many other similar devices are never conceived in advance; they all invariably depend upon the infectious atmosphere an accomplished dancer, an expert clarinettist, or a happily inspired vocalist can create when people are gathered together to make merry.

A great number of rhythmical patterns are to be found in the accompaniment provided by the *laghoúto* in the hands of a skilled performer. The melodies of a *periodic rhythmical type* are accompanied by the *laghoúto* with rhythmical patterns analogous to the intrinsic rhythm of the song or dance being performed. For melodies of *free rhythmical type,* such as the so-called table-songs *(tís távlas)* (generally performed by a seated gathering, at feast), the lutenist occasionally provides a drone by means of notes repeated at a slow tempo or as a tremolo; for others, he plays simple chord accompaniments at the opening of each phrase. He will also play a number of phrases derived from the melody as solo passages, when the melody is played instrumentally without the vocalist.

In the past, the harmonic accompaniment provided by the lute was restricted to a simple drone (*isokrátis,* pedal). The scales in which the principal melodic instruments (*violí, líra, klaríno,* etc.) played the different songs and dances were usually D, G, and C; these correspond to the D, G, and C strings of the *laghoúto.* Thus the lutenist was able to accompany the melody with ease, maintaining the drone *(íson),* on either one, two, or all three of the strings just mentioned. The harmonic accompaniment thus provided by the *laghoúto* consisted of a single tonic drone, a double drone in the tonic and the dominant or subdominant (to use the terminology of western music), or yet a more complex, multiple drone. This simultaneous sounding of an octave, a perfect fifth or a perfect fourth was consistent with the modal character of popular monophonic melody, retaining as they did the latter's traditional modal structure. In this ancient type of harmonic accompaniment, one can also recognise the drone *(íson)* of Byzantine music; of a music that shares many features in common with folk song in the intervals and scales that make up the latter.[396]

Today, the opposite holds true as far as the harmonic accompaniment provided by the *laghoúto* is concerned. The introduction of western harmonisation has altered the traditional style of Greek monophonic folk melody. This is especially true in the case of older tunes; in contrast to their modal structure, frequently based on tetrachords, these have been forced into a harmonisation based on the seven-tone major and minor scales of western european music.

In the fingering of the present day harmonic accompaniment provided by the *laghoúto,* the lutenist uses all four fingers and the thumb of his left hand, in different combinations, according to the nature of the harmony he wishes to provide.

The *laghoúto,* as an instrument providing both rhythmical and harmonic accompaniment, is in general use throughout all of Greece, especially in the islands, in coastal towns, and in the villages, where it appears at every kind of folk entertainment: festivals, weddings, baptisms, saints' days, etc. It is also to be heard in a very few popular taverns in such large cities as Athens, Piraeus and Thessaloniki, et alia, where for a few hours every evening folk music is played and sung for those who have not yet been completely cut off from the traditional forms of folk song — village dwellers visiting the city for business, and those victims of the city's lure who, for all their long years of residence in the different urban centres of Greece, have nevertheless remained spiritually close to the life of the village and its musical traditions.

Restricted to an instrument of accompaniment today, the *laghoúto* invariably requires the presence of a melodic instrument such as the *violí,* the *líra,* the *klaríno* and the *sandoúri.* Up until the present day, there have been two principal types of combination of the *laghoúto* with the different melodic instruments commonly to be found in the country. The first is the so-called *ziyiá,* consisting of the *laghoúto* in combination with either the violin or the pear-shaped *líra.* The second type of combination is the *companía* or *coumpanía,* the primary instrumental ensemble of mainland Greece; this ensemble consists of the clarinet, violin, lute, dulcimer *(klaríno, violí, laghoúto* and *sandoúri),* and is often joined by a vocalist (when one of the instrumentalists does not sing). The vocalist, either male or female, usually plays the tambourine *(défi)* as well.

Primadhóri lutenists

Its long neck and the frets, which extend upon the table almost as far as the instrument's rosette, indicate that the Greek *laghoúto,* today solely an instrument of accompaniment, was in the past a melodic instrument as well. The living proof of this was once to be found among the *primadhóri,* old-time lutenists, whose primacy and expertise was reflected by their name. They were capable of astonishing virtuosity: "The skilled *primadhóros* transformed the *laghoúto* into a violin". Such a musician would play entire dance melodies alone —without the aid of any melodic instrument, *violí* or *klaríno*— by dint of great technical dexterity in the left hand;

239

the same lutenist also simultaneously provided his own accompaniment. The melody as such was generally played on the first (A) string, along its entire range. The left hand would move up and down the instrument's neck with great dexterity, covering the full range of frets —including the *kalamákia*— as far as the rosette. At that time, the *kalamákia* served functionally as the moveable frets of the instrument's high register, unlike the *laghoúto* of the present day, where the fixed frets are merely decorative.[397] With the remaining three open strings —D, G, and C— the lutenist provided the harmonic accompaniment in the form of a simple, double, or multiple drone. However skilled a *primadhóros* may have been, he could never provide the entire musical entertainment for any festivities lasting many hours. His achievement, compared to what could have been wrought had he played together with another melodic instrument, was relatively poor. For this reason, he would usually play together with a violin, 'doubling' its part; in other words, the *laghoúto* and the violin would play the same melody simultaneously. When the violin stopped for some reason —to change a string or give the violinist a rest— the dancing and singing would continue to the music of the solo *laghoúto*. Today, *primadhóri* as such are nowhere to be found; those who are still alive have either retired years ago from the musical profession, or play the *laghoúto* only to provide a rhythmical and harmonic accompaniment for other instruments.

The laghoúto in the Greek world

According to the classification devised by ethnomusicology, the lute family of instruments includes all instruments possessing the following features: a soundbox, a neck with strings stretched parallel to the soundboard and to the neck itself, and which are played either with the fingers or with a plectrum *(pénna)*. A host of instruments, in other words, with significant differences between them, such as the *tambourás*, the *laghoúto*, the *oúti*, the *bouzoúki* and the *baghlamás*, the guitar, the mandolin, etc. Organologically speaking, all of these instruments can be divided into two basic categories — the long lutes and the short lutes.

Long-necked lutes, characterised by their small soundbox and long neck, are the most ancient members of the lute family (third millenium B.C., Mesopotamia). To this category belong the ancient Greek *tríchordhon* or *pandhoúra* (see *tambourás*).[398] Short-necked lutes, with a small soundbox continuing into a short neck without any distinction between the two parts, can be traced as far back as the eighth century B.C., where such instruments are represented in Elamite art.[399] Also belonging to the subdivision of short-necked lutes are those lutes with a large, pear-shaped soundbox and a short, separate neck, bent backwards, such as the Arabian lute, which is also to be found in Greece (see *oúti*). The Arabian lute was introduced to Europe following the conquest of Spain in the eighth century.

The present day Greek *laghoúto*, with its large, pear-shaped soundbox and long neck, is a relatively recent variant of the instrument; it was developed around the seventeenth century, probably in the Greek world. Morphologically, it is an amalgam of elements taken from the two basic types of *laghoúto*. From the first type, the long-necked *laghoúto* with small soundbox and long neck, the Greek lute of today retains the long neck; from the second type of lute, the short-necked *laghoúto* with large soundbox and short neck, it takes the large soundbox. In essence, the Greek *laghoúto* is a kind of *tambourás*; a *tambourás* retaining its traditional long, fretted neck, but with a large, pear-shaped soundbox derived from the Arabian lute ('ūd),[400] instead of the traditionally small, pear-shaped, round, or ovoid soundbox. The alteration described above took place for reasons of the quality of sound. The large soundbox of the *laghoúto* "better cultivates the voice", it "makes the instrument sing out better", claim the lutenists of yesteryear.[401]

Nor is it a matter of chance that the *laghoúto* is still known as the *tambourás* in certain regions of Greece. This, not only today or in the recent past, but long ago, as we are informed

101.   Lute and tambourás. "Chanteurs grecs". Drawn by Théodore Leblanc, 19th cent. Benaki Museum, Athens.

Marinaro Greco

L.tº Cuciniello, e Bianchi

102.   Lute. "Marinaro greco". Stackelberg, Costumes et usages des peuples de la Grèce moderne, Rome 1825.

104. Lute and nakers. Wall-painting: Praise ye the Lord (?) (detail), 17th cent.
Monastery of St. John the Baptist (Timiou Prodromou), Serres.

103. Shawm, lira (?), lute. Wall-painting: Jesus is mocked (detail), 16th cent.
← Varlaam Monastery, Katholikon, Meteora.

105. Lute. Wall-painting: Parable of Dives and Lazarus (detail), 16th-17th cent.,
Loukous Monastery, Astros, Kynouria.

106. Bouzoúki (instrument of the lute family) decorated with mother of pearl,
93 cm. long, body 25 cm. wide and 16 cm. deep. End 19th cent. →

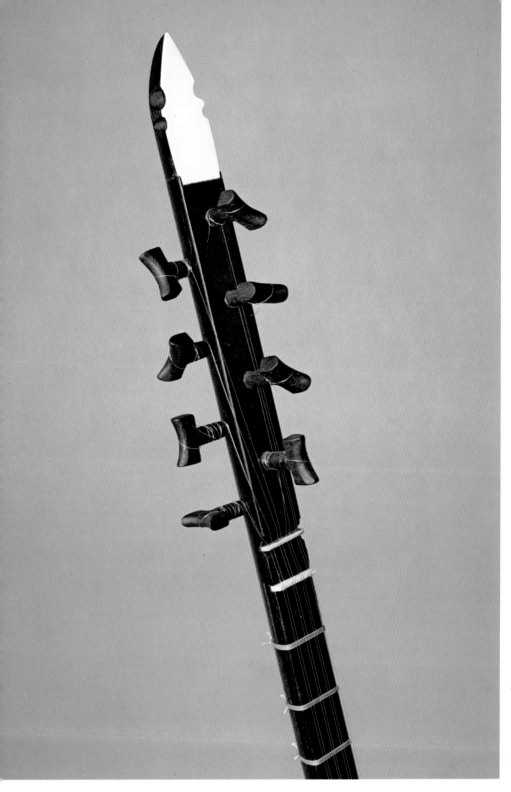

108. *Tambourás (instrument of the lute family),*
136 cm. long, body 30 cm. wide and 19 cm. deep.
Second half of 19th cent. →

107. *Pegboard of tambourás ((pl. 108).*

109.   Pear-shaped bowed three-stringed-instrument, 11th cent. Codex B26, f. 209 v. Great Lavra Monastery, Mount Athos.

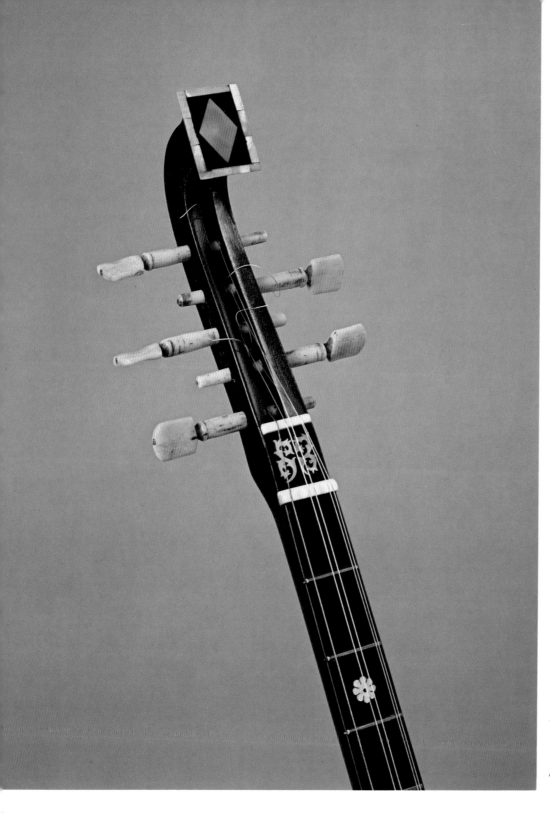

111. *Pegbox of baghlamás* *(pl. 112)*.

110. *Small tambourás. Wall-painting by Theophilos (detail), early 20th cent. Greek Folk Art Museum, Athens.*

←

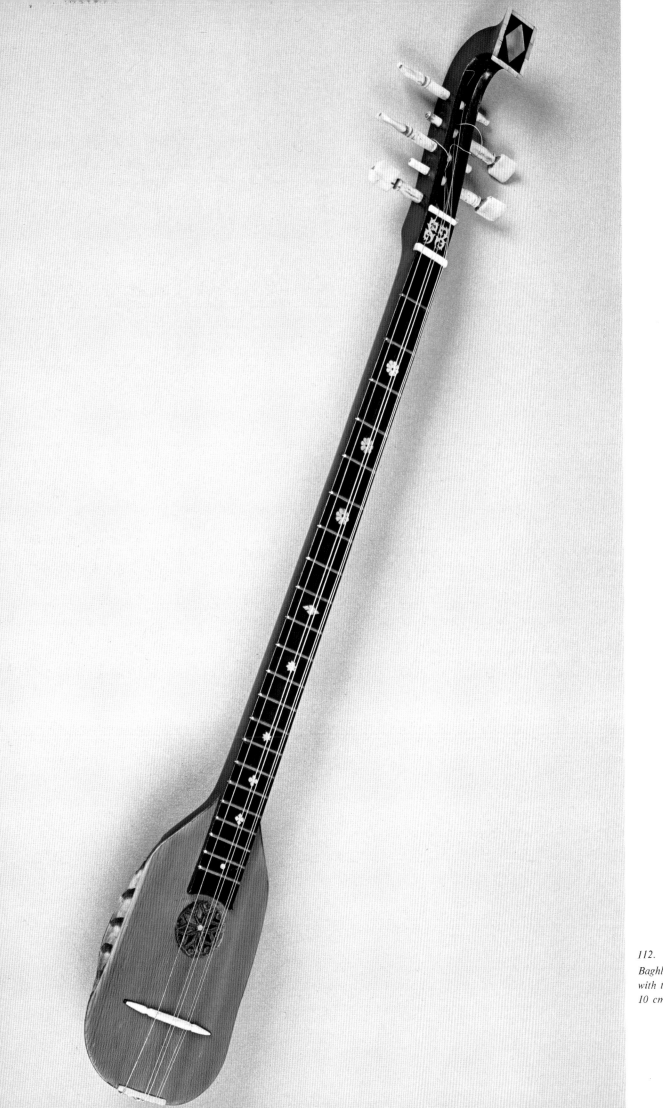

112.
*Baghlamás (instrument of the lute family)
with tortoise-shell soundbox, 76 cm. body
10 cm. wide and 6 cm. deep (1955).*

113. *Baghlamás (instrument of the lute family) with tortoise-shell soundbox, 43 cm. long, body 9 cm. wide and c. 6 cm. deep. Lutemaker: Georgios Panaghis, Aidonokhori, Epirus (1939).*

114. *Baghlamás (instrument of the lute family) with tortoise-shell soundbox, 50 cm. long, body 14.5 cm wide and 9 cm. deep. Inter-War years.*

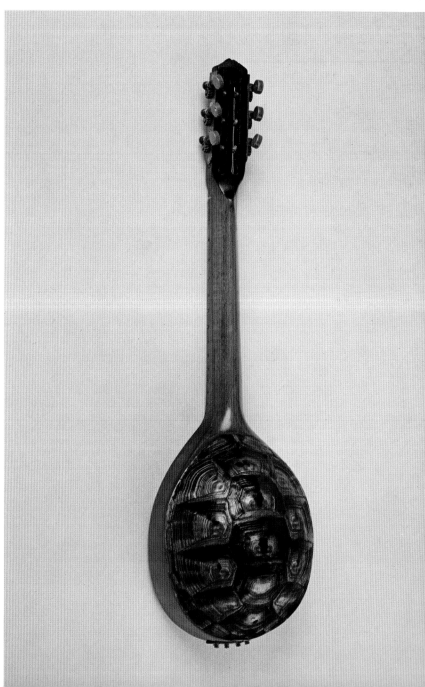

115.116. Baghlamás (instrument of the lute family) with gourd soundbox, 58 cm. long, body 15 cm. wide and 8 cm. deep. Lutemaker: Manolis Vlachakis or Maliotis, Iraklion, Crete, 1955 (front and rear).

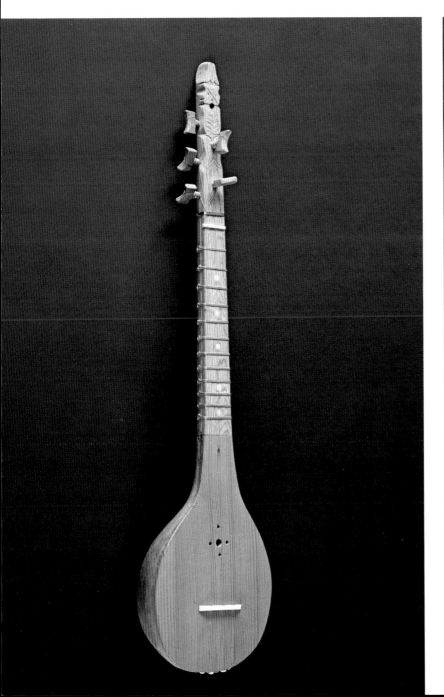 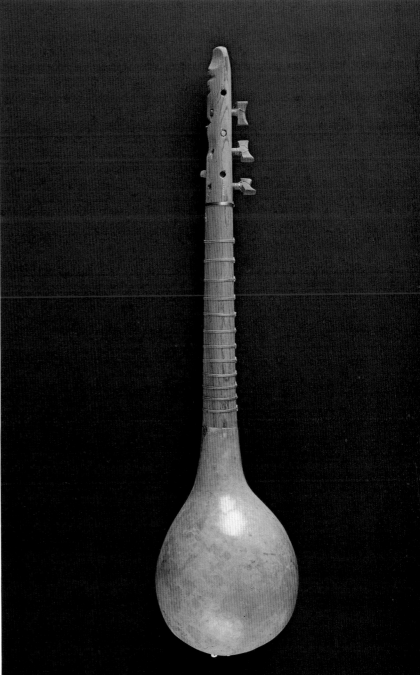

117. *Psaltery (kanonáki), tuning key, plectra and thimbles, wide base 92 cm. long, narrow base 29 cm. long, 37.5 cm.*
high. End 19th or early 20th cent.

119. *Baghlamádhes (instruments of the lute family): 1. 41.5 cm. long, body 7 cm. wide and 5 cm. deep. 2. 38.5 cm. long, body 8.5 cm. wide and 6 cm. deep. 3. 53 cm. long, body 6.5 cm. wide and 7 cm. deep. Inter-War years.*

→

118. *Dulcimer (sandoúri) and wooden sticks. Wide base 90 cm. long, narrow base 62 cm. long, 41 cm. high.*

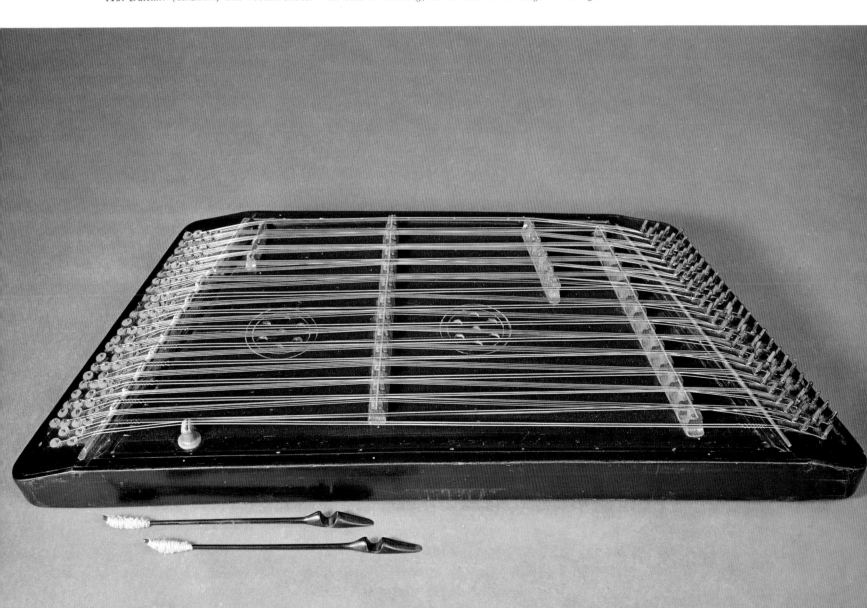

by the akritic Epic. In the Escorial manuscript (16th century), the lute is mentioned variously as the *lavoúto,* the *thamboúri,* the *tamboúri (tambourás).* In the passage where Digenis prepares to seek the fair maiden, the two terms *tamboúri* and *lavoúto* are used interchangeably for the same instrument, as is made clear from the sense of the text:

> *He jumped up and mounted his steed, and took his sword,*
> *And he took his tamboura (tamboúri) and readied it for play,*
> *And as he struck his lute (lavoúto), he sang like a nightingale.*[402]

The soundbox of the Greek *laghoúto* underwent a number of morphological alterations before finally assuming its present day form. In the past, influenced by the pear-shaped sound-box of the *tambourás,* the body of the instrument continued into the neck without any sign of a break between the two sections. With the passage of time, however, the neck became increasingly more distinct from the instrument's soundbox, which nonetheless has retained its pear-shaped outline up until the present day. The *laghoúto* without this clear distinction between neck and soundbox is no longer to be found today. Such instruments are known to us through iconographical sources (miniatures, wall-paintings, etc.), from photographic evidence, as well as information provided by older musicians. The same sources inform us that in the past the soundbox of the *laghoúto* was made in different sizes, with a wider or narrower base and greater or lesser in depth. The last, substantial change in the evolution of the Greek *laghoúto* concerned the neck of the instrument, and took place after the First World War, around 1920.

During that period, certain lutenists gradually abandoned the traditional, simple harmonic accompaniment provided by their instruments, and began to adapt to western harmonisation (tonic – fifth – tonic). In order to play these chords with greater ease, they shortened the neck of the *laghoúto* by some 2-2.5 cm. This shortening of the instrument's neck brought the intervals closer to each other and facilitated the fingering of the chords. Several musical 'influences' played a significant role in the movement towards western harmony: the so-called 'light music', which slowly but surely began to conquer first the larger cities, then the smaller cities and finally even the villages; the recently introduced jazz music; revue and operetta, with their oriental and pseudo-folk melodies; the foreign popular music groups (primarily those from Roumania and Hungary), with their harmonised popular melodies; and the grammophone record, that new means of communication which from the moment of its introduction began to replace live music at festivities, weddings, etc.[403]

The following are references to the *laghoúto* culled from popular poetry and literature. From an akritic song of Asia Minor:[404]

> *Bring me my lute (laghoúto) with its silver strings,*
> *That I may sing sorrowfully, and weep bitterly.*

From the Epic of Digenis (Escorial manuscript, 16th century):[405]

> *And he sat and made a fine, sweet-sounding lute (lavoúto).*

> *I have taken up my lute (lavoúto), and I will gently pluck its strings.*

From the anonymous *In Praise of Women* (early 16th century):[406]

> *And they want naught else*
> *save they beautify themselves*
> *and look upon men*
> *and hear them sing,*
> *and the lutes (lavoúta) they strike.*

From the *Lament of Phallidus the Poor* (17th century):[407]

> *Day and night I was with the musicians*
> *in the alleys and in the market-places,*
> *zithers (tsíteres), violins (violiá), lutes (laghoúta),*
> *harps (hárpes), bass (bássa) and flutes (fiaoúta),*
> *kladhotsímbana (?), trumpets (troumbétes),*
> *and now I compose verses...*

From the many verses of Vitsentzos Kornaros' *Erotokritos* (17th century) where the praises of the *laghoúto* are hymned, we give a mere five lines, all notable as well for their exquisite poetic expressiveness:[408]

> *He took his laghoúto and slowly walked along,*
> *and struck it most sweetly on his way to the palace.*

> *And this singer, this lutenist (laghoutáris),*
> *has a great power, has a great gift of grace.*

> *The strings of his laghoúto are birds that sing.*

The following surnames are derived from the professional *'laoutiéris'*: Laghoútos, Laghou-táris, Laghoútis, Laghoutiéris, Laoútas, Laoutatzís, Laoutáris, Laoutiéris, Lavoútas.[409]

OUTI (Short-necked Lute)

The *oúti* (from the Arabic *'ūd,* meaning wood) has a large, pear-shaped soundbox, a short, wide neck without frets, a head almost at right-angles to the neck, and lateral pegs. It is play-ed with a plectrum, or *pénna,* formerly fashioned from the bark of the cherry tree, or from ox-horn, but today generally made of plastic. The instrument is usually equipped with five pair of gut strings, each pair of which is tuned in unison. These are fastened to the bridge on the soundboard, and are tuned in fourths excepting the lowest-pitched string, which is tuned to an interval of one tone from its immediate neighbour. The manufacture of this instrument fol-lows the same procedure as that of the *laghoúto* (q.v.).

The *oúti* is played throughout Greece only to a limited extent. It was exclusively played by the Greeks of Asia Minor and Constantinople, who were ignorant of the Greek long-necked lute. In the wake of the Greco-Turkish War of 1922 and the subsequent exchange of ethnic pop-ulations between the two countries, the presence of the *oúti* in Greece was more widespread, especially at those feasts of the Asia Minor refugees and among those musical groups that also performed Turkish music. This never at any time affected the position occupied by the long-necked lute in Greece; the latter instrument remained firmly entrenched in the country, and at the present day continues to hold sway as the principal rhythmic and harmonic instrument of both the island *ziyiá* and the mainland *companía.*

LAOUTOKITHARA (Lute-guitar)

The *laoutokithára* (*laoúto,* lute; *kithára,* guitar) is a hybrid instrument of mixed ancestry; it is guitar-like in shape, but has the same number of strings and the same tuning as the *laghoúto.* The *laoutokithára* first appeared in Greece following the Second World War for two reasons: younger Greek lutenists were embarrassed at having to carry about so large and 'ugly' an instrument as they felt the *laghoúto* to be, and they were delighted with the ease with which the less unwieldy *laoutokithára* could be carried about and held during performance.

At the time when the *laoutokithára* first appeared upon the Greek musical scene, the true guitar had already been irrevocably established as the accompanist's instrument in the popular *rebétiko* group of song. Today, however, the *laoutokithára* is itself gradually dying out. Lutenists who decide to abandon the *laghoúto* —as happens ever more frequently— tend to change directly to the guitar proper, without passing through the intermediate stage represented by the *laoutokithára*.

MANDOLINO and KITHARA (Mandolin and Guitar)

The mandolin *(mandolíno)* and the guitar *(kithára)*, both members of the lute family,[410] do not, of course, belong to the popular *instrumentarium* of modern Greece. If they are mentioned here, that is because they have been played and continue to be played in the realm of folk music — the former as a melodic instrument, the latter solely as an accompanying instrument. The guitar has proved particularly important, insofar as in the years after the Second World War it has gradually been replacing the lute *(laghoúto)* in the two traditional Greek instrumental groups, the island *ziyiá* and the mainland *companía*.

When the *laghoúto* has been replaced by the guitar in this manner, the musical style of the folk song is transformed. With its sweet sound and different technique, the guitar infuses a misleading romanticism to Greek folk music, uncharacteristic of the pure folk songs and their traditional rendition. Without the restraining influence of the *laghoúto*, through its sound, its technique, and its 'psychology', as it were, as a traditional and well-tried instrument, Greek folk song has gradually acquired an all-persuasive harmonisation quite foreign to its nature. The islanders' songs have begun to acquire the tone of Italianate love-songs *(cantádhes)*, while the songs from Chimara (Epirus), Macedonia and Thrace, both the 'heavy' and the 'lighter' songs, are gradually losing their austere colour or their characteristic inner gaiety.

The mandolin and the guitar, as well as the *mandóla* and the *mandolocéllo* (the last two instruments are rarely used in folk song) were formerly made by the same craftsmen who made the lute-type members of the popular *instrumentarium*, the *laghoúto* and the various kinds of *tambourás*. Nowadays, the *mandóla* and the *mandolocéllo* are no longer manufactured in Greece; only guitars and —very rarely— mandolins are still made in the country.

LIRA (Pear-shaped Fiddle)

The *líra*[411] has a pear-shaped, hollowed-out soundbox and a short neck, without frets; the neck continues from the soundbox, and is equipped with rear pegs. The instrument also is fitted with a bridge, and is equipped with three single chords attached to the lower edge of the body, the tailpiece, or to a stringholder (*kténi*, comb); it is played with a bow. The *líra* is usually fashioned by the player himself, in different sizes, according to the dimensions of the wood he is able to find, his own bodily measurements (tall or short, with long or short fingers), and depending upon the 'voice' he wants his instrument to have — high and penetrating, or somewhat rougher and deeper. Fig. 155 lists the names given to the different parts of the *líra*, while fig. 156 gives the dimensions of the instrument culled from the measurement of over one hundred and fifty líres, representing all the regions of Greece and ranging from 1743 to the present day.[412]

Construction

To make the soundbox (*skáfi*, trough), neck (*chéri*, handle), and head *(kepháli)* of the *líra*, a single piece of wood is used, the most common being mulberry, oleander, pear, walnut, chestnut, maple, beech, plum, cypress, etc. Mulberry, ivy and wild pear are considered the best woods,

259

those that produce "a good voice" — "mulberry", it is said, "doesn't readily absorb moisture". The soundboard of the *líra* is usually made of coniferous wood, such as pine. As for the degree of dryness of the wood and the preferred methods of treating the wood, the reader is referrep to the relevant remarks made in the section of this book dealing with the lute (see *laghoúto* and *kementzés,* p. 214, 233 and p. 275).

The soundbox of the *líra* is not made of staves, as is the case with the *laghoúto,* but is invariably hollowed out; for this purpose small, sharp knives are used, or chisels, or any other suitable tools at the craftsman's disposal. The thickness of the walls of the soundbox ranges from approximately 3 mm to as much as a little over 1 cm, and are not necessarily consistent throughout. The soundbox of the *líra* is usually thinner around the edges and thickest at the bottom. In the past, one or more openings would be cut in the base of the soundbox "for the voice". Older *líra*-players continue to maintain that such holes —approximately 1.5-2 mm ui diameter— enabled the instrument "to sing out better" (fig. 157).

Of the neck, which is a continuation of the soundbox, and which terminates in a head equipped with pegs, there is nothing especially noteworthy. On the other hand, the table (*kapáki,* cover), of the *líra,* with its two soundholes (*mátia,* eyes), —whether it be flat or slightly curved— is always a source of great concern to every player. Especial care is taken that the wood be thoroughly dry, free of knots, and closely grained. It is restricted to a few millimetres in thickness, and care is taken that it be consistent throughout. In the past, *líres* could be found all the parts of which (body, neck, head and table) were made of the same kind of hardwood, either mulberry, walnut, cypress, etc. Made as they were with primitive technical means, the tables of such instruments were thicker and less consistently even as compared to the soundboards of the present day *líres,* which are cut by means of an electric band-saw. The table is glued to the soundbox of the instrument. Nevertheless, in the past the table was often affixed to the body by means of small metal nails or wooden pegs. Two hemispherical soundholes are always opened on the table of the *líra.* In the past, one or more holes (approximately 1.5-2 mm in diameter) were occasionally opened; these small holes resembled those made in the soundbox (fig. 158). The soundpost (*stýlos,* column) of the *líra* is wedged with one edge on the bottom of the soundbox and the other at the foot of the bridge, and not on the instrument's table, as is the case with instruments of the violin family (fig. 159).

The three pegs of the *líra* —most commonly known as the *striftália* (turners)— are made in various sizes, depending upon what suits the player as far as tuning his instrument is concerned. The tuning-pegs are made in a variety of shapes, according to the skill and the taste of the performer. The three strings of the *líra* are wound around these tuning-pegs; the strings rest upon the instrument's bridge and are fastened at the lower end of the *líra,* either to a projection of the soundbox especially constructed for this purpose —the tailpiece— or to a string-holder made of hardwood or bone.

The first string of the *líra,* the highest tuned, is called *cantí* or *cantíni* or *téli* (wire); the second or middle string is called the *messakí,* and the third and lowest tuned string is referred to as the *vourghára* or *bássa.* In the past, the three strings of the *líra* were made of gut, but nowadays players use commercially made strings similar to those used to equip the stringed instruments of 'art music'. Apart from these strings, the *líra*-players of yesteryear added as many as three *sympathetic strings* to their instruments. Wound around three additional pegs next to the three principal tuning-pegs of the instrument, these sympathetic strings were passed underneath the principal strings, through holes cut in the bridge, and were fastened in the same way as the main set of strings. Such sympathetic strings were usually tuned in unison with the principal strings, or an octave lower, and sounded 'sympathetically' when the main strings were played. In other words, the sympathetic strings would vibrate in response to the vibration of the instrument's three principal strings when the latter were bowed; this resulted in a 'sweeter' and stronger 'voice'. Today, it is rarely that one comes across *líres* equipped with sympathetic strings. In addition, a central peak *(messakós píros)* is added to the head of the *líra;* this supports the second, or middle string, thus bringing all three strings of the instrument into alignment (fig.

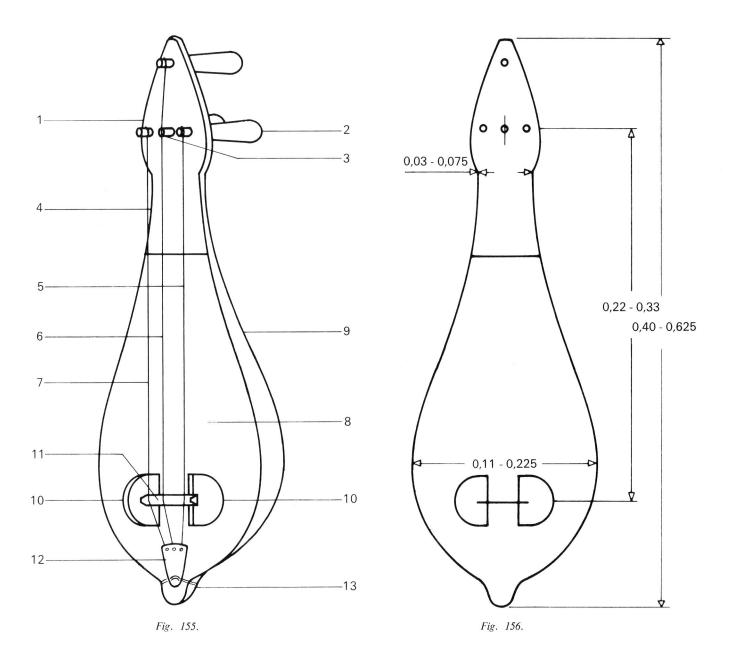

Fig. 155.

Fig. 156.

Fig. 155. Pear-shaped fiddle (líra): 1. Head (= kepháli, kephalí). 2. Pegs (striftália, striftária and stroufoúnia = turners; kourdhistíria = tuning devices; pĭri = pegs; passoúlia = poles). 3. Upper bridge (= páno kavaláris (rider); bássos = bass). 4. Neck (= lemós; piassoúdhi = handle). 5. First string (psilí = highest; cantí, cantíni). 6. Middle string (= messaki). 7. Lower string (vourghára, onomatopoeic?). Strings (= córdhes; télia = wires). 8. Soundboard (kapáki = cover). 9. Soundbox (kafkí, káfka = skull; koufári = carcass, shell; skáfi = trough; skáfos = vessel). 10. Soundholes (máthia, mátia = eyes; boúkes = holes, mouths). 11. Bridge (kavaláris = rider). 12. Stringholder (= cordhodhétis. piastrí tis córdhas; ourá = tail; kténi = comb; colodhétis). 13. Tailpiece (ourá = tail; rózos = knot; colodhétis; tsouní). Soundpost (psychí = soul; stýlos and colónna = pillar, column; gháïdharos = donkey fig. 159).

Fig. 156. Usual dimensions of the pear-shaped fiddle. Greatest depth of the soundbox 0.03-0.06.

160). The length of the strings that actually vibrates with the rubbing of the bow —the distance from the pegs to the bridge— generally ranges from 28-32 cm. It is also noteworthy that in the past many *líra*-players would open an additional hole in the heads of their instruments — besides the holes made to receive the pegs. Into this hole dancers would fit a lighted cigarette from time to time; thus the player could smoke without interrupting his performance, simply by lifting his instrument close to his mouth.

Until about the time of the Second World War, the bow of the *líra* was curved; it was made of different woods, and ranged in length from approximately 45-55 cm in most cases, to as much as 60 cm. The hairs of the bow consisted of hairs taken from the tail of a horse. Suspended from the curved wooden section of the bow were hung several small pellet-bells, *yerakokoúdhouna* or *lirarokoúdhouna*. With the movement of the bow, the bells were made to sound, thus providing rhythmical accompaniment to the melody played on the *líra*. The hairs of the bow were attached to the two ends of the bow in different ways (e.g. fig. 161a, b). For playing purposes they were rubbed with resin, or, as a substitute, with incense. The bow *(dhoxári)* of the *líra* is also known as the *liróxylo* in Ikaria (*xýlo* meaning wood) and the *vérgha* (stick) in Hydra. Today, most *líra*-players use violin bows to play their instruments.

The decoration of the *líra* is chiefly restricted to the back of the soundbox and the front of the instrument's head; such decorative motifs as incised geometric patterns and rosettes, carvings in bas relief (anchors, birds, vessels with flowers, etc.), and occasionally sculpted forms (the heads of birds or animals, for example, and more rarely those of human beings) are among the more common to be found. Apart from incised designs and bas relief, the *líra* of the past was also decorated by means of original poker-work and inlay. Geometric designs, such as circles, triangles, rhombi, etc., were executed in mother-of-pearl, tortoise-shell, rare woods, etc. Such incised and 'burnt' designs were also complemented by means of colours. In the past, either the wood used in the construction of the *líra* was allowed to retain its natural colouring, or the soundbox, neck and head of the instrument was dyed by means of natural dyestuffs — boiled leaves of the walnut tree, almond shells, pine bark, acorn cups, etc. Nowadays, the soundbox and the head of the *líra* —or the soundbox alone— are treated with commercial, european-type varnish.

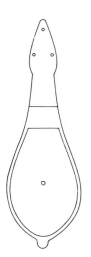

Fig. 157.

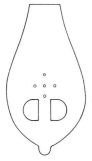

Fig. 158.

Fig. 159.

Playing technique

When the player is seated, the *líra* is usually played resting on his left thigh or between his two legs. In the latter case, the player keeps his legs together; the instrument is held leaning to one side or the other, or forwards or backwards, depending upon the position the *líra*-player is accustomed to. When the player is walking, he rests his instrument against his chest. In the past, the walking player would rest his *líra* upon the broad belt of the traditional Greek costume. The player of the *líra* is also known as the *liráris, liratzís, liritzís,* and *liristís.*

Technical and musical possibilities

The pear-shaped *líra* is tuned in perfect fifths. In the past, the pear-shaped *líra* was also tuned *alla turca* (intervals of perfect fifth and fourth), a tuning arrangement still encountered in the present day, albeit ever more rarely. In tuning his instrument, the *liráris* is not interested in the absolute pitch of the three strings, but in the relation of each string to the others. Until the present day, the A of the *líra* has always been lower than the A of the tuning-fork. It is especially low when the *líra* is played alone or when it is played together with a large tambourine *(dacharés)* or drum *(daoúli)*.[413] The strings of the *líra* are not stopped with the tips of the player's fingers —as is the case with the violin, for example— but the player's fingernails, are pressed against the strings.

The melody is generally played on the first and highest string of the *líra*. The second string —one fifth lower than the first string— is used only slightly for the melody, while the third string of the instrument —at an interval of a fifth or fourth from the second string— is rarely

262

used for the melody. In the course of playing, however, the bow often 'takes' — or rubs against— the second string together with the first string, upon which the melody is being played; or, the bow rubs against the second and the third strings together. Thus a rudimentary 'harmony', a kind of drone *(íson)* is provided by way of accompaniment.[414] Apart from the concordant intervals thus produced, this drone also creates momentary discordant harmonic strokes, according to the melody; such discordances impart the playing of the *líra* with a characteristic colour and nervous intensity, especially when the *líra* is played alone to accompany dance without song. The bridge of the *líra* is constructed so as to contribute to this technique of 'harmonic' playing. Slightly curved in shape, it allows the player to strike two or even three strings simultaneously, without any special effort on the part of the *liráris*. In the past, whenever the *líra* was played alone, its own 'harmonic' and rhythmic accompaniment was provided in the form of the drone, as well as by the beating of the player's right foot upon the floor or ground, and the jingling of the small pellet-bells attached to the bow as the latter was drawn back and forth across the strings.

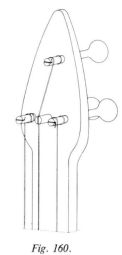

Fig. 160.

The pear-shaped *líra* is principally an instrument for quick tempi — in other words, for the performance of those dance melodies that are normally played with the point of the bow *(poúnta)*, with rapid, separate bow-strokes (détaché bowing). Slow melodies, in which two or three notes are sounded together by means of a single bow-stroke, are very rarely performed on the *líra*. It is also noteworthy that the *liráris* of old played his instrument in the *natural scale* rather than the tempered scale (see *Introduction*), and did not make use of vibrato. Today, on the contrary, most *líra*-players employ vibrato, use a violin bow, and order their instruments from factories established in the larger cities of the country in recent years.

The liráki — The vrondólira — The common líra

With the passage of years the pear-shaped *líra* underwent certain morphological modifications, an evolutionary process centred on the island of Crete. The original form of the pear-shaped *líra* is the *liráki,* or 'small líra' (fig. 162). The *liráki,* however, gradually became restricted to the playing of dance melodies, as the musical requirements of vocalists are different from those of the dance. The *liráki*, with its small and shallow soundbox, produces a sharp, penetrating sound — exactly what is necessary for the dance. However, the very different requirements for the accompaniment of song —especially in the past, at long-lasting gatherings and country fairs— led in time to the creation of a larger kind of instrument, which gradually evolved into the *vrondólira,* or 'thunderlira'.

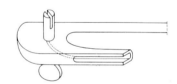

Fig. 161a.

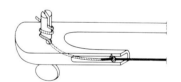

The *vrondólira* is constructed with a larger, deeper soundbox which is wider at the base of the instrument *(mághoula,* cheek). It produces a deeper sound, and is tuned lower than the *liráki*. The lower tuning of the *vrondólira* aids the player and the vocalist to sing for many consecutive hours without tiring easily. The *liráki*, on the other hand, is always tuned higher, and thus tires the vocalist more easily, as the latter cannot stand up to many hours of singing in the higher register.

In between the two above-mentioned instruments —the *liráki* and the *vrondólira*— an intermediate type of *líra* was created, the common *líra*. The common *líra* is larger than the *liráki* but smaller than the *vrondólira,* and is the variation of the instrument that finally prevailed. In the present day, despite the predominance of the intermediate type of *líra,* one also encounters —albeit ever more rarely— the archetypal *liráki,* as well as the *vrondólira*. In essence, there exist only two types of *líra* —the *liráki* and the *vrondólira*— as the third, intermediate type of the instrument, the common *líra,* is nothing more than a combination of the dimensions of the soundboxes of the former two. The emergence of the *liráki* and the *vrondólira* is the result of internal, purely musical demands. As we shall see below, the relatively recent changes in the shape of the *líra* were the result of external influences — particularly that of the violin, which is slowly but surely tending to replace the *líra*.

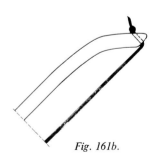

Fig. 161b.

The violin has provided the model for a series of additions to the soundbox, neck, and head of the *líra*. These additions assist in the playing of the instrument (through more reliable tuning and greater ease of fingering), and, together with the vibrato used by younger players, they contribute to the creation of a 'finer' sound. At the same time, however, such modifications tend to alter the character of the sound produced by the instrument; although they may have resulted in a 'sweeter' sound, because of such changes, the austere, rough, and unique timbre of the old *líra* has been lost. In the urban centres such new modifications assume a definite form and are firmly established as a result of the more obvious presence of the violin, the richer sound and perfection of manufacture of which instrument has had a decisive influence on the *líra*. There, too, are to be found the craftsmen and the workshops, where the daily observation, repair and manufacture of instruments enriches their experience as well as their technical capabilities.

To the archetype of the *líra*, the *liráki* (fig. 162), a stringholder is first added (*cordhodhétis* or *kténi*) (fig. 163). To this stringholder the strings of the instrument are fastened; subsequently, a fingerboard (*ghlóssa*, tongue), is added, while at the same time the neck of the *líra* is somewhat narrowed and elongated (fig. 164). The fingerboard and the longer and narrower neck all facilitate the player's fingering of the instrument, and assist the movements of the hand when striving to produce higher notes. Initially as a decorative feature, a scroll resembling that of the head of the violin is added to the head *(kepháli)* of the *líra;* this, without altering the customary position of the pegs of the instrument (fig. 165). Later, however, the entire head of the violin was added to the *líra,* a feature that decisively altered the form of the instrument. The old wooden pegs were abandoned, and were replaced by the pegs of the violin or the mandolin, positioned to the right and to the left of the head of the *líra* (fig. 166).

Alongside these additions a number of other modifications are to be observed: a) The soundbox of the *líra,* for reasons of sound quality, became progressively wider and deeper, while the wood from which it and the table of the instrument were made became thinner. b) A fourth string, again with the violin as the prototype, was added to the *líra.* In this way the *líra* came to have the same number of strings and the same tuning as the violin (G-D-A-E). However, the addition of a fourth string to the *líra* has not been widely imitated, and for all intents and purposes the practice has been abandoned. c) The *alla turca* tuning of the *líra* (D-A-D) has gradually been abandoned, and the tuning of the strings in fifths (D-A-E) has been generally adopted. d) Sympathetic strings are not longer used, due to the increased size of the soundbox with its concordant fuller and richer sound. e) Finally, as has been mentioned above, the old curved bow of the *líra* has been gradually replaced by the favoured use of the violin bow.

The violólira (violin-shaped líra)

All of the above-mentioned additions and modifications have one feature in common — the negative characteristic that not one of them affected the traditional pear-shaped soundbox of the *líra.* The opposite holds true in the case of the *violólira* (violin-shaped lira), a type of *líra* that was created around 1925. This instrument, the result of those attempts to develop a *líra* with the technical possibilities afforded by the violin, had the figure-eight-shaped soundbox of the violin in addition to the modifications described in the foregoing (fig. 167). The *violólira* is no longer made today, and is but rarely played. All of the other additions and modifications of the *líra* discussed above are to be found one next to the other. In other words, the *liráki* and the *vrondólira* still exist and are still played; *líres* with a stringholder, or fingerboard, or both; *líres* outfitted with the heads of violins; with or without lateral pegs, and so forth. Gradually, however, the *líra* manufactured in urban workshops, with a rather wide soundbox, with a stringholder, a fingerboard, and the head of a violin with lateral pegs, has come to predominate.

In the past, the pear-shaped *líra* was played alone.[415] In recent years, however, especially during the inter-bellum years and afterwards, the *líra* was played together with the lute *(laghoúto),* which was limited to the provision of a simple 'harmonic' and rhythmic accompaniment. In central and western Crete, the lute often plays the same melody together with the *líra,* provid-

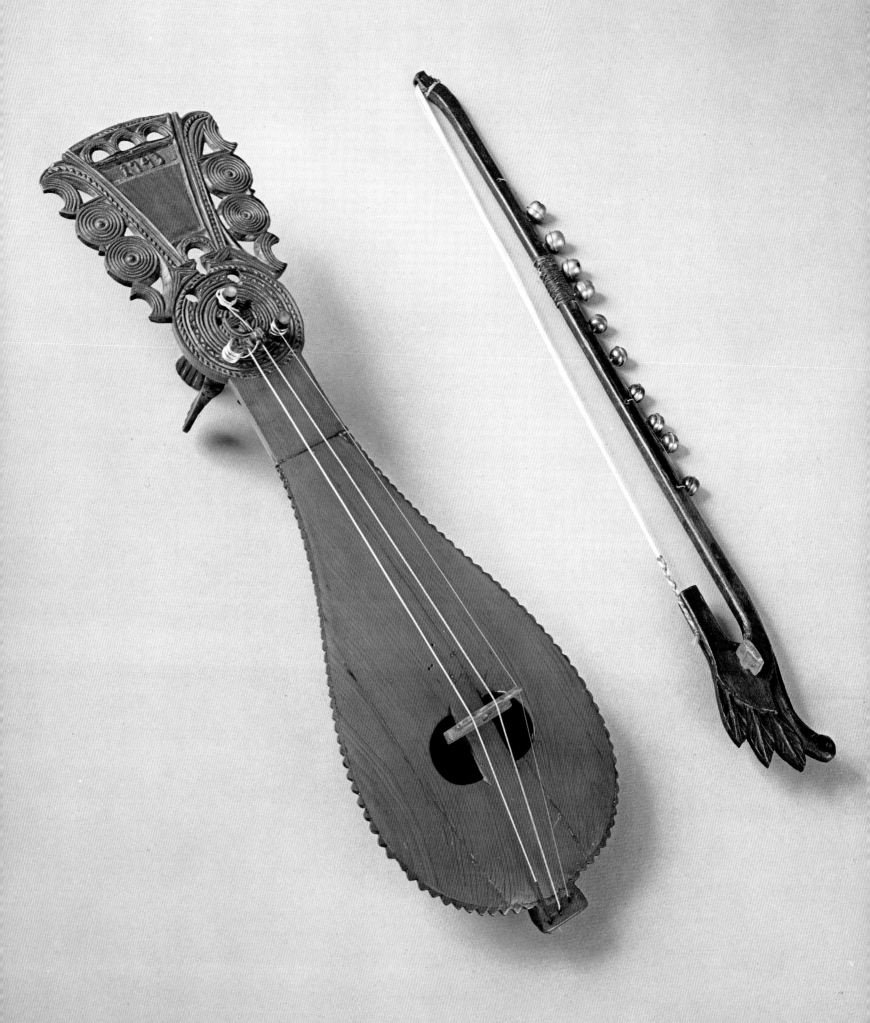

120.   Pear-shaped lira, 49.5 cm. long, body 15 cm. wide and
       4.5 cm. deep. Crete, 18th cent.(1743). Bow with
       pellet-bells, Inter-War years.

121.   Pear-shaped lira, 49 cm. long, body 13.5 cm. wide and
       4 cm. deep. Region of Iraklion, Crete, end 19th cent.

122.   Pear-shaped lira, large size (vrondólira), 58 cm. long,
       body 18.5 cm. wide and 5 cm. deep. Region of
       Rethymnon, Crete, early 20th cent.

123-124. *Pear-shaped lira, 45 cm. long, body 18 cm. wide and 3 cm. deep. Ikaria, 1946 (front and rear).*   124

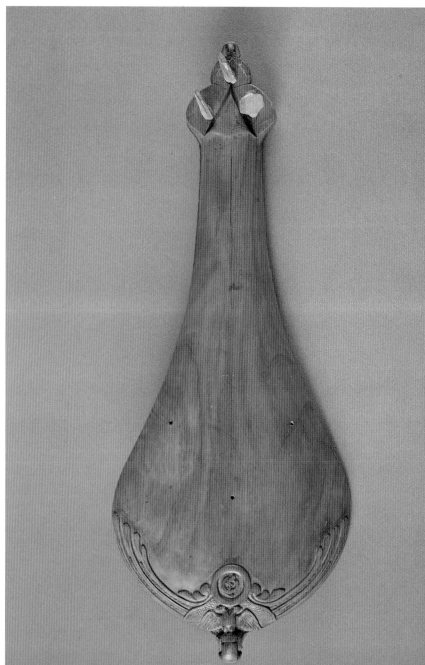

125 126

125.126. *Pear-shaped lira, 45 cm. long, body 16 cm. wide and 4 cm. deep. Dodecanese, 1925 (front and rear).*

127. *1. Bow of bottle-shaped lira (kementzés) of Greeks from Pontos (Black Sea area), 45.5 cm. long. 2-9. Bows of pear-shaped lira, with or without pellet-bells (yerakokoúdhouna), from various regions of Greece, 45-65 cm. long.*

128. *Pear-shaped lira, 63 cm. long, body 22 cm. wide and 3.5 cm. deep. Region of Lassithi, Crete (c. 1960).*

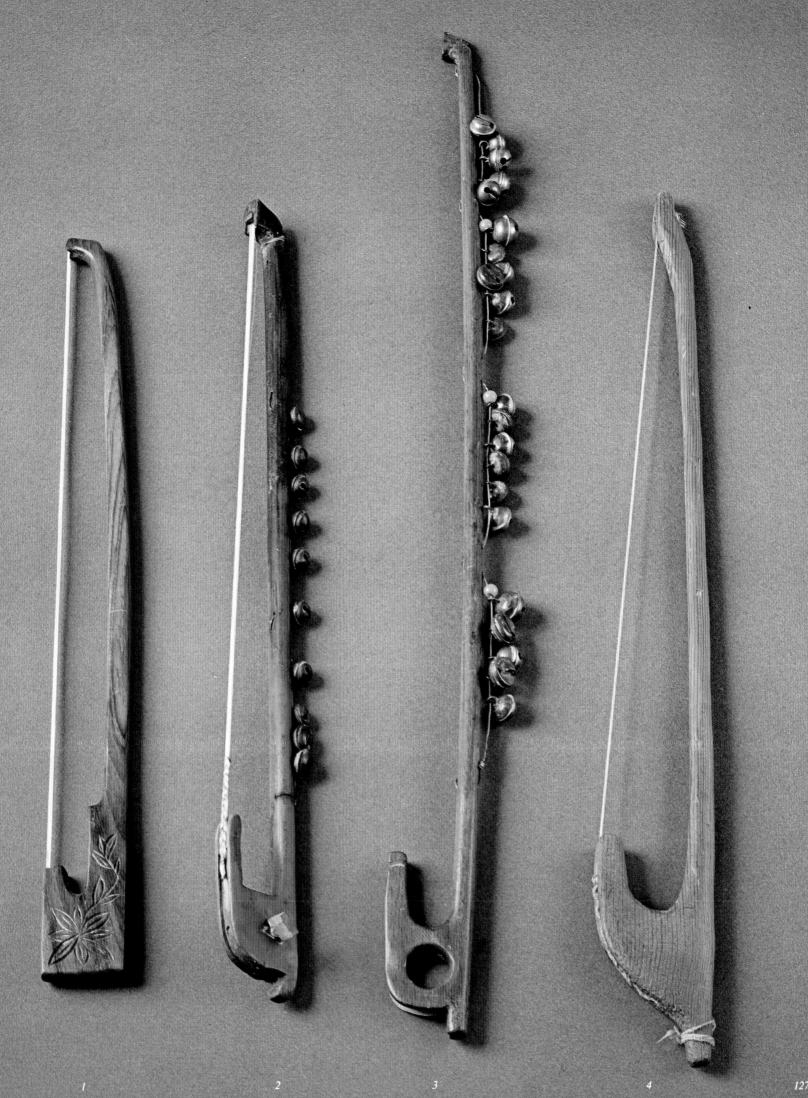

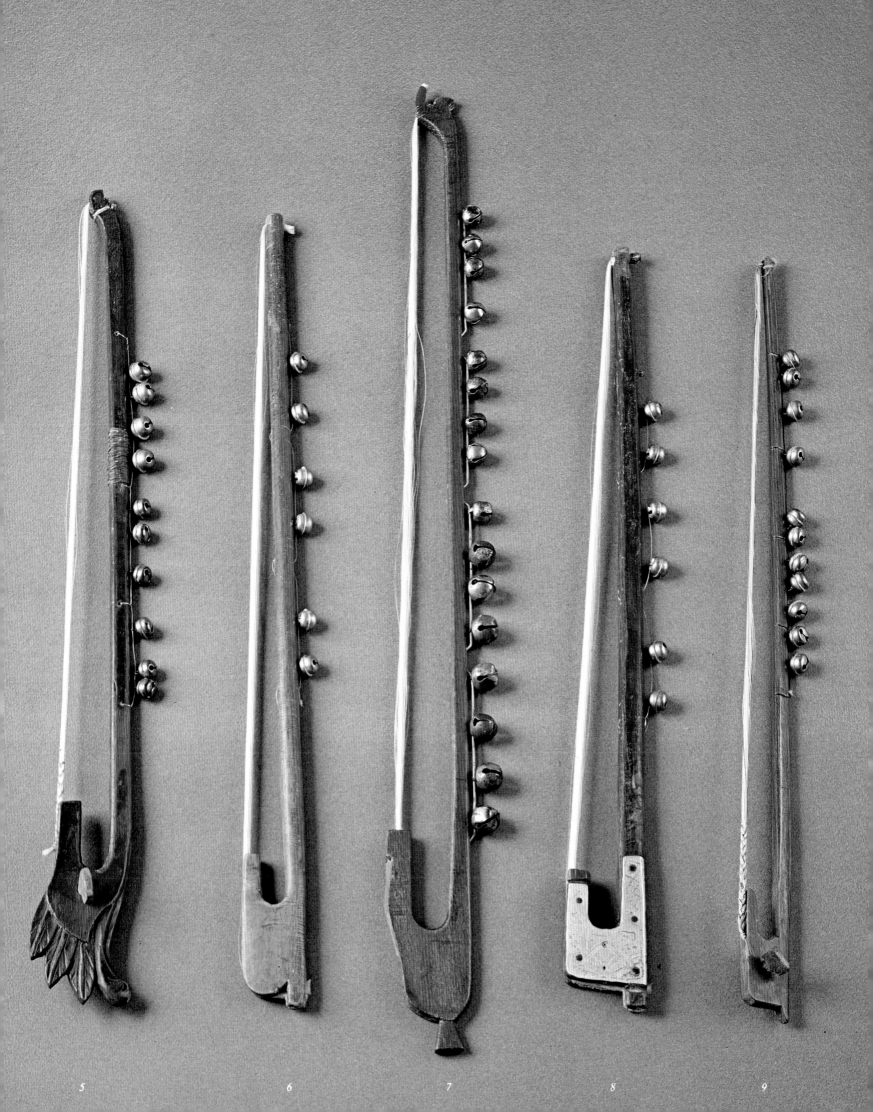

5   6   7   8   9

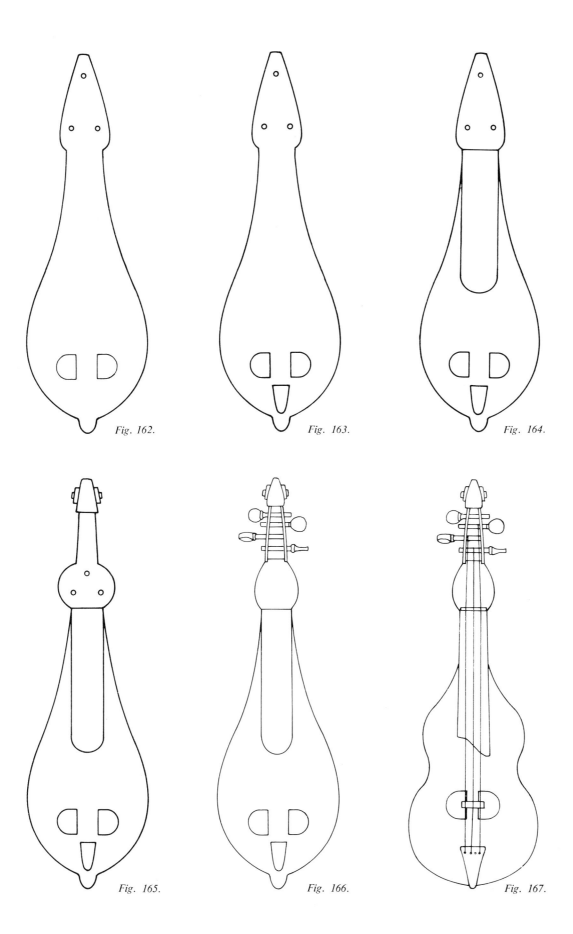

Fig. 162.

Fig. 163.

Fig. 164.

Fig. 165.

Fig. 166.

Fig. 167.

ing at the same time a rudimentary harmonic accompaniment.[416] In the eastern part of the island, the *líra* is accompanied by a small drum *(daoúli)*. Together with the *daoúli*, the *líra* is played today in northern Greece —in Macedonia and in Thrace. In the same region the *líra* is played together with a large tambourine *(dacharés)*— in other words, one *líra* is accompanied by either one or two *dacharédhes,* or two *líres* are accompanied by either one or two *dacharédhes.*

In addition to the combinations described in the foregoing —each of which is now regarded as an established *ziyiá,* as the *ziyiá* of violin and lute *(violí-laghoúto)*— older people recall hearing the *líra* played together with the *toubí* (small drum), with the *bouzoúki* (type of tamboura), with the *thiabóli* (ducted flute), with the mandolin, et alia, on certain of the Greek islands. They also recall the playing of two and occasionally of three *líres* together at feasts which lasted for several days. Nowadays, the pear-shaped *líra* is still played in the islands —especially in Crete and the islands of the Dodecanese— as well as in northern Greece, Macedonia and Thrace. In the past, however, the *líra* was played throughout mainland Greece.

The líra in the Greek world

The earliest mention of the name *líra* —referring to a stringed instrument played by means of a bow— can be traced to a report made at the close of the tenth century by the Persian Ibn Kurdādhbih to the Caliph Al-Mutamid, concerning the musical instruments of the Byzantines. In his report, Ibn Kurdādhbih refers to the *líra* among other Byzantine instruments, adding that it is a wooden five-stringed instrument similar to the Arabic *rebab.*[417] From that time on, there are many Byzantine and post-Byzantine iconographic and literary sources attesting to the existence of bowed, stringed instruments in Greece and the Greek world of the Near East; these references include mention of the pear-shaped *líra.*[418]

The following are representative examples of such iconographical and literary sources bearing upon the *líra:* a Byzantine ivory casket carved in relief (Museo Nazionale, Florence, 10th to early 11th century);[419] miniatures from eleventh century illuminated manuscripts;[420] and wall-paintings in sixteenth and eighteenth century monasteries.[421]

An akritic song has the following noteworthy lines:[422]

> *Give me my líra, my pityful bow,*
> *so that I can remember my love,*
> *as I am losing her today.*

Ptochoprodromos writes:[423]

> *If I do not hold my tongue, and bellow once again,*
> *I shall be taken for a líra, and thought full of inanity.*

In *Libistros and Rhodamne* (14th-15th century) we read:[424]

> *That craftsman stationed the others once again,*
> *one of them he set to playing a líra...*

Stefanos Sachlikis (14th century) wrote):[425]

> *So whoever desires to learn of Fate,*
> *how she plays upon the unfortunate man*
> *as a musician upon his líra —*
> *let him approach and read these verses (katalóghi)...*

> *And I played upon my liráki as a youth,*
> *like a fine young man...*[426]

274

There is also the following, from a Cretan *mantinádha* (distich):[427]

> *Play well, my líra, play with a full strong sound,*
> *so we may perhaps lead this black-eyed girl astray.*

Also noteworthy is the Greek proverb:

> *My líra plays certain things, while my violin plays others.*[428]

Many of those travellers who visited Greece in the more recent past —Pouqueville, Clarke, Chateaubriand, Chandler, and Löher, among others— refer to the *líra* in their chronicles.[429] The *líra* is also a recurrent motif in Cretan embroideries.[430]

The following surnames are derived from the words *líra* and *liráris:* Lýras, Lyratzís, Lyritzís, Lyrintzís, Lyristís, Lyrantzákis, Lyritzákis, Lyrákis, Lyrarákis, Lyrantonákis.[431]

KEMENTZES *(Bottle-shaped Fiddle)*

The *kementzés* or *líra,* played by the Greeks of the Black Sea region (Pontos) and from Cappadocia, is a bottle-shaped stringed instrument, with a long, narrow soundbox concluding in a short, unfretted neck. The pegs of the *kementzés* are inserted from the front. The instrument possesses a fingerboard, a bridge, and is equipped with three single strings fastened to a stringholder; it is played with a bow. Usually made by the player himself, the *kementzés* is constructed in different sizes, although the variations in length, breadth and bulk are not at all great. The terminology applied to the different parts of the *kementzés* is given in fig. 168, while fig. 169 refers to the dimensions of the instrument.

Construction

In the construction of the soundbox, neck, and head of the *kementzés,* mulberry, ivy, walnut, cedar, acacia, etc. are among the woods most commonly used. Of these, the best woods are considered to be, first of all plum *(kokkýmelon),* as "it provides a good voice," and then ivy *(kissós),* which also gives a good 'voice' to the instrument, though not as full as that given by the wood of the plum tree. The table of the *kementzés,* which is generally curved, is chiefly made of coniferous wood, such as pine or fir. The wood in any case must be clean, dry, and free of knots; it should also be close-grained. In the past, certain woods, such as ivy, were boiled in oil "so as to tighten up" and so resist splitting; alternatively, the wood to be used in the construction of a *kementzés* was placed in animal manure, a source of heat, in order to dry out rapidly. The safest method of preparation, however, is the gradual 'working' of the wood: first, a small section is carved from the block of wood that is to be the soundbox of the instrument; the newly exposed wood is allowed to dry before the block is hollowed out a little more, etc. — until the soundbox has been hollowed out to the required depth.

The walls of the soundbox should not be more than 3-4 mm thick, while the table of the *kementzés* should be even thinner, from 2-3mm. Two small holes are opened on each side of the soundbox and four holes *(tripía)* are made on the table, "for the voice". Two long, narrow soundholes *(rothónia,* nostrils), are also opened in the table; these are usually slightly curved towards the outside. A skilled craftsman/player *(kementzetzís)* carefully chooses the wood for the table of his instrument; he wants the wood to be closer-grained on the left side, where the highest tuned string is to be attached, and open-grained on the right-hand side, where the lower pitched strings will be stretched. In the past, some *kementzés*-players had two instruments — one with a close-grained table, and the other with less dense graining. The first of these, with its higher tuning and penetrating sound, was played to accompany dancing, whereas the latter, tuned to a lower pitch, had a 'sweeter' sound, and was used to accompany song. With the last-mentioned instrument, vocalists could sing for hours on end without tiring.

275

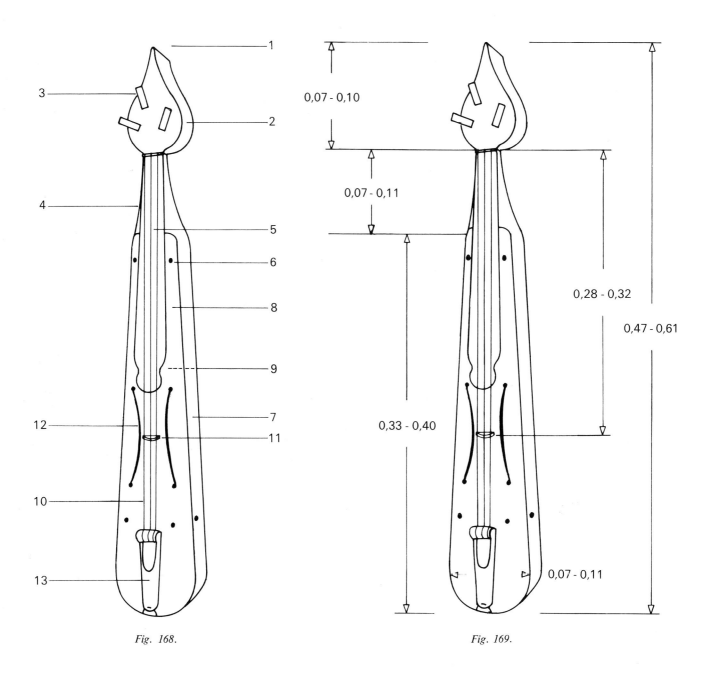

Fig. 168.   Fig. 169.

Fig. 168.   Bottle-shaped fiddle (Pontic líra = o kementzés or i kementzé; the terms in Pontic dialect): 1. The 'top' (=
i tepé). 2. Head (= to kiphál).3. Pegs (ta otía or ta tĺa = the ears). 4. Neck (= i ghoúla). 5. Fingerboard
(i ghlóssa = the tongue; to spalér = the slabbering-bib). 6. Small soundholes (ta tripía = the holes).
7. Ribs (to mágh'lon = the cheek). 8. Soundboard (to kapák = the cover). 9. Soundbox (i rácha = the
back). 10. Strings (= ta córdhas). 11. Bridge (to ghaïdhoúr or o gháïdharon = the donkey). 12. Soundholes (ta rothónia = the nostrils; ta skolékia = the worms). 13. Stringholder (to pallikár = the stal-
ward young man; to psár = the fish; o peïliavános = the wrestler). Soundpost (to stoulár, to tirék = the
pillar, the column). Bow (= to toxár). The hairs of the bow (ta tsária = the hairs of an animal's tail).
Ornaments (= ta ploumía).
Fig.169.   Usual dimensions of the bottle-shaped fiddle. Depth of the soundbox 0.032-0.07.

276

The three strings of the *kementzés* are wound onto the three pegs (*otía*, ears), usually arranged in a T-like pattern. The strings rest upon the nut (fig. 170) and the bridge, and are fastened to the stringholder, known as the *pallikár* (stalwart young man). The bridge of the *kementzés* — known as the *gháidaron* or *ghaidoúr* (donkey)— is thin, slightly curved, and much smaller than the bridge of the pear-shaped *líra*. Until approximately 1920, the strings with which the *kementzés* was equipped were often made of silk. Such strings resulted in the production of a beautiful, albeit weak, sound. The *kementzés* was equipped with either three silk strings, or the two higher-pitched strings were of silk and the third, lowest string, of gut. When the entire complement of strings were of silk, the two higher-tuned strings were thinner, whereas the third string was slightly thicker. In the course of time, the three strings of the *kementzés* were of gut; these subsequently were replaced by metal strings. Nowadays, the Pontic *líra* is equipped with three wire strings —the so-called *télia* (wires)— of equal thickness; or, with two *télia* of equal thickness and one *téli* slightly thicker; or, two *télia* of equal thickness and one wrapped wire string; or, finally, two *télia* of equal thickness and one string of gut.

Fig. 170.

The soundpost (*stoulár*, column), of the *kementzés* rests upon the table at its upper end —approximately beneath the left leg of the bridge, where the highest string is positioned— and with its lower end at the base of the soundbox. The sounding length of the strings of the *kementzés*, made to vibrate with strokes of the bow —i.e., the distance from the nut to the bridge— is approximately between 28 and 32 cm.

The bow —approximately 50-55 cm in length— is made of hardwood, and is slightly curved. In the past, the bow was strung with hairs from the tail of a horse; these were fastened at each end in different ways, usually by means of a small piece of linen cloth at the end where the bow is held by the player, and a knot at the other (fig. 171). Nowadays, many players of the *kementzés* use violin bows.

The decoration of the *kementzés* —with engraved or bas relief geometric designs, rosettes, stylised motifs from the natural world, etc.— is generally confined to the fingerboard (*ghlóssa*, tongue) and the pegbox of the instrument, and more rarely to the stringholder and to the back and ribs of the soundbox. The fingerboard is also decorated with carved openings, and, in the past, small mirrors and flat, decorative objects were glued to the head. What has been said respecting the varnishing of the pear-shaped *líra* holds true for the *kementzés* as well.

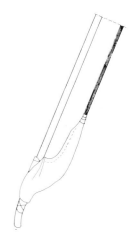

Fig. 171.

Playing technique — Technical and musical possibilities

The player *(kementzetzís)*, when seated, rests the instrument upon his left thigh or between his legs, which he holds together. In both instances, the *kementzés* is not held upright, but is held slanting slightly to the left or forwards. When the musician plays in a standing position, the instrument is supported by the thumb and forefinger of his left hand, which rests upon the head of the *kementzés*. Certain players are accustomed to lightly rest the lower end of the soundbox against their groin or upon their belt when they are playing while standing. Or again, they pass the left wrist through a loop made of a narrow ribbon which is tied to the head of the *kementzés* (fig. 172). This allows them to hold the instrument stable, and provides some resistance —necessary especially when they play the notes of the upper register with the extension of the fifth finger. This selfsame knotted ribbon, which often ends in a colourful tassel, is used to hang up the *kementzés* when the instrument is not being played, although some players prefer to protect the instrument in an embroidered velvet or silk cloth case.

The *kementzés* is invariably tuned by perfect fourths. However, as players of the instrument are not particularly concerned with the absolute pitch of the notes and hence do not use the tuning-fork, their tuning of the A string generally falls somewhat lower than the A of the regular diapason. The strings of the *kementzés* are stopped with the player's fingertips, as in the case of the violin, and the melody is mainly played on the first and second strings in the first position. Only rarely are one or two notes —higher than the first position— to be heard; when this is the case, it is done 'furtively', as the players claim, through the extension of the fifth finger. When the *kementzetzís* plays a melody, he often simultaneously stops the adjacent

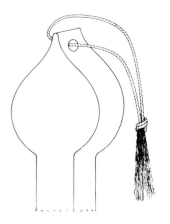

Fig. 172.

277

string with the same fingers. Something similar takes place in the case of the bow as well. Often, in the course of playing, the bow will rub against two strings, the string upon which the melody is played and the adjacent string. In this manner of playing, the role of the bridge is obvious. Its small dimensions (approximately 2-2.5 cm in length, and 1-1.5 cm in height) —dimensions still preserved without any change by *kementzés*-players— compel, as it were, the bow and the player's fingers to stroke and stop two strings simultaneously.[432]

Thus, one can distinguish the following modes of playing the *kementzés:* a) The melody is played on the highest string and is accompanied by a drone *(íson)* on the middle string (the player's fingers stop the highest string, while the bow touches both the highest string and the middle string). b) The melody is played on both strings in parallel perfect fourths (fingers and bow respectively stop and touch both strings simultaneously). c) The melody is played on the middle string, and is accompanied by a drone on the adjacent, higher string, (the fingers stop the middle string, while the bow simultaneously touches both the middle string and the neighbouring higher string). With the exception of the third mode of playing the *kementzés,* which is but rarely encountered, the remaining two modes of playing the Pontic *líra* are to be found in combination; at one moment the first mode of playing will predominate, at another the second mode, according to the taste of the musician and the mood of the moment, not to mention the particular tradition in which the musician happens to be versed. His performance is also influenced by the pressure he exerts upon the bow as it touches the string or strings he wishes to sound, as he tightens the usually slack hairs of the bow with the fingers of his right hand. Pontic players of the *kementzés* do not use vibrato, and all those who have remained uncontaminated by the influence of western music play in the *natural scale,* and not in the tempered scale. The Pontic *líra,* like the pear-shaped *líra,* is an instrument particularly suited to rapid tempi.

The *kementzés* is usually played alone, without any other instrumental accompaniment. When many people gather together for some festive event, especially in the case of open-air festivals, two or three and occasionally more *kementzédhes* are played together; the thin and rather weak sound of a single instrument would not be very audible. For the same reason, the *kementzés* is also played together with either the shawm *(zournás)',* the drum *(daoúli),* or the droneless bagpipe *(angíon)* or in different combinations of these instruments — e.g., *kementzés, angíon,* and *daoúli.* In such cases, the *kementzetzís* plays his instrument standing up, and is usually himself in constant motion. He follows the dancers with his own steps, in time with the dance rhythm, and often gives the impression that he himself is dancing; he rhythmically beats his bow against the soundbox of his instrument, and addresses hortatory syllables, words, or even entire phrases to the dancers.

The origins of the bottle-shaped fiddle

Ethnomusicological research has so far failed to arrive at any definite conclusions as to the origins of the bottle-shaped *líra.* However valuable they may be, the few iconographical and other sources of evidence —such as the Mozarabic illuminated manuscript of the tenth century, which depicts four people, each playing a large, bottle-shaped instrument with a bow (fig. 173)[433]— do not serve to compensate for the dearth of more concrete evidence. Thus, a number of theories proposing a possible link between the *kementzés* and the little 'pocket-violin' of eighteenth century dancing masters, or with the medieval *rebec,* lead nowhere.[434] Professor L.E.R. Picken has studied this very problem, although from a different viewpoint, in his work *Folk Musical Instruments of Turkey.* In a methodically presented argument, he maintains that the *kementzés* may have evolve from an archaic type of bowed, two-stringed instrument —the *iklíg*[435]— and that its presence in the Black Sea region is probably due to the Lazes.[436] The surname Kementzetzídhis is also worthnoting (Telephone Directory Attica, 1977).

Fig. 173.

KEMANES (Bottle-shaped Fiddle)

The *kemanés,* once played by the Greeks of Cappadocia, is a bottle-shaped stringed instrument played with a bow. It has a long, narrow, bottle-shaped soundbox, a short unfretted neck with a fingerboard, a head like that of the violin with lateral pegs, six strings, six sympathetic strings and two soundposts. In general terms, its construction resembles that of the *kementzés,* and it is made of the same materials: hardwood for the soundbox, neck and head, and soft-wood for the soundboard. The sympathetic strings run beneath the fingerboard (fig. 174), having been passed through holes cut in the bridge under the positions of the principal strings (fig. 175), and are fastened below the stringholder. In the past, the bow used to play this instrument was slightly curved, with hairs from a horse's tail; those who continue to play this instrument at the present day use a violin bow.

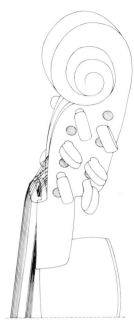

Fig. 174.

Like the *líra* and the *kementzés,* the *kemanés* is played resting on the left leg. The strings are stopped with the tip of the player's finger, and the six strings (formerly of gut, today they are metal) are tuned in perfect fifths and fourths. The tuning is as follows: three fifths and two fourths, or four fifths and one fourth, the fifths always being the lower intervals. The sympathetic strings are tuned in unison, or an octave higher or lower than the principal strings of the instrument. When the *kemanés* is played, the bow often touches the second string together with the first, or the second and third strings at the same time, thus providing a rudimentary 'harmony' in the form of a drone *(íson)* (see pear-shaped *líra* and *kementzés)* as accompaniment to the melody; the latter is usually played on the first, higher-pitched string.

The following surnames are derived from the word *kemanés:* Kemanés, Kemenés, Kemenídhis (Telephone Directory Attica, 1977).

VIOLI (Violin)

Terminology

Apart from the most common name given the violin throughout Greece, *violí,* the following are also used for this instrument, though more and more rarely: *dhiolí, violárin,*[437] *violoúdhin, vkiolín,*[438] et alia. When the terms *ta violiá* or *ta dhioliá* are used —"the *violiá* have arrived"; "let's go to the *violiá*"— not only the specific instrument (violin) is meant, but musical instruments in general, and especially the combination violin and lute *(ziyiá: violí, laghoúto)* and the ensemble clarinet, violin, dulcimer and lute *(companía: klarino, violí, sandoúri, laghoúto).*

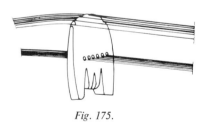

Fig. 175.

Playing technique — Technical and musical possibilities

The violin, both as a popular musical instrument and as an instrument played in the realm of 'art music', is manufactured in Greece based on models of western origin. As a popular musical instrument it was additionally equipped in the past with two or sometimes even four sympathetic strings (cf. *kemanés).* Moreover, it was tuned *alla turca* (the so-called "low *douzéni*"; i.e. G-D-A-D), and was played in a similar manner as the *líra,* resting on the player's left thigh. The present day violin is generally tuned in fifths (G-D-A-E), rarely is equipped with sympathetic strings, and is played resting on the violinist's shoulder. Older popular musicians maintain that the *alla turca* tuning of the strings (G-D-A-D) makes for 'sweeter' playing. The reasons given for this are twofold: first, the highest string is a whole tone lower than it would be were the instrument tuned in the western european manner *(alla franca* or "high *douzéni*", G-D-A-E); when the violin is tuned *alla turca,* the popular musician *(violitzís)* is not obliged to use the fifth finger of the left hand, but only the more easily manipulated, 'strong' forefinger, middle finger and ring-finger, with which he "licks the notes", "caresses the strings". In other words, this fingering arrangement enables the violinist to cover the intervals of the *natural scale* (see *Introduction*), the different micro-tones, and those imperceptible but characteristic glissandi from one note to another, and the variety of melodic ornamentation (appogiatura, trills, etc.).

The true popular violinist simply rests his instrument upon his shoulder, without pressing his left jaw upon the body of the violin as the manner of the violinists of 'art music'. The popular violinist holds his instrument essentially with his left wrist, using his thumb and forefinger and part of the palm of his hand. This, however, restricts the violinist to a rather limited and spare vibrato, always to a few notes only. The melody is usually played on the two upper strings (E and A), while the other two strings (D and G) were formerly used to maintain a drone *(íson)*. During the last few years —especially since the Second World War— the D and G strings of the violin have also come to be used for the melody as well.

The player's left hand remains fixed in the first position. This restriction, however, proves no obstacle to the 'furtive' playing of certain higher notes by bringing to bear the fifth finger should the melody call for it. In Epirus, in northern Greece, one comes across popular violinists who play certain melodies with their wrist held firmly in the second position. In this manner, they use only the 'strong' fingers —the forefinger, middle finger, and ring-finger. In other words, they play their instruments in a manner similar to that of those violinists whose instruments are tuned *alla turca*, as discussed in the foregoing passages. The forearm moves the bow of the popular violin, while the upper arm remains almost stationary, to such a degree that when the violinist wishes to touch the lower strings of his instrument, the violin itself is often moved — the instrument moves towards the bow, rather than the bow towards the strings. Until just a few years ago, there was a blind, popular violinist playing in the streets of Athens who did not move the bow at all. Quite opposed t o customary practice, his right hand —which held the bow— remained immobile; he moved the violin with his left hand instead. In other words, he did not rub the bow against the strings of his instrument, but the strings against the bow-hairs. His playing was correct, and had all the characteristics of the popular violin.[439]

As far as bowing technique is concerned, the popular violinist chiefly makes use of separate strokes (détaché bowing), a single bow-stroke for each note, together with some occasional use of the legato (two or more notes per each bow-stroke).[440] When playing his instrument, the popular violinist does not employ the full length of his bow, but only the half that extends from the middle section to the point; he especially makes use of the last third of the bow, the point *(poúnta)*, and he is ignorant of two-note chords (thirds, sixths, etc.), octaves, and of playing staccato, saltato, spiccato, etc. The popular violinist plays *forte* or *piano* according to the voice of the singer he is accompanying, whether he is playing in an enclosed or open area, whether he is playing together with another instrument, such as the *laghoúto*, or together with several other instruments, etc. True popular players are ignorant of dynamics: crescendi, diminuendi, a sudden drop to piano following a forte passage, are all unknown to them.[441]

When a feast or festive gathering has really got under way, the popular violinist, in the middle of his playing, will occasionally strike the back of his instrument's soundbox with the haft of his bow, thus momentarily transforming his violin into a rhythmical instrument. Many popular violinists, in order to forestall the necessity of interrupting their playing at such gatherings, keep a second E-string rolled up on the peg, the 'reserve', as they call it, ready for rapid attachment to the instrument should a string snap during play. Nowadays, popular violinists are generally influenced by western music —and especially by the performers of 'art music'— and are drawing ever farther away from the traditional techniques and style of playing through their gradual adoption of western violin technique.

As a melodic instrument, the violin is to be found in both the standard popular instrumental groupings throughout Greece, the *companía* of *violí, klaríno, sandoúri,* and *laghoúto,* and the island *ziyiá,* consisting of *violí* and *laghoúto.* In the case of the *companía,* the violin plays a far less dominant role, as the principal melodic instrument is the clarinet *(klaríno),* while as far as the island *ziyiá* is concerned, the violin is the basic melodic instrument. Today, the violin

130.131. *Pear-shaped lira, 40 cm. long, body 14.5 cm. wide and 4 cm. deep. Body, neck and pegboard decorated with tortoise-shell and mother of pearl. Region of Constantinople, 19th cent. (front and rear).*

132.   *Pear-shaped lira, 51 cm. long, body 16.5 cm. wide and 4 cm. deep. Region of Chania, Crete, early 20th cent.*

133.   *Above: Pear-shaped lira, 51 cm. long, body 24 cm. wide and 5 cm. deep, Dodecanese. Inter-War years.*
       Below: Pear-shaped lira, 52 cm. long, body 21.5 cm. wide and 5.5 cm. deep. Lutemaker: Frangias   →
       Christodoulakis, Athens (1969).

129.   *Lira on Cretan embroidery, 18th cent., Greek Folk Art Museum, Athens.*

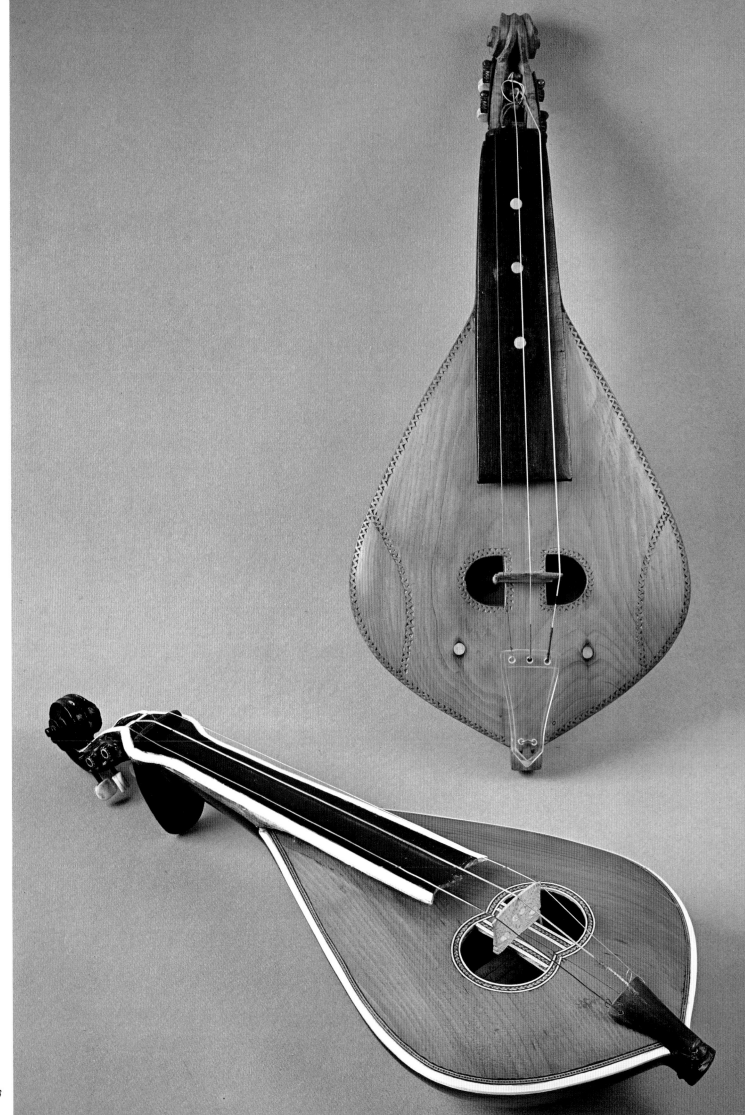

134. *Violin-shaped liras (violólires): 1. 55 cm. long, body 17 and 13 cm. wide, 4.5 cm. deep. 2. 58 cm. long, body 19.5 and 15.5 cm. wide, 4.5 cm. deep. Region of Iraklion, Crete. Inter-War years.*

135. *Bottle-shaped lira (kementzés) of Greeks from Pontos (Black Sea area), 56.5 cm. long, body 11 cm. wide and 6.5 cm. deep. Inter-War years.*

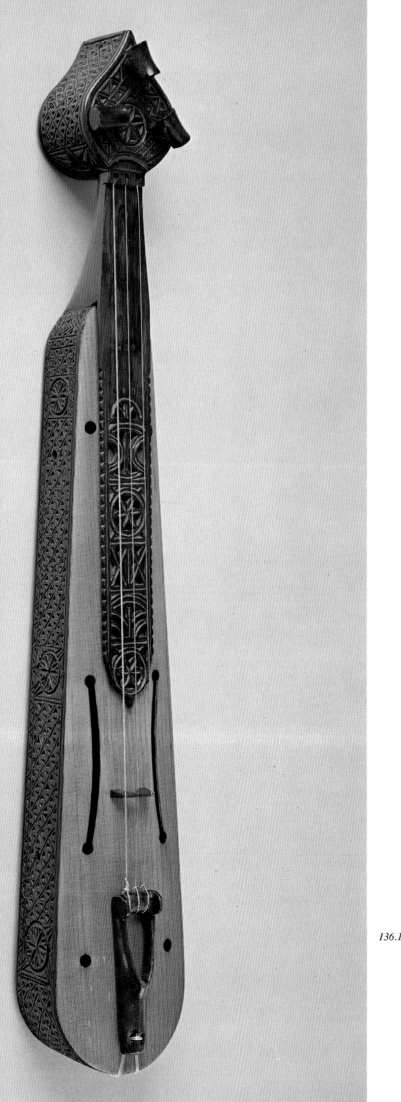

136.137. *Wood-carved bottle-shaped lira (kementzés)*
of Greeks from Pontos (Black Sea area),
54 cm. long, body 8 cm. wide and c. 4 cm. deep
(front and rear). Lutemaker: Ioannis Lyperidis (1900).

138

139

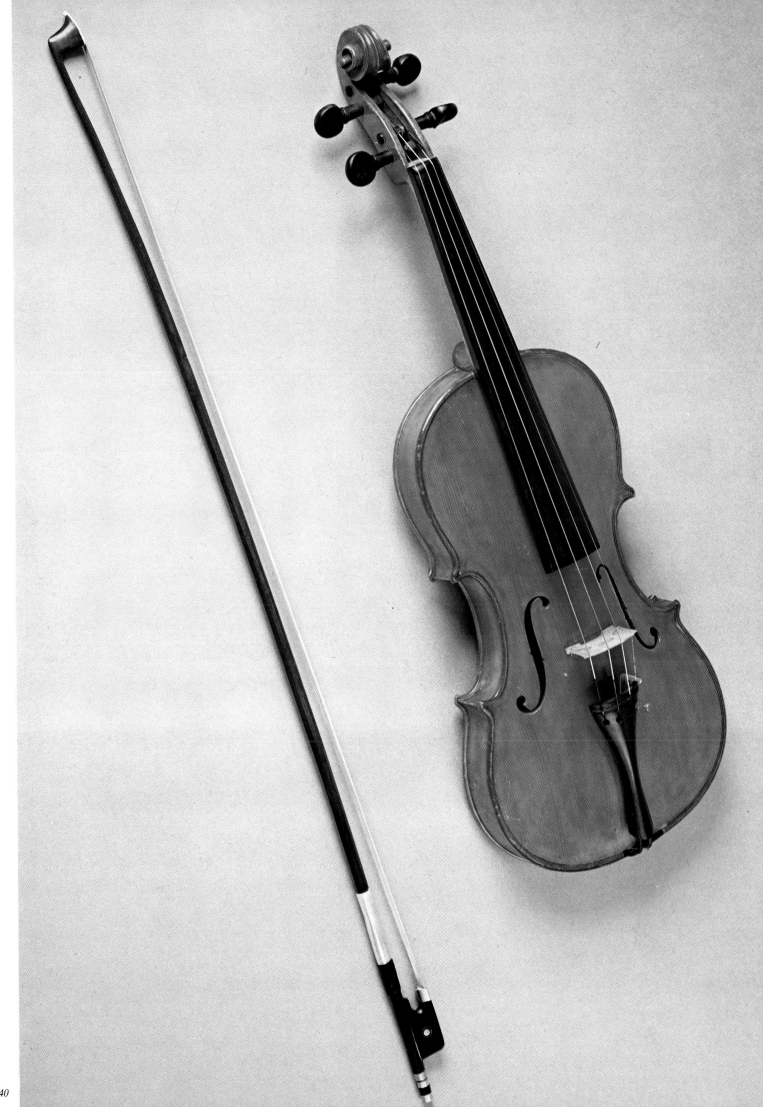

138. *Bottle-shaped lira (kemanés), with sympathetic strings, of Greeks from Pharassa, Cappadocia, 64 cm. long, body 11 cm. wide and c.7.5 cm. deep. Lutemaker: Pandelis Fortounidis, Platy, Thessaloniki (1967).*

139. *Bottle-shaped lira (kemanés), with sympathetic strings, of Greeks from Pharassa, Cappadocia· 63 cm. long, body 11 cm. wide and c.7.5 cm. deep. Lutemaker: Lazaros Koskeridis, Athen (1960).*

140. *Violin and bow. Lutemaker: Fotis Avyeris, Athens. Inter-War years.*

141. *Above: Mandóla, 86 cm. long, body 30 cm. wide and c. 17.5 cm. deep. Below: Mandolin (mandolino), 61.5 cm. long, body 19.5 cm. wide and c.14.5 cm. deep. Lutemaker: Ioannis G. Gombakis, Athens. Inter-War years.*

←

142. *Guitar (kithára), 95.5 cm. long. Lutemaker: Fotis Avyeris, Athens. Inter-War years.*

144.   *Pear-shaped lira, 50.5 cm. long, body 14 cm. wide and 5 cm. deep. Crete, 18th cent. (?).*

143.   *Barrel-organ (latérna), made in a Constantinople workshop. Inter-War years.*
←

145. *Mandolocello (a large lute), 96 cm. long, body 34 cm. wide and c. 20 cm. deep. Lutemaker: D. Mourtzinos, Athens. Early 20th cent.*

is the principal melodic instrument of the island *ziyiá,* as the *laghoúto* is restricted to providing the accompaniment. In the past, however, the melody was often shared between the violin and the *laghoúto* if the lutenist was a virtuoso performer *(primadhóros),* who could either play the melody along with the violin or upon his own, while simultaneously providing his own accompaniment.[442] The popular violin is still played in conjunction with other popular instruments. Such instrumental ensembles, however —such as the violin and a large tambourine *(tamboutsá,* q.v.),[443] a Cypriot ensemble made up when no *laghoúto* is available— do not comprise true instrumental *ziyiés,* but are fortuitous combinations of instruments born of the needs of the moment.

The violin in the Greek world

The presence of the violin among Greek popular musical instruments was noted several centuries ago, as much in Greek literary sources as in the chronicles and memoirs of foreign travellers. Even setting aside such lines from Greek folk songs as:

> *There they do not play violins, nor strike up their instruments*[444]

> *Silence all the violins and all the lutes (laoúta!)*[445]

there are many references to the violin in which that instrument is mentioned specifically by name. Thus, in the seventeenth century, Marinos Bounialis wrote:[446]

> *Violins and zithers (violiá, tsíteres) play on, lutes (laghoúta) sing out,*
> *enjoy yourselves all night long, without sleep.*

In the same century, two additional noteworthy references to the violin were made, one in the *Lament of Phallidus the Poor:*[447]

> *Day and night I was with the musicians*
> *in the alleys and the market-places,*
> *tsíteres, violiá, laghoúta...*

The second contemporary reference to the violin is made in John Covel's description of a night of merry-making on the island of Chios in 1677.[448] In the following century, the violin is mentioned by Kaisarios Dapontes (1714-1784): "There, for the three days (sc. Easter), the Greeks were granted permission to wear whatever they desired, to dance until the Phanari and outlying areas, to speak out in the alleys and to shout and sing to the accompaniment of violins and other musical instruments, carrying jugs of wine".[449]

At the end of the same century, in 1790, the freedom-fighter Panayis Skouzes wrote in his *Chronicle* of a certain violinist and good vocalist, one Dimitrios Karaoulanis, who... "went to Ali Pasha, and who was a violinist and had a fine voice".[450] The violin and other popular musical instruments also appear in the chronicles of Pouqueville and of Chateaubriand,[451] of Nikolaos Kasomoulis,[452] and of many other writers of that relatively recent period.

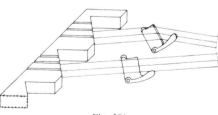

Proverbs — Adages

"I shall not say, my light, that the marriage is mine, unless the violins sound and the goat is slaughtered".[453]

Fig. 176.

"A piss without a fart, that's a marriage without a violin".[454]

"As the violinist plays, so goes the tune".

Surnames

Violákis, Violantzís, Violáris, Violatzís, Violás, Violidhákis, Violídhis, Violitzís, Dhiolís, Dhiolitzís, Dhiolitzópoulos.[455]

KANONAKI (Psaltery)

Terminology — Construction

The *kanonáki*, also known as the *kanóni*, or *psaltíri*,[456] is made in different sizes of maple or similar hardwood. It is constructed in the shape of a trapezoid, with its right side perpendicular to the large base, and with its strings —made of either gut or plastic— running lengthwise along its two parallel sides. On the soundboard —which is also constructed of wood, excepting the right-hand section (approximately 15 cm wide), which is fashioned from skin— one or more round or ovoid holes are cut out for the sound, or 'voice'; these are often highly decorated.

Alongside the keys of the instrument, on the left side, the *kanonáki* is equipped with a set of pegs *(mandalákia,* latches, clothes-pegs), a kind of moveable bridges that can be moved up or down to raise or lower the pitch of the various notes by a quarter-tone (fig. 176). To the right, on the section made of animal skin, the bridge is placed. The *kanonáki* is tuned by means of a moveable metal key — in the past, according to the mode *(trópos)* of the music being played, today, in the diatonic scale. The melodic range covered by the *kanonáki* is usually three octaves and three notes, but there do exist *kanonákia* with a smaller melodic span, such as those instruments that are not equipped with *mandalákia*.

Playing technique

The *kanonáki* is usually laid upon the thighs of the performer, and is played by means of two plectra *(pénnes,* or *nýchia),* which are attached to the forefinger of each of the player's hands with metal thimbles *(dhactylýthres);* the latter implements were formerly made of silver, or even, in certain instances, of gold. The plectra, nowadays made of plastic, were once fashioned from tortoise-shell, ox-horn,[457] or some similar material. By means of these plectra —which are nothing more than artificial finger-nails (hence the Greek *nýchia*)— the performer plucks the strings of his instrument with greater ease and certainty, playing the lower notes with his left hand and the higher notes with his right. The use of such plectra results in an improved technique and a stronger sound. The inlaid decoration of the sides of the instrument's soundbox, together with the carved openings on the soundboard for the 'voice', are influenced by the decorative art of the Orient.

The kanonáki in the Greek world

In the past, the *kanonáki (qanun, qanoun,* etc.) was known chiefly under the name of *psaltírion,* especially in medieval times. Just when the term *kanonáki* replaced that of *psaltírion* is unknown, although it is clear that this change of nomenclature occurred through the expansion of Islam and the resultant contact of the Arabs and Turks with the peoples of Europe.

The origin of the *psaltírion* have been traced back to the Asian world, many conturies before the period of classical Greece.[458] From ancient Greece herself, many references to musical instruments similar in type to the *kanonáki* have been gleaned. These are to be found in the works of such writers as Aristotle (*Problemata,* 19.23.2), Theophrastus (*Natural Histories,* 5.7.6),[459] Athenaeus, and others, and refer to the instrument by such names as the *tríghonon psaltírion, epighóneion, mághadis* and *simíkion.*[460] However, as there exists no iconographical evidence of these instruments, only hypothetical conjectures (which still await verification) have been possible regarding the link between the ancient Greek *psaltírion* and the modern *kanonáki*.

On the other hand, the Byzantine and post-Byzantine periods, the two great sources of the history of the modern Greek *instrumentarium* —illuminated manuscripts and religious wall-paintings[461]— are rich in information concerning the triangular or trapeziform *psaltírion,* including the manner in which it was held and played, etc. This, despite the fact that with many of these miniatures or wall-paintings it is not always easy to ascertain whether the instrument depicted is a *kanonáki* or a harp. The *psaltírion,* among other musical instruments, is mentioned as having been played at the Hippodrome in Constantinople in a Scandinavian chronicle of the twelfth century.[462] Philippe du Fresne-Canaye, writing in his *Journey* that he saw "a Greek harp" played at the wedding of a rich merchant at Pera, in Constantinople, in 1573, actually meant *kanonáki.*[463]

SANDOURI (Dulcimer)

Construction

The *sandoúri* (dulcimer),[464] an isosceles trapeziform, has triple, quadruple, or quintuple metal strings running lengthwise along the instrument's two parallel sides, and tuned in unison. The *sandoúri* is played by means of two light sticks, called *bagétes;* in the past, the ends of the sticks were wrapped around with a strip of animal skin, but today they are generally wrapped in cotton (fig. 177). The *sandoúri* is made in different sizes, and is constructed from several kinds of well-dried woods. The soundboard is made of coniferous wood, close-grained and free of knots. Onto the soundboard are affixed the bridges (*colonákia,* columns, or *yéfyres,* bridges); one or more soundholes, usually round in shape, are cut into it. Hardwood is used to construct the two sides (*balcónia,* balconies) of the instrument. On the right side, the so-called *dákos* (block), the tuning pegs are placed; small, headless nails are fixed to the left side of the instrument, not quite flush with the surface of the wood. These nails, on the left side (*koútsouro,* stem) of the *sandoúri,* support the strings. Both the tuning pegs and the small nails are fixed slightly aslant —i.e., not at right angles to the soundboard— as thus they can withstand the tension of the strings. The strings are made to sit on 'cushions' (*maxilária*) on the right-and left-hand sides, as this ensures that they remain a constant distance away from the soundboard. The bottom of the instrument (*pláka,* plate, or *pátos,* bottom), and the front and rear side-pieces are made of different kinds of wood. Skilled *sandoúri*-makers, in order to ensure that the instrument will not warp because of humidity or the tension of the strings, make each of the sides from a piece of wood that they have first sliced in half and then glued the two halves together again, but with the grain opposed.

Playing technique — Technical and musical possibilities

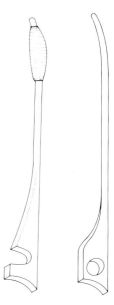

The *sandoúri* is laid upon the thighs of the player *(sandouriéris),* or is played resting upon a table, or even suspended from the player's neck, when, for instance, he accompanies the bridegroom's party on its way to collect the bride, or during the singing of *patinádhes* (distichs), etc. The usual melodic range of the *sandoúri* covers three whole octaves and a few additional notes. However, there do exist smaller instruments with a corresponding smaller melodic range.

The playing sticks *(bagétes)* —with one end slightly turned upwards— are held with the aid of the thumb, between the performer's forefinger and middle finger. Playing technique calls for more use of the wrist than of the two fingers. Both wrist and fingers must be supple and relaxed, as with the clenching of the player's hand the sound produced by the instrument is far from beautiful, and the playing will be heavy and stiff. In the past, musicians often played the *sandoúri* "with their forearms", using sticks that were relatively straight and with a hole in one end; the player's forefinger was inserted into this opening (see fig. 177).

Originally, the *sandoúri* was principally a melodic instrument. It would carry the melody along with other instruments such as the violin, or the clarinet *(klaríno),* while at the same time —according to the nature of the melody played— it would provide a drone *(íson)* in the tonic or fifth, or it would provide a simple harmonic accompaniment to the melody (intervals of an octave, of a fifth, and of a fourth). With the passage of time, and with the influence of western harmonisation, such simple harmonies gave way to common chords or chords of the seventh, with the result that the traditional Greek 'modal' idiom became unfamiliar.

Fig. 177.

299

The *sandoúri* is, in essence, a variant form of the *kanonáki* (psaltery), although it differs from the latter instrument in certain significant aspects. In the case of the *kanonáki*, the sound is produced by the plucking of its strings, and is relatively weak. When the *kanonáki* is played, the repetition of a single note, however rapid the execution, does not give the impression of continuous sound. With the *sandoúri*, however, the sound is produced when the strings of the instrument are struck, and therefore is relatively loud. This playing-technique allows for a great variety of effects: different attacks, nuances of sound, subtle accentuations, melodic ornamentation and diverse rhythmical patterns. Moreover, a skilled *sandouriéris* manages to create the impression of continuous sound through the rapid repetition of a single note.

The sandoúri in the Greek world

The widespread distribution of the *sandoúri* throughout the Greek world is due to the influence of the Greeks of Asia Minor, who fled to Greece as refugees following the Greco-Turkish War of 1922. It is from Asia Minor that both the skilled players of the *sandoúri* and the master-craftsmen of the instrument came to Greece. Nevertheless, the *sandoúri* was played on the Greek mainland and in the islands even before the arrival of the Greeks from Asia Minor; the testimony of older musicians corraborates this. Albeit indirectly, there is evidence that the instrument existed in Athens as early as 1802, according to Edward Daniel Clarke's *Travels,* where the author notes that few Greeks know how to play the dulcimer.[465]

Thanks to its technical and expressive potential, the *sandoúri* soon became an indispensable member of the ensemble: violin, clarinet, dulcimer, lute *(companía: violí, klaríno, sandoúri, laghoúto)*. As it is both a melodic and a polyphonic instrument, the *sandoúri* may be played either alone or as a 'doubling' instrument; in the latter case, it plays the melody in conjunction with either one or with both of the two other melodic instruments, the clarinet and the violin. Again, it can be limited to the simple harmonic under-pinning of the melody played; this was especially the case following the First World War, when the folk song began to strongly reflect the influence of western harmonisation. The *sandoúri* can also be played in such a manner as to mark the rhythmical structure of the melody, according to the demands of the mood of the moment. These various possibilities, together with the ease which the *sandouriéris* can pass from one manner of playing to another, or combine the different effects simultaneously — gradually granted the *sandoúri* an almost 'managerial' position in the *companía*, a position that the instrument continues to occupy up until the present day.[466] Apart from being an important member of the *companía*, the *sandoúri* can also be played in conjunction with the island *ziyiá* (violin, dulcimer, lute), or together with other makeshift combinations of instruments.

Tsímbalo (Cimbalom)

The *tsímbalo* is a large version of the *sandoúri*, permanently stationed on four legs. Its melodic range usually consists of four octaves and a few additional notes, and the arrangement of its strings differs from that of the *sandoúri* in order to facilitate its playing. The *tsímbalo* is also equipped with a pedal —much like the piano— that enables the performer *(tsimbalístas)* to control the resonance and the dynamics (piano-forte) of the sound produced. In order to gain the same advantages, certain *sandoúri*-players have added a similar pedal to their instruments as well, although this innovation has not —at least to date— found many imitators.[467] The following surnames are also worth noting: Sandoúris, Sandourtzís (Telephone Directory Attica, 1977).

LATERNA (Barrel-organ)

The barrel-organ *(latérna)*, like the mandolin and the guitar, is not a traditional Greek popular instrument. Nevertheless, from the last century up until the present day, its cylinders have had folk melodies inscribed —'printed', as they say— upon them, in addition to other kinds of music, for the merry-makers of the urban centres; people who, in addition to the quadrilles and other fashionable dance-tunes so characteristic of that period, sought some pleasant way of returning to the roots of their own indigenous culture at moments of sentimental intensity and nostalgia.

What is most significant about the popular and folk music 'printed' on the cylinders of the *latérna,* however, is its harmonisation. Most skilled 'printers' *(stampadhóri)* —the craftsmen who make up the cylinders by affixing the small pins that describe the melodies— were of foreign extraction, and were born or lived in the urban centres of the nineteenth and twentieth centuries —Constantinople, Smyrna, Piraeus, Syra, Athens et alia. Reared on Italian and Italianate music— opera, canzonetta, and the *cantádhes* of the Ionian islands and Athens[468] — far removed from the tradition of Greek folk song, these *stampadhóri* harmonised the folk melodies they 'printed' in the same manner they did the fashionable western european songs of the day, on the basis of the principles of western music. This harmonisation, so very different from the modal character of Greek folk music, had a certain significance, despite the fact that only a small number of folk songs were 'printed' on the cylinders of the *latérna.* Its importance lies in the fact that the *latérna,* intended to appeal to the broad masses of the people, succeeded through such harmonisation in alienating them from the wholesome tradition of musical aesthetics that had characterised Greek folk song until its introduction. It is true that the treatment folk song received at the hands of the *stampadhóri* constitutes but one of many aspects of the history of the barrel-organ in Greece, and by no means the most important aspect at that. It is equally clear that a more general review of the history of the *latérna* in Greece does not fall within the scope of this book.

Today, out of the vast number of *stampadhóri* of an earlier age, only Nikolaos Armaos is still alive. Born in Constantinople in 1890, he has worked continuously for over fifty years in Piraeus, where he settled in 1923 upon his arrival in Greece. It is to him that one rushes to repair or tune the few *latérnas* that still exist in defiance of the changing times. These few specimens, hounded from the centre of Athens, can still be heard in a few remote neighbourhoods; they are usually tastelessly decorated and poorly tuned, and are played without the once common accompaniment of the tambourine *(défi)* — a faded relic of the romantic Athens of a bygone era.

The *latérna* is also known in Greece as the *orghanáki,* or *romvía;* the last is derived from the manufacturer's trademark, the Italian factory POMBIA, inscribed on the instrument in Latin characters and read according to the Greek values of these letters, ROMVIA.

Some of the chordophones described above are also made as children's sound-producing-toys, often by the children themselves. They use many different materials, from cane and easily worked soft woods to plant fibres, threads, wires, tacks, and whatever else can be of use to a child who wishes to make his very own violin, *líra,* or *tambourás.*

ARTIKOLIRA

The *artikólira* is made in Crete. Constructed by children from *Ferula narthex (ártikas),* a kind of cane native to the island —a light wood that is easily worked— this 'instrument' is equipped with three strings of thread or wire, three pegs, and a bridge. The hairs of the bow are fashioned from strands taken from a donkey's tail or from plant fibres, which are rubbed with resin or even, upon occasion, with incense. When this 'instrument' is equipped with wire strings or old strings from a genuine *líra* it produces a whistling sound of, naturally, indefinite pitch. The *artikólira* is the instrument with which the shepherds' children train themselves until "their fingers go right ahead" and they deserve to hold in their hands a true, finely decorated *líra* of hardwood.

In Crete, the children also make a *líra* with a soundbox consisting of a dried gourd; to this gourd a piece of wood is affixed, serving as the neck of the 'instrument'. The other parts —pegs, strings, bridge and bow— are just like those of the *artikólira*. Older children —from ten to twelve years of age— add to their 'instruments' a soundpost with the assistance of an adult.

TAMBOURAS

In many regions of mainland Greece the children also make the 'instrument' which they call *tambourás*. Onto a long, narrow piece of planking, approximately 40 cm long and 4-7 cm wide, they nail three or four tacks at each end. An equivalent number of strings made of wire or thread are stretched between these nails, from end to end of the board. This 'instrument' is played either with the fingers or with a plectrum made from dried bark or cane. Children who are skilled in wood-carving shape the wood from which the instrument is constructed so that it resembles the true *tambourás* — oviform at one end, and straight at the other end.

DHIOLI

The *dhiolí (violí* or *sándouras)* is to be found throughout Greece, both on the mainland and in the islands. To make this 'instrument', a thick piece of cane is cut out from between two knots. The children then peel off two or four narrow strips of shiny bark from this piece of cane, leaving a slight space between the strips. These are held in an upright position, by means of small wooden bridges positioned at both ends (fig. 178). The bow is fashioned in the same manner, and is rubbed with resin to improve its sound. Some children hack out that section of the cane immediately below the 'strings' in imitation of the hollow soundbox of the violin and the *líra*. The *dhiolí* gives out a whistling sound, the pitch of which is, of course, indefinite.

Fig. 178.

146. Cymbals, shawm and stringed-instrument (?). Greek dance. Du Mont, Nouveau voyage du Levant (1694).

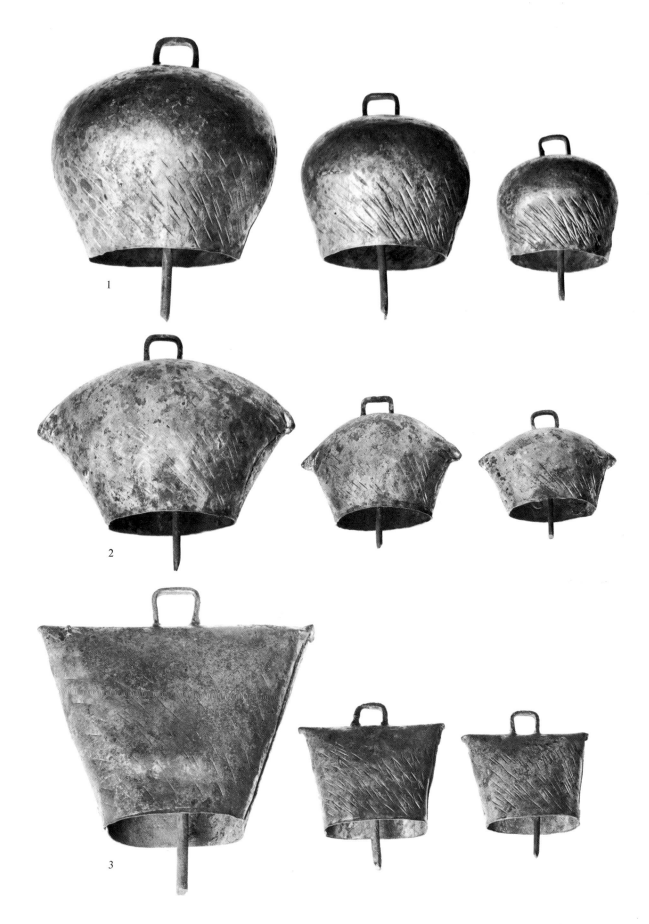

147. Forged bells: 1. "Koudhoúnia" of Amphissa. 2. Bells of Ioannina "with ears". 3. Tsokánia.

148. Forged bells: 1. Léria and 2. Sklavéria of Crete.

149. *Forged bells: 1. Large "koudhoúni" with a small kýpros as a clapper. 2. Large "koudhoúni" of Ioannina "with ears" and with a small kýpros as a clapper.*

150. Forged bells: 1. Tsokáni (fouchtokoúni) of Cyprus. 2. "Koudhoúni" formerly used by the Sarakatsani.

151. Cast-bells: 1. Monós kýpros (single kýpros). 2. Dhiplókypros (double kýpros). 3. 4. Single kýpros with a protruding upper base.

1

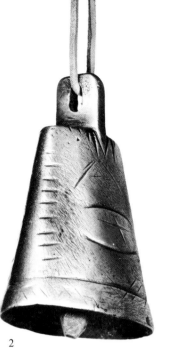

2

152. *Cast-bells: 1. Kýpros with slightly upward turned lips and a curved upper base (type of rabaoúni). 2. Plakerós monós kýpros(single kýpros) with elliptical the two bases. 3. Plakerós dhiplókypros (double kýpros) with elliptical bases. 4. Triplókypros (triple kýpros).*

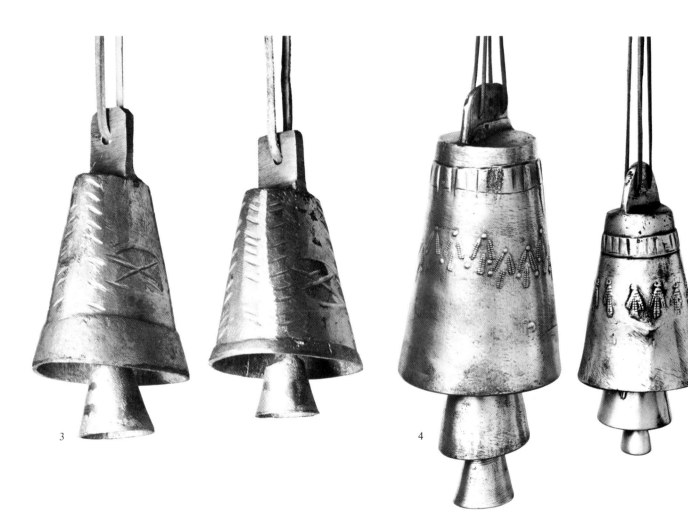

3

4

153. Cast-bells: 1.2. Kambanéli. 3. Pellet-bells.

154. 155. *Choosing bells at a fair in Larissa.*

156. Beast of burden wearing a bell. J.F. Lewis, Illustrations of Constantinople (1835-36).

159. *Cast-bells and forged bells hung around the waists of the "karnavália" in a traditional ritual. Carnival. Nikissiani, region of Pangeon (Cavala) (1972).*

160. *Mock death and dirges. Carnival. Nikissiani, region of Pangeon (Cavala) (1972).*

161. *Triangle and cymbals. Carols in Metsovo.*
→

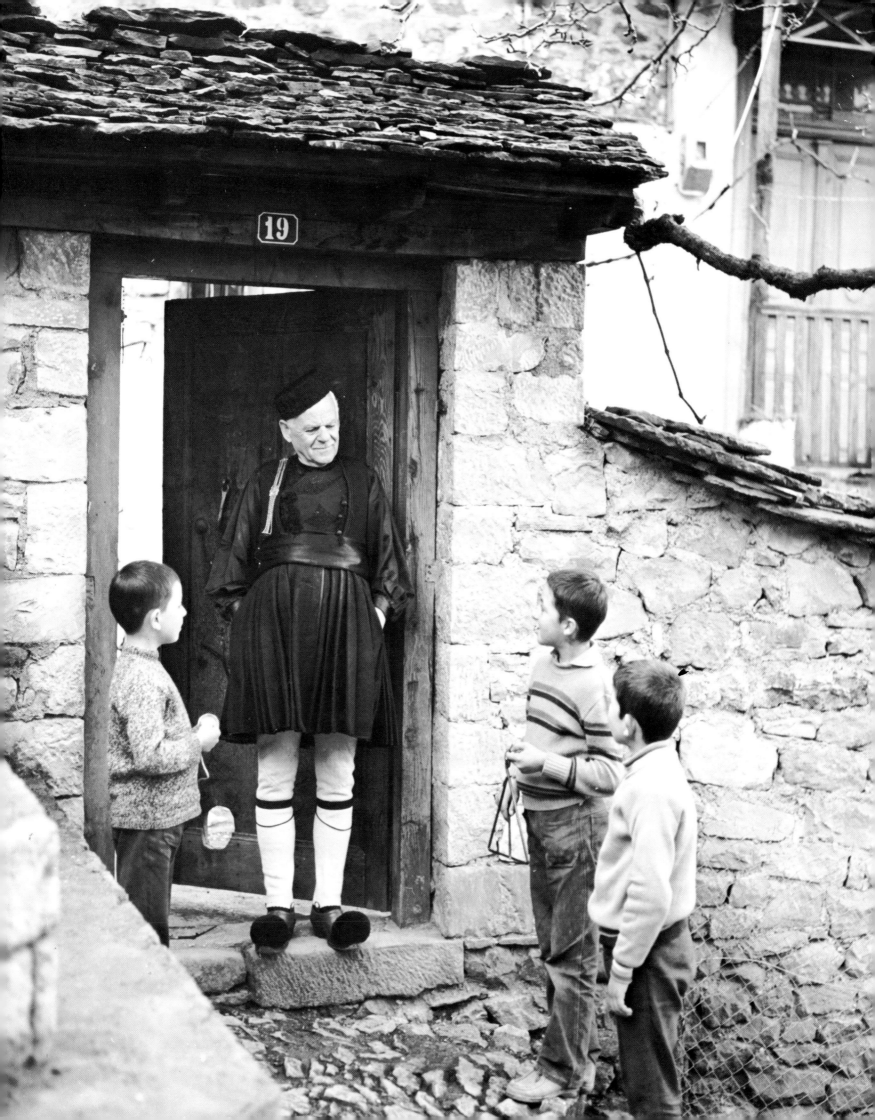

163. Wooden semanterion (kópanos). Monastery Great Lavra, Mount Athos.

162. Iron semanterion (símandro). Monastery of Aghios Nicolaos, Metsovo.

←

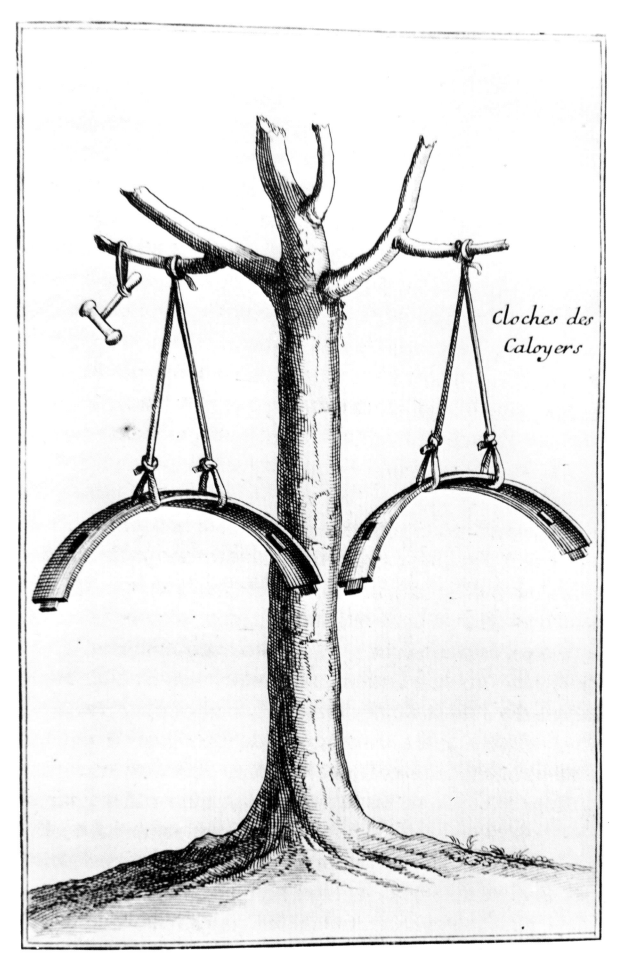

Cloches des
Caloyers

164. Iron semanteria. Tournefort, Relation d'un voyage du Levant (1717).

165. Réndela (wooden clapper). Historical Museum, Galaxidi.

166. Bells on a scarecrow. Metsovo.

→

167. 168. Wine glasses. How they are played, alone or with worry-beads.

169. 170. 171. Wooden spoons. How they are held and manner of playing them.

173. *Hand-clapping (K), tambourine, kemantzá, tambourás (I). "A Grecian Wedding". Aaron Hill, A full and just account of the Ottoman Empire (1709).* →

172. *Sound-producing device in the braids of a dancer. A. De La Motraye, Voyage en Europe, en Asie et en Afrique (1727).*

A GRECIAN WEDDING

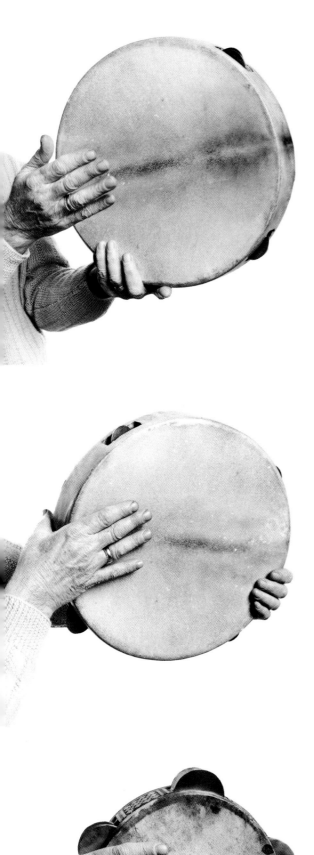

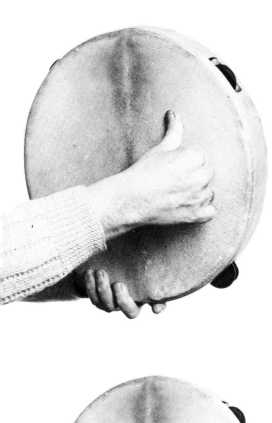

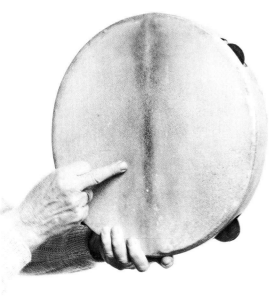

174. Tambourine (défi). Manner of playing.

175. *Shawms and drum. A Greek wedding procession. W. Eton, Schilderung des türkischen Reiches (1805).*

176. Large tambourine with jingles. Dance "Páno-Káto". Stackelberg, Trachten und Gebräuche der Neugriechen (1831).

177. Pottery drum (toumbeléki). Manner of playing.

178. *Pottery drum.*
Carols in Mytilene.

ἐ

σου

λόγι

μ(ι)α

ΤΗϹϹ

λαζ̄ε

πόμ

ἀν

αὐπ

ΤΗθε

179. *Double aulos. Initial letter in the Ms Sinai Gr. 1047, Liturgy, fol. 3 v. Library of Congress, Washington.*

180. *Bagpipe with drone. Greek musician of Athens. Anonymous, Drawings (1810). Gennadius Library, Athens.*

181. *Shawm and tambourine. Greek dance. H.W. Williams, Travels in Italy, Greece and the Ionian Islands (1820).*

182. *Bagpipe with drone. Drawing by Stefanos Mandalos, Makronissos (1950).*

183. *Greek dance accompanied by a droneless bagpipe. M. Guys, Voyage littéraire de la Grèce (1783).*

184. *Greek peasant with bag-pipe with drone. Nicolas de Nicolay, Les navigations, peregrinations et voyages (1577).*

Villageois Grec

185. *Shawms and drum. Traditional ritual "Maïdhes", Pelion.*

186. *Zournás-player of Pelion.* →

187. *Bagpipe with drone (gáida) of Thrace. Different positions of the drone. (Player: Theodoros Kekes).*

188. *Greek islander with tambourás. De Ferriol, Recueil de cent estampes (1714).*

→

189. *Lute. Miniatures of the Ms Erotokritos (1710), Harley 5644, British Museum, London.*

191. *Pear-shaped lira. Model for a Byzantine style icon. 18th/19th cent. (?).*
→

190. *Pear-shaped lira. Engraved design on a bowl. Greek Folk Art Museum, Athens.*

192. *Pear-shaped líra and lute (laghoúto). Crete.*

193. Bottle-shaped lira of Greeks from Pontos (Black Sea area). (Player: Alecos Akrivopoulos).

194. 195. *Pear-shaped lira. Manner of holding the bow. The strings of the lira are not stopped with the tips of the player's fingers, but the player's fingernails are pressed against the strings.*

196. *Psaltery (kanonáki). The strings are plucked by means of two plectra which are attached to the fore-*
    fingers of the player's hands with metal thimbles.

1   2

197. *1. Children's líra with soundbox made from a dried gourd. 2. Artikólira, children's líra made of ártika (kind of cane).*

←

198. *Dulcimer (sandoúri). Manner of playing (positions of the hands). (Player: Tassos Diakoyiorgis).*

199. Liras and drum (daoúli). Anastenaria. Aghia Eleni, Serres (1970).

200. *Nicolaos Armaos in his workshop. Reparing the hammers of a barrel-organ.*

201. *Yiannis Paleologos, maker of instruments of the lute family in his workshop.*

202. *Barrel-organ (latérna) and tambourine (défi).* →

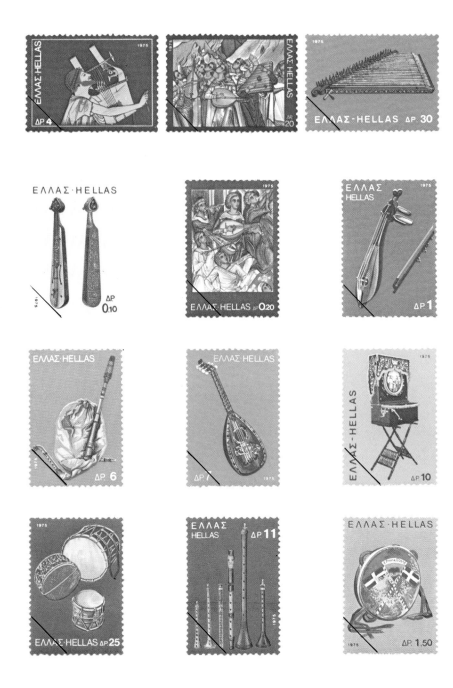

In December 1975, a series of postage stamps depicting Greek popular musical instruments went into circulation. The series consists of twelve stamps, designed by Panayiotis Gravalos and Vassiliki Constantinea. The instruments represented come from the collection of Fivos Anoyanakis, and, with only one exception, are to be found illustrated in this volume.

NOTES

1. The popularly accepted date for the outbreak of the Greek War of Independence is March 25, 1821. Although the Greek proclamation of Independence was made in January 1822, it was not until the Convention of London in 1830 that the great powers officially recognised Greece as a sovereign and independent state. Thus, from a peripheral province of the Ottoman Empire, Greece became a small nation state on the European model.

2. *Paraloghés* constitute a category of narrative songs or 'ballads' of imaginary ("fictitious") contents, such as Μάννα μὲ τοὺς ἐνιὰ ὑγιούς [The Mother with Nine Sons], Τοῦ νεκροῦ ἀδελφοῦ [The Song of the Dead Brother], Τῆς "Αρτας τὸ γεφύρι [The Bridge of Arta], Γυρισμὸς τοῦ ξενιτεμένου [The Exile's Return]. Linos Politis, *A History of Modern Greek Literature*, Oxford 1973, 85.

3. S.P. Kyriakidis, Αἱ Ἱστορικαὶ ἀρχαὶ τῆς δημώδους νεοελληνικῆς ποιήσεως [The Historical Origins of Modern Greek Poetry], Thessaloniki 1954. K. Th. Dimaras, Ἱστορία τῆς νεοελληνικῆς λογοτεχνίας [History of Modern Greek Literature], 6th edn., Athens, 3-22. Linos Politis, *A History of Modern Greek Literature*, 85, 88.

4. Thr. Georgiadis, *Der griechische Rhythmus, Musik, Reigen, Vers und Sprache*, Hamburg 1949.

5. S. Baud-Bovy, "L'accord de la lyre antique et la musique populaire de la Grèce moderne", *Revue de musicologie*, 53/1 (1967), 3-20.

6. S. Baud-Bovy, "Équivalences métriques dans la musique vocale grecque antique et moderne", *Revue de musicologie*, 54/1 (1968), 3-15.

7. A. Keramopoullos, "Ἡ ἐθνική μας μουσικὴ καὶ οἱ χοροὶ" [Our National Music and Dances], Ἡμερο-λόγιον Μεγάλης Ἑλλάδος, 1925.

8. S. Baud-Bovy, *Chansons populaires de Crète occidentale*, Geneva 1972.

9. S.P. Kyriakidis, Ἑλληνικὴ Λαογραφία [Greek Folklore], Part I, Μνημεῖα τοῦ λόγου [Texts], 2nd edn., Athens [Academy of Athens, Publications of the Folklore Archives, No 8], 1965, 5-118. Ἑλληνικὰ δημοτικὰ τραγούδια (Ἐκλογὴ) [Greek Folk Songs (Selection)], I, Introduction by G. Spyridakis, Athens [Academy of Athens, Publications of the Folklore Archives, No 7], 1962, p. ε΄-λα΄. G. Spyridakis and Sp. Peristeris, Ἑλληνικὰ δημοτικὰ τραγούδια (Μουσικὴ Ἐκλογὴ) [Greek Folk Songs (Musical Selection)], III, Athens [Academy of Athens,

Publications of the Greek Folklore Research Centre, No 10], 1968.

It should be noted that ethnomusicological research has yet to furnish a generally acceptable solution of the problem of how folk song came into existence. It is unknown whether the genre's original creator was a single individual, whose name is now lost, or many people, and whether the person or people concerned were of agricultural, pastoral or urban background. Nowadays the majority of scholars are less concerned with identifying the original bearer of a folk melody than with the melody itself. See C. Braïloïu, "Le folklore musical", *Musica aeterna*, Zürich 1949. "Folk music is, above all, the art of variation", and the people's contribution to its creation is indirect. When a song is felt to belong to a people, to express some aspect of their world, the song will be worked over again and again in performance: the superfluous is removed, additions are made, poetic and musical phrases are rounded off, rhymes and rhythm are corrected, words are changed, etc. These and other processes are what give a folk song its perfection.

10. The term "ethnic musical instruments" has been adopted by the "International Committee on Museums and Collections of Musical Instruments", a branch of the UNESCO (International Council of Museums); see *Ethnic Musical Instruments. Identification-Conservation*, ed. by Jean Jenkins, London 1970.

11. The scientific division of the *natural* and *tempered* scale. The natural scale has intervals of a major tone, minor tone and minim-minor tone, whereas the tempered scale only has intervals of a tone and a semitone.

By *interval*, we mean the quotient that results from dividing the number of vibrations of the higher note by the number of vibrations of the lower note. For the intervals of the byzantine music, see N. Ath. Chrysochoidis, "Τὰ τονιαῖα διαστήματα τῶν κλιμάκων τῆς βυζαντινῆς μουσικῆς μετὰ καὶ σχε-τικῶν διαγραμμάτων" [The Intervals of the Scales of Byzantine Music], *Mélanges offerts à Octave et Melpo Merlier*, III, Athens 1957, 235-253.

12. Sp. Peristeris, "Δημοτικὰ τραγούδια Δροπόλεως Βορείου Ἠπείρου" [Folk Songs of Dropolis, Northern Epirus], Ἐπετηρὶς τοῦ Λαογραφικοῦ Ἀρ-χείου, 9-10 (1955-1957) [Athens 1958], 105-133. Ant.

Lavdas, "Πεντάφθογγοι κλίμακες ἐν τῇ δημώδει μουσικῇ τῆς Ἠπείρου" [Five-tone Scales in the Folk Music of Epirus], Ἠπειρωτικὴ Ἑστία, 7 (Ioannina 1958), 135-141. D. Stockmann— W. Fiedler— E. Stockmann, Albanische Volksmusik, I: Gesänge der Çamen, Berlin 1965.

13. S. Baud-Bovy, Chansons du Dodécanèse, II, Paris 1938, 226-227, 231-238, 243-244, 251-252.

14. Zyiá, zýia, zy(i)a, zýi: from ζυγὸς = balance, ζευγάρι = pair as of two instruments.

15. Companía or coumpanía: from the Italian compagnia. Originally, during the first decade of the 20th century, the instruments of the companía were the clarinet, the violin and the lute. The dulcimer was added a little later, around 1920.

16. In Greek there is no equivalent term for luthier, the instrument - maker, first of lutes, and then in time of all the stringed instruments. The 'learned' words instrument - maker and instrument - factory were used on cards and labels together with the name of the maker. There were affixed on inside the soundbox of the instruments. Such terms were not used in the everyday speech of popular musicians or instrument - makers; they always say craftsman (mástoras), workshop (erghastíri).

17. 1922 witnessed the loss of the territories in Asia Minor awarded to Greece by the treaty of Sèvres (1921) and the defeat of the Greek Army by the Turks. The final act in the tragedy was the carefully prepared offensive of the Turks in August 1922. In two weeks they destroyed the Greek Army and drove the survivors to Smyrna, which was given up to fire and sword. The exodus of one and a half of million of Greeks refugees that followed marked the end of centuries of Hellenism in Asia Minor.

18. The dates 1811-1840 in the Great Greek Encyclopaedia (Pyrsos) aud the Helios Encyclopaedic Dictionary (Helios) are wrong, according to E. Veloudios' grandchildren Thanos Veloudios and Marika Veloudiou. The oldest known dated lute of E. Veloudios was made in 1862 (F. Anoyanakis' Collection of Greek Popular Instruments).

19. F. Anoyanakis, "Νεοελληνικὰ χορδόφωνα. Τὸ λαγοῦτο" [Neohellenic Chordophones. The Lute], Λαογραφία, 28 (Athens 1972), 217-218, 223 (with a summary in French, 483-499).

20. Dim. Loucopoulos, Γεωργικὰ τῆς Ρούμελης [Rural Life in Roumeli], Athens 1938, 50-61. K. Biris. Οἱ Γύφτοι. Μελέτη λαογραφικὴ καὶ ἐθνογραφικὴ [The Gypsies. Ethnological Study], Athens 1942. Idem, Ρὼμ καὶ Γύφτοι. Ἐθνογραφία καὶ ἱστορία τῶν τσιγγάνων [Rom and Gypsies. Ethnography and History of the Gypsies], Athens 1954. J.L.S. Bartholdy, Voyage en Grèce, fait dans les années 1803 et 1804, II, Paris 1807, 232. Edward Daniel Clarke, Travels in Various Countries of Europe, Asia and Africa, III, London 1814, 644. F.C.H.L. Pouqueville, Voyage dans la Grèce, I, Paris 1820, 292-297; II, 162, 167, 335-337, 375-376; V, Paris 1821, 191, 193.

21. Despina Mazaraki, Τὸ λαϊκὸ κλαρίνο στὴν Ἑλλάδα [The Popular Clarinet in Greece], Athens 1959, 50-52.

22. S. Baud-Bovy, Études sur la chanson cleftique, Athens 1958, 78, 83.

23. S. Baud-Bovy, Chansons populaires de Crète occidentale, Geneva 1972, 298-299.

24. Sp. Skiadaressis, "Ἀριέττα καὶ καντάδα στὴ γνήσια Κεφαλλονίτικη μορφή της" [The true Cephalonian Arietta and Cantádha], Ἠώς, 3rd period, 5, No 58-60 (Athens 1962), 146-148.

25. G. Lambelet, La musique populaire grecque. Chants et danses, Athens 1934, 93, 139, 192. See also L.A. Bourgault-Ducoudray's collection, Trente mélodies de Grèce et d'Orient [mostly urban songs], Paris 1876. S. Baud-Bovy, "Grèce moderne", Encyclopédie de la musique (Fasquelle), II, Paris 1959, 342-343.

26. From: rebétis, rebeskés = escapist, lazy, a good-for-nothing, Ioannis Stamatakos' Dictionary of the Modern Greek Language (Λεξικὸν τῆς Νέας Ἑλληνικῆς Γλώσσης), 3 vols., Athens 1971. According to N.P. Andriotis' Etymological Dictionary of the Modern Greek Language (Ἐτυμολογικὸ λεξικὸ τῆς κοινῆς νεοελληνικῆς), Athens 1951, the word is "perhaps from the same theme as the Slavic rebenok = boy, young man".

27. The origin of the rebétiko song can be traced back to the closing decade of the nineteenth century. In our opinion, however, the roots of the genre should be sought in an earlier period. Up to now, no strict musicological investigation has been carried out on the history of the rebético song. Nor, for that matter, has any research or study been made of the considerable number of gramophone recordings in circulation before the beginning of the Second World War. A variety of instruments, including, among others, a dulcimer, a violin, a short-necked lute (oúti), a bouzoúki were used to accompany rebetika songs during the period between World Wars I and II. See: G.D. Skouriotis, "Εἰσαγωγὴ στὴν κοινωνιολογικὴ ἐξέταση τοῦ δημοτικοῦ τραγουδιοῦ" [Introduction to the Sociological Study of the Folk Song], Κοινωνιολογικὴ Ἔρευνα, I (Athens 1957), No 1, 55-66; No 2/3, 142-152. T. Vournas, "Τὸ σύγχρονο λαϊκὸ τραγούδι" [Contemporary Popular Song], Ἐπιθεώρηση Τέχνης, 13 (Athens 1961), 297-285. F. Anoyanakis, "Γιὰ τὸ ρεμπέτικο τραγούδι" [On the Rebétiko], Ἐπιθεώρηση Τέχνης, 14 (Athens 1961), 11-20. E.I. Machairas, "Τὸ ρεμπέτικο καὶ τὸ σύγχρονο λαϊκὸ τραγούδι" [The 'Rebétiko' and Contemporary Popular Song], Καινούργια Ἐποχή, 6 (Athens 1961), 84-99. D. Christianopoulos, Ἱστορικὴ καὶ αἰσθητικὴ διαμόρφωση τοῦ ρεμπέτικου τραγουδιοῦ [Historical Evolution of the Rebétiko Song], edn. Διαγώνιος, Thessaloniki 1961 (with an extensive bibliography, 1-18). El. Petropoulos, Ρεμπέτικα τραγούδια [Rebétika Songs], Athens 1968. M. Vamvakaris, Αὐτοβιογραφία [Autobiography], Athens 1973. Two biographies of Rebétika-Singers (G. Rovertakis and K. Roukounas, Samiotaki) by T. Schorelis - M. Ikonomidis, Ἕνας ρεμπέτης Γ. Ροβερτάκης, Athens 1973, and Ἕνας ρεμπέτης, Κ. Ρούκουνας, Σαμιωτάκι, Athens 1974. T. Schorelis, Ρεμπέτικη Ἀνθολογία [Anthology of Rebética], Athens

1977. G.G. Papaioannou, "Ἡ μουσικὴ τῶν ῥεμπέτικων, ἀνανέωση ἢ ἐπιστροφὴ στὶς ρίζες;" [The Music of the Rebétiko Song. Rebirth or Return to the Roots?], Χρονικὸ '73 [Art Gallery ORA] Athens 1973, 282-296. M. Dragoumis, Ἑλληνικὴ παραδοσιακὴ μουσική. Τὸ ρεμπέτικο τραγούδι [Traditional Greek Music. The Rebétiko Song], edn. Wander, Biochemie, Athens 1974 (with an extensive bibliography). Gail Holst, Road to the Rembetica, Athens 1974. S. Damianakos, Κοινωνιολογία τοῦ ρεμπέτικου [Sociology of the Rebétiko], (Athens) 1976.

28. Introductory notes by Manos Hadjidakis in his record, Τὰ «Πέριξ», παλιὰ λαϊκὰ τραγούδια ["Ta Perix", Old Folk Songs], 1974.

29. Apart from plucked tambourás-type instruments (bouzoúki and baghlamás) and the instruments used for 'art music' (piano, electric guitar, etc.), both rebétiko and the more recent popular 'art music' have turned in the last few years to such traditional popular instruments as the dulcimer (sandoúri) and the clarinet (klaríno) as well. The use of such instruments is a kind of musical fashion, a form of 'folklorismus'— "which includes the tendency to falsification as though the latter were an inherent part of its identity"; see M.G. Meraklis, "Τί εἶναι [What is] Folklorismus", Λαογραφία, 28 (1972), 27-38.

30. 'Old Greece' refers to the territory comprising the young Greek state, extending from the Peloponnese to Mt. Olympos (see note 1).

31. Haxthausen's Collection, although it was compiled earlier (1814), was only published in 1935: Neugriechische Volkslieder, gesammelt von Werner von Haxthausen, Münster i. W. 1935.

32. C. Fauriel, Chants populaires de la Grèce moderne, 2 vols., Paris 1824-1825.

33. L.A. Bourgault-Ducoudray, Trente mélodies populaires de la Grèce et d'Orient, Paris 1876.

34. See Melpo Merlier, Essai d'un tableau du folklore musical grec, Athens 1935. P.E. Formozis, Contribution à l'étude de la chanson et de la musique populaire grecque, Thessaloniki 1938. G. Spyridakis and Sp. Peristeris, Ἑλληνικὰ δημοτικὰ τραγούδια (Μουσικὴ ἐκλογή) [Greek Folk Songs (Musical Selection)], III, Athens [Academy of Athens, Publications of the Greek Folklore Research Centre No 10], 1968, p. η'-ια'.

35. Despina Mazaraki, Τὸ λαϊκὸ κλαρίνο στὴν Ἑλλάδα [The Popular Clarinet in Greece], Athens 1959. Idem, "Some Notes on Greek Shepherd Flutes", Bulletin de l'Institut de musique, 13 (1969), [Académie Bulgare des Sciences], 275-284.

36. G. Spyridakis and Sp. Peristeris, Ἑλληνικὰ δημοτικὰ τραγούδια (Μουσικὴ Ἐκλογή) [Greek Folk Songs (Musical Selection)] III, p. ια'. We should also note Stavros Karakassis' Ἑλληνικὰ μουσικὰ ὄργανα [Greek Musical Instruments], Athens 1970. For comments on the latter, see F. Anoyanakis, "Ἡ ἔρευνα γιὰ τὰ ἑλληνικὰ μουσικὰ ὄργανα" [Research on Greek Musical Instruments], offprint from Νεοελληνικὸς Λόγος, Athens 1973, 142-159.

37. A. Schaeffner, "Les instruments de musique", Larousse de la Musique, Paris 1957, 468. Bruno Nettl, Music in Primitive Culture, 2nd edn., Cambridge, USA 1969, 90-95.

38. C. Sachs, Geist und Werden der Musikinstrumente, Berlin 1929. A. Schaeffner, Origine des instruments de musique, Paris 1936.

39. C. Sachs, World History of the Dance, New York 1937, 10-203.

40. Older systems of notation (even including that of ancient Greece), though of value to us today, are no more than simple mnemonic aids. See also Jaap Kunst, Ethnomusicology, 3rd edn., The Hague 1959, 1. Kurt and Ursula Reinhard, Turquie, Paris 1969, 91-92. A. Daniélou, Inde du Nord, Paris 1966, 42. Tran Van Khe, Viêt-Nam, Paris 1967, 64-66.

41. For a list of relevant books, records and films, see: A. Schaeffner, Origine des instruments de musique, 1936. Jaap Kunst, Ethnomusicology, 3rd edn., The Hague 1959. Idem, Supplement to the third edition of Ethnomusicology, The Hague 1960. J. Chailley, Précis de musicologie, ouvrage collectif publié sous la direction de J. Chailley, Paris 1958, Encyclopédie de la Pléiade, Ethnologie générale, volume publié sous la direction de J. Poirier, Paris 1968, 1375.

42. In the case of these musical cultures (those of China, Japan, Indochina, Indonesia, the Arabs, etc.), traditional music is the music cultivated in the various regal and princely courts and, more generally, in the patricians' palaces, as opposed to the popular music of the people.

43. J.J.M. Amiot (1718-1794, Jesuit missionary), Mémoire sur la musique des Chinois, Paris 1779.

44. G.A. Villoteau (1759-1839), De l'état actuel de l'art musical en Égypte, Paris 1812. Idem, De l'état actuel de l'art musical en Égypte, Paris 1826. Id., Description historique, technique et littéraire des instruments de musique des Orientaux, Paris 1813.

45. A.J. Ellis (1814-1890), "On the Musical Scales of Various Nations", Journal of the Society of Arts, 1885.

46. J. Kunst, Ethnomusicology, 3rd edn., The Hague 1959, 12.

47. G. Herzog, "Research in Primitive and Folk Musik in the United States", Bulletin of the American Council of Learned Societies, 24 (1936).

48. H. Pernot, Mélodies populaires de l'île de Chio, Paris 1903. See Melpo Merlier, "La chanson populaire grecque", Acta musicologica, 32, fascicles II/III (Basel 1960), 68-77. G. Spyridakis and Sp. Peristeris, Ἑλληνικὰ δημοτικὰ τραγούδια [Greek Folk Songs], III, p. η'.

49. (K. Psachos), 50 δημώδη ἄσματα Πελοποννήσου καὶ Κρήτης. Συλλογὴ Ὠδείου Ἀθηνῶν [Fifty Folk Songs from the Peloponnese and Crete. Collection of the Athens' Conservatory], Athens 1930.

50. On the history of the Musical Section (formerly the "National Musical Collection") of the Greek Folklore Research Centre (formerly the "Folklore Archives"), see G. Spyridakis and Sp. Peristeris, Ἑλληνικὰ δημοτικὰ τραγούδια [Greek Folk

Songs], III, p. στ'-ζ'.

51. Despina Mazaraki, *Τὸ λαϊκὸ κλαρίνο στὴν Ἑλλάδα* [The Popular Clarinet in Greece], Athens 1959.

52. Sp. Peristeris, "Ὁ ἄσκαυλος (τσαμπούνα) εἰς τὴν νησιωτικὴν Ἑλλάδα'" [The Bagpipe *(tsaboúna)* in the Islands of Greece], *Ἐπετηρὶς Λαογραφικοῦ Ἀρχείου*, 13/14 (1960-1961), 52-72.

53. F. Anoyanakis, "Νεοελληνικὰ χορδόφωνα. Τὸ λαγοῦτο" [Neohellenic Chordophones. The Lute], *Λαογραφία*, 28 (Athens 1972), 175-240 (with a summary in French, 483-499). Comparable studies of the drum, the bell, the pear-shaped *líra* and other instruments are now awaiting publication.

Fig. 179.

54. Many of the names of modern Greek musical instruments are derived from related Turkish terms. Examples: *zíli* (zil), *massá* (maşa), *daoúli* (davul), *défi* (tef), *toumbeléki* (dümbelek), *zournás* (zurna), *gáida* (gayda), *bouroú* (boru), *baghlamás* (baglama), *kementzés* (kemençe), *kemanés* (keman), *sandoúri* (santur).

This borrowing of words is the result of long years of Greek contact with the Turks, especially during the two centuries leading up to the War of Independence of 1821. During this period, the Turkish ruling class frequently employed Greek popular musicians for their entertainment. Good Greek players were much in demand at Turkish festivities until quite recently, as we learn from older Greeks from Macedonia, the Black Sea area and Asia Minor. E.D. Clarke's remark that he found Greek musicians playing Turkish music in January 1803, is a case in point (E.D. Clarke, *Travels in Various Countries of Europe, Asia and Africa*, IV, London 1816, 439).

Today, according to the conclusions of ethnomusicology we are aware of the fact that all the instruments to be found in ancient Greece (lyra, aulos, etc.) existed prior to the birth of ancient Greek civilisation, and were imported to the Greek world from other countries ("No instrument originated in Greece", C. Sachs, *The History of Musical Instruments*, New York 1940, 128). The same holds true for the instruments used by the Greek people in the post-Byzantine era, and more recent times as well. An instrument, however, has its place in the musical tradition of a country, only when its people have sung their joys and sorrows on it, especially in crucial times in their history, regardless of whether this instrument has come from abroad, from a near or far country. Neohellenic instruments, regardless of their origins, have been deeply loved and have been made with love and care and craftsmanship by local craftsmen and players, from the Byzantine era until the present day.

55. S.P. Kyriakidis, *Ἑλληνικὴ Λαογραφία* [Greek Folklore], Part I, *Μνημεῖα τοῦ λόγου* [Texts], 2nd edn., Athens 1965, 62.

56. E.M. von Hornbostel and C. Sachs, "Systematik der Musikinstrumente", *Zeitschrift für Ethnologie*, 46 (1914), 553-590. See also the translation of this same study by Antony Baines and Klaus P. Wachsmann, "Classification of Musical Instruments", *The Galpin Society Journal*, No 14, March 1961 (offprint, Amsterdam 1969), 3-39.

We use the term sound-producer (Schallgeräte, Germ.,) — as other writers have already done — for sound-producing devices, as for example bull-roarers, whistles, the semanterion, which cannot be considered musical instruments.

See also *Musikinstrumente der Völker*, Aussereuropäische Musikinstrumente und Schallgeräte: Systematik und Themenbeispiele, Sammlungskatalog des Museums für Völkerkunde, Wien 1975.

57. For the order: terminology, construction, etc., we followed the way each musical instrument was presented in the *Handbuch der Europäischen Volksmusikinstrumente*, edited by Ernst Emsheimer and Erich Stockmann, Stockholm-Berlin. (In this edition see Serie I, vol. I, Bálint Sárosi, *Die Volksmusikinstrumente Ungarns*, Leipzig 1967).

58. *Kemantzá* or *rebábi* or *ribápi*. Stringed bowed instrument, with long neck, an usually round soundbox, and with a rather long and pointed tail-pin and two strings. It is played in the same way as the pear-shaped *líra* (see adjacent figure 179).

This instrument used to be encountered— though not very often— in Greece. It is no longer used nowadays.

"Noblemen dancing... holding in their hands the so-called *fengía*". According to Vogt, *fengía*, probably are "a stick surmounted by a crescent" ("un bâton surmonté d'un croissant"), see Constantin Porphyrogennetus, *Le livre des cérémonies,* ed. Albert Vogt, II, Paris 1939, 103. Vénétia Cottas regards *fengía* as a type of castanets and identifies them with *vomvonária*, see Vénétia Cottas, *Le théâtre à Byzance*, Paris 1931, 12, 33.

On *vomvonária*, "probably instruments producing a bruzzing sound", see Ph. Koukoules, *Βυζαντινῶν βίος καὶ πολιτισμὸς* [Byzantine Life and Civilisation], III, Athens 1949, 116 footnote 2, 187: "While the *tzoukánes* were playing, the others were singing and together they approached the maiden". The *tzoukánes* were probably wind instruments. The same observation is made by the editor of the Epic of Digenis Akritas, see P.P. Kalonaros, *Βασίλειος Διγενὴς Ἀκρίτας,* II, Athens 1970, MS Escorial, lines 1033-1034.

"The donkey sounded the trumpet, the camel is dancing, the mouse on top beats on the *tavlabássia*", see *Διήγησις παιδιόφραστος τῶν τετραπόδων ζώων* [Playful Tale about Quadrupeds], ed. G. Wagner, *Carmina graeca medii aevi,* Lipsiae 1874, p. 178, lines 1068-1069. *Tavlabássia:* probably a type of drum, from the Arabic *tabla* = drum, see C. Sachs, *Reallexikon der Musikinstrumente.*

59. Eudokia Miliatzidou-Ioannou, "Οἱ καμπάνες τῆς Θεσσαλονίκης. Πληροφορίες γιὰ τοὺς τεχνίτες καὶ τὴν τέχνη τους" [The Bells of Thessaloniki. Information about the Craftsmen and their Art], *Μακεδονικά*, 12 (Thessaloniki 1972), 234-263.

60. *Zilia*, from the Turkish *zil* = cymbal. In Megara, and the area around it, the large *zilia* (diam. 12-14 cm) were called *sachánia* or *sachanákia* because they

362

resemble a small frying-pan with two handles, *saghanáki* (from the Turkish *sahan*). The player was called *sachanatáris*.

61. In Megara, until the Second World War, the following popular lines on the fees paid popular musicians were sung: "Put your right hand inside your silver pocket/Take a 'kosipentari' (= 25 Drachmae), give it to the *sachanatáris*".

62. When children had no money with which to buy *zília*, they made *zília* from the round tops of tin-cans or they used the lids from kettles.

63. Lavignac, *Encyclopédie de la musique*, Part I, *Histoire de la musique. La musique arabe*, V, Paris 1922, 2794, 2936. J. Blades, *Percussion Instruments and their History*, London 1970, 86, 108, 176, 180, 185, 314, 386.

64. For the part played by the 'café-aman' in the propagation of the *companía*, see Despina Mazaraki, *Tò λαϊκὸ κλαρίνο στὴν Ἑλλάδα* [The Popular Clarinet in Greece], Athens 1959, 48-50. Café-aman: place of entertainment equipped with a stage, where popular musicians play "alla turca" and female performers (usually two in number) dance and sing.

65. Gr. P. Efthimiou, "Ὁ Κιοπὲκ Μπέης Διδυμοτείχου" [The 'Kiopek Bey' in Didymotichon], *Ἀρχεῖον τοῦ Θρακικοῦ λαογραφικοῦ καὶ γλωσσικοῦ θησαυροῦ*, 19 (1954), 155, 156. Katerina I. Kakouri, *Dionysiaka*, Athens 1965, 95: "This procession was made up of women only led off by the 'kadina' wearing a red dress... castanets on her fingers", i.e. small cymbals wrongly translated in English as 'castanets' (first edition in Greek 1963).

66. M. Wegner, "Griechenland", *Musikgeschichte in Bildern*, Leipzig 1963, 60-61. J. Blades, *Percussion Instruments and their History*, London 1970, 179, Pl. 70, 71. In addition see A. Inodgrass, *Early Greek Armour and Weapons*, Edinburgh University Press 1964, 38-51, where the author convincingly maintains that the greater number of archaeological finds believed until today to be cymbals "may, with varying degrees of certainty, be called shield-bosses". Among these are to be considered the finds from the graves of Mouliana (near Sitia, Crete), Minoan period (circa 1200 B.C.), which according to Inodgrass were erroneously thought to be cymbals. See S. Xanthoudidis, "Ἐκ Κρήτης (Οἱ Τάφοι τῶν Μουλιανῶν)", *Ἀρχαιολογικὴ Ἐφημερίς*, 1904, 46-48.

67. Clement of Alexandria, *Λόγος δεύτερος*, Chap. IV: Πῶς χρὴ περὶ τὰς ἑστιάσεις ἀνίεσθαι, ed. Otto Stählin, I, Leipzig 1905, 181.

68. Gregory the Divine, *Ἔπη ἱστορικά*, Migne, *P.G.* 37, line 1211.

69. John Chrysostom, *Ἅπαντα*, Migne, *P.G.* 51, line 211.

70. Gregory, Bishop of Nyssa, Migne, *P.G.* 44, line 484.

71. *Τῆς ἐν Λαοδικείᾳ συνόδου Κανὼν ΝΓ* [Canon 53 of the Council of Laodicea (360 A.D.)], see G.A. Rallis and M. Potlis, *Σύνταγμα τῶν θείων καὶ ἱερῶν κανόνων* [Collection of the Divine and Sacred Canons], III, Athens 1853, 220.

72. Constantine Porphyrogennetus, *Le livre des cérémonies*, ed. Albert Vogt, II, Paris 1940, 180, 181, and *Commentaire*, 184, 185.

73. Nikitas Choniatis, *Ἱστορία*, ed. Bekker, Bonn 1835, 655.

74. P.P. Kalonaros, *Βασίλειος Διγενὴς Ἀκρίτας*, II, Athens 1970, MS Grottaferrata (14th century), p. 63 lines 845-850. G.N. Hadjikostis, "Κυπριακὰ ἄσματα" [Songs of Cyprus], *Λαογραφία*, 15 (1953-1954), 436.

75. Leo Deacon, *Ἱστορία*, Bonn 1828, 133.

76. Franz Drexl, "Das anonyme Traumbuch des cod. Paris. Gr. 2511" (14th century), *Λαογραφία*, 8 (1921), 358, line 135. See also Ph. Koukoules, *Βυζαντινῶν βίος καὶ πολιτισμός* [Byzantine Life and Civilisation], V, Athens 1952, 193.

77. From the multitude of representations with cymbals in illuminated byzantine manuscripts and wall-paintings in churches we shall note only those that are characteristic in form, dimensions, and manner of playing the cymbals during the Byzantine and post-Byzantine era:
Henri Omont, *Miniatures des plus anciens manuscrits grecs de la Bibliothèque Nationale, du VIe au XIVe siècle*, Paris 1929, Pl. V (Greek MS 139, fol. 5v, 10th cent.); Pl. XLII (Greek MS 510, fol. 264v, circa 880); MS Coislin 239 (fol. 121-122v, 12th century). Suzy Dufrenne, *L'illustration des psautiers grecs du Moyen Age*, I, Paris 1966, Pl. 29 (MS 61, Pantocrator Monastery, Mount Athos, fol. 206r, 9th cent.). Jean Ebersolt, *La miniature byzantine*, Paris-Bruxelles 1926, 19, Pl. XIII. See also Hugo Buchthal, *The Miniatures of the Paris Psalter*, London 1938 (Nendeln Liechtenstein 1968, reprint) [Studies of the Warburg Institute, vol. 2], 23. *Greek Psalter, circa 1090*, British Museum, MS Add. 36928, fol. 46v. Ernest T. de Wald, *The Illustrations in the Manuscripts of the Septuagint*, III: *Psalms and Odes*, Part I: *Vaticanus graecus 1927* (12th cent.), Princeton-London-The Hague 1941, Pl. LXIV (fol. 264r), Pl. XXXIX (fol. 170v), Pl. LXX (fol.279v), Pl. LXV (fol. 265r), Pl. XLII (fol. 178v); Part II: *Vaticanus graecus 752* (11th cent.), Princeton-London-The Hague 1942, Pl. IX (fol. 7v), Pl. VI (fol. 5r), Pl. LIV (fol. 449v), Pl. V (fol. 3r). Sieur du Mont, *A new Voyage to the Levant*, London 1696, 281-300 (The Dancing of the Greeks).
Wall-paintings: "Jesus is mocked", in the Katholikon of the following monasteries of Mount Athos: Iwiron (Dormition of the Virgin), Stavronikita (Saint Nicholas), Koutloumoussiou (Transfiguration), Dionysiou (Timiou Prodromou = St. John the Baptist), Karakalou (Holy Apostles), Great Lavra (Annunciation); "The Ark carried by the priests and the king" in the Sanctuary of the Karakalou Monastery; "Jesus is mocked" in the Chapel of Koukouzelissa, Great Lavra Monastery (Mount Athos), in the Monasteries of the Transfiguration (Meteora), Phaneromeni (Salamine), et alia.

78. See note 66.

79. Aeschylus, *Seven against Thebes*, 386, 399. Sophocles, *Ajax*, 17. Euripides, *Rhesus*, 308. Aristophanes, *The Peace*, 1078.

80. For a more detailed description of the making of bells, the belling of flocks, and the use of bells in

general, a monograph "Neohellenic Idiophones—The Bell, Sound-producer and Musical Instrument" is being read for publication by the author of this work.

81. Angeliki Hadjimichali, Σαρακατσάνοι (The Sarakatsani), A/I, Athens 1957, p. ηγ΄-σγ΄. See also Georges B. Kavadias, *Nomades méditerranéens. Les Saracatsans de Grèce,* Paris 1965.

82. The variants of the *tsokáni*-type also have certain elements of form common with the 'koudhoúni'-type.

83. *Léri* = bell for animals; verb *lerízi* = to sound. *See* "Κρητικαὶ λέξεις" [Cretan Words], *Φιλίστωρ,* 4, fascicle 6 (Athens 1863). *Sklavéri* = a slave's *léri (Skláviko léri, sklavoléri, sklavéri),* with the means which the Byzantines gave to the words *sklávos* or *sklavikós* = *slávos* (Slav). S. Xanthoudidis, *Ποιμενικὰ Κρήτης* [Pastoral Life in Crete], Athens 1920, 34.

84. "The *léri,* the bell of sheep, goats, he-goats or rams, also called *sklavéri* and *tsáfaron", Pavlos Vlastos' Archives (Various Vocabularies)* 45, (1852) [Historical Archives of Crete, Chania].

85. K. Iliopoulos, "Ποιμενικὰ τῆς Ἠλείας" [Pastoral Life in Elis], *Λαογραφία,* 12 (Thessaloniki 1938-1948), 253-285.

86. This type of bell was hung on hunting falcons during the Byzantine and post-Byzantine times. In later years, when people ceased to hunt with falcons, the original meaning of the word *yerakokoúdhouno (yeráki* = falcon; *koudhoúni* = bell) was forgotten, and ever since then this word simply means pellet-bell. We come accross the word *yerakokoúdhouno* in its original sense, in a folk song of Epirus: "The falcon's bell tinkles and the black horse neighs calling the young lord to the hunt".
    P. Aravandinos, *Συλλογὴ δημοτικῶν ἀσμάτων τῆς Ἠπείρου* [Collection of Folk Songs of Epirus], Athens 1880, 201. See also *Pavlos Vlastos' Archives,* 21 (1850), 199.

87. A.M. Karanastasis, "Ποιμενικὰ τῆς Κῶ" [Pastoral Life on Kos Island], *Λαογραφία,* 16 (Athens 1956), 54.

88. S. Baud-Bovy, *Études sur la chanson cleftique,* Athens 1958, 48-117.

89. Despina Mazaraki, *Τὸ λαϊκὸ κλαρίνο στὴν Ἑλλάδα* [The Popular Clarinet in Greece], Athens 1959, 21-48, 79-81.

90. In the monophonic Greek folk melody, it is obvious that the word chromatic bears no relation to the western chromatic scale. See "Chromatique (Genre)", *Larousse de la Musique* I, Paris 1957.

91. K. Makris, "Metalwork", *Greek Handicraft,* Athens, [National Bank of Greece], 1969, 220-239.

92. For more details, see Angeliki Hadjimichali, *Σαρακατσάνοι* [The Sarakatsani], A/II, Athens 1957, 120-121.

93. C. Sachs, *The History of Musical Instruments,* New York 1940, 169-172. H. Hickmann, *Catalogue général des antiquités égyptiennes du musée du Caire, No 69201-69852: Instruments de musique,* Cairo 1949. J. Blades, *Percussion Instruments and their History,* s.v. Bell. See also *Die Musik in Geschichte und Gegenwart,* V, Kassel 1956, s.v. Glocken (with an extensive bibliography). *Encyclopaedia of Religion and Ethics* (Editor J. Hastings), VI, s.v. Gongs and Bells.

94. For the bell in ancient Greece see: Daremberg-Saglio, *Dictionnaire des antiquités grecques et romaines,* s.v. tintinnabulum (κώδων = bell); Pauly-Wissowa-Kroll, *Real-Encyclopädie der klassischen Altertumswissenschaft,* s.v. κώδων. Max Wegner, "Griechenland", *Musikgeschichte in Bildern,* Leipzig 1963, Pl. 34, p. 60.

95. Angeliki Hadjimichali, *Σαρακατσάνοι* [The Sarakatsani], A/II, 114, 115.

96. Verbs for 'belling': *armatóno* = to equip (a flock); *koudhounóno* = to 'bell'; *sidheróno* = to put on 'irons', i.e. bells; *sklaveróno* = to equip a flock with *sklavéria* (as bells are called in Crete).

97. *Takími,* from the Turkish "takim" = entirety, group, host. In this case, a set of tuned bells chosen to match.
    Douzína, in our opinion, a bastardised version of the word *douzéni* from the Turkish "düzen" = order, harmony.
    In the text, whenever the weight of bells is mentioned, we use the term for the old unit of weight: "oka" and "dram" (1 oka = 400 drams; 1 dram = 3,2 grams). Whenever the unit of weight now in use (gram and kilogram) is mentioned, it has been taken from recent sources of information.

98. From the MS of Grottaferrata, 14th century, P.P. Kalonaros, *Βασίλειος Διγενὴς Ἀκρίτας,* II, Athens 1970, p. 43-44, lines 232-236.

99. Despina Mazaraki, "Some Notes on Greek Shepherd Flutes", *Bulletin de l'Institut de musique,* 13 (1969), [Académie Bulgare des Sciences], 275-284.

100. Musicologist Despina Mazaraki is preparing a monograph on the matching of the shepherd flute *(floyéra),* with the bells of the flock. In the present work the subject is dealt with in a general sense only.

101. The terms 'accompaniment' and 'harmonisation'—borrowed from the western music— do not correspond with the nature of Greek monophonic melody. Nor does a Greek shepherd function in this way when improvising upon his pipe. These terms were used as they are more familiar to the general reader.

102. G.A. Megas, "Ἀναστενάρια καὶ ἔθιμα τῆς Τυρινῆς Δευτέρας εἰς τὸ Κωστῆ καὶ τὰ πέριξ αὐτοῦ χωρία τῆς Ἀνατολικῆς Θράκης" [Anastenaria and Customs of Cheese-Monday in Kosti, and surrounding villages, in Eastern Thrace], *Λαογραφία,* 19 (1960-1961), 472-534. Katerina I. Kakouri, *Dionysiaka,* Athens 1965.
    Tiriní Dheftéra (= Cheese-Monday): the Monday of the last week of Carnival when only dairy products are eaten.
    Katharí Dheftéra (= Clean-Monday): the first day of Lent.

103. G. Spyridakis, "Τὸ ἄσμα τῆς χελιδόνος (χελιδόνισμα) τὴν πρώτην Μαρτίου" [The Swallow-Song of the First March], *Ἐπετηρὶς τοῦ Κέντρου Ἐρεύνης Ἑλληνικῆς Λαογραφίας,* 20/21 (Athens 1967-1968),

364

15-54, with an extensive bibliography. In this detailed study there is no mention of the use of the bell, even though it is quite vividly remembered by older people. See the figur of the wooden swallow, with the pellet-bell on its neck, in K. Chourmouziadis' study, "Τὸ Τσακήλι τῶν Μετρῶν" [Village Tsakili, Metrai (Thrace)], Θρακικά, 11 (1939), 347-413; see also Angelos D. Metrinos, "Τὸ ἄσμα τῆς χελιδόνος" [The Swallow-Song], Θρακικὴ Ἐπετηρίς, 1 (1897), 166-167. Bertrand Bouvier, Le mirologue de la Vierge, Geneva 1976, 36, footnote 2 (bibliography).

104. Museum of Greek Folk Art, Athens.

105. R.M. Dawkins, "The Modern Carnival in Thrace and the Cult of Dionysos", The Journal of Hellenic Studies, 26 (1906), 206.

106. B.J. Vikas, "Ἔθιμα παρὰ Βλαχοφώνοις" [Customs of the Vlachs], Λαογραφία, 6 (1917), 176.

107. Ph. Koukoules, "Μεσαιωνικοὶ καὶ νεοελληνικοὶ κατάδεσμοι. Μέρος Γ′: Οἱ κατάδεσμοι κατὰ τὴν σημερινὴν ἐποχήν" [Medieval and Neohellenic Spells. Part III: Spells in the Modern Age], Λαογραφία, 9 (1926), 462-463.

108. Anna Hadjinikolaou, "Gold Embroidery", Greek Handicraft, Athens [National Bank of Greece], 1969, Pl. 180.
Prelate's copes with pellet-bells are also to be found in the vestries of the Mount Athos monasteries (three in the Great Lavra, one in the Pantocrator Monastery, etc.). It is strange that Pitton de Tournefort, whose descriptions and designs are so detailed, does not mention the use of pellet-bells in his book, even though he does deal with the subject of priests' vestements and censers. Pitton de Tournefort, Relation d'un voyage du Levant, I, Paris 1717.

109. S. Kyriakidis, "Τὸ σκλάβωμα" [The 'Enslavement' = dedication to a Saint], Λαογραφία, 13 (Thessaloniki 1951), 350-351, 354-355.

110. S. Kyriakidis, "Ἰωάννης ὁ Χρυσόστομος ὡς λαογράφος" [John Chrysostom as Folklorist], Λαογραφία, 11 (Thessaloniki 1934-1936), 634, 637.

111. J. Doubdan, Le voyage de la Terre Sainte, Paris 1666, 366. There is a similar description in Sieur Poullet's Nouvelles relations du Levant, Paris 1667, 139-141.

112. Katerina I. Kakouri, Dionysiaka, Athens 1965.

113. G.K. Spyridakis and G. Aikaterinidis, "Λαϊκαὶ λατρευτικαὶ τελεταὶ εἰς τὴν Μακεδονίαν (Χωρίον Καλὴ Βρύσις Δράμας) ἀπὸ 5-8 Ἰανουαρίου" [Popular Worship in Macedonia; Kali Vrissi, near Drama, January 5th-8th], Preliminary announcement by A.K. Orlandos, Minutes of the Academy of Athens, 40 (1965), 237-240.

114. J.C. Lawson, "A Beast-dance in Skyros", Annual of the British School at Athens, 6 (1899-1900), 125-127. R.M. Dawkins, "A Visit to Skyros, I: The Carnival", Annual of the British School at Athens, 11 (1904-1905), 72-74. D. Papageorgiou, "Αἱ Ἀπόκρεω ἐν Σκύρῳ" [The Carnival in Skyros], Λαογραφία, 2 (1910), 35-47. Joy Coulentianou, The Goat-dance of Skyros, Athens 1977. In the Skyros' Carnival, in contrast with other carnivals, each "yéros" hangs around his waist many bells of various types

('koudhoúnia', tsokánia, kýpri). The great number of bells— sometimes more than 60 bells are hung— was, and still is, a sign of manliness and bravery. In older times these bells were 'tuned' and matched. Nowadays they are rarely so.

115. "Λαογραφικὰ Μαυροκκλησίου Διδυμοτείχου" [Folklore of Mavroklissi, near Didymotichon], Θρακικά, 44 (1970), 239.

116. N. Rodoinos, "Ἀπὸ τὰ ἔθιμα τῆς πατρίδος μου Ὀρτάκιοϊ (Ἀδριανοπόλεως). Τὰ Δημήτρια (Ὁ Μπέης)" [Customs of my Homeland Ortakioi (Adrianopolis). The 'Dimitria' (The Bey)], Θρακικά, 13 (1940), 315.

117. Charilaos S. Doulas, "Λαϊκὴ λατρεία. Ἔθιμα τοῦ Δωδεκαημέρου ἐν Θεσσαλίᾳ: Τὰ Ρογκάτσια ἢ Ρογκατσάρια" [Popular Worship. Customs of the Twelfth-day in Thessaly: the Rogatsia or Rogatsaria], Λαογραφία, 17 (1957-1958), 628.

118. Vassilios Kalfantzis, "Ὁ γάμος τοῦ Καραγκιόζη στὴ Γονούσσα τῆς Κορινθίας" [The Karagioz' Wedding in Gonoussa, near Corinth], Λαογραφία, 17 (1957-1958), 636.

119. Kyriakos Stergiou, musician, Kyprou-Str. 3, Alexandropolis (1965).

120. Panayotis E. Papanis, "Ἡ Ἀποκριὰ καὶ τὰ Καρναβάλια εἰς τὴν Ἀγιάσον τῆς Λέσβου" [The Carnival and the Mummers (karnavália) in Ayiassos, on Lesbos], Λαογραφία, 17 (1957-1958), 638.

121. Nikos Angelis, Στὸν ἴσκιο τῆς μαδάρας. Οἱ Κουκουγέροι [Collection of short stories: "Under the Madara-rock Shadow". The Koukouyéri], Athens 1961, 76.

122. Th. D. Athanassiadis, "Ἡ ἑορτὴ τοῦ Λαζάρου ἐν Δραγαρίῳ" [The Feast of Lazarus in Dragarion], Λαογραφία, 5 (1915), 403-404. Ch. J. Soulis, "Τὰ τραγούδια τοῦ Λαζάρου" [Songs of Lazarus], Ἠπειρωτικὰ Χρονικά, 2 (1927), 182. Angeliki Hadjimichali, Σαρακατσάνοι [The Sarakatsani], A/II, 134-135. Bertrand Bouvier, Le mirologue de la Vierge, Geneva 1976, 37, 38.

123. D. Archigenis, "Πρωτοχρονιάτικα κάλαντα στὴν Μικρὰ Ἀσία πρὸ τοῦ 1922" [New Years' Carols in Asia Minor before 1922], Προσφυγικὸς Κόσμος, Athens, Jan. 1, 1961.

124. D. Papageorgiou, Ἱστορία τῆς Σκύρου ἀπὸ τῶν ἀρχαιοτάτων χρόνων [History of Skyros], Patras 1909, 157.

125. Yiannis Balabourdas, Café-owner, Koundouriotou-Str. 17, Alexandropolis (1965).

126. See note 124.

127. On the sign over the shop in Thessaloniki of Afendoulis I. Kantartzis (member of an old family of Pontic bell-makers) is written: Λαϊκὴ Τέχνη [Popular Art], and in English: "Bellmakers — Brass Souvenirs from Greece, Thessaloniki".

128. In Myli on Karystos (Euboea), in the garden of the mason Andonis I. Sarlanis (b. 1927), whose father was a cattle-breeder, we saw a kýpros hanging from a cypress-tree, jangling when ever the wind blows. (August 1972).

129. The signboard over Alexis Tambakis' shop, Zinonos-Str. 23, Athens, reads: "Café-Bar 'Karditsa',

Coal-broiled Souvlaki, free wheaten bread" 1972.

130. Lavignac, *Encyclopédie de la musique,* Part I. *Histoire de la musique,* I, *Égypte,* Paris 1913, 7. H. Hickmann, *Catalogue général des antiquités égyptiennes du Musée du Caire. No 69201-69852: Instruments de musique,* Cairo 1949, 34-36, Pl. XXII. J. Blades *Percussion Instruments and their History,* London 1970, 167, Pl. 63.

131. *Die Musik in Geschichte und Gegenwart,* VII, Kassel 1958, 985-986, 1619.

132. C. Mc Phee, *Music in Bali,* New Haven and London 1966, 121, Pl. 32, 34.

133. Dimitrios Manakas, "Καρνάβαλος τῆς ᾿Απόκρεω" [The Mummer of Carnival], *Θρακικά,* 31 (1959), 269-272. The author of this article writes that the girls in the Kiopek-Bey ritual "hold *krótala* [clappers] in their hands". But, as he told me, these *krótala* are *massés* (tongs with cymbals), which I was able to confirm from other sources as well.

134. *Tzamála* = camel, from the Arabic "gmal", which is pronounced "gamal" and "dzamal" as well. On Christmas Eve and on the eve of St. Demetrius, the inhabitants of the villages and towns of Thrace disguise themselves "for the good year" as "tzamáles" (camels). Or they perform what is known as the "tzamála", that is, they carry from house to house in the village the figurative representation of a camel, bestowing upon their fellow villagers their wishes for a good year, wealth and health, and accepting small gifts such as food, wine, money. In Thrace, masquerades apart from the "karnavália" "koudhounáti", etc., are generally called "tzamáles". The heavyset and clumsy woman was also called "tzamáles" in former times. In addition, the "dance of the tzamála" in western Thrace is also noteworthy.

Ph. Koukoules, "Καλλικάντζαροι" [Imps], *Λαογραφία,* 7 (1923), 315-328. Σύμμεικτα, "᾿Ερωτήματα διὰ τὴν λαϊκὴν λατρείαν" [Various Questions regarding Popular Worship], *Λαογραφία,* 11 (Thessaloniki 1934-1937), 661-664. Elpiniki Saranti-Stamouli, "Προλήψεις καὶ δεισιδαιμονίες τῆς δυτικῆς Θράκης" [Prejudices and Superstitions in Western Thrace], *Λαογραφία,* 13 (Thessaloniki 1951), 109-110. P. Kavakopoulos, "Χοροὶ καὶ μελωδίες τῆς δυτικῆς Θράκης" [Dances and Melodies of Western Thrace], Offprint from the *Minutes of the Second Symposium of Folklore in the Region of Northern Greece.* Thessaloniki 1976 [Institute for Balkan Studies Thessaloniki], 99.

135. When the triangle is closed at all three of its angles, then it produces sound resembling that produced by a small bell. In other words, it changes timbre and loses the rather clear and penetrating sound it normally has. This particular secret was known to the skilled iron-workers of old by means of their experience. Thus they would make the triangle, leaving one of its angles open, saying "in this manner a better voice was produced".

136. Today, one finds a single child singing the *kálanda* (carols) and accompanying himself upon the triangle. In addition, a horseshoe is used in the event no triangle is available.

137. The same holds true for 'art music' as well. See J. Blades, *Percussion Instruments and their History,* London 1970, 389.

138. D. Archigenis, "῾Ο λαογραφικὸς θησαυρὸς Σμύρνης, Χριστούγεννα εἰς τὴν Σμύρνην" [A Treasury of Smyrna Folklore. Christmas in Smyrna], *Προσφυγικὸς κόσμος,* Athens, Dec. 17 and 24, 1967.

139. J. Blades, *Percussion Instruments...,* 388. R. Donington, *The Instruments of Music,* London 1951, 119.

140. In Europe, on the other hand, the triangle is known to have existed as such from the Middle Ages. The triangle having three ore more metallic rings attached to its base is the form in which this instrument is usually encountered in many miniatures and other illustrations — thus bearing witness to its relationship to the ancient sistrum, its remote ancestor. See J. Blades, *Percussion Instruments...,* 191. F.W. Galpin, *Old English Instruments of Music,* London 1965, Pl. 53. A. Baines, *European and American Musical Instruments,* London 1966, Pl. 824.

141. A. Schaeffner, *Origine des instruments de musique,* Paris 1936, 14, 30. C. Sachs, *World History of the Dance,* New York 1937, 175-203. Idem, *The History of Musical Instruments,* New York 1940, 26.

142. *Stráka* (plur. *Strákes*), finger-snapping: the sound created by the beating of the middle finger against the fourth finger and the palm of the hand, after its violent rubbing against the thumb. In Crete, *strákes* are also known as *balónia* (baloons), *Pavlos Vlastos' Archives,* 58 [Historical Archives of Crete, Chania], 45, footnote. *Stráka* is also the name given to the sound produced when the forefinger, held loosely, strikes the middle finger following the abrupt shaking of the entire hand. In this instance, the forefinger and the middle finger act as the two sections of a *krótala* (clappers).

143. Migne, *P.G.* 55, line 208.

144. Migne, *P.G.* 37, line 1438.

145. G.A. Rallis and M. Potlis, *Σύνταγμα τῶν θείων καὶ ἱερῶν κανόνων* [Collection of the Divine and Sacred Canons], III, Athens 1853, 221.

146. *Photius, Patriarch of Constantinople, Λόγοι καὶ ῾Ομιλίαι* [Homelies], ed. by S. Aristarchos, II, Constantinople 1900, 254.

147. *Pseudo-Nonnus Commentary,* Patriarchal Library, Jerusalem, Codex Taphou 14, fol. 310v, 11th century. K. Weitzmann, *Greek Mythology in Byzantine Art,* Princeton 1951, 38, 40, Pl. XII fig. 36. W. Bachmann, *The Origins of Bowing and the Development of Bowed Instruments up to the Thirteenth Century,* London 1969, 37, Pl. 10. P. Lekatsas, *Διόνυσος* [Dionysos], Psychico 1971, 69-70.

Regarding the five corybants K. Weitzmann writes: "In the Jerusalem manuscript [Cod. Taphou 14, fol. 310v] five Corybantes are lined up: the first dances with cymbals in the hands, the second plays a viola, the third a drum, the fourth a transverse flute, and the fifth dances without an instrument". Nevertheless, the position of the fifth corybant does not bear out this interpretation. This particular corybant is depicted standing upright, supported by his right leg, exactly as is Rhea a little further on. Just how much this position differs from the dancing movement we see in the case of the first corybant, who is playing cymbals while simultaneously dancing, characteristically extending his left foot forward. The fifth corybant can be said to be clapping his hands. The position of his hands justifies this interpretation, which moreover agrees with the text of Pseudo-Nonnus: "But Zeus she [Rhea] carried to Crete and she placed the Curetes and Corybantes round the babe, so that they might dance and rattle and make their weapons resound and thus produce the greatest possible noise in order to conceal and drown the crying of the child, so that Cronus might not learn the hiding place of the infant and take and swallow it". (Migne, *P.G.* 36, col. 1065). The contents of this text do not justify the interpretation the movement of the corybant's hands as a gesture of supplication or as apotropaic. On the practice of hand-clapping in Byzantine times see the detailed bibliography in Ph. Koukoules, Βυζαντινῶν βίος καὶ πολιτισμός [Byzantine Life and Civilisation], A/II, 101; V, 233-234. See also S. Baud-Bovy, *Chansons du Dodécanèse,* I, Athens 1935, 334, 338-339.

148. Vitsentzos Kornaros, Ἐρωτόκριτος, κριτικὴ ἔκδοσις Στ. Ξανδουδίδου [Erotokritos, critical edition by S. Xanthoudidis], Iraklion, Crete 1915, 161, line 2157.

149. Sitsa Karaiskakis, "Das Lehrgedicht Λόγοι διδακτικοὶ τοῦ πατρὸς πρὸς τὸν υἱὸν von Markos Depharanas, 1543", Λαογραφία, 11 (Thessaloniki 1934-1937), 55, line 570.

150. This face-to-face dance was witnessed by Clarke in Athens in the December of 1802. Edward Daniel Clarke, *Travels in Various Countries of Europe, Asia and Africa,* IV, London 1816, 5.

151. N.G. Politis, Μελέται περὶ τοῦ βίου καὶ τῆς γλώσσης τοῦ ἑλληνικοῦ λαοῦ. Παροιμίαι [Studies on the Life and Language of the Greek People. Proverbs], I, Athens 1899, 575; III, Athens 1901, 376, 579.

152. Ph. Koukoules, Βυζαντινῶν βίος καὶ πολιτισμὸς [Byzantine Life and Civilisation], VI, Athens 1955, 262-266. Popi Zora, *Embroideries and Jewellery of Greek National Costumes* [Museum of Greek Folk Art], Athens 1966, 19. Ioanna Papandoniou, *Greek Costumes,* [Peloponnesean Folklore Foundation], (Athens) 1973 (women's costumes), 1974 (men's costumes).
Apart from the breast, the head, the torso, etc., one also encounters instances where coins are fastened to the laces of women's footwear: bride's wedding gown from Kephalovrysso (Argolid, Peloponnese), Peloponnesean Folklore Foundation, Folk Art Museum, Nafplion.

153. J. Spon and G. Wheler, *Voyage d'Italie, de Dalmatie, de Grèce et du Levant fait ès années 1675 et 1676,* II, Amsterdam 1679, 55.

154. See note 152 (Popi Zora).

155. P.L. Fourikis, "Ἑλληνοαλβανικαὶ λαογραφικαὶ ἔρευναι" [Greco-Albanian Folklore Researches], Λαογραφία, 10 (Thessaloniki 1929), 4-19.

156. D. Kambouroglou, Ἱστορία τῶν Ἀθηνῶν [History of Athens], III, Athens 1959, 38.

157. Melpo Merlier, *Essai d'un tableau du folklore musical grec,* Athens 1935, 36-37.

158. S. Baud-Bovy, *Chansons du Dodécanèse,* I, Athens 1935, 338.

159. Elias Petropoulos, Ρεμπέτικα τραγούδια [Rebétika Songs], Athens 1968, 24.

160. K. Makris, "Woodcarving", *Greek Handicraft,* Athens [National Bank of Greece], 1969, 73.

161. John Rupert Martin, *The Illustration of the Heavenly Ladder of John Climacus,* Princeton 1954, Pl. XIV, fig. 60 (fol. 169v: Solitude, MS Princeton, Univ. Lib. Garrett, MS 16, 11th cent.); Pl.XXXVI, fig. 114 (fol. 95v: Methods of Wakefulness, MS Vatican. Cod. Gr. 394, 11th cent.); Pl. CXII, fig. 300 (Vatican Gallery, The Dormition of Ephraim Syrus, by Emm. Tzanfournari, circa 1600).

162. Grelot, *Relation nouvelle d'un voyage de Constantinople,* Paris 1680, 206-207.

163. A.M. Karanastasis, "Οἱ ζευγάδες τῆς Κῶ. Ἡ ζωὴ καὶ αἱ ἀσχολίαι των" [The Ploughmen of Kos Island], Λαογραφία, 14 (1952), 303.

164. S. Baud-Bovy, *Chansons du Dodécanèse,* I, Athens 1935, 168. Bartok and Lord provide a similar description: "Old Dula used to roll a large copper pan on a short wooden table... The rumble of the pan furnished a weird and crude accompaniment...": Bela Bartok and Albert B. Lord, *Serbo-Croatian Folk Songs,* New York 1951, 251-252.
In neither of these two sources of information is made clear the manner in which the *tapsí* (baking-pan) is turned nor in what manner the sound buzzing produced by the pan accompanies the song made clear. Professor Baud-Bovy, to whom we directed our questions, informed us that he himself had never had an opportunity to see the *tapsí* used as a musical instrument with his own eyes, and that the description in his book is based upon secondhand evidence.
Recent research unknown to us when this book went to press in the Greek edition provides illuminating answers to the above questions. See Wolf Dietrich "Über das Singen zur sich drehenden Pfanne", *Studien zur Musik Südost-Europas* [Beiträge zur Ethnomusikologie], 4, Hamburg 1976, 71-78.

165. The Greek Folklore Research Centre, MS 236, p. 56 (Pan. Makris, Συλλογὴ ζώντων μνημείων ἐξ αὐτοῦ τοῦ στόματος τοῦ λαοῦ τῆς κωμοπόλεως Κατιρλί, Λεξιλόγιον καὶ ἀραί [Living Popular Texts of Katirli (Thrace). Vocabulary and Curses], 1888).

166. Du Cange, *Glossarium,* s.v. σήμαντρον. C.D. Ioannides, "Quasi-Liturgical Hymns", Κυπριακαὶ σπουδαί, 33 (1969), 124. G.A. Rallis and M. Potlis, Σύνταγμα τῶν θείων καὶ ἱερῶν κανόνων [Collection of the Divine and Sacred Canons], IV, Athens 1854, 521.

167. C. Sachs, *The History of Musical Instruments,* New York 1940, 168-169.

168. Information (1951) from Christos Makkas, Akamatra. This sound-producer is a membranophone.

169. For the form and the function of the first semanteria, their history and their symbolic meaning, see F. Cabrol, *Dictionnaire d'Archéologie Chrétienne et de Liturgie*, III, Paris 1914, s.v. Cloche, Clochette (with an extensive bibliography). See also K.N. Kallinikos, Ὁ χριστιανικὸς ναὸς καὶ τὰ τελούμενα ἐν αὐτῷ [The Christian Church and its Rituals], Alexandria 1921, 74-76. Palladius, Λαυσαϊκὴ Ἱστορία [The Lausiae History], Chap. ρδ΄, Migne, *P.G.* 34, line 1210 (C. Butler, *The Lausiae History of Palladius*, 1894-1904). N.B. Tomadakis, "Ἀποθησαυρίσματα" [Anthology]", Ἀθηνᾶ, 70 (1968), 13.

170. C.D. Ioannides, "Quasi-Liturgical Hymns", Κυπριακαὶ σπουδαί, 33 (1969), 123, 124.

171. Τὰ Ἅπαντα τοῦ Ἀλεξάνδρου Παπαδιαμάντη [Complete Works of Alexandros Papadiamandis], revised by G. Valetas, II, (Athens) 1954, 117.

172. Rather different is the opinion of the French botanist, doctor, and philosopher, Pitton de Tournefort. In his book *Relation d'un voyage du Levant*, I, Paris 1717, 115, he finds the simultaneous sounding of the metal and wooden semanteria anything but pleasant.

173. G.N. Aikaterinidis, "Ὁ ἑορτασμὸς τοῦ Ἁγίου Γεωργίου εἰς Νέον Σούλι Σερρῶν" [St. George's Day in Neon Souli, near Serres], Σερραϊκὰ Χρονικά, 5 (1969), 129-148.

174. The church-bell *(kambána)* was first used in the churches of the East from the 9th century onwards.

175. Migne, *P.G.* 99, line 1784.

176. I, Bonn 1839, 334.

177. G.A. Rallis and M. Potlis, Σύνταγμα τῶν θείων καὶ ἱερῶν κανόνων [Collection of the Divine and, Sacred Canons], Athens 1853, IV, 520-521. Migne, *P.G.* 138, line 1073.

178. John Rupert Martin, *The Illustration of the Heavenly Ladder of John Climacus*, Pl. LXXX, fig. 221, fol. 7v, Chap. I (MS Paris. Bibl. Nat. Cod. Coislin 263, 11th cent.).

179. G. and M. Sotiriou, *Icônes du Mont Sinaï* [Collection de l'Institut Français d'Athènes, No 100], I, Athens 1956, Pl. 108; II, Athens 1958, 242.

180. John Rupert Martin, *The Illustration...*, Pl. LXIX, fig. 200 (MS of Mount Sinai Monastery, Gr. 415, fol. 170r, 12th cent.).

181. Mount Athos: Great Lavra Monastery (Refectory) "The Dormition of Blessed Father Athanasios"; in the monasteries Karakalou (Lite), Dochiariou (Narthex), Dionysiou (Refectory), Vatopediou (Refectory), Pantocrator (Refectory) "The Dormition of Hosios Ephraim the Syrian; in the Lite of Grigoriou and Xiropotamou Monasteries "Noah enters the Ark". P.M. Mylonas, *Athos und seine Klosteranlagen in alten Stichen und Kunstwerken,* Athens 1963, Plates 11, 14, 23, 31, 35, 38, 46, 48, 52, 54, 64, 66, 74, 78, 79. In the Katholikon of St. Nicholas Anapafsas Monastery, Meteora (1527), "The Burial of Ephraim the Syrian". See also A. Xyngopoulos, Σχεδίασμα ἱστορίας τῆς θρησκευτικῆς ζωγραφικῆς μετὰ τὴν ἅλωσιν [Notes toward a History of Religious Painting after the Fall of Constantinople], Athens 1957, Pl. 21, fig. 2.

182. B. de Khitrowo, *Itinéraires russes en Orient, Antoine Archevêque de Novgorod, Le livre du pèlerin (1200),* Geneva 1889, 97. Émile Legrand, *Description des îles de l'Archipel par Christophe Buondelmonti, Version grecque par un anonyme,* Paris 1897, 93. Henri Castela, *Le sainct voyage de Hierusalem et Mont Sinay faict en l'an du grand Iubilé 1600,* 2nd edn., Paris 1612, 310-311. J. Doubdan, *Le voyage de la Terre Sainte,* Paris 1666, 279-280. Grelot, *Relation nouvelle d'un voyage de Constantinople,* Paris 1680, 179. F.C.H.L. Pouqueville, *Voyage dans la Grèce,* I, Paris 1820, 382.

183. Ἑλληνικὰ δημοτικὰ τραγούδια (Ἐκλογὴ) [Greek Folk Songs (Selection)], I [Athens Academy of Athens, Publications of the Folklore Archives, No 7], 1962, 125.

184. Ch. I. Papachristodoulou, "Δημοτικὰ τραγούδια τῆς Ρόδου" [Folk Songs of Rhodes], Λαογραφία, 18 (1959), 316.

185. Ph. Koukoules, Βυζαντινῶν βίος... Παράρτημα: Ἡ νέα ἑλληνικὴ γλώσσα καὶ τὰ βυζαντινὰ καὶ μεταβυζαντινὰ ἔθιμα [Byzantine Life... Appendix: The Neohellenic Language, and Byzantine and post-Byzantine Customs], V, Athens 1952, 7.

186. F. Drexl, "Das anonyme Traumbuch des cod. Paris. 2511", Λαογραφία, 8 (1921), 372.

187. D. Loucopoulos, "Σύμμεικτα λαογραφικὰ Μακεδονίας" [Folklore of Macedonia], Λαογραφία, 6 (1917-1918), 139.

188. *Pavlos Vlastos' Archives,* 14 [Historical Archives of Crete, Chania], 607. See also Telephone Directory of Attica, 1977.

189. Perhaps from *kóndhion* or *kondhýlion* see Ph. Koukoules, Βυζαντινῶν βίος... [Byzantine Life...], V, 156. see also Τὰ τοῦ ὁσίου πατρὸς Ἐφραὶμ τοῦ Σύρου πρὸς τὴν Ἑλλάδα μεταβληθέντα, Ἐν Ὀξονίᾳ 1709, Λόγος εἰς τὸν Πάγκαλον Ἰωσήφ, Oxford 1709, p. Σμε, Κ.

190. *Pavlos Vlastos' Archives,* 37, 540-541.

191. Theodosios K. Sperantzas, Κυκλαδικὲς ἱστορίες: Ἡ Παναγιὰ ἡ Χρυσοπηγὴ τῆς Σίφνου [Cycladic Stories], Athens 1949, 31-32.

192. A small *kýpros* was used instead of the *kóndio* by the priest Ioannis M. Panayiotou (b. 1890) in the church of St. Nicholas at Kambos (Fourni islands, Ikaria). A heroic figure, the teacher-priest (even though he only finished four years of schooling) Papa-Yiannis managed to build a school on Agathonissi (Dodecanese) and to 'bring-out', in his words, other teachers, while he was continuously persecuted for his patriotic activities, now by the Italians (the Dodecanese being then under Italian rule), now by the Turks, on the opposing coast of Asia Minor where he would seek refuge every so often, hidden in the hold of some caique: "Thus we found it, traditions helps (us)", he said of the *kóndio* when the author met him in his church for the first time in 1970.

193. K.N. Kallinikos, Ὁ χριστιανικὸς ναὸς καὶ τὰ τελούμενα ἐν αὐτῷ [The Christian Church and its Rituals], Alexandria 1921, 225.

194. F.C.H.L. Pouqueville, *Voyage dans la Grèce,* Paris 1820, I, 382.

195. A.G. Vrondis, "Ροδιακὴ λαογραφία" [Folklore of Rhodes], *Λαογραφία,* 11 (1934-1937), 533, footnote 5.

196. R. Brancour, *Histoire des instruments de musique,* Paris 1921, 227. Fr. W. Galpin, *A Textbook of European Musical Instruments,* London 1956, 54. Em. Winternitz, *Instruments de musique du monde occidental,* Paris 1972, 57. C. Sachs, *Reallexikon,* s.v. Ratsche.

197. As far as we know, in the Greek Orthodox monasteries no one recall the monks being summoned by means of the ratchet.

198. We have taken the shape and the dimensions from the *réndela* belonging to the Historical Museum of Galaxidi.

199. For the various local terms used for this form of fishing see Ph. Koukoules, *Βυζαντινῶν βίος...* [Byzantine Life...], V, 335-336. See also P. Vlastos, *Συνώνυμα καὶ συγγενικά* [Synonyms and Related Words], Athens 1931, 310.

200. For information concerning the history of this idiophone from the village Lafkos, we are obliged to the folklorist Kitsos Makris, Volos.

201. Gerasimos D. Kapsalis, "Λαογραφικὰ ἐκ Βερμπιάνης" [Folklore of Verbiani], *Λαογραφία,* 4 (1913), 407.

202. Gerasimos I. Salvanos, "Λαογραφικὰ συλλεκτὰ ἐξ Ἀργυράδων Κερκύρας" [Folklore of Argyrades, Corfu], *Λαογραφία,* 10 (Thessaloniki 1929), 116-117.

203. N.G. Politis, "Ὠκυτοκία" [Easy Birth], *Λαογραφία,* 6 (1917), 338, footnote 1.

204. V.I. Vikas, "Ἔθιμα παρὰ Βλαχοφώνοις" [Customs of the Vlachs], *Λαογραφία,* 6 (1917), 118.

205. K.A. Romaios, "Τὸ ὑνὶ κατὰ τὸν γάμον" [The Plough-share at the Wedding], *Λαογραφία,* 7 (1913), 357.

206. A. Stefopoulos, "Παιδικὰ παραδοσιακὰ παιχνίδια ἀπὸ τὴ Χρυσὴ Καστοριᾶς" [Traditional Children's Games in Chryssi, near Kastoria], *Μακεδονικά,* 12 (1972), 375-378.

207. This nomenclature is due to the acute sound of the small drum *(daoúli)* in the Messolonghi region, a sound resembling that produced by the small forged bell-type, the *tsokáni* (see *Koudhoúni* = Bell). K.S. Konstas, "Ἡ ζυγιὰ στὴ Δυτικὴ Ρούμελη" [The *Ziyiá* in Western Roumeli], *Λαογραφία,* 19 (1960-1961), 329.

208. P. Aravandinos, *Ἠπειρωτικὸν γλωσσάριον* [Glossary of Epirus], Athens 1909, 25.

209. F. Harrison and J. Rimmer, *European Musical Instruments,* London 1964, 15.

210. See note 14.

211. The *Anastenaria* take place from the eve of St. Constantine and St. Helen, May 20th, through 23rd, and the *Kaloyeros,* on Cheese-Monday (see note 102). See A. Chourmouziadis, *Περὶ τῶν Ἀναστεναρίων καὶ ἄλλων τινῶν παραδόξων ἐθίμων καὶ προλήψεων* [On the Anastenaria and some other Strange Customs and Superstitions], Constantinople 1873. Katerina I. Kakouri, *Dionysiaka,* Athens 1965.

212. Georgios Phrantzes, *Ἑάλω ἡ Πόλις, Χρονικὸν* [The City (Constantinople) has fallen, Chronicle] according to the edition J.-P. Migne, Athens (undated), 49.

213. *Διήγησις ὡραιοτάτη τοῦ θαυμαστοῦ ἀνδρὸς τοῦ λεγομένου Βελισαρίου,* ed. G. Wagner, *Carmina graeca medii aevi,* Lipsiae 1874, line 258-259.

214. Stratigós [General] Ioannis Makryannis, *Ἀπομνημονεύματα* [Memoirs], Text, Introduction, Notes by G. Vlachoyiannis, 2nd edn., I, Athens 1947, 261.

215. *Pictures from the War of Independence (1821)* J. Makriyannis – Pan. Zographos, Athens [National Historical Museum], 1966.

216. Suzy Dufrenne, *L'illustration des psautiers grecs du Moyen Age,* I, Paris 1966, Pl. 11 (MS 61, fol. 85r, Pantocrator Monastery, Mount Athos, 9th cent.), Pl. 47 (fol. 7v. MS Add. 40731 of the British Museum "Psalter of Bristol", late 10th or beginn of 11th century. British Museum, Greek Psalters, MS Add. 19352, fol. 191 (11th century) and MS Add. 36928, fol. 46v (ca 1090).

J. Strzygowski, *Der Bilderkreis des griechischen Physiologus, des Kosmas Indikopleustes und Oktateuch nach Hansdschriften der Bibliothek zu Smyrna,* Leipzig 1899, Pl. XI, fig. 52. Ernest T. de Wald, *The Illustrations in the Manuscripts of the Septuagint,* III, *Psalms and Odes,* Princeton-London-The Hague (1941-1942), Part I: *MS Vaticanus graecus 1927,* Pl. XVIII (fol. 68v, 12th century); Part II: *MS Vaticanus graecus 752,* Pl. LIV (fol. 449v, 11th century).

Sirarpie Der Nersessian, *L'illustration du roman de Barlaam et de Joasaph,* Paris 1937, Album: Pl. LI, fig. 192 (Cod. Paris. Gr. 1128, fol. 19, 14th century), Pl. LXXXIX, fig. 358 (fol. 169), Pl. XC, fig. 360 (fol. 174).

217. In Byzantine and post-Byzantine times wall-paintings, the drum and the nakers are to be found primarely in the representations of "Jesus is mocked", "Praise ye the Lord", in the parable "The Dive and Lazarus".

218. Leo Deacon, *Ἱστορίαι,* 1828, 133.

219. Nikitas Choniatis, *Ἱστορία,* edn. Bonn 1835, 655.

220. P.P. Kalonaros, *Βασίλειος Διγενὴς Ἀκρίτας,* II, Athens 1970, MS Grottaf., 62, line 828.

221. *Τὰ κατὰ Λύβιστρον καὶ Ῥοδάμνην,* ed. W. Wagner, *Trois poèmes grecs du Moyen-âge,* Berlin 1881, line 3749-3750.

222. G. Chortatsis, *Κατζοῦρμπος,* Comedy, Critical edition, Notes, Glossary by Linos Politis, Iraklion 1964, 20, lines 23-24.

223. Vitsentzos Kornaros, *Ἐρωτόκριτος,* Critical edition by S. Xanthoudidis, Iraklion 1915, 307, line 1970.

224. Marinos Tzanes Bounialis, *Κρητικὸς πόλεμος,* ed. Agathangelos Xirouchakis, Triest 1908, 279, linc 11.

225. See *Ambassade en Turquie de Jean de Gontaut Biron de Salignac, 1605 à 1610. Voyage à Constantinople — Séjour en Turquie.* Relation inédite, précédée de la vie du baron de Salignac par le Comte Théodore de Gontaut Biron, Paris 1888, 37 (Chios, 1604). *Voyage en Turquie et en Grèce* du R.P. Robert de Dreux, aumônier de l'Ambassadeur de France (1665-1669), publié et annoté par Hubert

Pernot, Paris 1925, 104 (near Larissa, 1669). (R. Sauger), *Histoire nouvelle des anciens ducs et autres souverains de l'Archipel,* Paris 1699, 711 (Cyclades, 1698). *Lettres sur Constantinople,* de M. L'Abbé Sevin, Lettre XVII, 1755, Paris 1802, 107 (Mistras, 1705).

226. Ph. Koukoules, *Βυζαντινῶν βίος...* [Byzantine Life...], V, 407.

227. Pseudo-Kodinos, *Traité des offices,* Introduction, texte et traduction par Jean Verpeaux, Paris 1966, 172. See also A. Xyngopoulos, *Les miniatures du roman d'Alexandre le Grand dans le codex de l'Institut Hellénique de Venise,* Athens - Venice 1966, Plates p. 13, fig. 26 (fol. 28v); p. 27, fig. 55 (fol. 47v); p. 14, fig. 27 (fol. 29r); p. 9, fig. 18 (fol. 21v), 14th century.

228. N.G. Politis, *Μελέται περὶ τοῦ βίου καὶ τῆς γλώσσης τοῦ ἑλληνικοῦ λαοῦ. Παροιμίαι* [Studies on the Life and Language of the Greek People. Proverbs], III, Athens 1901, 369, 370, 380.

229. Ch. P. Konstantinou, "Κατάραι" [Curses], *Λαογραφία,* 15 (1953-1954), 455.

230. K.S. Konstas, "Ἡ ζυγιὰ στὴ Δυτικὴ Ρούμελη" [The *Ziyiá* in Western Roumeli], *Λαογραφία,* 19 (1960-1961), 329.

231. P. Vlastos, *Συνώνυμα καὶ συγγενικά* [Synonyms and Related Words], Athens 1931, 69, 181.

232. Ioannis D. Stamatakos, *Λεξικὸν τῆς Νέας Ἑλληνικῆς Γλώσσης* [Dictionary of the Modern Greek Language], 3 vols, Athens 1971.

233. Kythnos, Serifos, Sifnos, Mykonos, Naxos, Santorini, Amorgos, Paros, Milos, Tinos, Andros, et alia.

234. *Διήγησις ὡραιοτάτη τοῦ θαυμαστοῦ ἀνδρὸς τοῦ λεγομένου Βελισαρίου,* ed. G. Wagner, *Carmina graeca medii aevi,* Lipsiae 1874, 304-321.

235. Ph. Koukoules, *Βυζαντινῶν βίος...* Παράρτημα: *Ἡ νέα ἑλληνικὴ γλῶσσα καὶ τὰ βυζαντινὰ καὶ μεταβυζαντινὰ ἔθιμα* [Byzantine Life... Appendix: The Neohellenic Language, and Byzantine and post-Byzantine Customs], V, Athens 1952, 38.

236. Telephone Directory of Attica, 1977.

237. The corpse that would swell up like a baloon instead of decomposing was called *doubí,* for when it was struck it sounded like a drum *(týmpano),* writes R.P. François Richard in his journal, *Relation de ce qui s'est passé de plus remarquable à Saint-Erini, isle de l'Archipel, depuis l'établissement de Pères de la Compagnie de Jésus en icelle,* Paris 1957, 225. P. Vlastos, *Συνώνυμα...* [Synonyms...], Athens 1931, 181. S. Vios, "Χιακαὶ παραδόσεις" [Traditions of Chios], *Λαογραφία,* 9 (1926), 224, 228.

238. See notes 235 and 237.

239. Euripides, *Helene,* 1347; *Cyclops,* 65, 205. Aristophanes, *Wasps,* 119, etc. See also C. Sachs, *The History of Musical Instruments,* New York 1940, 148-149. E. Wellesz, *A History of Byzantine Music and Hymnography,* 2nd edn., Oxford 1962, 107. M. Wegner, "Griechenland", *Musikgeschichte in Bildern,* Leipzig 1963, 9, 36, 52.

240. "The *dairés* (frame drum) played with the clarinet was known as *tagharáki*". Information from Dimitrios Boglis (Trigono) and Constantinos Fotiou (Oxya), both villages near Florina (1950).

241. P. Gentil de Vendosme et Ant. Achélis, *Le siège de Malte par les Turcs en 1565,* ed. H. Pernot, Paris 1910, 105, line 736. See also *Pavlos Vlastos' Archives* 44 (1850), *Vocabulary,* s.v. *taghári.*

242. *Ambassade en Turquie de Jean de Gontaut Biron, baron de Salignac, 1605 à 1610. Voyage à Constantinople — Séjour en Turquie,* Paris 1888, 37. F.C. H.L. Pouqueville, *Voyage en Morée, à Constantinople, en Albanie, et dans plusieurs autres parties de l'empire Othoman pendant les années 1798, 1799, 1800 et 1801,* I, Paris, 272, 306. Idem, *Voyage dans la Grèce,* Paris 1820, I, 383; IV, 435. F.A. de Chateaubriand, *Itinéraire de Paris à Jérusalem,* II, Paris 1811, 81.

243. *Defitzís* and *deftzís* one who plays the *défi* (frame drum) terms rarely used in Greece today, unlike *liráris* (*lira*-player), *laoutiéris* (lute-player), *violitzís* (violin-player).

244. We have yet to encounter in our researches a *défi* where bells are used instead of or together with *zília* (cymbals), nor do any of the older musicians recall any such instance. Perhaps it was a sole exception, or perhaps the word 'bells' referred to *zília.* The sound given by the *zília* is truly bell-like, and resembles the sound produced by pellet-bells. See also Elias Petropoulos, *Καλιαρντά, ἤτοι τὸ γλωσσικὸ ἰδίωμα τῶν κιναίδων* [Kaliarda, i.e. the idiom/slang of the homosexuals (in Greece)], Athens 1971, 164—where the name *tsiganoromvia* (= gypsy's barrel-organ) is given to the *défi* (tambourine), perhaps because the Gypsies often accompany the barrel-organ with the tambourine.

245. *Μυκονιάτικα Χρονικά,* No 18, Athens, Sept. 23, 1934.

246. *Toumbeléki* or *toumberléki, toumbilék, tymberléki, tsimbourléki, doubeléki, tioubiouléki.*

247. *Taraboúka* or *tarboúka, talboúka, travoúka, darboúka, draboúka, dardaboúka.* See P.A. Bibelas, *Λαογραφικὰ Κυδωνιῶν (Αἰβαλῆ), Μοσχονησίων (Νησί) καὶ Γενητσαροχωρίου (Χωριό)* [Folklore of Kydoniai, Moschonissia and Yenitsarochori, Asia Minor], Athens 1956, 32. E.A. Bogas, *Τὰ γλωσσικὰ ἰδιώματα τῆς Ἠπείρου (Δωρείου, Κεντρικῆς, καὶ Νοτίου), Α΄: Γιαννιώτικο καὶ ἄλλα λεξιλόγια* [Idioms of Epirus: Glossary of Ioannina and other Glossaries], Ioannina 1964, 269. D. Archigenis, "Ὁ λαογραφικὸς θησαυρὸς Σμύρνης πρὶν ἀπ' τὸ 1922" [A Treasury of Smyrna Folklore (before 1922)], *Προσφυγικὸς Κόσμος,* Athens, Dec. 17, 1967, Jan. 28, 1968, Oct. 6, 1968, Nov. 10, 1968. S.P. Kyriakidis, "Δεισιδαιμονίαι καὶ δεισιδαίμονες συνήθειαι (ἐκ Γκιουμουλτζίνας τῆς Θράκης)" [Superstitions and Superstitious Customs in Gioumoultzina, Thrace], *Λαογραφία,* 2 (1910-1911), 410, 421.

248. G.A. Megas, *Σιάτιστα, τ' ἀρχοντικά της, τὰ τραγούδια της καὶ οἱ μουσικοί της* [Siatista: Mansions, Songs and Musicians], Athens 1963, 21.

249. In the past, in certain regions of Greece (Drama, Kavala, etc.), the pottery drum was known solely as the *taraboúka.* In the same regions, the small nakers *(anakarádhes)* were referred to as *toumbe-*

lékia. Today, the pottery drum is generally known as *toumbeléki* or *taraboúka,* without any distinction between the two terms.

250. Skin of a cat, rabbit, sheep; bladder of an animal (ox, cow, etc.); crop of pelican or heron; skin of still-born kid.

251. See note 248.

252. G. Valetas, *Ἀνθολογία τῆς δημοτικῆς πεζογραφίας* [Prose Anthology], I, Athens 1947, 470.

253. Regarding eastern Crete we have no information.

254. *Nounoúra* (onomatopoeic). *Chochlionounoúra* (from *chochliós* = snail). *Karáolas* and *Karívolas* = snail. *Chochlopádouro (chochliós* and *padoúra).*

255. The different pipes: the *floyéra,* the *sourávli* and the *madoúra* are made from the varieties of cane growing in Greece, *arundo donax* and *arundo plinii.* Tubes made of plastic material are used even by good popular instrumentalists, who have neither the time nor patience to search out good canes or the appropriate wood. "The plastic is ready and at hand" they claim. "It is easily worked, quickly fashioned, and sounds the 'voices' well".

256. Hardwood or softwood: elder, maple, walnut, apple, chestnut, olive, arbute, cornel, beech, oak, cedar, fir, alder, boxwood, heather.

257. Angeliki Hadjimichali, *Σαρακατσάνοι* [The Sarakatsani], A/II, Athens 1957, 149.

258. For every aerophone (flute, shawm, bagpipe, etc.) the part of the instrument that is near the mouth of the player is considered the 'upper-part', while the section furthest away from the player's mouth is regarded as the 'lower part'. In addition, the descriptive 'right' and 'left' always is in relation to the musician playing the instrument.

259. Yiannis P. Gikas, *Μουσικὰ ὄργανα καὶ λαϊκοὶ ὀργανοπαῖκτες στὴν Ἑλλάδα* [Musical Instruments and Popular Performers in Greece], Athens 1975, 43-44.

260. Information regarding the 'voices' — that is the intervals of sound encompassed given by the *floyéra* — have been culled from the study of the musicologist Despina Mazaraki, "Some Notes on Greek Shepherd Flutes", *Bulletin de l'Institut de musique,* 13 (1969) [Académie Bulgare des Sciences], 275-284. In this work, Despina Mazaraki distinguishes four types of the Greek shepherd's flute based on the length of the pipe and of the timbre of the sound produced. These are: the *kalámi* (from 15-20 cm to 36-38 cm in length), and having a "clear voice", the *floyéra* (40-45 cm long), with a "heavy voice", the *tzamára* (60-85 cm long), with a "hoarse voice", and the *darvíra* (approximately 63 cm long), with a "deep voice".
The classification we propose — short *floyéra* and long *floyéra* — we believe to be both simpler and more objective, while neglecting neither the length of the instrument nor the timbre of the sound produced (see text). We do not feel that the length of the instrument can be considered the *chief* characteristic upon which its classification is based, as is the case in the study of Despina Mazaraki, where the *kalámi* (15-38 cm long) and the *floyéra*

(40-45 cm long) are to be classified as two different types, for both instruments give the intervals of the diatonic scale. Neither should the instrument be divided into types based on differences in the timbre of the sound produced. Such differences are difficult to ascertain — when they exist — such as in the case of two instruments differing in length by a mere 2-7 centimetres. On the other hand, the descriptions "heavy voice" for the *floyéra* and "deep voice" for the *darvíra* are based on very subjective criteria, difficult to discern, as we know, while at the same time the words 'heavy' and 'deep' in this case can be considered synonymous.
In the same study Despina Mazaraki also provides the fingering positions — *dhactyliés* or *piassímata,* as they are called — of the *floyéra.*

261. E.A. Bogas, *Γλωσσικὰ ἰδιώματα τῆς Ἠπείρου, Α΄, Γιαννιώτικα καὶ ἄλλα λεξιλόγια* [Idioms of Epirus. Glossary of Ioannina and other Glossaries], I, Ioannina 1964, s.v. *tzamára.*

262. Girolamo Germano, *Grammaire et vocabulaire du grec vulgaire,* publiés d'après l'édition de 1622 par H. Pernot, Paris 1907, *Flauto da sonare, πλαγιαύλι (τό).* A.G. Paspatis, *Τὸ Χιακὸν γλωσσάριον* [Glossary of Chios], Athens 1888, s.v. *payiavlízo* =to play the *payiávli.*

263. With the exception of the study of Despina Mazaraki (see note 260), the sole disciplined musicological work dealing with the Greek shepherd's flute, whatever else has been written for that instrument, the *sourávli* or the *madoúra,* is restricted to simple, more or less interesting, informative tidbits. See: Carsten Høeg, *Les Saracatsans, une tribu nomade grecque,* I, Paris-Copenhague, 1925. D. Loucopoulos, *Ποιμενικὰ τῆς Ρούμελης* [Pastoral Life of Roumeli], Athens 1930. Angeliki Hadjimichali, *Σαρακατσάνοι* [The Sarakatsani], A/II, Athens 1957, 143-154. K.P. Hadjiioannou, "Γεωργικὰ καὶ ποιμενικὰ τῆς Κύπρου" [Pastoral Life of Cyprus], *Λαογραφία,* 11 (1934-1937), 67-111. Melpo Merlier, *Essai d'un tableau du folklore musical grec,* Athens 1935. K.N. Iliopoulos, "Ποιμενικὰ τῆς Ἠλείας" [Pastoral Life of Elis], *Λαογραφία,* 12 (Thessaloniki 1938-1948), 253-285. A.N. Karanastasis, "Ποιμενικὰ τῆς Κῶ" [Pastoral Life on Kos], *Λαογραφία,* 16 (1956), 21-104. B. Lamnatos, *Ἡ ζωὴ στὰ χειμαδιὰ* [Sheep-fold Life in the Winter], Athens 1973, et alia. See also: Du Cange, *Glossarium,* s.v. *sourávlion.* A. A. Sakellarios, *Τὰ Κυπριακά,* II, Athens 1891: *Μεσαιωνικαὶ καὶ νέαι κυπριακαὶ λέξεις* [Medieval and Modern Language (words) of Cyprus], s.v. *pidhiávlin; pidhiavlízo* = to play on the *pidhiávli.*

264. *Pavlos Vlastos' Archives,* 44 (1850) and 45 (1852), *Vocabularies,* s.v. *pandhoúra, chabióli, pabióli.*

265. Three kinds of reed (made from cane, wood, metal or plastic) are used in certain aerophones, popular instruments and those instruments used to perform 'art music', for the production of sound: they are the free reed, the single-beating reed, and the double-beating reed. The free reed *(eléfthero ghlossídhi)* slightly smaller than the opening at the base to which it is affixed, beats both inside and out of that

opening, as in the case of the harmonica, the accordion, the harmonium, etc. The single-beating reed *(monó epikroustikó ghlossídhi)*, slightly larger than the opening at the base where it is attached, when beating strikes against a fixed body. The clarinet-type pipe of Crete *(madoúra)*, the island and mainland bagpipes *(tsaboúna* and *gáida)*, the clarinet, *(klaríno)*, etc. all are equipped with single-beating reeds. In the case of the double-beating reed *(dhipló epikroustikó ghlossídhi)* its two cane 'lips' beat, i.e. open and close against each other; instruments such as the shawm *(zournás)*, the oboe, the bassoon, are fitted with double-beating reeds.

It is also noteworthy that, in the case of the vocalist, the vocal cords function much as a reed made of membrane. The same holds true for the lips of the musician in the playing of certain wind instruments, such as the cornet, the trumpet, the trombone, etc.

266. V. Kornaros, Ἐρωτόκριτος [Erotokritos], ed. S. Xanthoudidis, Iraklion, Crete, 1915, 593.

267. "*Kondiliá:* a short section of a Cretan melody upon which the *mandinádhes* [distichs] are sung", Maria Lioudaki, Λαογραφικὰ Κρήτης. Μαντινάδες [Folklore of Crete, Mandinádhes], Athens 1936, 350, 395. G.I. Hadjidakis, Κρητικὴ μουσικὴ [Cretan Music], Athens 1958, 236.

268. *Zymbraghós, tzymbraghós, azymbraghós* = twin. S. Xanthoudidis, Ποιμενικὰ Κρήτης [Pastoral Life of Crete], Athens 1920, 30. For the etymology of the word *padoúra, madoúra*, S. Xanthoudidis (Ἀθηνᾶ, 28 (1916), "Λεξικογραφικὸν Ἀρχεῖον," Παράρτημα [Lexicographical Archives, Appendix], 140) writes that "it is derived from the musical stringed instrument called *pandhoúra* or *pandhouris*".

269. Migne, *P.G.* 51, line 211.

270. Migne, *P.G.* 30, line 373.

271. Pseudo-Kodinos, *Traité des offices*. Introduction, texte et traduction par Jean Verpeaux, Paris 1966, 197. See also Du Cange, *Glossarium*, s.v. *sourávlion*.

272. S. Baud-Bovy, *Chansons du Dodécanèse*, I, Athens 1935, 265.

273. Bergadis, Ἀπόκοπος. Ἡ Βοσκοπούλα [Apokopos. Voskopoula = the shepherdess], revised by S. Alexiou, Athens 1971, lines 445-446.

274. Marcos Antonios Foskolos, Φορτουνᾶτος [Fortunatos], ed. by S. Xanthoudidis, Athens 1922, act III, scene 4, lines 335-336.

275. Petros Spandonidis, Τὸ κλέφτικο τραγούδι καὶ ἡ ἀρχαία τέχνη [The Klephtic Song and Ancient Art], Thessaloniki 1952, 60.

276. Τὰ κατὰ Λύβιστρον καὶ Ροδάμνην [Libistros and Rhodamne], ed. W. Wagner, *Trois poèmes grecs du Moyen-âge*, Berlin 1881, line 892; see also lines 793-798, 2187-2189.

277. Συναξάριον τοῦ τιμημένου γαδάρου [Synaxarion of the Estimable Donkey], ed. G. Wagner, *Carmina graeca medii aevi*, Lipsiae 1874, lines 341-342.

278. J. Théodore Bent, *Early Voyages and Travels in the Levant, Extracts from the Diaries of Dr. John Covel, 1670-1679*, London 1893, 170.

279. Edward Daniel Clarke, *Travels in Various Countries of Europe, Asia and Africa*, III, London 1814, 759.

280. G. Millet, *Recherches sur l'iconographie de l'Évangile aux XIVe, XVe et XVIe siècles*, 2nd edn., Paris 1960, 114-135. From the illuminated manuscripts published to date we refer to the following: G. de Jerphanion, *Les églises rupestres de Cappadoce*, Paris, I, 1925, 1932; II, 1936, 1942, and 3 Albums; see Pl. 68 in Album I, Paris 1925.
Suzy Dufrenne, *L'illustration des psautiers grecs du moyen-âge*, Paris 1966, Pl. 47 (fol. 7v, MS Add. 40731, British Museum, 10th-11th century). H. Omont, *Évangiles avec peintures byzantines du XIe siècle*, I-II (Reproduction des 361 miniatures du manuscrit grec 74 de la Bibliothèque Nationale Paris), fol. 4, p. 6; fol. 108, p. 96; fol. 108v, p. 97. Kurt Weitzmann, *Aus den Bibliotheken des Athos*, Hamburg 1963, MS 14 of Esphigmenou Monastery, fol. 393v (11th-12th century). Ernest T. de Wald, *The Illustrations in the Manuscripts of the Septuagint*, III, *Psalms and Odes*, Part I: *Vaticanus graecus 1927*, Princeton-London-The Hague 1941, Pl. LXIV (fol. 264r, Psalm CL, 12th century). H. Omont, *Miniatures des plus anciens manuscrits grecs de la Bibliothèque Nationale, du VIe au XIVe siècle*, Paris 1929, Pl. XCII (MS Gr. 54, fol. 13v, 14th century).
For the wall-paintings, see G. Millet, *Monuments byzantins de Mistra*, Paris 1910, Pl. 118, fig. 2: Nativity (detail) in Perivleptos, 14th century; Pl. 133, fig. 5: Nativity (detail) in Aghia Sophia, 14th century. G. Millet, *Monuments de l'Athos*, I, *Les peintures*, Paris 1927, Nativity, 83, 198, 222, 250. A. Xyngopoulos, *Les miniatures du roman d'Alexandre le Grand dans le codex de l'Institut Hellénique de Venise*, Athens-Venice 1966, Plates: p. 29, fig. 59 (fol. 49v); p. 45, fig. 91 (fol. 75r); p. 54, fig. 109 (fol. 91r), 14th century.

281. British Museum, London: Greek Psalter ca. 1090, MS Add. 36928 (fol. 46v); Greek Psalter 11th century, MS Add. 19352 (fol. 189v). Patriarchal Library, Jerusalem, Cod. Taphou 14, fol. 33v, 11th century. W. Bachmann, *The Origins of Bowing..*, London — New York — Toronto 1969, Pl. 10, Cod. Taphou 14, fol. 310v, 11th century. H. Omont, *Miniatures des plus anciens manuscrits grecs de la Bibliothèque Nationale, du VIe au XIVe siècle*, Paris 1929, Pl. CIV (MS Gr. 533, fol. 34v, 11th century); Pl. CXVII (MS Coislin 239, fol 26v, 12th century). Ernest T. de Wald, *The Illustrations in the Manuscripts of the Septuagint*, III: *Psalms and Odes*, Part II, *Vaticanus graecus 752*, 11th century, Princeton - London - The Hague 1942, Pl. XV, fol. 53v; Pl. IX, fol. 7v; Pl. LIV, fol. 449v; Pl. VI, fol. 5r; Pl XIII, fol. 18v.

282. Kurt Weitzmann, *Ancient Book Illumination*, Cambridge, Massachusetts 1959, Pl. XVI, fig. 36 (Mount Sinai Cod. 3, fol. 8r, 11th century). Paul Buberl, *Die byzantinischen Handschriften*, I: *Der Wiener Dioskourides und die Wiener Genesis*, Leipzig 1937, Pl. XXXVII, fig. 34 (Wiener Genesis, Cod. Theol. graec. 31, fol. XVII). Patriarchal Library, Jerusalem, Cod. Taphou 14, fol. 33v, 11th century.

283. The pipes of the *syrinx* (Pan-pipe) are closed at their lower end, they have no fingerholes, and each pipe gives only one note.

284. Michail Chourmouzis, Ἡ νῆσος Ἀντιγόνη [Antigone's Island], Constantinople 1869, 57.

285. N.G. Kyriazis, Κυπριακαὶ παροιμίαι [Cypriot Proverbs], Larnaca 1940, 288.

286. G.M. Vizyinos, "Οἱ Καλόγεροι καὶ ἡ λατρεία τοῦ Διόνυσου ἐν Θράκῃ" [The Kaloyeri and the Dionysian Worship in Thrace], Θρακικὴ Ἐπετηρίς, 1 (1897), 126-127. See also Skarlatos D. Vyzantios, Ἡ Κωνσταντινούπολις [Constantinople], III, Athens 1869, 462 ("Phrygian aulos..."). A. Chourmouziadis, Περὶ τῶν Ἀναστεναρίων καὶ ἄλλων τινῶν παραδόξων ἐθίμων καὶ προλήψεων [On Anastenaria and other Strange Customs and Superstitions], Constantinople 1873, 9. G. D. Pachticos, 260 δημώδη ἑλληνικὰ ᾄσματα [260 Greek Folk Songs] Athens 1905, 183, 185, 186, 188, 189, 190 f.

287. We have also come across instances of the *zournás* fashioned from thick cane, with a bell made from tin, in Mytilene, the Peloponnese, Macedonia, etc.

288. K.S. Konstas, "Ἡ ζυγιὰ στὴν Δυτικὴ Ρούμελη" [The *Ziyiá* in Western Roumeli], Λαογραφία, 9 (1960-1961), 325-359.

289. Daremberg-Saglio, *Dictionnaire des antiquités grecques et romaines*, s.v. tibia.

290. C. Sachs, *The History of Musical Instruments*, New York 1940, 138. M. Wegner, "Griechenland", *Musikgeschichte in Bildern*, Leipzig 1963, 30, 68, 78, 84, 126. H. Becker, *Zur Entwicklungsgeschichte der antiken und mittelalterlichen Rohrblattinstrumente*, Hamburg 1966, 19.

291. For the ancient Greek *aulos*, see K. Schlesinger, *The Greek Aulos*, London 1939. M. Wegner, "Griechenland"..., Leipzig 1963.

292. See opinions of Basil the Great, Clement of Alexandria, Epiphanius, Gregory the Divine, and others, in Ph. Koukoules, *Βυζαντινῶν βίος...*[Byzantine Life...], V, Athens 1952, 239-240.

293. *Ambassade en Turquie de Jean de Gontaut Biron, baron de Salignac, 1605 à 1610, Voyage à Constantinople — Séjour en Turquie*, Relation inédite précédée de la vie du baron de Salignac par le Comte Théodore de Gontaut Biron, Paris 1888, 37.

294. *Voyage en Turquie et en Grèce* du R.P. Robert de Dreux aumônier de l'ambassadeur de France (1665-1669) publié et annoté par H. Pernot, Paris 1925, 104.

295. *Travels in Asia Minor and Greece or an Account of a Tour Made at the Expense of the Society of Dilettanti*, by R. Chandler, 3rd edn., II, London 1817, 151.

296. F.C.H.L. Pouqueville, *Voyage dans la Grèce*, IV, Paris 1820, 435.

297. Takis Lappas, Ἡ Ἀράχωβα τοῦ Παρνασσοῦ [Arachova], Athens 1961, 36-37. J. C. Hobhouse, *A Journey Through Albania and Other Provinces of Turkey in Europe and Asia, to Constantinople, during the Years 1809 and 1810*, London 1813, 254-255.

298. Dinos Konomos, "Ἀνέκδοτα ἀπομνημονεύματα τοῦ Παύλου Καρρὲρ" [Unpublished Memoirs of the Heptanesian Composer Pavlos Karrer, 1829-1896], Φιλολογικὴ Πρωτοχρονιά, Athens 1962, 241-242.

299. P. Gentil de Vensdome et Ant. Achélis, *Le siège de Malte par les Turcs en 1565,* ed. H. Pernot, Paris 1910, 131, line 1445.

300. Marinos Zanes Bounialis, Ὁ Κρητικὸς Πόλεμος [The Cretan War], ed. Agathangelos Xirouchakis, Triest 1908, 156, lines 17-18. See also Συναξάριον τοῦ τιμημένου γαδάρου [Synaxarion of the Estimable Donkey], lines 341-342, and Διήγησις ὡραιοτάτη τοῦ θαυμαστοῦ ἀνδρὸς τοῦ καλουμένου Βελισαρίου [Tale of Belisarius], lines 258-259, ed. G. Wagner, *Carmina graeca medii aevi*, Lipsiae 1874.

301. A. Banck, *Byzantine Art in the Collections of the U.S.S.R.*, Leningrad-Moscow 1966, 368.

302. M. Michailidis, "Καθολικὸ Μονῆς Ὁσίου Νικάνορος (Ζάβορδας) Γρεβενῶν" [Katholikon of the Monastery of Hosios Nicanor, Zavorda, near Grevena], Ἀρχαιολογικὰ ἀνάλεκτα ἐξ Ἀθηνῶν, IV (Athens 1971), 346-352.

303. A. Xyngopoulos, Σχεδίασμα ἱστορίας τῆς θρησκευτικῆς ζωγραφικῆς μετὰ τὴν ἅλωσιν [Notes toward a History of Religious Painting after the Fall of Constantinople], Athens 1957, 114-121.

304. T.A. Gritsopoulos, "Ἡ κατὰ τὴν Κυνουρίαν Μονὴ τῆς Λουκοῦς" [Loukous Monastery, Kynouria], Πελοποννησιακά, 6 (1963-1968), 129-190.

305. N.G. Kyriazis, Κυπριακαὶ Παροιμίαι [Cypriot Proverbs], Larnaca 1940, 288.

306. A.A. Papadopoulos, "Παροιμίαι Πόντου" [Proverbs of Pontos], Λαογραφία, 6 (1917), 26.

307. See Telephone Directory of Attica, 1977.

308. *Pavlos Vlastos' Archives*, 44 (1850), *Vocabulary*.

309. Du Cange, *Glossarium*. Girolamo Germano, *Grammaire et vocabulaire du grec vulgaire* publiés d'après l'édition de 1622 par H. Pernot, Paris 1907.

310. The skin of the sheep is nowhere near as strong as that of the goat.

311. Propolis = bee-glue, a brown sticky resinous substance gathered by bees from trees and used by them as cement and varnish.

312. H. Balfour, "The Old British 'Pidcorn' or 'Hornpipe' and its Affinities", *Journal of the Anthropological Institute*, 20 (London 1890).

313. A. Baines, *Bagpipes*, Oxford 1960, 45.

314. N. Bessaraboff, *Ancient European Musical Instruments*, New York 1964, 79, Pl. I, 87. See also F.W. Galpin, *Old English Musical Instruments*, London 1965, 128.

315. C. Sachs, *The History of Musical Instruments*, New York 1940, 212.

316. See plates of fingering-position and musical examples in the study of S. Peristeris, "Ὁ ἄσκαυλος (τσαμπούνα) εἰς τὴν νησιωτικὴν Ἑλλάδα" [The Bagpipe *(tsaboúna)* in the Islands of Greece], Ἐπετηρὶς Λαογραφικοῦ Ἀρχείου, 13-14 (1960-1961), 63-71.

317. See W.L. Landowski, *Le travail en musique*, Paris 1949.

318. In 1959, when we met at Tzermiado, Andonis G. Tzermias was 84 years old. He lived with his memories, taken from his life, together with his wife,

known throughout the village as Madouraraina (= wife of the *madouráris* = *madoúra*-player).

319. For the importance of such vent-holes in the family of aerophones, see A. Baines, *Bagpipes,* 22.

320. C. Sachs, *The History of Musical Instruments,* 141. A. Baines, *Bagpipes,* 63-67.

321. Ernest T. de Wald, *The Illustrations in the Manuscripts of the Septuagint,* III, *Psalms and Odes,* Part II: *Vaticanus graecus 752,* Princeton-London-The Hague 1942, Pl. IX, fol. 7v.

322. Baron Rodolphe d'Erlanger, *La musique arabe,* II, Paris 1935, 234.

323. A.H.S. Megaw-A. Stylianou, *Zypern: Byzantinische Mosaiken und Fresken,* New York 1963, Pl. XXIV.

324. G.N. Aikaterinidis, '"Ο Ἅγιος Φανούριος εἰς τὴν λαϊκὴν παράδοσιν τῆς Κρήτης" [St. Phanourios in the Popular Traditions of Crete], *Κρητικὴ Πρωτοχρονιὰ* 1965, 168.

325. Nicolas de Nicolay, *Les navigations, peregrinations et voyages, faicts en la Turquie,* Antwerp 1577, 171-172.

326. *Ambassade en Turquie de Jean de Gontaut Biron, baron de Salignac, 1605 à 1610, Voyage à Constantinople – Séjour en Turquie.* Relation inédite, précédée de la vie du baron de Salignac par le Comte Théodore de Gontaut Biron, Paris 1888, 37. In addition, see S. Baud-Bovy, "La cornemuse du tsar", *Ἑλληνικά,* 19 (1966), 116-117 (correction of the translation of a line in the text of 1612).

327. (Robert Sauger), *Histoire nouvelle des anciens ducs et autres souverains de l'Archipel...,* Paris 1699, 386.

328. F.C.H.L. Pouqueville, *Voyage en Morée, à Constantinople, en Albanie et dans plusieurs autres parties de l'empire Othoman, pendant les années 1798. 1799. 1800 et 1801,* I, Paris 1805, 272; *Voyage dans la Grèce,* I, Paris 1820, 383.

329. A.G. Paspatis *Τὸ Χιακὸν γλωσσάριον* [Glossary of Chios], Athens 1888, s.v. *tsabounáris.* See also *Μυκονιάτικα Χρονικὰ* No 50-51, April 21, 1935. A.E. Florakis, *Τῆνος. Λαϊκὸς πολιτισμὸς* [Tinos' Folklore], Athens 1971, 388-389. William Haygarth, *A Book of Original Sketches Mostly Costumes (1810)* [Greek musician of Athens].

330. *Διήγησις παιδιόφραστος τῶν τετραπόδων ζώων* [Playful Tale about Quadrupeds], ed. G. Wagner, *Carmina graeca medii aevi,* Lipsiae 1874, lines 199, 322, 1014.

331. *Γαδάρου, λύκου καὶ ἀλουποῦς διήγησις ὡραία* [Tale of the Donkey, the Wolf and the Fox], ed. G. Wagner, *Carmina graeca..* line 345. See also P. Vlastos, *Συνώνυμα καὶ συγγενικά* [Synonyms and Related Words], Athens 1931, s.v. *tsabounízo, tsabounó* (verbs).

332. Ph. Apostolidis, "Κύρια ὀνόματα κ' ἐπίθετα τῆς Τσαντῶς" [Proper Names and Adjectives of Tsanto, Thrace], *Θρακικά,* 13 (1940), 350.

333. S. Baud-Bovy, *Chansons du Dodécanèse,* II, Paris 1938, 407.

334. Despina Mazaraki, *Τὸ λαϊκὸ κλαρίνο στὴν Ἑλλάδα* [The Popular Clarinet in Greece], Athens 1959.

335. Throughout the islands of Greece, even if one does occasionally encounter the clarinet *(klaríno),* the instruments that continue to reign today are those

of the ensemble violine and lute *(ziyiá: violí-laghoúto).*

336. A relatively similar period is also to be found in the history of Byzantine music of the 13th-14th centuries, with the *melurgí* and *maístores*; see E. Wellesz, *A History of Byzantine Music and Hymnography,* Oxford 1962, 145, 238, 329.

337. Paul Faure, *La vie quotidienne en Crète au temps de Minos (1500 av. J.-C.),* (Paris) (édit. Hachette-Littérature) 1973, 242, and in addition 350-354.

338. N. Angelis, *Στὸν ἴσκιο τῆς μαδάρας. Μηνύματα θανάτου* [Collection of short stories: "Under the Madara-rock Shadow". Death Messages], Athens 1961, 35-39.

339. R.M. Dawkins, "A Visit in Skyros, I: The Carnival", *Annual of the British School at Athens,* 11 (1904-1905), 72-74.

340. The publisher of Theognis, J.M. Edmonds (Loeb Classical Library, Greek Elegy), refers to a verse of Athenaeus, who interprets the lines 1229-1230 as referring to the *kóchlos* (= conch), today known as the *bouroú*. Information pertaining to the lines of Theognis, as well as their translation, we owe to the archaeologist Stylianos Alexiou. For the use of the *bouroú* as a sound-producing device during the Minoan period, see A. Evans, *The Palace of Minos,* I, London 1921, 581.

341. Euripides, *Iphigeneia in Tauris,* 303.

342. Theokritus, *Idyllia,* 22, 75.

343. Odysseas Elytis, *"Ήλιος ὁ πρῶτος* [Helios the First] (Poems), Athens 1943, 21.

344. P. Vlastos, *Συνώνυμα καὶ συγγενικά* [Synonyms and Related Words], Athens 1931, 304.

345. J. Jegerlehner, "Beiträge zur Verwaltungsgeschichte Kandias im 14. Jahrhundert", *Byzantinische Zeitschrift,* 13 (1904), 460).
For the use of the *voúkino* as sound-producer in former times as a signaling device, see Irini Oustayiannaki-Tachataki, *Λαογραφικὰ σταχυολογήματα* [Folklore in Crete], Archanes (near Iraklion, Crete) 1976, 12.

346. J. Porte, *Encyclopédie des musiques sacrées,* I, Paris 1968, 494-499.

347. Angeliki Hadjimichali, *Σαρακατσάνοι* [The Sarakatsani] A/II, 432. Kitsos Makris, "Ποιμενικὰ ξυλόγλυπτα" [Carvings by Shepherds], *Δίαυλος,* No 1, (Volos, November-December 1965).

348. H. Castela, *Le sainct voyage de Hierusalem et Mont Sinay en l'an du grand Iubilé 1600,* 2nd edn., Paris 1612, 532.

349. Nicolas de Nicolay, *Les navigations, peregrinations et voyages faicts en la Turquie,* Antwerp 1577, 75. Anonyme, *The Travels of Certain Englishmen into Africa, Asia, Troy, Bythinia, Thracia...,* London 1609, 12-13. De Thévenot, *Relation d'un voyage fait au Levant,* Rouen 1665, 191. See also Ph. P. Argentis and S.P. Kyriakidis, *Ἡ Χίος παρὰ τοῖς γεωγράφοις καὶ περιηγηταῖς* [Chios, according to Geographers and Travellers], Athens 1946, I: 20, 264, 300, 311, 331, 424, 555; III: 1402, 1419, 1424, 1446, 1464, 1479.

350. *Πουλολόγος* [Tale about Birds], ed. G. Wagner, *Carmina graeca medii aevi,* Lipsiae 1874, 198, lines 629-630.

374

351. A. Stefopoulos, "Παιδικὰ παραδοσιακὰ παιχνίδια ἀπὸ τὴ Χρυσὴ Καστοριᾶς" [Traditional Children's Games from Chryssi, Kastoria], Μακεδονικά, 12 (1972), 369.

352. G.D. Pachtikos, 200 δημώδη ἑλληνικὰ ἄσματα [200 Greek Folk Songs], Athens 1905, 187.

353. Yiannis Vlachoyiannis, Ἱστορικὴ ἀνθολογία [Historical Anthology], Athens 1927, 85.

354. This sound-producing device, known as the bull-roarer (rhombe or planche ronflante in French, and Schwirrholz in German), is still to be found today in many of the so-called primitive societies, in their religio-magical functions. Members of such societies believe that the sound produced by the bull-roarer is either the voice of their ancestors or the voice of certain deity. A similar sound-producing device has been preserved in the Museum of St. Germain-en-Laye in France. It is fashioned from the horn of a reindeer, 14,000 years old, and was discovered in a cave in Dordogne. See A. Schaeffner, "Les instruments de musique", La musique des origines à nos jours, Paris, Larousse, 15. C. Sachs, The History of Musical Instruments, 40-43.

355. "Tambourás or tamboúri, instrument with télia (= strings); Pavlos Vlastos' Archives, 44, Vocabulary. In Nikissiani (region of Pangeon) the tambourás is also called tsamboúras, according to Theodor Papaloudis (born 1897).

356. Angeliki Hadjimichali, Σαρακατσάνοι [The Sarakatsani], A/II, 154.

357. S.I. Karas, Γένη καὶ διαστήματα εἰς τὴν βυζαντινὴν μουσικήν [Genera and Intervals in the Byzantine Music], Athens 1970, 16-19.

358. J.P. Sideris, "Οἱ ζεϊμπὲκ (Ἔθιμα τῶν Ἀπόκρεων ἐν Σύρῳ) [The Zeimbek. The Customs of the Carnival on Syros], Λαογραφία, 4 (1913-1914), 567.

359. The kavónto, the tzivoúri and the karadouzéni are known to us solely through literary sources and the oral descriptions older people. For the number of strings and the tuning of the following musical instruments: tambourás, sázi, bouzoúki, baghlamás, yiongári, boulgarí, kíteli, kavónto, tzivoúri and karadouzéni see also R. Yekta, "La musique turque", Encyclopédie Lavignac, Part I, V (Le Tanbour, 3015-3017; Le Meydan-Sazi, 3018). C. Sachs, Reallexikon, s.v. Tanbur, Tampuras, Saz, Mpuzuki, Baghlama, Yonghar, Tanbur bulghari [boulgarí is one of the names by which the tambourás is known in Bulgaria], Kitelis (kíteli, from the Turkish: iki+tel = two télia = wires, strings), Cavonto, Tsiburi, Qaradüzen.
In addition we include the names given to the bouzoúki and the baghlamás in the idiom/slang ("kaliardi") of the homosexuals. For bouzoúki: kaimókouto (kaimós = pain, longing + koutí = box), kaimochélono (kaimós + chelóna = tortoise, because the sound-box is often made of tortoise-shell). For baghlamás: chelonóbouro (chelóna = tortoise + bouró, from tó bouriári = song in the idiom "kaliardí"). choumsokaimoú (choumsi = jail in the "kaliardí" + kaimós = pain, longing — because the baghlamás was the par excellence instrument of convicts), Elias Petropoulos, Καλιαρντά, ἤτοι τὸ γλωσσικὸ ἰδίωμα τῶν κιναίδων [Kaliarda, i.e. the idiom/slang of the homosexuals (in Greece)], Athens 1971, 52, 175-176, 177.
H.G. Farmer, "The Music of Islam", The New Oxford History of Music, I, London 1957, 447. R. Wright, "Tanbour boulghari", Dictionnaire des instruments de musique, London 1941. Kurt and Ursula Reinhard, Turquie, Paris 1969, 109-110, 129-130. M. Todorof, Blgarski Narodni Musikalni Instrumenti [Bulgarian Popular Musical Instruments], (in Bulgarian), Sofia 1973, 124-130. L. Picken, Folk Musical Instruments of Turkey, London 1975, see Index, 637ff. and 647ff.

360. "...the tríchordhon [three stringed]. which is called by the Assyrians pandhoúra", Polydeukes D, 60. "pandhoúra or pandhourís: musical instrument", Hesychius, cf. Athenaeus 183 F (Liddell-Scott Dictionary) (Greek - English). Also see pandhourás, pandhourízo, pandhoúrion, pandhouristís, pándhouras, phándhouros (Stamatakos'Dictionary) (in Greek).

361. National Archaeological Museum, Athens, Themis' Room, No 216.

362. R.A. Higgins, R.P. Winnington-Ingram, "Lute-players in Greek Art", The Journal of Hellenic Studies, 85 (1965).

363. H.G. Farmer, Oriental Studies, Mainly Musical. An Early Greek Pandore, London 1953, 61-63.

364. F. Anoyanakis, "Ein byzantinisches Musikinstrument", Acta Musicologica, 37, No 3-4 (Basel 1965), 158-165.

365. Sachs traces the etymological origins of the word pandoúra (pantura) from the Summerian pantur = 'small-bow'. He believes that the ancient Greek pandhoúra could have descended from the musical instrument mousikó tóxo (= musical bow), both as an instrument and as terminology. C. Sachs, The History of Musical Instruments, 137.

366. Constantine VII Porphyrogennetus, Le livre des cérémonies, ed. Albert Vogt. II: Commentaire, Paris 1940, 182-183, 188.

367. Paul Riant, Expéditions et pèlerinages des Scandinaves en Terre Sainte au temps des croisades, Paris 1865, 200.

368. Ph. P. Argentis and S.P. Kyriakidis, Ἡ Χίος παρὰ τοῖς γεωγράφοις καὶ περιηγηταῖς [Chios according to Geographers and Travellers], Athens, I (1946), 307. The English "a great kind of citern" is incorrectly translated in the Greek text "a kind of large guitar", (apparently referring to a tambourás).

369. N. K. Kassomoulis, Ἐνθυμήματα στρατιωτικὰ τῆς Ἐπαναστάσεως τῶν Ἑλλήνων, 1821-1823 [Military Souvenirs of the Greek War of Independence, 1821-1823], Athens, I (1940), 270; II (1941), 539; III (1942), 74-75.

370. Ἀπομνημονεύματα Στρατηγοῦ Μακρυγιάννη [Memoirs of General Makriyannis], Text - Introduction - Notes by G. Vlachoyiannis, I, Athens 1947, 285, footnote 2.

371. Dimitrios Paschalis, "Οἱ δέκα Λόγοι τοῦ Διγενοῦς Ἀκρίτα" [Ten Episodes from the Life of Digenis Akritas], Λαογραφία, 9 (1926), 403.

372. Chrysanthus, Archbishop of Dyrrachion. Θεωρητικὸν μέγα τῆς μουσικῆς [Theory of Music], Triest

375

1832, 194.

373. P.P. Kalonaros, Βασίλειος Διγενῆς 'Ακρίτας, I-II, Athens 1970, Escor. line 832; Acritic Song 233, lines 123, 141.

374. N.G. Politis, 'Εκλογαὶ ἀπὸ τὰ τραγούδια τοῦ ἑλληνικοῦ λαοῦ [Selections from the Songs of the Greek People], 3rd edn., Athens 1932, 68. Claude Fauriel, Τὰ ἑλληνικὰ δημοτικὰ τραγούδια [The Greek Folk Songs], Athens 1956, 247. K.A. Psachos, Δημώδη ᾄσματα Γορτυνίας [Folk Songs of Gortynia], Athens 1923, 120. B. Bouvier, Δημοτικὰ τραγούδια ἀπὸ χειρόγραφο τῆς Μονῆς 'Ιβήρων [Folk Songs from a Manuscript of the Iwiron Monastery], Athens 1960, 23. A. Melachrinos, Δημοτικὰ τραγούδια [Folk Songs], Athens 1946, 163. S. Karakassis, 'Ελληνικὰ μουσικὰ ὄργανα [Greek Musical Instruments], Athens 1970, 76. (See note 36).

375. A. Xyngopoulos, Les miniatures du roman d'Alexandre le Grand dans le codex de l'Institut Hellénique de Venise, Athens-Venice 1966, Plates: p. 29, fig. 59 (fol. 49v); p. 45, fig. 91 (fol. 75r); p. 54, fig. 109 (fol. 91r), 14th century.

376. Choiseul-Gouffier, Voyage pittoresque de la Grèce, Paris 1782, I: Pl. 18, fig. 33; 1822, II: p. 2, Pl. 70 and 81; Ibid., Planches, Brussels (circa 1830), "Seconde vue du Bosphore, prise à Kandilly". Pl. 20.

377. Greek Painters of the Nineteenth Century, Texts and supervision of the painter Errikos Frantziskakis, Athens [Commercial Bank of Greece], 1957: P. Lembessis, "The Evzone", 121; Nikiphoros Lytras, "The Milkman", 64, and "Return from Pentelikon", 70.

378. Theodor Vryzakis (1814-1878), "Le camp de Caraïskakis (au Pirée, en 1827)", Lithography, National Historical Museum, Athens. Theophilos, Athens [Commercial Bank of Greece], 1966, Pl. 53, 56, 66, 212. See also : wall-painting by Theophilos in the Museum of Greek Folk Art, Athens; coloured lithography, "Arnautes", by Th. Leblanc, Historical Museum of Pylos; Calender of the National Bank of Greece 1968, Peter von Hess, "Theodoros Kolokotronis".

379. Angeliki Hadjimichali, 'Ελληνικὴ λαϊκὴ τέχνη, Σκῦρος [Greek Folk Art, Skyros], Athens 1925, 119-120. Publications of the Benaki Museum: Embroideries of Epirus and the Ionian Islands, Athens 1965, fig. 5; Embroideries of Skyros, Athens 1965, fig. 13.

380. Yiannis Tsarouchis, "'Η tapisserie καὶ οἱ ζωγράφοι" [The Tapestry and the Painters], Ζυγός, 2nd period, fascicle IX (Nov.-Dec. 1965), 15-49.

381. N.G. Politis, Μελέται, Παροιμίαι [Studies, Proverbs], II, 662.

382. Telephone Directory of Attica, 1977.

383. Nicholas Bessaraboff, Ancient European Musical Instruments, 2nd edn., New York 1964, 222. Curt Sachs, The History of Musical Instruments, 253.

384. In mountainous regions or areas isolated from urban centres: Ierisso (Chalkidiki), certain villages of Epirus, in Nikissiani (Pangeon, Kavalla), Agoriani (Parnassos region), in villages of the region of Tyrnavos (Thessaly), etc.

385. The large and deep soundbox provides a corresponding great and loud sound; this however, is not always sweet and beautiful.

386. The oldest known Greek lute (laghoúto) studied to date was made in 1862 by Emmanuel Veloudios (Collection of Greek Popular Musical Instruments, belonging to Fivos Anoyanakis). See note 18 as well.

387. The older lute-players and craftsmen, such as Demosthenes Papaconstantinou (b. 1885, Vilia, Attica), Yiannis Paleologos (b. 1904, Constantinople), among others, recall lutes fashioned from rosewood. Today, the lute is not made from such wood.

388. The lute belonging to Demosthenes Papaconstantinou, renowned lute-player, was made in 1912, by Manolis Kopeliadis. With an ebony body, this instrument was equipped with 39 staves — narrow and very thin — in order to keep the instrument from being too heavy.

389. The importance of the natural method of drying the wood in affecting the quality of the sound produced by the instrument is also underlined in recent, relevant studies. See Émile Leipp, Le Violon. Histoire, esthétique, facture et acoustique, Paris 1965, 61-63.

390. According to the workshop, this obtuse angle is either smaller or greater, generally ranging between 145-160 degrees. In the case of the western lute (Renaissance and Barok), the great degree of the 'break' backwards which often served to create an acute angle with the player's hand, not only facilitated the player's tuning of his instrument, but also served to distribute more evenly the weight of the instrument. See F.W. Galpin, A Textbook of European Musical Instruments, 4th edn., London 1956, 93. N. Bessaraboff, Ancient European Musical Instruments, 225.

391. The moveable frets (berdédhes) are often mistakenly referred to as tásta. Tásta is the name given only to those permanent, metallic 'bindings' affixed to the neck of the instrument, such as those to be found today on certain instruments of the lute family, the present-day bouzoúki, the guitar, etc.

392. See S.I. Karas, Γένη καὶ διαστήματα εἰς τὴν βυζαντινὴν μουσικήν [Genera aud Intervals in the Byzantine Music], Athens 1970.

393. The custom of fashioning the first two moveable frets from thicker material is today to be found only among the older lute-players. The importance of this technique towards the production of a 'cleaner' sound is also underlined by the English theoritician and lutist Thomas Mace, in 1676, in his valuable writings upon the construction and technique of the lute, Musick's Monument, or, Remembrancer of the best Practical Musick both Divine and Civil, that has ever been known to have been in the world, London 1676, 68.

394. The uncles of the renowned popular musician Iakovos Ilias (b. 1906 in Megara), themselves well-known lute-players and violonists, tune their instruments upon the sound given by the bell of the Church of the Virgin's Dormition at Megara: that is E, albeit slightly lower than the E given by the tuning-fork. In addition, see F. Anoyanakis, "Τὸ γενεαλογικὸ δέντρο ἑνὸς λαϊκοῦ μουσικοῦ" [The Geneological Tree of a Popular Musician], Λαογρα-

φία, 29 (1974), 93-113.

395. Such ensembles, through playing in different night-spots where they often accompanied western musical instruments tuned to the G of the tuning-fork, were obliged to accept the high G of Europe in tuning their own instruments.

396. N.A. Chrysochoidis, Τὰ τονιαῖα διαστήματα τῶν κλιμάκων τῆς βυζαντινῆς μουσικῆς μετὰ καὶ σχετικῶν διαγραμμάτων [The Intervals of the Scales of the Byzantine Music], Athens 1956. G. Spyridakis and S. Peristeris, Ἑλληνικὰ δημοτικὰ τραγούδια [Greek Folk Songs], III, p. κα΄-λε΄.

397. In the case of one post-war Cretan lute in particular, while the maker of the instrument, G.E. Frangedakis (Chania), has affixed the first two fixed cane frets (kalamákia) as usual, the following three were made not from cane but from plastic. These he joined from the side, thus giving them an abstract geometric form. This is a characteristic example of how a certain part of the instrument, originally directly related to the actual playing of the instrument, gradually loses its practical significance, instead slowly being tranformed into a decorative motif.

398. Claudie Marcel-Dubois, "Luth", Encyclopédie de la musique, (Fasquelle), III, Paris 1961. Joan Rimmer, Ancient Musical Instruments of Western Asia, London 1969, 22-23. H. Turnbull, "The Origin of the Long-necked Lute", The Galpin Society Journal 25 (July 1972), 58-66.

399. A Banck, Byzantine Art in the Collection of the U.S.S.R., Leningrad-Moscow 1966, 368 ,"Lid from a Vessel with Musicians, Dancers and Acrobats, 12th century, Silver".

400. The Greek of the middle ages found himself in constant communication with the surrounding Arabic and Islamic world. Byzantine and Islamic commerce are indistinguishable: the one begins where the other leaves off (E. Perroy, Le Moyen-âge [Histoire générale des civilisations], III, Paris 1955, 155). In addition, entire regions under Byzantine dominion would from time to time break away from her sovereignty, only to return to the sheltering wings of the empire following a shorter or longer period of independence. Such was the case of the island of Crete, which was subject to Arabic rule for more than a century (823-961), and which was greatly influenced by her conqueror (K. Paparrigopoulos, Ἱστορία τοῦ Ἑλληνικοῦ Ἔθνους [History of the Greek Nation], IV, Athens 1932, 93, 95-96). Byzantium influenced and was in turn influenced by the East (Cambridge Mediaeval History, IV, Cambridge 1923, 152, 173). It is not too difficult for one to unterstand how, among such a constant inter-communication, there also took place an exchange of influences in the sphere of music. And this, especially in the case of musical instruments, for the most part common to the peoples of the Balkan peninsula. Furthermore, it should not be forgotten that musical instruments were — and always are — among the most "circulated objects in the world" (A. Schaeffner, Larousse de la Musique, I, Paris 1957, 468). L. Picken, Folk Musical Instruments of Turkey, London 1975, 557.

401. During the same period traditionalTurkish music was solely based on the use of the oúti (short-necked lute with a large soundbox). The long-necked lute (laghoúto) with a large soundbox as well — known in Turkey as lavouta or lavta — was used on a limited scale, and never in the classical traditional music of the country. Certain musicologists believe that the laghoúto "does not have a clearly Turkish character", while others do not refer to the instrument at all among the instruments making up the Turkish instrumentarium, See: R. Yekta, "La musique turque", Encyclopédie de la musique (Lavignac), Part I: Histoire de la musique, V, Paris 1922, 3015, 3017-3018. K. and U. Reinhard, Turquie, Paris 1969, 112. A. Adnan Saygun, "Musique turque", Encyclopédie de la Pléiade, Histoire de la musique, I, Paris 1960, 601-603, 613-616. A similar opinion is shared by Professor Laurence Picken (Jesus College, Cambridge). In his answering letter to the author, related to the position of the lavouta or lavta in the traditional music of Turkey, he writes: "My impression is that, as your authorities suggest, this instrument made no detectable impact on Turkish music... It was perhaps derived from an instrument of either the Italian or the Greek communities in Pera or Galata" (Oct. 16, 1972). Also see Laurence Picken, Folk Musical Instruments of Turkey, London 1975, 284.

402. P.P. Kalonaros, Βασίλειος Διγενὴς Ἀκρίτας, II, Escor., lines 831-833, 1145-1150.

403. F. Anoyanakis, "Νεοελληνικὰ χορδόφωνα. Τὸ λαγοῦτο" [Neohellenic Chordophones. The Lute], Λαογραφία, 28 (1972), 207-214 (with a summary in French, p. 483-499).

404. Ἑλληνικὰ δημοτικὰ τραγούδια (Ἐκλογὴ) [Greek Folk Songs (Selection-Texts)], I, Athens, 1962, 114.

405. P.P. Kalonaros, Βασίλειος Διγενὴς Ἀκρίτας, II, lines 627, 1145. For the dating of the Escorial manuscript (16th or 15th or 14th century) see II, p. η΄, footnote 18.

406. S. Alexiou, Κρητικὴ Ἀνθολογία [Cretan Anthology], 2nd edn., Iraklion, Crete 1969, 63.

407. S. Alexiou, ibid., 211. See also S. Xanthoudidis, "Ὁ Φαλλίδος", Ἐπετηρὶς Ἑταιρείας Βυζαντινῶν Σπουδῶν, 4 (1927), 100, lines 44 ff.

408. Vitsentzos Kornaros, Ἐρωτόκριτος, Critical edition by S. Xanthoudidis, Iraklion, Crete 1915, I, lines 391-392, 647-648; II, line 1349.

409. Telephone Directory of Attica, 1977.

410. F. Anoyanakis, "Νεοελληνικὰ χορδόφωνα..." [Neohellenic Chordophones...], 222, 233.

411. Apart from the pan-hellenic líra, the instrument was also known in the past as the lioúra among the Greeks of Sozopolis, (in Eastern Thrace), and zíga or gíga in the region of Serres.

412. The oldest líra we have studied has the date 1743 inscribed on its head in low-relief (Collection of Greek Popular Musical Instruments of Fivos Anoyanakis).

413. For the influence had upon the chordophones (bowed or plucked), the tuning of the compania (violin-clarinet-lute-dulcimer) and the island zyiá (violin-lute) by gut strings in comparison with modern metallic

strings, their construction, etc. see F. Anoyanakis, "Νεοελληνικὰ χορδόφωνα..." [Neohellenic Chordophones...], 191-192.

414. S. Baud-Bovy, *Chansons du Dodécanèse*, II, Paris 1938, 284-285, 291, 304.

415. N. Mavris — E. Papadopoulos, Δωδεκανησιακὴ λύρα [The Dodecanesian Lira], Port-Said 1928, p. ιζ΄. S. Baud-Bovy, *Chansons du Dodécanèse*, II, 226.

416. F. Anoyanakis, "Νεοελληνικὰ χορδόφωνα" [Neohellenic Chordophones...], 194-199.

417. H.G. Farmer, *Byzantine Musical Instruments in the Ninth Century*, London 1925, 3-7.

418. For the origins and the presence of the first bowed stringed instruments in the 10th century A.D., in the world of the Byzantine and Islamic empires, see W. Bachmann, *The Origins of Bowing and the Development of Bowed Instruments up to the Thirteenth Century*, London 1969, 24-42.

419. Florence, Museo Nazionale, Collection Carrand 26. W. Bachmann, *The Origins of Bowing...*, p. VIII, Pl. 9. In *Byzantine Art, an European Art*, (Catalog of the 9th Exhibition of the Council of Europe), Athens 1964, 157, No 50, this casket (reliquary) is attributed to the 11th-12th century.

420. E.T. de Wald, *The Illustrations in the Manuscripts of the Septuagint*, III, *Psalms and Odes*, Part II: *Vaticanus graecus 752*, Pl. VI (fol. 5r), Pl. IX (fol. 7v). J. Lassus, "Les miniatures byzantines du Livre des Rois, d'après un manuscrit de la Bibliothèque Vaticane", *Mélanges d'Archéologie et d'Histoire, École Française de Rome*, 45 (1928), 38-74, Pl. VII, fig. 11c (Cod. Vat. Gr. 333 formerly 238, fol. 45v, No 85c).

421. Philanthropinon Monastery (Ioannina), Exterior Narthex: "Jesus is mocked"; Zavorda Monastery (Grevena): "Jesus is mocked", both of the 16th century (see M. Michailidis, "Καθολικὸν Μονῆς Ὁσίου Νικάνορος (Ζάβορδας) Γρεβενῶν" [Katholikon of the Monastery of Hosios Nikanor (Zavorda) Grevena], Ἀρχαιολογικὰ Ἀνάλεκτα ἐξ Ἀθηνῶν, IV (1971), 346-354. Meteora: Varlaam Monastery, Katholikon: "Jesus is mocked" (see N.A. Bees, "Συμβολὴ εἰς τὴν ἱστορίαν τῶν Μονῶν τῶν Μετεώρων" [Contribution to the History of the Meteora's Monasteries], Βυζαντίς, I (Athens 1909), 191-331. G. Sotiriou, "Βυζαντινὰ μνημεῖα τῆς Θεσσαλίας ΙΓ΄ καὶ ΙΔ΄ αἰῶνος" [Byzantine Monuments of Thessaly of the 13th and 14th centuries], Ἐπετηρὶς Ἑταιρείας Βυζαντινῶν Σπουδῶν, 9 (1932), 382-515. See also in the Monasteries of Mount Athos: Philotheou: "Praise ye the Lord", 18th cent.; Grigoriou: "Praise ye the Lord", 18th cent.; Karakalou, Sanctuary: "The Ark carried to Jerusalem", 18th century.

422. Ἑλληνικὰ δημοτικὰ τραγούδια [Greek Folk Songs], I, Athens 1962, 116. In the same collection, page 114, the same song in a version from Asia Minor, has the word *laghoúto* (lute) substituted for *lira*: "Bring me my lute *(laghoúto)* with its silver strings, that I may sing sorrowfully, that I may cry bitterly".

423. D.-C. Hesseling and H. Pernot, *Poèmes prodromiques*, Amsterdam 1910, 40. See also Hans-Georg Beck, *Geschichte der byzantinischen Volksliteratur*, Munich 1971.

424. Τὰ κατὰ Λύβιστρον καὶ Ροδάμνην, ed. W. Wagner, *Trois poèmes grecs du Moyen-âge*, Berlin 1881, 242-349, lines 793-794.

425. S. Papadimitriou, Στέφανος Σαχλίκης καὶ τὸ ποίημα αὐτοῦ «Ἀφήγησις παράξενος» [Stefanos Sachlikis and his poem "Strange Story"], Odessa 1896, 16. Announcement made during the Fourth International Cretan Congress (Sept. 1976): "Ὁ Δικηγόρος τοῦ Χάνδακα Στέφανος Σαχλίκης, ποιητὴς τοῦ 14ου καὶ ὄχι τοῦ 15ου αἰώνα" [The Lawyer of Chandax (Iraklion, Crete), Stefanos Sachlikis, poet of the 14th and not of the 15th century].

426. *Pavlos Vlastos' Archives*, 14, 606.

427. Maria Lioudaki, Μαντινάδες, I, 527.

428. N.G. Politis, Μελέται, Παροιμίαι [Studies, Proverbs], I, 527.

429. F.C.H.L. Pouqueville, *Voyage en Morée, à Constantinople, en Albanie, et dans plusieurs autres parties de l'empire Othoman, pendant les années 1798, 1799, 1800 et 1801*, I, Paris 1805, 272, 279-280, 306, 311-312, 315-316, 521. Idem, *Voyage dans la Grèce*, Paris 1820, II, 261-262, 311-313; III, 33; IV, 129-130; Paris 1821, V, 193. E.D. Clarke, *Travels in Various Countries of Europe, Asia and Africa*, IV, London 1816, 121-122. F.A. de Chateaubriand, *Itinéraire de Paris à Jérusalem*, II, Paris 1811, 16, 73, 81. R. Chandler, *Travels in Asia Minor and Greece*, 3rd edn., II, London 1817, 151. Franz von Löher, *Kretische Gestade*, Bielefeld and Leipzig 1877, 145.

430. Museum of Greek Folk Art, Athens. See also Laura F. Pesel, "Cretan Embroidery", *The Burlington Magazine for Connoisseurs* 10, No 45 (December 1906), 155-161.

431. Telephone Directory of Attica, 1977. Telephone Directory of Crete, 1973.

432. The few instances of the *lira* from the Black Sea region we have encounrered in the last fifteen years or so, having a larger bridge, constitute an exception, an unacceptable "modernism", as characterised by older musicians from the Black Sea region.

433. Mozarabic manuscript, Biblioteca Nacional, Madrid, Hh 58, fol. 127r, circa 920-930. See W. Bachmann, *The Origin of Bowing...*, London 1969, Pl. I. The illustration in the text (fig. 173) is a copy from a photograph (detail).

434. C. Sachs, *The History of Musical Instruments*, New York 1940, 275. Kurt and Ursula Reinhard, *Turquie*, Paris 1969, 127-128. Kurt Reinhard, "Musik am Schwarzen Meer", *Jahrbuch für musikalische Volks- und Völkerkunde*, 2 (Berlin 1966) ed. Fr. Bose, 25-27.

435. From the archaic types of stringed bowed instruments the *iklig* (Turkish) or *kemantchá* belong to the family of the lute with a long thin neck and hemispheric soundbox (originally half the shell of a coconut) covered with skin. The neck passes through the soundbox and terminates in a 'foot' which enables the player to rest the instrument on the ground when it is played. It has two strings which are tuned in fifths and is played with a curved bow (see fig. 179).

436. Laurence Picken, *Folk Musical Instruments of*

Turkey, London 1975, 296-337. It is also noteworthy that more recent comparative musicological research indicates that the musical 'idiom' of the Greeks and Turks of the Black Sea region differs radically from that of other regions of both Greece and Turkey. S. Baud-Bovy, "Chansons d'Épire du nord et du Pont", *Yearbook of the International Folk Music,* 3 (1971), 120-127.

437. D.M. Sarros, Περὶ τῶν ἐν Ἠπείρῳ, Μακεδονίᾳ καὶ Θράκῃ συνθηματικῶν γλωσσῶν [On Cryptic Idioms of Epirus. Macedonia and Thrace], Λαογραφία, 7 (1923), 541.

438. Ath. A. Sakellarios, *Τὰ Κυπριακὰ (Λεξιλόγιον)* [Cypriot Vocabulary], II. Athens 1891.

439. This manner of playing is not exceptional. In certain countries the popular violin is played in this fashion. See Oszkar Dincsér, *Két csiki hangszer, Mozsika és gardon (Zwei Musikinstrumente aus dem Komitat Csik),* Magyar Történeti Muzeum, Budapest 1943.

440. F. Anoyanakis, "Νεοελληνικὰ χορδόφωνα..." [Neohellenic Chordophones...], 224-227, 231-233.

441. See note 440, p. 193-194.

442. See note 440, p. 206.

443. Sozos Tombolis, Κυπριακοὶ ρυθμοὶ καὶ μελωδίες [Cypriot Rhythms and Melodies], Nicosia, Cyprus 1966, 17.

444. N.G. Politis, Ἐκλογαὶ ἀπὸ τὰ τραγούδια τοῦ ἑλληνικοῦ λαοῦ [Selections from the Songs of the Greek People], 219.

445. A. Melachrinos, Δημοτικὰ τραγούδια [Folk Songs], Athens 1946, 145.

446. Marinos Tzanes Bounialis, Ὁ Κρητικὸς πόλεμος [The Cretan War], ed. Agathangelos Xirouchakis, Triest 1908, 570.

447. S. Alexiou, Κρητικὴ Ἀνθολογία [Cretan Anthology], 2nd edn., Iraklion, Crete 1969, 211.

448. Ph. P. Argentis and S. Kyriakidis, Ἡ Χίος παρὰ τοῖς γεωγράφοις καὶ περιηγηταῖς [Chios according to Geographers and Travellers], I, Athens (1946), 307. In the same work, page 317, the word fiddle is translated as *violi* (violin). Fiddle, however, is the generic name for every bowed stringed instrument, such as vielle, violin, *lira,* etc.

449. Th. N. Philadelpheus, Ἱστορία τῶν Ἀθηνῶν ἐπὶ Τουρκοκρατίας, ἀπὸ τοῦ 1400 μέχρι τοῦ 1800 [The History of Athens during Turk Dominion, from 1400 to 1800], I, Athens 1902, 330.

450. Χρονικὸ τῆς σκλαβωμένης Ἀθήνας στὰ χρόνια τῆς τυραννίας τοῦ Χατζαλῆ, γραμμένο στὰ 1841 ἀπὸ τὸν ἀγωνιστὴ Παναγῆ Σκουζέ, ἀποκαταστημένο ἀπὸ τὸν Γ. Βαλέτα [Chronicle of the Enslaved Athens during the Years of Tyranny under Hadjali, written in 1841 by Panayis Skouzes, revised by G. Valetas], Athens 1948, 83.

451. F.C.H.L. Pouqueville, *Voyage dans la Grèce,* IV, Paris 1820, 435. F.A. de Chateaubriand, *Itinéraire de Paris à Jérusalem,* II, Paris 1811, 74.

452. N.K. Kassomoulis, Ἐνθυμήματα στρατιωτικὰ τῆς Ἐπαναστάσεως τῶν Ἑλλήνων, 1821-1833 [Military Souvenirs of the Greek War of Independence, 1821-1833], I, Athens 1939, 207.

453. N.G. Politis, Μελέται, Παροιμίαι [Studies,

Proverbs], III, 375.

454. Neoklis G. Kyriazis, Κυπριακαὶ παροιμίαι [Cypriot Proverbs], Larnaca 1940, 110.

455. Telephone Directory of Attica, 1977.

456. *Kanonáki* or *kanóni,* derived from the word *canón* = measure: the single-stringed instrument use to measure intervals during the ancient Greek years. *Psaltírion* or *psaltíri,* from the verb *psállo* which means to touch, to play a stringed instrument with the fingers, and not with a plectrum, (Liddell-Scott Dictionary).
The following are also derived from the Greek word *canón: qanun (kanun, kanoun), cano, kanon, meo canno, micanon, medicinale,* etc.

457. They would throw the ox-horns into the fire, as a result of which 'layers' of horn would peel off. From these thin peels they would fashion plectra, both for the psaltery *(kanonáki)* and the short-necked lute *(oúti).*

458. F.W. Galpin, *A Textbook of European Musical Instruments,* 4th edn., London 1956, 84. Idem, *Old English Instruments of Music,* 4th edn., London 1965, 43. N. Bessaraboff, *Ancient European Musical Instruments,* 2nd edn., New York 1964, 211.

459. Albin Lesky, *Geschichte der griechischen Literatur,* Bern-München 1963, 620, 737.

460. C. Sachs, *The History of Musical Instruments,* 136, 137, 257, 292.

461. By way of example we refer to the following: Psalter and other texts, Jerusalem, Greek Orthodox Patriarchal Library, Cod. Taphou 53, fol. 203, 11th century.
E. de Wald, *The Illustrations in the Manuscripts of the Septuagint,* III, *Psalms and Odes,* Part I: *Vaticanus graecus 1927:* Pl. XXXIX (fol. 170v, Psalm XCI), Pl. XLII (fol. 178v, Psalm XCVII, 12th cent.). *Book of Job,* with Commentary, Paris, Bibliothèque Nationale, Gr. 135, fol. 150v (14th cent.). The wall-painting "Praise ye the Lord" in the narthex of the Monastery Varlaam (Meteora), etc.

462. Paul Riant, *Expéditions et pèlerinages des Scandinaves en Terre Sainte au temps des croisades,* Paris 1965, 200.

463. Philippe du Fresne-Canaye (1573), *Le voyage du Levant,* Paris 1897, 114-115.

464. *Sandoúri* from the Persian-Arabic *santir* or *sintir* or *santur,* words derived from the Greek *psaltírion.*

465. Edward Daniel Clarke, *Travels in Various Countries of Europe, Asia and Africa,* IV, London 1816, 4.

466. A corresponding role — we are not making a comparison — was played by the piano in the older instrumental ensembles of the so-called 'light music' of the period between the two World Wars.

467. *Tsímbalo* with a pedal was made for the first time in 1870 in Hungary, by the Hungarian dulcimer-maker Vencel Jozsef Schunda. See Gyorgy Gabry, *Old Musical Instruments,* Budapest 1969, 18. Janos Manga, *Hungarian Folk Song and Folk Instruments,* Budapest 1969, 60.

468. F. Anoyanakis, Ἡ μουσικὴ στὴ νεώτερη Ἑλλάδα [Music in Modern Greece], offprint from *Histoire de la musique* by Karl Nef, Translation — Additions by F. Anoyanakis, Athens 1960, 2-9. 10-28.

BIBLIOGRAPHY

Anoyanakis, F. *Instruments de musique populaires grecs*, Athens 1965. [Ministère de l'Éducation Nationale et des Cultes].

— *"Νεοελληνικὰ χορδόφωνα. Τὸ λαγοῦτο"* [Neohellenic Chordophones. The Lute], with a summary in French, 483-499; *Λαογραφία*, 28 (1972).

— "Ein byzantinishes Musikinstrument", *Acta Musicologica*, XXXVII/III-IV (1965), 158-165.

Archives, see *Pavlos Vlastos' Archives*.

Argentis, Ph. P. and Kyriakidis, S.P. *'Η Χίος παρὰ τοῖς γεωγράφοις καὶ περιηγηταῖς* [Chios according to Geographers and Travellers], I-III, Athens 1946.

Bachmann, W. *The Origins of Bowing and the Development of Bowed Instruments up to the Thirteenth Century*, London — New York — Toronto 1969.

Baines, A. *Bagpipes*, Oxford 1960.

— *European and American Musical Instruments*, London 1966.

— *Catalogue of Musical Instruments*, Victoria and Albert Museum, II, London 1968.

Banck, A. *Byzantine Art in the Collections of the USSR*, Leningrad — Moscow 1966.

Baud-Bovy, S. *Chansons du Dodécanèse*, 2 vols., Athens—Paris 1935-1938.

— *La chanson populaire grecque du Dodécanèse, Les textes*, Paris 1936.

— "Sur la strophe de la chanson cleftique", *Mélanges H. Grégoire*, 2, Brussels 1950, 53-78.

— "La strophe de distiques rimés dans la chanson grecque", *Studia memoriae Belae Bartok sacra* (Academia Budapest) (1957), 355-373.

— *Études sur la chanson cleftique*, Athènes 1958.

— "L'accord de la lyre antique et la musique populaire de la Grèce moderne", *Revue de musicologie*, 53/1 (1967), 3-20.

— "Équivalences métriques dans la musique vocale grecque antique et moderne", *Revue de musicologie*, 54/1 (1968), 3-15.

— "Chansons d'Épire du Nord et du Pont", *Yearbook of the International Folk Music Council*, 3 (1971), 120-127.

— *Chansons populaires de Crète occidentale* (with a disc), Geneva 1972.

— "L'évolution parallèle de la construction, de la technique et du répertoire de la lyra crétoise", *Studia instrumentorum musicae popularis*, V, Stockholm 1977, 127-130.

— *Essai sur la chanson populaire grecque*, Note liminaire de Fivos Anoyanakis, Fondation Ethnographique du Péloponnèse, Nauplie 1983.

Becker, H. *Zur Entwicklungsgeschichte der antiken und mittelalterlichen Rohrblattinstrumente*, Hamburg 1966.

Bessaraboff, N. *Ancient European Musical Instruments*, 2nd edn., New York 1964.

Blades, J. *Percussion Instruments and their History*, London 1970.

Bounialis, Marinos Tzanes *'Ο Κρητικὸς πόλεμος* [The Cretan War], edit. Agathangelos Xirouchakis, Triest 1908.

Chryssochoidis. N. Ath. *Τὰ τονιαῖα διαστήματα τῶν κλιμάκων τῆς βυζαντινῆς μουσικῆς* [The Intervals of the Scales of Byzantine Music], Athens 1956.

Constantin VII Porphyrogennetus, *Le livre des cérémonies*. edit. Albert Vogt, II: *Commentaire*, Paris 1940.

D'Erlanger, R. *La musique arabe*, 6 vols., Paris 1935.

Der Nersessian, Sirarpie *L'illustration du roman de Barlaam et Joasaph*, Paris 1937.

De Wald, E. *The Illustrations in the Manuscripts of the Septuagint*, III: *Psalms and Odes*, Princeton — London — The Hague 1941-1942.

Dimaras, K. Th. *'Η ἱστορία τῆς νεοελληνικῆς λογοτεχνίας* [History of Modern Greek Literature], 6th edn., Athens 1975.

Dufrenne, Suzy *L'illustration des psautiers grecs du Moyen Age*, Paris 1966.

Drexl, F. "Das anonyme Traumbuch des Cod. Paris. Gr. 2511", *Λαογραφία*, 8 (1921), 347-375.

Ellis, A.J. "On the Musical Scales of Various Nations", *Journal of the Society of Arts*, 1885.

Farmer, H.G. *Byzantine Musical Instruments in the Ninth Century*, London 1925.

— *Oriental Studies, Mainly Musical. An Early Greek Pandore*, London 1953.

— "The Music of Islam", *The New Oxford History of Music*, I, London 1957.

Fauriel, C. *Chants populaires de la Grèce moderne*, 2 vols., Paris 1824-1825.

Galpin, F.W. *A Textbook of European Musical Instruments*, London 1956.

— *Old English Instruments of Music*, London 1970.

Georgiades, Thr. *Der griechische Rhythmus, Musik, Reigen, Vers und Sprache*, Hamburg 1949.

Gikas, Y.P. *Μουσικὰ ὄργανα καὶ λαϊκοὶ ὀργανοπαῖκτες στὴν 'Ελλάδα*. [Musical Instruments and Popular Performers in Greece], Athens 1975.

[Greek Folk Songs (Selection)] *'Ελληνικὰ δημοτικὰ*

τραγούδια ('Εκλογή), I, Athens 1962 [Academy of Athens. Publications of the Folklore Archives, No 7].

Hadjimichali, Angeliki Σαρακατσάνοι [The Sarakatsani], A/I-II, Athens 1957.

Hickmann, H. Catalogue général des antiquités égyptiennes du musée du Caire, No 69201-69852: Instruments de musique, Cairo 1949.

Jenkins, Jean (edit.), Ethnic Musical Instruments, Identification-Conservation, London 1970.

Kakouri, Katerina J. Dionysiaka, Aspects of the Popular Thracian Religion of Today, Athens 1965 (First publication in Greek 1963).

— Προϊστορία τοῦ Θεάτρου ἀπὸ τὴ σκοπιὰ τῆς κοινωνικῆς ἀνθρωπολογίας [Prehistory of the Theatre from the Viewpoint of Social Anthropology], with a summary in English of the anthropologist Prof. John K. Campbell, Athens 1974.

Kalonaros, P.P. Βασίλειος Διγενὴς Ἀκρίτας [Vassilios Digenis Akritas], 2 vols., Athens 1970.

Karas, S. Γένη καὶ διαστήματα εἰς τὴν βυζαντινὴν μουσικὴν [Genera and Intervals in the Byzantine Music], Athens 1970.

Kornaros, Vitsentzos Ἐρωτόκριτος [Erotokritos], Critical edition by S. Xanthoudidis. Iraklion, Crete 1915.

Koukoules, Ph. Βυζαντινῶν βίος καὶ πολιτισμός [Byzantine Life and Civilisation], I-VI, Athens 1948-1955.

Kunst, J. Ethnomusicology, 3rd edn., The Hague 1959.

— Supplement to the Third Edition of Ethnomusicology. The Hague 1960.

Kyriakidis, S.P. Αἱ ἱστορικαὶ ἀρχαὶ τῆς δημώδους ἑλληνικῆς ποιήσεως [The Historical Origins of Modern Greek Folk Poetry], Thessaloniki 1954.

— Ἑλληνικὴ Λαογραφία [Greek Folklore], I, Athens 1965.

Lavignac, Encyclopédie de la Musique, Part I: Histoire de la Musique, Paris, I, 1913; V, 1922.

Liddell-Scott, A Greek - English Lexicon, Oxford, Edn. 1940.

Lioudaki, Maria Μαντινάδες [Mantinadhes (distichs)], Athens 1936.

Martin, J.R. The Illustration of the Heavenly Ladder of John Climacus, Princeton 1954.

Mazaraki, Despina Τὸ λαϊκὸ κλαρίνο στὴν Ἑλλάδα [The Popular Clarinet in Greece], Athens 1959.

— "Some Notes on Greek Shepherd Flutes", Bulletin de l'Institut de Musique, 13 (1969) [Académie Bulgare des Sciences], 275-284.

— "Ein Aulos der Sammlung Karapanos", Mitteilungen des Archäologischen Institutes, Athenische Abteilung, 89 (1974), 105-121.

Merlier, Melpo Essai d'un tableau du folklore musical grec, Athens 1935.

Michaelidis, Solon The Music of Ancient Greece. An Encyclopedia, London 1978.

Migne, J.-P. Patrologia Graeca, 1857-1866.

Millet, G. Monuments byzantins de Mistra, Paris 1910.

— Monuments de l'Athos, I: Les peintures, Paris 1927.

— Recherches sur l'iconographie de l'Évangile, aux XIVe, XVe et XVIe siècles, 2nd edn., Paris 1960.

Musik in Geschichte und Gegenwart (Die). I-XIV, Kassel — Basel — Paris — London — New York 1949-1968.

Omont H. Miniatures des plus anciens manuscrits grecs de la Bibliothèque Nationale, du VIe au XIVe siècle, Paris 1929.

Pachticos, G.D. 260 δημώδη ἑλληνικὰ ἄσματα [260 Greek Folk Songs], Athens 1905.

[Pavlos Vlastos' Archives] Ἀρχεῖον Παύλου Βλαστοῦ, Historical Archives of Crete, Chania (unpublished)

Peristeris. Sp. Ὁ ἄσκαυλος (τσαμπούνα) εἰς τὴν νησιωτικὴν Ἑλλάδα [The bagpipe (tsaboúna) in the Islands of Greece], Ἐπετηρὶς Λαογραφικοῦ ἀρχείου, 13-14 (1960-61), 63-71.

Pernot, H. Mélodies populaires grecques de l'île de Chio, Paris 1903.

Picken, L. Folk Musical Instruments of Turkey, London 1975.

Politis. N.G. Μελέται περὶ τοῦ βίου καὶ τῆς γλώσσης τοῦ ἑλληνικοῦ λαοῦ. Παροιμίαι [Studies on the Life and Language of the Greek People. Proverbs], 4 vols., Αthens 1899-1902. Παραδόσεις [Traditions], 2 vols., Athens 1904.

Politis, Linos A History of Modern Greek Literature, Oxford 1973.

Psachos, K.A. Δημώδη ἄσματα Γορτυνίας [Folk Songs of Gortynia], Athens 1923.

— 50 δημοτικὰ ἄσματα Πελοποννήσου καὶ Κρήτης [Fifty Folk Songs from the Peloponnese and Crete], Collections of the Athens' Conservatory, Athens 1930.

Pseudo-Kodinos, Traité des offices. Introduction, texte et traduction par Jean Verpeaux, Paris 1966.

Rallis, G.A. and Potlis, M. Σύνταγμα τῶν θείων καὶ ἱερῶν κανόνων [Collection of the Divine and Sacred Canons], Athens, III, 1853; IV, 1854.

Reinhard, K. "Musik am Schwarzen Meer", Jahrbuch für musikalische Volks - und Völkerkunde, 2 (Berlin 1966), edit. Fr. Bose.

Reinhard, Ursula and K. Turquie, Les traditions musicales, Paris 1969 [Institut international d'études comparatives de la musique].

Sachs, C. Reallexikon der Musikinstrumente, Berlin 1913.

— Geist und Werden der Musikinstrumente, Berlin 1929.

— World History of the Dance, New York 1937.

— The History of Musical Instruments, New York 1940.

Saygun, A.A. "Musique turque", Encyclopédie de la Pléiade, Histoire de la musique, I, Paris 1960.

Schaeffner, A. Origine des instruments de musique, Paris 1936.

— "Les instruments de musique", La musique des origines à nos jours, Larousse, Paris 1946.

Schlesinger, Kathleen The Greek Aulos, London 1939.

Spyridakis, G. and Peristeris, Sp. Ἑλληνικὰ δημοτικὰ τραγούδια (Μουσικὴ ἐκλογὴ) [Greek Folk Songs (Musical Selection)], (with 5 discs) III, Athens

1968 [Academy of Athens. Publications of the Greek Folklore Research Centre, No 10], Summary in English p. 417-430.

Themelis, D.G. *Tὸ "κανονάκι", ἕνα λαϊκὸ μουσικὸ ὄργανο. Ἔρευνα γιὰ τὴν προέλευσή του"* [The "kanonáki" (psaltery), a popular musical instrument. An investigation on its origins]. *First Symposium of the Folkore of Northern Greece (Epirus-Macedonia-Thrace)*, Thessaloniki 1974. [Offprint of the Institute for Balkan Studies, Thessaloniki 1975, No 153].

Wagner, G. *Carmina graeca medii aevi,* Lipsiae 1874.

Wagner, W. *Trois poèmes grecs du Moyen-âge,* Berlin 1881.

Wegner, M. "Griechenland", *Musikgeschichte in Bildern,* Leipzig 1963.

Weitzmann, K. *Greek Mythology in Byzantine Art,* Princeton, 1951.

— *Aus den Bibliotheken des Athos,* Hamburg 1963.

— *Ancient Book Illumination,* Cambridge, Massachusetts 1959.

Wellesz, A. *A History of Byzantine Music and Hymnography,* 2nd edn., Oxford 1963.

Winternitz, Em. *Instruments de musique du monde occidental,* Paris 1972.

Xanthoudidis, S. *Ποιμενικὰ Κρήτης* [Pastoral Life in Crete], Athens 1920.

Xyngopoulos, A. *Les miniatures du roman d'Alexandre le Grand dans le Codex de l'Institut Hellénique de Venise.* Athens — Venice 1966.

— *Σχεδίασμα ἱστορίας τῆς θρησκευτικῆς ζωγραφικῆς μετὰ τὴν ἅλωσιν* [Notes towards a History of Religious Painting after the Fall of Constantinople], Athens 1957.

Yekta, R. "La musique turque", *Encyclopédie Lavignac,* Part I: *Histoire de la musique,* V, Paris 1922.

SELECTIVE DISCOGRAPHY

ACADEMY OF ATHENS — GREEK FOLKLORE RESEARCH CENTRE

Ἀκριτικὰ καὶ Ἱστορικὰ [Akritic and Historical Songs] PR7 T 110/111

Κλέφτικα καὶ Παραλογὲς [Klephtic and Narrative Songs or Ballads]   PR7 T 112/113

Λατρευτικὰ καὶ Ἐρωτικὰ [Devotional and Love-Songs] PR7 T 114/115

Τοῦ Γάμου, Σατυρικὰ καὶ Ξενιτειᾶς [Wedding – Satyric – Exile's Songs]   PR7 T 116/117

Μοιρολόγια, Ἐργατικά, Νανουρίσματα καὶ Ταχταρίσματα [Dirges, Work-Songs, Lullabies and "Tachtarismata"]   PR7 T 118/119

(These 5 recordings accompany the book *Greek Folk Songs (Musical Selection)*, III, G. Spyridakis and Sp. Peristeris [Academy of Athens—Publications of the Greek Folklore Research Centre. No 10, 1968])

SOCIETY FOR THE DISSEMINATION OF NATIONAL MUSIC (ATHENS)

Songs of Epirus . . . .   SDNM 111

Songs of Eastern Macedonia . . . .   SDNM 117

Songs of Western Macedonia . . . .   SDNM 109

Songs of Thrace (Part I) . . . .   SDNM 106

Songs of the Peloponnesus . . . .   SDNM 113

Songs of Crete . . . .   SDNM 114

Songs of Kasos and Karpathos . . . .   SDNM 103

Songs of Rhodes, Chalki and Symi . . .   SDNM 104

Songs of Amorgos, Kythnos and Sifnos   SDNM 105

Songs of Mytilene and Chios . . . .   SDNM 110

Songs of Thasos, Lemnos and Samothrace   SDNM 108

Songs of the Ionian Islands . . . .   SDNM 115

Songs of Constantinople and the Sea of Marmara . . . .   SDNM 118

(These recordings were released between 1972-1978. Additional recordings of this Series are forthcoming)

THE MERLIER COLLECTION

Authentic Greek Folk Music from early recordings of 1930-1931   POLYDOR — 24 21 079, 1976.

PELOPONNESIAN FOLKLORE FOUNDATION (NAFPLION)

Greek Folk Music, Vol. I,   P.F.F./1, 1975
Music from Macedonia. Thrace, Epirus, Sterea, Peloponnesus, Dodecanese and Cyprus.

Greek Folk Music, Vol. II,   P.F.F./2, 1976
Music from Macedonia, Thrace, Epirus, Peloponnesus, Dodecanese and Asia Minor.

Greek Folk Music, Vol. III,   P.F.F./3, 1977
Music from Macedonia, Thrace, Peloponnesus, Cyclades, Dodecanese, Sterea and Asia Minor. Wedding Songs.

(Additional recordings of this Series are forthcoming)

LYCEUM CLUB OF GREEK WOMEN (ATHENS)

Folk Music. Dances — Songs (Naoussa, Macedonia, Limassol / Cyprus)   LCGW 101, 1975

Folk Music. Dances — Songs (Megara / Attica) LCGW 102, 1976

LE CHANT DU MONDE — ETHNOLOGIE VIVANTE

Grèce — Documents recueillis par Domna Samiou G.U. LDX 74425, 1970-1971

* *Songs of my Country*. Travelling in Greece with Domna Samiou   LYRA 3252, 1972

* Ἔχε γειὰ Παναγιὰ [Eche Yeiá Panayiá = Farewell, Virgin Mother]   EMI 14C 064 — 70115, 1973

* *Great Solos — Souravli* [Instrumental music] 12 Masterpieces selected by Domna Samiou EMI 14C 054 — 70816, 1977

* *Greek Carols* (Christmas, New Year, Epiphany, Lazarus) selected by Domna Samiou   EMI 2J 062 — 70139, 1974

* *Greek Folk Songs and Music*. Τῆς πικροδάφνης ὁ ἀνθὸς [By the Flowering Oleander] selected by Domna Samiou EMI 2J 062 — 70253, 1975-1976

* = Recordings edited by Greek Records Companies

383

ORIGINAL FOLK AND ETHNIC MUSIC OF THE PEOPLES OF EUROPE

Folk Music of Northern Greece (Epirus, Macedonia) collected and edited by Wolf Dietrich
ALBATROS VPA 8298, 1976

Folk Music of the Dodecanese Islands (Field recordings from Kos, Simi, Nisiros, Rhodes, Karpathos) collected and edited by Wolf Dietrich
ALBATROS VPA 8295, 1976

Folk Music of Greece, collected and edited by Wolf Dietrich   TOPIC 12TS231

ORIGINAL ETHNIC MUSIC OF THE PEOPLES OF THE WORLD

Folk Music of Cyprus. Greek Music — Turkish Music (Traditional Songs and Dances of the Greek, Turkish and Maronite Communities) collected and edited by Wolf Dietrich   ALBATROS VPA 8218, 1974

MUSEUM COLLECTION BERLIN — Editor ARTUR SIMON

Music of the Pontic Greeks TELDEC MC5—TST 78071

ETHNIC FOLKWAYS LIBRARY

Folk Music of Greece, recorded by James A. Notopoulos (Crete, Cyprus Naxos, Pontus, Rhodes, Peloponnesus, Macedonia, Epirus. Songs and Dances)
FOLKWAYS FE 4454, 1955

The following recordings of the Rebetic Music were selected by Markos F. Dragoumis:

A) OLD PERFORMANCES — REPRINTS FROM 78 RPM RECORDINGS

Τὸ ρεμπέτικο τραγούδι [The Rebetiko Song], 1-2, Centre of Research and Study of Rebetika Songs
CBS 82290, 1977

Τὰ πρῶτα ρεμπέτικα [The earliest Rebetika, 1900-1913] T. Schorelis   CBS 53753, 1976

Ρεμπέτικη Ἱστορία [Rebetic History], 1-6,
K. Hadjidoulis   EMI, 1975-1976

Οἱ μεγάλοι τοῦ ρεμπέτικου [Great Rebetes], 1-5,
K. Hadjidoulis   MARGO, 1975-1976

Ἀφιέρωμα [Dedication to Papaioannou, Bellou, Ninou],
K. Hadjidoulis   EMI, 1977-1978

Ἀφιέρωμα στὸ Μάρκο [Dedication to Marko (Vamvakaris)]   MINOS, 1972

Markos Vamvakaris MELOPHONE SMEL 5, 1969

Vassilis Tsitsanis, 1-6, K. Hadjidoulis   EMI, 1975-1978

Ioanna Georgakopoulou, Rebetika.   EMI, 1976-1977

Marika Ninou at "Fat Jimmy's Tavern"
UNIVOX   SLX 2003, 1977

Stellakis Perpiniadis, Autobiography, K. Hadjidoulis
EMI, 1976

Nikos Armaos, Laterna and Ntefi (Barrel-organ and Tambourine)   EMI, 1977

B) CONTEMPORARY PERFORMANCES

Λουκᾶς Νταραλᾶς, Ἕνας ρεμπέτης [Loukas Daralas, A Rebetis]   SONORA 571, 1974

Λουκᾶς Νταραλᾶς, Ἐγὼ καὶ τὸ ρεμπέτικο [Loukas Daralas, The Rebetiko and I]   SONORA 64, 1975

Στρᾶτος Παγιουμτζῆς, Τὸν παληὸ ρεμπέτικο καιρὸ [Stratos Payioumtzis. In the old days of the Rebetiko]
PHILIPS 6483012, 1969.

Τὰ τραγούδια τοῦ πατέρα μου. Παλιὲς ἐπιτυχίες τοῦ Γιάννη Παπαϊωάννου [My Father's Songs. Old successes of Yiannis Papaioannou] edited by
Markos F. Dragoumis   EMI, 1974

Mouflouzelis, The old Rebetiko Song
ZODIAC 88025, 1972.

Mouflouzelis, Old Rebetika Songs, No 2,
ZODIAC 88044, 1974.

Mouflouzelis, Old Rebetika Songs, No 3.
ZODIAC 88053, 1975.

Τὰ μεράκια τοῦ Μουφλουζέλη [The 'moods' of Mouflouzelis]   ZODIAC 88061, 1977.

LIST OF PLATES

Frontispiece: Pandhoúra or tríchordhon. A fourth century B.C. relief from Mantineia. National Archaeological Museum, Athens.

1. Triangular psaltery. Miniature, 12th cent.
2. Bowed stringed instrument, lute, trumpet, lute, psaltery. Wall-painting, 16th cent.
3. Bagpipe, flute (?). Icon, 17th/18th cent.
4. Pellet-bells on silver incense-boat (c. 1800).
5. Pellet-bells on silver gold-plated censer (1622).
6. 1. Flute, trumpet, tambourás. 2. Flute, tambourás. 3. Tambourás, flute, clappers, harp. Miniatures, 14th cent.
7. Shawm. Wall-painting, 16th/17th cent.
8. Small bell. Wall-painting, 14th cent.
9. Hand-semanterion. Wall-painting, 16th cent.
10. Cymbals, horn. Wall-painting, 16th cent.
11. Handsemanterion.
12. Tambourás. Wall-painting, 19th cent.
13. 14. Líras and drum. Anastenaria, Aghia Eleni, Serres (1970).
15. Hand-cymbals, bowed stringed instrument, drum, flute and hand-clapping (?). Miniature, 11th cent.
16. Ornament of hair-braids (massoúr-plexídhes). Attic costume.
17. Construction of forged bells in a workshop in Amphissa. (Pl. 1-8).
18. Casting of bells in a workshop in Ioannina. (Pl. 1-14).
19. Bronze double cast-bell (dhiplókypros) on leader he-goat.
20. Bronze bell (rabaoúni).
21. Bronze pellet-bells.
22. Bronze double cast-bells (dhiplókypri).
23. Small silver pellet-bells hung around the sacred icon. Anastenaria, Aghia Eleni, Serres (1970).
24. Small pellet-bells on censers.
25. Silver pellet-bells on woman's costume of Astypalea (Dodecanese).
26. Cast-bells and forged bells hung at the waists of men in costume (karnavália). Popular painting (c. 1950).
27. Pellet-bells on swallow-shaped sound-producer (chelidhóna).
28. Cast-bells and forged bells hung at the waists of men in costume (karnavália). Carnival, Nikissiani (1972).
29. Coins hung on chests of men in 'foustanella' (Boúles). Carnival, Naoussa (1972).
30. Coins on bridal costume of Attica.
31. Ornament on headscarf of a woman's costume (sourghoút).
32. Iron tongs (massá) with finger-cymbals (zília).
33. Wooden ratchet (rokána).
34. Wooden spoons (koutália).
35. Bronze cymbals (zília).
36. Tambourine. Wall-painting by Theophilos, early 20th cent.
37. Small drum. Wall-painting, 16th cent.
38. Drum. Wall-painting, 16th/17th cent.
39. Bowed stringed instrument, shawm (?), triangular harp (psaltery ?), hooked trumpet, bowed stringed instrument, drums, shawm (?), hooked trumpet, ornament (sound-producer) on the plait of a dancer. Wall-painting, first half of 18th cent.
40. Small drum and shawm. Wall-painting, 17th cent.
41. Trumpet and drum. Wall-painting, 16th cent.
42. Mirlitons (made of shell: nounoúra; made of carton: ghourghoúra).
43. Small drum. Wall-painting, 17th cent.
44. Drums (daoúlia): 1. Sitia (Crete). 2. Naoussa 3. Messolonghi.
45. Drum (daoúli) of Amphissa.
46. Drum with snares (toubí) and beaters. Kythnos.
47. Drum (daoúli) and beaters. Sitia (Crete).
48. Tambourine (défi) with jingles (zília). Thrace.
49. Tambourine (toumbanás). Chryssomilia (Fourni, Ikaria).
50. Tambourines (défia) with jingles (zília): dacharés, Macedonia; défi, Epirus.
51. Pottery drum (toumbeléki). Mytilene.
52. Pottery drum (toumbeléki). Sifnos.
53. Pottery drums (toumbelékia). Mytilene and Macedonia.
54. Pottery drum (toumbeléki). Didymotichon(Thrace).
55. Long flute. Wall-painting, 16th cent.
56. Bowed stringed instrument, lute, pan-pipe, psaltery, tambourine, shawm, bagpipe with drone (gáida). Wall-painting, 16th cent.
57. Pan-pipe and transverse flute. Miniature, 11th cent.
58. Long flute. Wall-painting, 16th cent.
59. Straight trumpet and hooked trumpet. Wall-painting, 18th cent.
60. Shawm, tambourine. Carved wooden iconostasis (1803).
61. Horn, small drum, bowed stringed instrument, trumpet, lute. Wall-painting, 16th cent.
62. Long flutes (tzamáres) of Epirus. Cane flutes (floyéres).

63. Cane flutes (floyéres) from various regions of Greece.
64. Wooden carved flute (floyéra) with serpent-like stick for cleaning. Ligourio (Argolid).
65. Bronze flute (floyéra). Aghali, near Tripolis.
66. Cane ducted flutes (sourávlia) from Cyprus and Santorini.
67. Flutes made from wingbones of birds of prey from various regions of Greece.
68. Cane ducted flute (thiambóli). Rethymnon area, Crete. Wooden ducted flute (sourávli). Skopia, near Florina.
69. 70. Wooden and cane ducted flutes (sourávlia). Doumbia (Chalkidiki).
71. Cane folk-clarinets: madoúra from Crete and monotsábouno from other Aegean islands.
72. Shawms: zournás (Macedonia) and karamoúza (Attica).
73. Shawms: karamoúza, brass (Attica) and zournádhi, wood (Messolonghi).
74. Bagpipe (tsaboúna). Symi (Dodecanese).
75. Up-cut and down-cut single reeds of bagpipes (1, 3). Shawm staples with double reeds (2). Cane from which shawm double reeds are made (4). Stages of making of a shawm double reed (5).
76. Bagpipe (tsaboúna). Naxos.
77. Bagpipe with drone (gáida). Soufli (Thrace).
78. Bagpipe with drone (gáida). Macedonia.
79. Bagpipe (bladder). Andros. Children's bagpipe (bladder), Kythnos.
80. Sound-producing devices of island bagpipe (tsaboúna).
81. Trough-like yoke of a sound-producing device of a Cretan bagpipe (askomadoúra).
82. Trumpet made of horn (voúkino). Brass trumpet (troumbéta).
83. Conch (bouroú).
84. Whistling water-pots (lalítses).
85. Whistle on animal-shaped handle of a shepherd's crook.
86. Lute (laghoúto). Athens, early 20th cent.
87. Lute (laghoúto). Constantinople, end 19th cent.
88. Pegbox of lute (Pl. 87).
89. Soundboard of lute (Pl. 87).
90. Pegbox of 'úd (Pl. 91).
91. 'Úd (oúti). Athens 1971.
92. Lute-guitar (laoutokithára). Inter-War years.
93. Sázi (instrument of the lute family). Caesarea, Cappadocia, early 20th cent.
94. Tambourás. Copper engraving (1782).
95. Baghlamádhes (instruments of the lute family). End 19th cent.
96. Island Greek with tambourás. Lithograph, 19th cent.
97. Bouzoúkia (instruments of the lute family). Early 20th cent.
98. Tambourás on a Skyrian embroidery.
99. Bouzoúki (instrument of the lute family). Early 20th cent.
100. 1. Baghlamás. 2. Bouzoúki. End 19th or early 20th cent.
101. Lute and tambourás. Lithograph, 19th cent.
102. Lute. Lithograph (1825).

103. Shawm, lira (?), lute. Wall-painting, 16th cent.
104. Lute and nakers. Wall-painting, 17th cent.
105. Lute. Wall-painting, 16th/17th cent.
106. Bouzoúki (instrument of the lute-family). End 19th cent.
107. Pegboard of tambourás (Pl. 108).
108. Tambourás (instrument of the lute family). Second half of 19th cent.
109. Pear-shaped bowed three-stringed instrument. Miniature, 11th cent.
110. Small tambourás, Wall-painting by Theophilos. Early 20th cent.
111. Pegbox of baghlamás (Pl. 112).
112. Baghlamás (instrument of the lute family) with tortoise-shell soundbox (1955).
113. 114. Baghlamás (instrument of the lute family) with tortoise-shell soundbox. Inter-War years.
115. 116. Baghlamás (instrument of the lute family) with gourd soundbox (1955).
117. Psaltery (kanonáki), tuning key, plectra and thimbles. End 19th or early 20th cent.
118. Dulcimer (sandoúri).
119. Baghlamádhes (instruments of the lute family). Inter-War years.
120. Pear-shaped líra. Crete, 18th cent. (1743). Bow with pellet-bells. Inter-War years.
121. Pear-shaped líra. Crete, end 19th cent.
122. Pear-shaped líra, large size (vrondólira). Crete, early 20th cent.
123. 124. Pear-shaped líra. Ikaria (1946).
125. 126. Pear-shaped líra. Dodecanese (1925).
127. 1. Bow of bottle-shaped líra (kementzés) of Greeks from Pontos (Black Sea area). 2-9. Bows of pear-shaped líra from various regions of Greece.
128. Pear-shaped líra. Crete (1960).
129. Líra on Cretan embroidery, 18th cent.
130. 131. Pear-shaped líra. Region of Constantinople, 19th cent.
132. Pear-shaped líra. Crete, early 20th cent.
133. Pear-shaped líra. Dodecanese, Inter-War years (above). Pear-shaped líra (Athens 1969).
134. Violin-shaped líras (violólires).
135. Bottle-shaped líra (kementzés) of Greeks from Pontos (Black Sea area). Inter-War years.
136. 137. Wood-carved bottle-shaped líra (kementzés) of Greeks from Pontos (Black Sea area) (1900).
138. Bottle-shaped líra (kemanés), with sympathetic strings, of Greeks from Pharassa, Cappadocia (1967).
139. Bottle-shaped líra (kemanés), with sympathetic strings, of Greeks from Pharassa, Cappadocia (1960).
140. Violin and bow. Athens, Inter-War years.
141. Mandolin (mandolíno) (below). Mandóla, Athens, Inter-War years.
142. Guitar (kithára). Athens, Inter-War years.
143. Barrel-organ (latérna). Constantinople, Inter-War years.
144. Pear-shaped líra. Crete, 18th cent. (?).
145. Mandolocello (a large lute).
146. Cymbals, shawm and stringed instrument (?). Copper engraving (1694).
147-150. Forged bells.

SOURCES OF INFORMATIONS
INSTRUMENT-MAKERS AND PLAYERS

INDEX OF AUTHOR'S NAMES

INDEX OF GEOGRAPHICAL NAMES

GENERAL INDEX

Please note: in order to help the reader decipher the maze of Greek names of instruments and their components, the author has listed all related terms under general headings.

accordion, 47, n.265
'accompaniment', as a term, n.101.
acheloniá (tortoise-shell, bell), 58
aerophones, 27, 46, 147-206
afalós (rosette, lute), 214, 233, 235, 240, fig.149/15
afipnistírion símandron (semanterion), 95
afouklári, áfouklas (double-chanter), 179
Africa, 45
agathós (double-chanter), 179
aghiosídheron (semanterion), 95
aïdhonáki (water-whistle), 205
akritic cycle (songs), see folk songs
Alcestes, 16
alepú ('valve'), 177, 179
alla franca or "high *douzéni*" (kind of tuning), 279
alla turca or "low *douzéni*" (kind of tuning), 262, 264, 279, 280
ambeliá (forged bell's staple), 60
America, 45, 64
anakarádhes (nakers), 130
anapniá ('valve'), 177, 179
Anastenária, see rituals, traditional
anastenáridhes (participants in the *Anastenária),* 78
anemodhíktis-skiáchtro (wind-blown scarecrow), 113, Pl.166
anemológhos (mouth of ducted flute), 150
anemológhos ('valve'), 177, 179
angará (bagpipe's drone), 198
angíon (bag of droneless bagpipe), 168
angíon (bagpipe, droneless), 168
angitzís (bagpiper), 181
angopón (bagpipe, droneless), 168
angóxylo (double-chanter), 179
ánighma (rosette, lute), 214, 233, 235, 240, fig.149/15
apotropaic properties of sound, 52, 64, 77, 78, 80, 89, 103, 114
apotropaic significance, 95, 114
Arabia, 44
Arabian lute, 240
Arabic rebab, 274

Arabic ʿūd, 212
Arabs, contact with, 298, n.42, 400
archaeological evidence, see references
árghana (ta), see instrumental ensembles
árghano (drum), 117
armáta, takími, douzína, see belling
artikólira (children's 'musical instrument'), 301, Pl.197/2
arundo donax, arundo plinii, n.255
askáki, askávli, áskavlos (bagpipe, droneless), 168
áskavlos (bagpipe with drone), 198
askí (bag of bagpipe with drone), 198
askí (bag of droneless bagpipe), 168
askobadoúra, see *askomadoúra*
askomadoúra (bagpipe, droneless), 52, 93, 168, 184.
askomadouráris (bagpiper), 180
askotsábouno, askotsaboúrna, askozaboúna (bagpipe, droneless), 168
asterískos (liturgical implement used as struck bell), 113
Athenian *cantádha,* see song, popular
Athens and Piraeus Musicians' Society ʿMutual Aidʾ, 32
Atlantic Ocean, 182
aulos *(avlós),* ancient Greek, 161, 165, 166, 167
Australia, 45
avdhéla (forged bell's clapper), 60
avláki (mouth of ducted flute), 150
avlós (shawm), 163

babióli (ducted flute), 151
badoúra (clarinet-type pipe), 152
baghlamás, see tamboura(s), variants
bagétes (dulcimer's sticks), 299
bagpipe, droneless, island- *(tsaboúna),* 26, 46, 52, 93, 152, 168, 177, 179-184, 201; Pl.74, 76
terminonology and regional distribution: *angíon, angopón, askáki, askávli, áskavlos, asko-*

(bagpipe, droneless, island-)
badoúra, askomadoúra, askotsábouno, askotsaboúrna, askozaboúna, dhiplotsábouno, flaskomadoúra, gáida, káida, klotsotsábouno, moskotsábouno, saboúna, saboúnia, skortsábouno, touloúm - zournás, touloúmi, tsaboúna, tsabounáskio, tsabounofyláka, tsamoúnda, tzaboúrna, 168
—— components of, terminology distribution, dimensions, construction, materials used:
 – bag: *angíon, askí, dhermáti, fyláki, póst, thylakoúri, touloúmi, výrsa* (= untreated skin), 168, n.310
 – cane pipes (long section): (plural) *bibikománes, chabiólia, kalámia, lámnes, mánes, stimónia,* 180, fig.113
 – cane pipes (small section = single-reed-bearer): (plural) *bibíkia, chabiolákia, madourákia, madoúres, pirpíngia, tsaboúnes, tsaboúnia, tsambiá, tsibónia, tsoubónia,* 180, fig.113
 – double - chanter (grooved base): *afouklári, áfouklas, agathós, angóxylo, madouróxylo, márta, mártha, náv, potamós, skáfi, thikári, tsabounokáfkalo, váthra,* 179, Pl.80, 81
 – mouthpipe: *boúzounas, flómos, fouskotári, fyseró, fysitári, fysitíri, kurélli, kókkalo, masoúri, pibóli, sifoúni, stomotíra,* 179
 – reed, single-, (up-cut, down cut): *bibíki, ghlossídhi, fteroúla, tsambí,* 180, n.265, Pl.75.
 – single-reed-bearer, see cane pipes, small section
 – 'valve' (fig.108): *alepú, anapniá, anemológhos, flómos,*

393

398

(folk songs)
—— love-songs *(tis agápis)*, 25, 104
—— lullabies *(nanourísmta)*, 43
—— narrative song *(paraloghí, -és)*, 16, 25, n.2
—— *mandinádhes* (distichs), n.267
—— shepherd's songs: *tsopanárika*, 76; *vláchika*, 76; *skáros*, 77; *'mirolóyia'*, 76
—— shallow-song *(chelidhónisma)*, 78, n.103
—— *tachtarísmata*, 43
—— table-songs *(tis távlas)*, 27, 129, 238
—— wedding-songs, 25
      (see also song, popular
foniás (mouth of ducted flute), 150
foot, stamping of, 43, 90, 91
foúrla, fourlídha or *forlídha* (disc/pirouette, shawm), 165
fouchtokoúni (bell, forged), 54
foúka, foúska (pellet-bell), 58
fouskotári (mouthpipe), 179, 198
frame drum, see drum
France, 200
friction drum, see drum
fráouro (ductless flute), 149
fteroúla (single-reed, up-cut, down-cut, 180
fthiabóli, ftiabóli (ducted flute), 151
fyláki (bag of droneless bagpipe), 168, 177
fysári (mouthpipe), 198
fyseró (mouthpipe), 179, 198
fysitári, fysitíri (mouthpipe) 179
fysolátis (mouthpipe), 198
fytsi (mouthpipe), 198

gáida, see bagpipe with drone
gáida (bagpipe, droneless), 168
gaidanáki, gaidanítsa, gaidanoúla (chanter), 199
gaidatzís or *gáidatzis* (bagpiper), 181, 198
gáidha or *gháidha* (bagpipe with drone), 198
gaidháris, gaidhiéris, gaidiéris (bagpiper), 198, 199
gaidhoúrka (chanter), 199
gaidofloyéra (chanter), 198
garóxylo (bagpipe's drone), 198
garózi (bagpipe's drone), 198
Gaza (Palestine), 204
gbanéli (drum), 117
gháidharon (o) or *ghaidhoúr (to)* (bridge, bottle-shaped fiddle), 277, fig.168/11
gháidharos (soundpost, pear-shaped fiddle), fig.155/- and 159
geography, musical, 44
Germany, 64
gesticulator, 16

ghargháli (pellet-bell), 58
ghavál (ductless flute), 149
ghlóssa (forged bell's clapper), 60
ghlóssa (i) (fingerboard, bottle-shaped fiddle), 275, fig.168/5
ghlóssa (fingerboard, pear-shaped fiddle), 264
ghlossídhi, dhipló epikroustikó (double-beating reed), n.265
ghlossídhi, eléfthero (free reed), n.265
ghlossídhi, monó epikroustikó (single-beating reed), n.265
ghlossídhi (forged bell's clapper), 60
ghlossídhi (plug of ducted flute), 150
ghlossídhi (single-reed, up-cut, down-cut), 180, n.265
ghlossídhi (single-reed-bearer), 199
ghlossocháboulo (ducted flute), 151
ghorghára (ducted double flute), 151
ghoúla (i) (neck, bottle-shaped fiddle), fig.168/4
ghourghoúra or *troumbéta*, see drum, friction
ghouviastíras (hollower, forged bell), 58, see also Pl.17/1-8
ghreveláki (pellet-bell), 58
gíga (pear-shaped fiddle), n.411
glousnítsa (ducted double flute), 151, 162
Greco-Turkish War (Debacle of Asia Minor) of 1922; 32, 41, 210, 258, 300; n.17
Greece, ancient, 44; — 'old', 32, 114; n.30
Greece, mainland, 27, 30, 52, 54, 58, 129, 149, 151, 166, 168, 184, 198, 201, 239, 274, 300, 302; — islands, see Index of Geographical Names (Islands)
Greek, ancient music, 16, 27; — musical instruments, 25, 52, 53, 91, 133, 161, 165, 166, 167, 202, 203, 211, 240, 298; n.54, 360; — rhythmical genera (dhiplasion/hemiolic), 25
Greek folk music, see folk song and song, popular
Greek Folklore Research Centre of the Academy of Athens, 45, 47
Greek War of Indenpendence of 1821; 15, 251, 130, 205, 206; n.1, 54
Greeks of Asia Minor, the Black Sea area (Pontos), Cappadocia, see Index of Geographical Names
gringarídhi (pellet-bell), 58
guitar, electric, 47, n.29
guitar *(kithára)*, 25, 28, 29, 30, 31, 211, 233, 240, 258, 259, 300, n.391; Pl.142

gunshots *(pyrovolismí)*, 114
—— apotropaic properties attribute to, 114
—— in traditional customs, 114
—— today: firecrakers, fireworks, 114
Gypsies, 29, 89, 201, n.244
—— as instrument-players, 29, n.244
—— contribution of, to Greek folk music, 29
—— Turkish-, 201

hand-clapping *(palamákia)*, 43, 90-92, n.147
      terminology: *koúrtala, kourtalísmata*, 91
—— accompaniment of dance and song, and funeral processions, 91
—— proverbs referred to, 92
—— references, iconographical and literary, 91, n.147, Pl.15, 173
hand-cymbals, see cymbals
hand-semanterion, see semanterion
harmonica, n.265
'harmonisation', as a term, n.101
harmonium, n.265
harp, see psaltery
headband ornament *(sourghoút* or *serghoútsa)*, as 'musical instrument' and as sound-producer, 92, 93, Pl.31
hartákia (strips of paper), see children's sound-producing toys
Hellenic-Roman culture, 44
Heptanesian *cantádha,* see song, popular
Heptanesian Islands = Ionian Islands, see Index of Geographical Names
heroic hexameter, 25
heterophony, 27
hieró xilo (semanterion), 95
historical songs, see folk songs
Homeric epics, 25; — era, 167
horn, natural, 203
horn *(troumbéta* or *voúkino)*, sound-producer made of horn, used as a signalling device 203, Pl.61, 82
hornpipes, 182, fig.121
horseshoe, used as a triangle, n.136
hypertéleioi auloí, 166

iambus, 102
iconographical references, see references
idiophones, 46, 51-114
iklíg or *kemantchá,* see fiddle, spike bowl
ikíteli, see tamboura(s), variants
!ndia, 44
Indian Ocean, 182

401

404

405

406

ACKNOWLEDGEMENTS

The work "Greek Popular Musical Instruments" contributes to the study, research and preservation of our popular musical instruments, the principal bearers of Greek popular music.

The fruit of three years of labour, the publication of this work owes a great deal to the many collaborators and friends, as well as to those scientific and religious institutions which aided us in our efforts:

The Brotherhoods of the monasteries Stavronikita and Great Lavra (Mount Athos), Timiou Prodromou (Serres), Varlaam and Transfiguration (Meteora). The General Direction of Antiquities and Restoration of the Ministry of Culture and Science, and the Ephors of Byzantine Antiquities. The director of the Greek Institute of Byzantine and post-Byzantine Studies in Venice, Prof. Manoussos Manoussakas.

The curators of the Museums: National Historical Museum, Athens, Ioannis Meletopoulos; Museum of Greek Folk Art, Athens, Popi Zora; Benaki Museum, Athens, Angelos Delivorias.

The president of the Peloponnesian Folklore Foundation, Nafplion, Ioanna Papandoniou and the folklorist Kitsos Makris.

The directors of the Gennadius Library (Athens), the National Library of Paris, the British Museum, the Library of Congress, the Patriarchal Library of Jerusalem.

Invaluable for the author were the opinions and the aid concerning musicological, historical, linguistic and other problems, give by the professors: Samuel Baud-Bovy (Geneva), Laurence Picken (Cambridge), and Dimitrios Loukatos, Dimitrios Pallas, Linos Politis (Athens); Popi Zora, curator of the Museum of Greek Folk Art (Athens), Stylianos Alexiou, curator of the Archaeological Museum of Iraklion (Crete); the Byzantinists Anna Hadjinikolaou and Manolis Chatzidakis (Athens); the musicologists Despina Mazaraki, Simos Karras and Spiros Peristeris (Athens).

Yiannis Venardis, Dimitrios Letsios, Dimitris Tloupas, D. A. Charissiadis, the Brothers Houtzaiou, the painter Georgios Manoussakis and the folklorist Joy Coulentianou willingly provided us with photographs from their private archives.

Hundreds of popular musicians and instrument-makers contributed to the preparation of this work with their knowledge and sensitivity. Among them, especially: Christos Parassidis, Vassilis Skenderidis and Michail Skenderidis (Caesarea, Cappadocia), Costas Angelidis, Nicolaos Armaos, Elias Kanakis and Yiannis Paleologos (Constantinople), Pantelis Fortounidis (Pharassa, Asia Minor), Victor Dekavallas (Thessaloniki), Manolis Stagakis (Iraklion, Crete), Ioannis Papadakis (Rethymnon, Crete), Manolis Frangedakis (Chania, Crete), Charalambos Paraskoulakis (Armeni, Chania), Nicolaos Kodonas (Kozani), Tassos Diakoyiorgis, Iakovos Ilias, Nikos Kopeliadis, Loukas Bertsos, Vassilis Panayis and Georgios Panayis (Athens), as well as the craftsmen of the workshop "Theodoros Stamatelos – Ilias Flokos" (Amphissa) and "G.K. Papanikolaou" (Ioannina), who with patience and love allowed us to follow the construction of bells.

This work owes a great deal to the invaluable assistance — contribution in the investigations and coordination of labour for the publication — of Fivi Caramerou, as well to the photographers Makis Skiadaressis, Romilos Parissis and Konstantinos Paschalidis for their dedication and the quality of their work, and the sculptoress-painter Anna Vafia for the scientific accuracy and sensitivity of her drawings.

F. A.

DRAWINGS

Anna Vafia

PHOTOGRAPHS

M. Skiadaressis: 1, 2, 4, 5, 7, 8, 9, 11, 12, 16, 24, 32, 38, 41, 43, 44, 45, 46, 47, 51, 52, 53, 54, 55, 58, 59, 62, 63, 64, 65, 66, 67, 68, 72, 73, 74, 76, 77, 78, 79, 80, 81, 87, 88, 89, 90, 91, 92, 95, 96, 100, 101, 103, 105, 106, 109, 111, 112, 113, 114, 115, 116, 119, 120, 121, 122, 123, 124, 125, 126, 127, 128, 130, 131, 132, 133, 134, 135, 136, 137, 138, 139, 140, 141, 142, 156, 163, 173, 175, 176, 180, 181, 183, 184, 188.

R. Parissis: 13, 14, 17, 18, 20, 21, 22, 23, 25, 26, 27, 28, 29, 30, 31, 33, 34, 35, 36, 42, 48, 49, 50, 69, 70, 71, 75, 82, 83, 84, 85, 94, 98, 102, 110, 117, 118, 129, 143, 144, 145, 146, 147, 148, 149, 150, 151, 152, 153, 159, 160, 164, 167, 168, 169, 170, 171, 172, 174, 177, 182, 187, 190, 191, 194, 195, 196, 197, 198, 199.

K. Paschalidis: 3, 10, 15, 19, 37, 39, 40, 56, 57, 60, 61, 86, 93, 97, 99, 104, 107, 108, 161, 162, 165, 166.

D.A. Charissiadis: 192.
N. Gizikis: 193.
D. Tloupas (Larissa): 154, 155, 202.
D. Letsios (Volos): 185, 186.
Y. Venardis (Skyros): 157.
Houtzaiou Brothers (Mytilene): 178.
G. Manoussakis: 200, 201.
Joy Coulentianou: 158.

The photographs 6, 179, 189 were contributed respectively by the Greek Institute of Byzantine and Post-byzantine Studies (Venice), the Library of Congress, the British Museum.

The photographs 36, 182, 193 were taken from the archives of the author.

The instruments which appear in this work belong to the collection of Greek popular instruments of Fivos Anoyanakis.